MOLLY MCGOLLY AND MOTHER NATURE

(An Earth Day Story)

by Virginia Marie Capps

Scriptures taken from The Jerusalem Bible © 1966 by Darton Longman & Todd Ltd and Doubleday and Company Ltd.

New Revised Standard Version Bible: Catholic Edition, copyright © 1989, 1993, Division of Christian Education of the
National Council of the Churches of Christ in the United States of America. Used by permission. All rights reserved.

ISBN: 978-1-4834-6066-6 (sc)
ISBN: 978-1-4834-6067-3 (e)

Lulu Publishing Services rev. date: 10/19/2016

DEDICATION

To the Virgin Mary (Queen of Heaven, Queen of Peace, Our Heavenly Mother). I dedicate this book to our Mother Mary for bringing me back to the TRUTH of the Catholic faith. For many years I fell prey to becoming a cafeteria Catholic. It was my Heavenly Mother who woke me up and led me back to the fullness of the Catholic faith... back to Her Son Jesus and His bride The Catholic Church.

I remember many years ago on one of my trips to Sterrett Alabama, to be present during apparitions of the Virgin Mary (one of the visionaries from Medjugorje Bosnia came to Caritas of Birmingham), of a conversion that took place between a woman I met and myself.

At one point in our walk and conversation the woman asked me "Do you know what I love most about the Catholic religion?" At which I stated "No, what?" She proceeded to tell me "Because it tells you what to believe." Although I had been to these apparitions before and had started my conversion, I couldn't agree with her at that time. I replied "Nooo. I believe in most of what the Catholic Church teaches but not all of it." We kept walking and she looked at me and kindly stated "Really?" We reached our destination and then separated and went in different directions. I never saw that woman again.

Through my continued prayers and conversion I now whole heartily agree with her. Just look at how the world is and you can see how far we of free will have veered from the path to Heaven.

If only we would live the 10 Commandments and the teachings of Jesus in the Gospels.

I originally started writing this book as an Earth Day story. Then I decided to make Molly a little Irish Catholic girl so I could remind Catholics of some of the truths of the faith (like why we baptize our babies, why we go to confession with a Catholic priest/s and why our marriages are considered sacred).

After a while I started including my opinion (like a journal) because 'the world' didn't want to hear the TRUTH. People in my life (family, friends, co-workers, neighbors, people from my past that I still keep up with from time to time) only want to be told that whatever they are doing in their life is just fine. I found that trying to be charitable while guiding them to the TRUTH...did not work. My motto 'Charity through Truth', most of the time ended with them no longer talking to me or asking for my opinion, yelling and being told in varied ways that I am too righteous. So my thoughts and feelings came out in this book. TRUTH is TRUTH. God has not changed, only man has changed.

Mother Mary led me back to the TRUTH of the Catholic faith and I am so very grateful. I've repented for my mortal and venial sins and have changed my ways (I have taken the spike out of my own eye). I also state the truth and am trying my best to lead the young (who many times don't have good examples close to them but have been taught the truth and will still be held to the truth) and the old (who have allowed the evil one to deceive them and need to come back to the TRUTH of the Catholic faith like myself) back to the TRUTH found in the Magisterium of the Catholic Church.

Thank you Mother Mary for gently and lovingly guiding me to TRUTH and your Son Jesus. I pray and hope that this book will lead others to the path of redemption and light, even if at first they get angry and think I'm way to righteous. Each person will have a storm to go through before humbling themselves to the point of putting God first which is a must in order to get into Heaven.

I love you Mother Mary,

Your daughter,
Virginia Marie

Molly McGolly was of Irish descent,
she bathed in spring water and her breath smelled of green mint.
Molly's parents were good practicing Catholics and were richly blessed.
Not much money, but they had 10 lively children, no less.
Mr. Fitzgerald McGolly wore a green stove pipe hat on his head.
His odd sense of fashion covered most of his curly hair that was red.
He looked like a cross between Abe Lincoln and a leprechaun.
On occasion Dad sported a kilt, a plaid skirt which is not very long.
Maureen McGolly, Molly's Mom, had firey red hair; like a campfire she wore in a puffy bun;
accompanied by a smile she wore dusk til dawn.
That's right!
Mom only smiled at night.
During the day her mouth led her children by commanding orders, praying and trying to keep the peace.
Mom was very busy especially feeding the mouths that didn't yet have teeth.
Maureen McGolly's long legs could out run anyone in town,
a skill she acquired chasing after 10 children in 10 directions on the front lawn.
When you're the mom, you can't wave the white flag, throw in the towel or give up!
All you can do is stop, step back, take a deep breath (sigh or cry) and re-group.

(LUCK OF THE IRISH)

The older children were starting to take up the slack,
keeping the younger ones out of danger by teaching and correcting to keep them on the right track.
They would feed, babysit and play with the younguns,
freeing Mom up so she could cook dinner in the oven.
Mr. McGolly worked at the Pulley Zip Line Factory as the financial advisor.
Some might say he was a money miser.
If you have a large family to raise;
you learn early how to reduce, reuse, recycle and save.
Mrs. McGolly was known as the thrifty queen.
She even saved every scrap of bread in the freezer; then made bread pudding.
Left over applesauce turned into applesauce cake the next day.
Kids had to eat almost everything on their plate before they could go outside and play.

(LUCK OF THE IRISH)

They lived at the top of a hill;

decreasing the chance the main course was made of road kill.

       A penny saved is a penny earned;

in the McGolly household a lesson well learned.

       Molly was the oldest child in the McGolly clan.

She shared a room with her 4 year old twin sisters, Miriam and Maryann.

Two sets of twin brothers all shared a bedroom.

They were accustomed to close quarters, it started in their mother's womb.

Mike and Mark were 7 years old and slept in the top bunks.

John and Joseph were 2 years old and kept rolling off the lower bunks KERPLUNK!

Molly thought they should be renamed Lumpy and Bumpy;

or perhaps they should just sleep on the floor and keep each other company.

The cribs were occupied by the newest mouths to be fed.

Thirty fingers, thirty toes and three bobbing heads;

Triplets: Leo, Patrick and Shawn.

If the family keeps growing, some will be sleeping on the front lawn.

They were one big happy family as the saying goes;

through the joy, sorrow, triumphs and whaos.

Bells rang, song filled the air and birds chirped; on the day Fitzgerald McGolly and

Maureen McFrugal got married in the Catholic Church.

Lawful marriage raised to the dignity of a sacrament by Christ.

Meaning a Catholic Christian man and woman unite for life.

The bond of holy matrimony can not be dissolved by any human power.

The marital vows they profess to each other, they are to honor.

Part of the vow asks: Will you accept children lovingly from God, and bring them up according

to The law of Christ and His Church?

Natural conception or adoption for family growth.

The marital act is sacred between husband and wife,

and must remain that way the rest of their life;

Remember 'til death do we part' or the Catholic Church grants an annulment.

The only birth control method approved by the law of Christ and His Church is the natural

family plan;

simply because it is the only natural method available to man.

The Holy Bible condemns all other forms of contraception;

only God is to have the power for creation.

The natural family plan helps determine the woman's fertile period.

During this time the married couple (marriage is a sacrament in the Catholic Church) may choose

to embrace the marital act if they want their family to grow;

or choose to abstain from the marital act during the woman's fertile period, for family growth control.

Perhaps finances, physical problems or other dilemmas warrant holding off having more children for awhile.

Maybe the married man and woman want to conceive and have children but so far have been unfruitful.

Planning your family with natural family planning may take a little more work but the benefits are immeasurable.

No pain, no gain;

whether to exercise the marital act or refrain.

Couples who practice the natural way learn to communicate better with each other.

The wife feels loved and cherished and this includes her fertility.

Abstaining (voluntarily doing without) from the sexual act before marriage is very important.

Even if you have fallen for the ways of the world and have had in the past very lax standards;

it is time to pick yourself up (wherever you are) and your physical body become the temple of the Holy Spirit.

Being a virgin on your wedding day is as God intended for women and men.

Having multiple sexual partners before marriage makes it difficult to work out life's trials once they begin.

For those people tend to want to turn around and run;

or spend time wishing or getting a divorce, their marriage vows undone.

If a married man and woman truly love each other and are committed, knowing they get one spouse;

for it is a mortal sin to divorce and marry someone else.

Divorce is part of the culture of death; for what God has joined together no human power can denounce.

The evil one through the birth control pill (and other forms of birth control other than N.F.P.) and multi media is tearing marriages apart and breaking up the family.

The best way to stop this destructive pattern is to do GOD's Will by being true to your holy matrimony spouse and natural family planning.

Annulment in the Catholic Church is far from a divorce.

Something has to be fundamentally wrong from the beginning nullifying the union should have ever taken place.

You are actually held to the vow you took on your wedding day.

Remember it is the vow that is the matter in the sacrament of holy matrimony.

The vow you pronounced to God and your spouse,

in God's house.

What God has put together let no man put asunder.

+++

I heard that Pope John Paul II wrote that the skills needed for a successful relationship are the virtues. So do a checklist of virtues on your future spouse AND on YOURSELF.

A few virtues are humility, chastity, patience, faith, charity;
the areas lacking will be the way/s they will hurt you in your marriage and cause great strife.
Maybe each of us should do a little work on ourselves before we become someone's husband or wife.

+++

Natural family planning is not full proof but about 97% is pretty good!
These odds are about the same as finding trees in the woods.
Mother Teresa of Calcutta did the field work. She and her nuns taught natural family planning to about 30 thousand people (Christians/Muslims/Hindus). The results were about 97% effective. These people had no other forms of contraception available to them, so they were very motivated. Remember they had much difficulty providing the necessities of life to their children (a good reason to hold off having children).

+++

There are different ways to achieve natural family planning; one requires a thermometer, one a calendar and a third way requires 2 fingers.
Natural Family Planning (N.F.P.) is cheap, efficient and has no physical side effects.
There are many wonderful reasons to use (N.F.P.) for birth control, as opposed to other forms of contraceptives (not approved of by the Catholic Church such as birth control pills, I.U.D.'s etc…).

Read what the CATECHISM OF THE CATHOLIC CHURCH has to say about Contraception
CATECHISM OF THE CATHOLIC CHURCH
Contraception: see Matrimony: purpose
Periodic continence and contraception: 2370
Please get a copy of the CATECHISM OF THE CATHOLIC CHURCH and look this up!

==

According to the Family Research Council, pointing to a collection of studies from the last several decades: Devout, married Catholics have the best sex of any demographic group.

==

How about that: Devout married Catholics have the best sex of any demographic group;
NOT cafeteria Catholics!
There could be added benefits to treating your body like it is the temple of the Holy Spirit.
Also, the divorce rate for cafeteria Catholics is 50% plus; the same as the general population.
The divorce rate is about 3% for devout Catholics.
Embracing the marital act is a holy union, between one man and one woman.
If you don't believe me, open your Holy Bible to 1 CORINTHIANS Chapter 6 Verses 9-20 and Chapter 7 Verses 1-40.
If we love God we should obey all of His Laws and not stand in the way of creation.

To be clear, only natural conception of a holy union between a husband and his wife.

To be clearer: no birth control pills, no plan B pill, no morning after pill, no binding, no IUD's or other devices.

Without the approval of the Catholic Church; no tying of fallopian tubes or hysterectomies.

No condoms, no crushing of testicles, no castration, no spilling of seed, no Viagra or the like etc..., no vasectomies.

Also no in-vitro-fertilization, no artificial insemination and no sperm bank donating.

No surrogate mothers and no cloning.

To be crystal clear: 1 CORINTHIANS Chapter 6 verse 18-20

Keep away from fornication. All the other sins are committed outside the body; but to fornicate is to sin against your own body. Your body, you know, is the temple of the Holy Spirit, who is in you since you received him from God. You are not your own property; you have been bought and paid for. That is why you should use your body for the glory of God.

===

We all have free will, so it is up to each one of us;

to be humble enough to obey our Father's Will or are we too selfish?

Perhaps God wants to bless you with a child who will become a Catholic nun or priest;

to spread the good news of salvation to people in other lands North, South, West or East.

Maybe God will give you a child with severe disabilities:

to teach your whole family to have great humility.

This grace of a handicapped child may be the reason your whole family goes to Heaven.

Their siblings will learn from an early age to put others needs first; like they are all united in holy communion.

Caring for others and sharing responsibility helps develop virtues like patience and perseverance.

Caring for elderly family members can have the same beautiful consequences.

Every marital act should be open to love and life.

Natural family planning (N.F.P.) is incredibly bonding...

I'm giving my whole self to you, and only you!

A husband should love, honor and cherish his one and only beloved wife.

Each of the McGolly children's birth story was different;

even if the birth time was only one minute.

A few came out roaring, some rooting for food with mouths opened.

Others looking around trying to figure out what just happened!

Who turned on the lights, where am I and who are you guys?

Why suddenly can I see with these 2 things called eyes?

Mrs. McGolly (Mom) recorded each of her children's reaction to the first few moments of life in their baby books.

It was the first and last entry for most of the books.

Only Molly's book (being the first born) included each milestone date.

First word, first crawled, first steps, first tooth and each doctor visit height and weight.

The day the first set of twins were born, literally the bubble burst.

It was like all the sudden everyone forgot Molly was the center of the universe.

She now had to share her parents, with two infant brothers.

One might think it was downhill from there, when later came all the others.

But Molly learned the more the merrier.

Dad always loved Mom and both loved all the children; life could not be happier.

Mr. McGolly planted a fruit tree for each of his children on the day of their birth.

He planted the small trees into the good fertile brown earth.

Molly's was an apple tree and the twins were in pairs.

Mike and Mark's trees were a pair of pears.

Miriam and Maryann had two cherry trees

next to the hives full of bees.

The pecan trees belonged to Joseph and John.

Molly's apple tree was surrounded by the fruit orchard on the front lawn.

Kind of like the Garden of Eden;

except Molly's apples were suppose to be eaten.

This tradition started with a peach tree;

Mr. McGolly planted for his new bride when they built the log cabin at the top of the highest hill.

He would say to his wife everyday "You're a peach" and every time Maureen his bride would blush; still a romantic thrill.

Ten lively children later and there's something still there only they feel!

The triplet's trees have a theme:

one lemon, one orange and one grapefruit a citrus team.

It was no wonder that Dad had a wood work shop.

He planted so many trees but what to do with the ones that he chopped?!

In the winter he chopped wood for the fireplaces, so they would not freeze.

Since the house was located on a hill; Spring and Summer there was a nice breeze,

which served as their air conditioning, along with assorted shade trees.

Mr. McGolly preferred natural energy sources like solar and wind power.

The large windmill scooped up fresh water from the spring into their very own water tower.

It looked like a giant bucket on stilts which piped in water into the house and outdoor shower.

On the top of the barn they collected energy from the sun through solar panels.

Sunny days were great but on cold cloudy days better to wear pajamas made of flannel.

(LUCK OF THE IRISH)

Mr. McGolly saved lots of money on wind and solar energy;

since the sunshine and wind are free.

The wood shop was his hobby, where he worked with his hands;

crafting beautiful functional furniture, toys for the tots and wooden ceiling fans.

Under the wood shop was the root cellar;
preserving a few bottles of homemade wine and the vegetables that were grown during the summer.
In addition to the veggie garden Mrs. McGolly had an herb garden next to the kitchen door.
They also have a grape vineyard and guess what's next in store?!
Mr. McGolly wants to add on to the house a nursery for babies and a mother-in-law suite.
They will be right next to each other, so hopefully he can get more sleep.
His brothers are lumberjacks and they're going to bring more logs.
This time next year it will look like a log cabin lodge.
Grandma McFrugal (Maureen's Mom) is moving in to stay.
Since Grandpa McFrugal a couple of years ago passed away.
Molly remembered Grandpa McFrugal,
he liked to play and make Molly giggle!
Grandpa could snatch her nose with his hand and always found a coin in her ear.
However, true to his last name McFrugal, the coin always disappeared.
For safe keeping he put it back in the other ear.

(LUCK OF THE IRISH)

Molly had her nose back again, right in the middle of her face.
Good thing it didn't get lost, her little nose would have been difficult to replace.
Although there is an advantage to not being able to smell;
especially if your downwind of the triplets diaper pail.
No disposable diapers in the McGolly household.
Just reusable all cotton cloth diapers; rinse, wash, dry and fold.
The cloth diapers were washed over and over to be recycled;
then hung out on the pulley system clothes line to be dried.
So the McGolly children were use to hand-me-downs almost from the moment they were born.
Hand-me-down clothing was a must to be worn.
Since Molly was the oldest her recycled clothing came from the Clothes Closet at school and her cousins from another school district.

(LUCK OF THE IRISH)

Molly was pretty good with a needle and thread since her cousins clothes did not fit.
Her cousins were much taller and more round.
So Molly had to use belts to keep her pants from falling down.
The shirts looked like dresses and the dresses as long as evening gowns.
Molly cut them in half and made matching dresses for Miriam and Maryann.
This trick Molly learned from Grandma McFrugal who was thrifty with left over material.
Grandma made clothes for Molly that matched the curtains, pillows and the cloth that covered the dining room table.
Molly's mother wore Grandma McFrugal's wedding dress on the day she said "I do".

Then packed it away so her sisters and future daughters could wear it too!

After Molly's parents were married and the honeymoon commenced;

after his proposal and after her consent:

The blushing bride selected a crucifix

and her new husband had it blessed by a Catholic priest.

Post nuptials the crucifix was placed over their bed;

to remind them there are three in this marriage now wed.

God, one man and one woman united in holy matrimony;

What God has joined together, let no man put asunder.

Before Fitzgerald McGolly and Maureen McFrugal were married they agreed;

Mr. McGolly as head of the household would take the lead.

He would make all the major decisions

and his bride would make all the minor decisions.

(LUCK OF THE IRISH)

There have been no major decisions made in the McGolly household to this day!

Baffling how things have turned out this way.

The day Fitzgerald McGolly took Maureen McFrugal for his beloved wife,

turned out to be the best day of his life.

At least until judgment day when he hopefully will enter Heaven through the pearly gate.

After living a good and just life following all the Commandments and teachings of Jesus Christ

... sometimes he could hardly wait!

Then he would remember: Natural Conception to Natural Death

God has a plan for him and it's not complete yet.

★★

Scripture: JOHN 3:16-21

Yes, God loved the world so much

That he gave his only Son,

So that everyone who believes in him may not be lost

but may have eternal life.

For God sent his Son into the world

not to condemn the world,

but so that through him the world might be saved.

No one who believes in him will be condemned;

but whoever refuses to believe is condemned already,

because he has refused to believe

in the name of God's only Son.

On these grounds is sentence pronounced:

that though the light has come into the world

men have shown they prefer

darkness to the light

because their deeds were evil.

And indeed, everybody who does wrong

hates the light and avoids it,

for fear his actions should be exposed;

but the man who lives by the truth

comes out into the light,

so that it may be plainly seen that what he does is done in God.

■■■

Mr. McGolly knew every day is a battle for the soul.

Living God's laws according to the Bible is the goal.

Prayer, fasting, Bible reading and (at least) once a month confession with a Catholic priest

and receiving Holy Eucharist in (and ONLY in) the state of grace.

These are the ways that will lead us to Heaven and tame our hearts

to be in the right place.

Just like the Red Sea in the story of Moses; someday the sky will part.

If we have prepared our bodies to be the temple of the Holy Spirit and a dwelling place

for Jesus in our heart.

Then and only then can we follow Jesus to the other side;

if the teachings of Christ and all 10 Commandments we did abide.

Even when everyone mocks, laughs or condemns you,

continue to be obedient to your Heavenly Father.

Just like Jesus when they put a heavy wooden cross on His shoulder.

The wound on Jesus's shoulder from carrying the cross which inflicted on Thee

an anguish greater than any other wound of Thy Most Blessed Body.

Since the cross represents our sins;

it is each one of us who hurt Jesus.

To come back to God's good grace

we must repent with true sorrow and ask forgiveness;

do our penance and change our ways.

We have to do more than just believe in Jesus Christ.

Demons believe in Jesus and they must kneel before Him.

■■■

Mother Teresa of Calcutta stated something like...

      Follow Jesus when carrying your cross, don't try to lead Him.

■■■

Like Jesus, we are to pick up our cross everyday and carry it uphill along the narrow path.

If we of free will choose not to, someday we'll face God's wrath.

God puts no one in Hell, we each do it to ourselves.

Only those who live their lives doing God's Will, not their own;

will be able to ascend to Heaven to be close to God on His throne.

Remember: You have to be let into Heaven, we can't get there on our own.

∙∙∙

Saint Faustina's Diary (Divine Mercy in My Soul)

Notebook I Part # 153

Please get a copy of Saint Faustina's Diary (Divine Mercy in My Soul)

Saint Faustina was a mystic. One day she saw two roads.

*Notebook I Part # 153;

One day, I saw two roads. One was broad, covered with sand and flowers, full of joy, music and all sorts of pleasures. People walked along it, dancing and enjoying themselves. They reached the end without realizing it. And at the end of the road there was a horrible precipice; that is, the abyss of hell. The souls fell blindly into it; as they walked, so they fell. And their number was so great that it was impossible to count them. And I saw the other road, or rather, a path, for it was narrow and strewn with thorns and rocks; and the people who walked along it had tears in their eyes, and all kinds of suffering befell them. Some fell down upon the rocks, but stood up immediately and went on. At the end of the road there was a magnificent garden filled with all sorts of happiness, and all these souls entered there. At the very first instant they forgot all their sufferings.

^^^

Mr. McFrugal (Maureen's father) read this passage from St.Faustina's Diary (Part 153) to all of his children a few days before his daughter Maureen was to be married.

No one in the family (Mrs. McFrugal, Robert, Kevin, Martha, Carolyn, Rosie, Ivan, Maureen) took a breath for about 20 seconds nor flinched a muscle.

When finally Carolyn asked "Isn't there a third road?"

Mr. McFrugal calmly stated "No mention of a third road; just two. It's Heaven or Hell.

Sounds like there will be no cafeteria Catholics in Heaven ever. You're either in the state of grace or the state of mortal sin. I'm just going to say this once and then repeat it a thousand times. As Catholics, we know it only takes one mortal sin to take you to Hell. Something you refuse to repent for that you know to be against your Father in Heaven's Will. That part of your soul the light has gone out, withered or has died. You no longer feel guilty because you have (of free will) separated yourself from God.

Mortal sin is the only thing that separates us from God;

therefore it only takes one mortal sin to separate us from God; and each of us does it to ourselves by doing our will over God's. God has an ocean of mercy to forgive us but we must ask for forgiveness with true sorrow and have a firm purpose to amend our ways to be forgiven."

Mr. McFrugal continued as every member of his family seemed to be sitting at the edge of their seat "I can think of a few serious/mortal sins that the world seems to be turning a blind eye to: lust, fornication, living together before marriage. None of my children better ever 'shack up' or I'll cut them right out of the will. Other serious sins: taking birth control pills or any other form of birth control (other than N.F.P. in a holy matrimony marriage and only for a good reason). Why can't the world see the effects of this intrinsically evil mortal sin. So many souls are on a path to Hell because of promiscuity brought about since contraception has been widely accepted in the secular world. It seems to me that most of the bad things of this world are the result of people using their body for their own will and not as a temple of the Holy Spirit. The virtues need to be encouraged, and lived. I pray all my children will live according to God's Will and be living examples of virtue. Humility, charity, chastity (for your state in life)...to mention just a few. Also for the work you do in this life to be pleasing to God. People that make their living pulling souls away from God will find themselves in Hell some day and for eternity if they do not repent and change their ways. Some examples would be
drug dealers, directors/producers/actors that encourage any of the mortal sins (like lust,
fornication, living together before marriage, abortion, homosexuality, divorce,
murder (even if your pretending to be the good guy/the investigator),
witchcraft (even if trying to push the show off as benign/no harm to the innocent).
Sacrilege is mortal sin. Also anything to do with birth control or abortion (including
prescribing birth control if you're a physician). I want my family to promote a
culture of life. Examples of a culture of life:
Movies, books, music that are life sustaining and nourish,
holy matrimony marriages that flourish,
keeping families together through thick and thin,
recognizing the dignity of every human life at every stage from the beginning to the end.
Natural conception to natural death; a right to be born and a right to age.
My children, question your vocation to God,
whether it's single life/married life/or religious life;
are you doing it in a way that is pleasing to God.

^^

Look up in the CATECHISM OF THE CATHOLIC CHURCH:
Catechism of the Catholic Church # 1857

For a sin to be mortal, three conditions must all be met: "Mortal sin is sin whose object is grave matter and which is also committed with full knowledge and deliberate consent."

^^

Mr. McFrugal reminded his children that grave matter is according to God. God's word is in the Bible is case you're confused,
you don't get the option to choose.

The Catholic Church tells you what to think;

popularity does not rule, there is no voting booth.

Our Father who art if Heaven hallowed be Thy name,

Thy kingdom come, Thy Will be done

on earth as it is in Heaven.

No one in Heaven is telling God what to do, one third of the angels tried that once and were cast out of Heaven forever.

We must be obedient to our Father in Heaven, for He knows what is best for all of us.

Mr. McFrugal walked over to the bookshelf and opened a book and took out a political cartoon.

It showed a little feeble old man freshly in Hell looking at satan.

The little old man said "Why am I here? I'm a good man".

The devil looked at him and clearly stated "Yes, you're a good man, but you made some bad choices in which you never repented."

Although this cartoon was created to be funny it is theologically correct.

The picture of the cartoon was passed around to each family member to get the full effect.

Mr. McFrugal added "All those little old ladies going to church cramming for finals; would do well to ask for forgiveness for all mortal sins and not hold on to their wills.

It helps to look how your sins have impacted others to sin and has led to the immorality of the world today.

God is merciful and wants to forgive; all we need to do is ask for forgiveness with true sorrow.

So go to confession today! Don't put it off today thinking you can go tomorrow...

but tomorrow never comes.

Remember my children, Purgatory is for people who are sorry for their sins and have something to pay off. A purging, cleansing since all sins must be atoned.

Maybe a little bit will be swept under the rug, but not mortal sin.

Hell is for people who refuse to repent for something serious they know offends God.

They are attempting to tell God, He has to change to their way because

they love their sin/sins more than they love God.

There are no examples of God giving into popular demand in the Bible:

1). One third of the angels cast out of Heaven for siding with satan; never allowed back.
2). Adam and Eve cast out of the Garden of Eden for eating the fruit from the tree of the knowledge of good and evil.
3). Sodom and Gomorrah destroyed by fire (now a desolate wasteland by the Dead Sea).
4). Noah's Ark and the Great Flood (Everyone who was not on the Ark perished).

★There is an example of the people changing their ways and their lives being spared;

Jonah and the Big Fish. Proving there is always hope for people who of free will, change their ways to God's Will.

Through St. Faustina, Jesus tells her it is the last appeal. THE LAST NICE WAY GOD IS PLEADING WITH US!

WHAT COMES NEXT IF WE DO NOT RETURN TO GOD'S WAY!? MAY NOT BE SO NICE!

Jesus through Saint Faustina is reminding us that Divine Mercy is for everyone.

Mr. McFrugal had the Novena and Chaplet to the Divine Mercy pamphlet in his hand.

He read from the back cover: "Priests will recommend it to sinners as their last hope of salvation. Even if there were a sinner most hardened, if he were to recite this Chaplet only once, he would receive grace from My infinite mercy... I desire to grant unimaginable graces to those souls who trust in My mercy...Through the Chaplet you will obtain everything, if what you ask for is compatible with My will."

After Mr. McFrugal gave his fatherly advice powerfully worded but softly spoken, as was his usual demeanor. He asked "So, who wants to go to confession with me?"

Everyone grabbed their coats and packed into the family van;

off they went... to repent!

Maureen was the driver and took the ordinary route to the church,

but the road was blocked due to construction.

She asked "Which road should I take?" in all the confusion.

All the passengers in the vehicle stated in unison

"The narrow road strewn with thorns and rocks."

til this day it remains a family inside joke.

If you ask for directions, someone will blurt out "Take the narrow road strewn with thorns and rocks."

Every time this statement comes up it stirs up a mixture of emotions. On one hand it's humorous and reminds them of that wonderful night.

On the other hand the loving calm lesson Mr. McFrugal gave to his grown children was the last serious Christ centered conversation before he passed away.

... so the phase "Take the narrow road strewn with thorns and rocks" is bitter sweet.

A few days after the spiritual enlightenment by Mr. McFrugal, he gave his daughter Maureen away in Holy Matrimony to Fitzgerald Paul McGolly.

WEDDING DAY for Maureen Marie McFrugal:

Before the day is night,

She will be Fitzgerald Paul McGolly's wife.

Maureen slowly emerged from her bedroom coming down the stairs with her eyes opened wide; stating out loud "I'm going to be someone's bride."

Her sister Martha made hot cocoa for everyone in the McFrugal household.

It was a surprise for everyone after the first sip, I am told.

Martha served the mugs and raising hers with a tight fist, toasted her older sister "To much joy and wedding bliss!"

Everyone took a sip of hot cocoa

and after the first gulp they wanted to know
what's in there...it taste different from what
we were expecting....WHOA!!!!

Martha stated "I'm glad you asked, so now I will explain.

This cup of cocoa is much like the marriage covenant.

You think you know what you're getting yourself into until you try it.

You're all drinking Mexican hot cocoa, it has a few more ingredients.

It starts with the usual warm white milk for nourishment

and melted chocolate for love's sweetness.

Then BAM a little pepper spice for life's unforeseen surprises;

sprinkled with cinnamon representing true grit in tough times.

Mixed all together it's pretty nice.

Although sometimes it is scalding hot but most of the time it's fine.

In other words, sometimes it's comfort food

and sometimes it's the spice of life.

So, here's to you my dear sister Maureen, whom this day will begin her vocation

for God.

Of the 3 choices (single life, married life, religious life);

She of free will has chosen married life as her vocation to God.

May your married life to Fitzgerald Paul McGolly be full of joy!

Dear Sister, always be obedient to God and leave the consequences to Him."

Mr. McFrugal "Good words to live by."

Mrs. McFrugal "I'll drink to that."

Maureen's mouth was as wide open as her eyes!

If Martha's breakfast toast was just a taste of what she might dish out at the wedding reception;

maybe Maureen should call off the wedding and elope, that was a brief consideration.

Then she saw her wedding dress draped over the dining room table and her veil suspended from

the chandelier looking like a wispy white cloud and the tiara a floating white dove.

Maureen was pampered first with a bubble bath then her long red hair shampooed, conditioned

and curled. On top of her head was a beautiful bun which flowed down to her left shoulder

with long cascading ringlets in the front.

The tiara was a complete circle, more like a wreath around her head encompassing her mid-forehead.

The veil was puffed up from the back of the wreath tiara with ivory tulle.

Maureen wore her mother's wedding dress; handmade in the old country of Ireland.

The ivory colored satin bodice was covered with a handmade lace jacket with floral motifs and

shamrocks that buttoned all the way up in front with satin covered buttons.

Maureen's mother and grandmother worked many loving hours making the roses and shamrocks

lace used to make this beautiful dress fit for a queen.

The main body of the dress was a long full skirt that opened like a flower with soft pleats

of folding lace forming a Victorian style semi-bustle at the back, extending with a short train

measuring eight feet in length.

This was the day Maureen had waited for her whole life;

today she was going to become Fitzgerald Paul McGolly's wife!

The finishing touches of a pedicure, nails manicured, powdered, perfumed, hair puffed,
make up artfully applied (not too much);
then chauffeured to the Catholic Church.
Bridesmaids were singing:

> I'M GETTING MARRIED IN THE MORNING
> DING DONG THE BELLS ARE GOING TO RING
> PULL OUT THE STOPPERS
> LA-LA-LA-LA-LA
> GET MAUREEN TO THE CHURCH ON TIME

They didn't know all the words but everyone got the point.
Upon arriving to the Catholic Church, Maureen was enclosed into her wedding gown,
veil and slippers.

> Something old...the wedding gown, tiara and veil
> Something new...the pearl necklace from her beloved Fitzgerald Paul McGolly
> Something borrowed... earrings from Aunt Ruth
> Something blue...

Oh my! Maureen didn't have anything blue.
She accidentally left her blue garter at home with no time to retrieve it before the wedding started!
The bridesmaids all had red velvet Victorian style dresses...nothing remotely blue.
In a panic five minutes before she was to walk down the aisle;
the sunlight peered through a window illuminating a mosaic of the Mother of God,
and at Mary's feet was a small crystal clear glass with a royal blue candle nestled inside.
Maureen said "Mother Mary, thank you for the something blue.
I love you Mother Mary, please guide me my whole marriage through".
Maureen took the small crystal glass and blue candle and placed it in the middle of her
white roses and gardenia floral wedding bouquet.
Mother Mary saved the day!
Maureen down deep in her heart, knew things would not always work out so well.
There would be trials with unhappy endings but she asked Mother Mary to be with her
and give her the strength to endure whatever was to be put in front of her...
to do God's Will with love and joy; even when difficult, even when difficult for a long
period of time, even if called to suffer for the glory of God.
Following a prayer led by her maid of honor, her sister Martha;
it was time to get married.
Maureen really started to feel the seriousness of making a wedding vow to God and her
soon to be husband in front of God, and her family and friends.
A covenant to be lived out the rest of her life from this new beginning to end.
She felt a moment of serious conviction before her father escorted her down the aisle
into the arms of the man she would share her life; til death do they part.

The tower bells were ringing,
>				birds singing.

Now if you think about it, the bird nests were probably located in the bell tower.

So when the bells are ringing, the birds have to be awake,
>				singing in the bird church choir!

Gerald (short for Fitzgerald) wore a black tuxedo with top hat and coat with tails.

His top hat was black instead of the usual green.

Today was a special day; for he was getting married to the girl of his dreams!

But enough about Gerald for all eyes were on Maureen.

^^^

Catechism #1625–1631: Declaration of Consent

Look up in the CATECHISM OF THE CATHOLIC CHURCH

(Author Note): It is the vow in the sacrament of Holy Matrimony that is the matter. The priest/s must say the right words and the right matter must be present in all 7 sacraments. Catholics are not allowed to pick and choose the Declaration of Consent of marriage vows.

^^^

>   The sacrament of Holy Matrimony for Maureen and Fitzgerald was celebrated within the
>   Holy Mass with the Liturgy of the Eucharist.

They were both in the state of grace and felt like their souls were lifted during the celebration of their love and commitment to God and each other.

Remember there are three in this marriage (God, one man and one woman) now wed.

Now it was time for the wedding reception held in the reception hall at the church.

The best man Clement and the maid of honor Martha gave their toasts to the newly wed couple.

Clement completed his tribute to his best friend and brother Gerald…everyone clapped and and laughed. His speech was heartfelt and humorous, after all they're Irish.

Before I tell you about Martha's wedding toast; first a little history lesson.

When Maureen and her best friend Clare were in high school they decided one night;
to sneak out and live on the wild side.

They were good girls their whole lives, so what's one night of a little mischief?!

However there was a little problem; Maureen shared a room with her little sister Martha.

Martha was trying her best to sleep but the two older girls were making too much noise.

They kept the light on while planning their escape,
waiting for the parents to go to sleep.

They had to get the keys to the family van and sneak out of the house through the window.

When the two were ready to execute their plan,

Martha got out of bed pretending to go to the bathroom.

Instead she went straight downstairs, grabbed the camera and walked out the front door
and hid in the far backseat of the family van.

She was going to get these two back for keeping her awake almost every Friday night that entire school year.

Martha took 2 floral bed sheets, a pillow and a blanket; she planned to be comfortable.

Finally Maureen and Clare got into the van, started the engine and off they went for a night of fun and excitement!

First they went to the midnight viewing of 'JAWS' at the drive-in-theater.

Maureen and Clare spent most of the time flirting with guys outside of the van.

This allowed Martha to get some snap shots, some close up without getting caught.

Maureen and Clare had no reason to be on guard,

they didn't know the little sister was a domestic 'narc'.

After the movie, they decided to go to the lake and skinny dip (like the girl in the movie).

They wanted to prove how brave they were;

even though they swam in the lake and not in a shark infested ocean.

They were victims of Martha's revenge and not a man eating shark;

which all took place at night in the dark.

Martha got out of the van and took their clothes and hid them in the van.

Maureen and Clare sobered up fast, although neither had not a drop of alcohol to drink.

Who took their clothes? Who was watching them without their clothes?

The van wheels burned rubber, they were off lickey split!

(LUCK OF THE IRISH): They did not get a speeding ticket!

It was time to depart and they were rightly scared out of their wits!

(LUCK OF THE IRISH): They found 2 floral bed sheets in one of the back seats.

One size fits all.

Floral togas on the go…

Enough adventure for one night, they were on their way home…or so they thought.

The van ran out of gas and they had to walk a mile at night in togas to get the gas can filled.

This allowed the photographer to get great shots of the 2 toga queens returning;

without any suspicion of a 'stow away' on board.

The three girls arrived at the McFrugal home front in time to get rid of the evidence and pretend nothing out of the ordinary happened.

Maureen and Clare thought they got away with their caper undetected.

UNTIL TODAY!

When it was Martha's turn to give her toast, she made her grand entrance.

She changed her clothes from the red velvet bridesmaid dress into a toga consisting of two floral bed sheets.

Clare looked at Maureen with eyes wide open like the headlights of a car

"Dejavu, I feel like we're back in high school."

Maureen could barely speak but managed to say "I knew we should have eloped."

Martha had a slide projector all prepared in the reception hall just waiting for the flip of a switch.

The SWITCH being from nice McFrugal family photos of Maureen growing up to photo evidence of the night Maureen decided to take a walk on the wild side.

Martha began her wedding toast:

"Dear Gerald, I just want to share a few things that I've learned over the years of

sharing a room with my sister Maureen.

First of all, after 6pm at night don't give her anything with caffeine.

She will be awake all night and you will get no sleep.

I have a story to tell you all about one night she had a cola to drink

and that night neither Maureen, Clare nor I got any sleep…not even one wink!"

She proceeded to tell the story of sneaking out the house, going to the midnight

movie in the van, skinny dipping in the lake to prove they were brave,

becoming toga queens and running out of gas…

and thinking that was a secret well kept…no one was the wiser.

Martha showed the pictures she took that night several years ago

concluding with Maureen and Clare individually coming out of the confessional.

Martha lovingly stated "Honestly Gerald, Maureen is a great person to be around all the

time. You are truly blessed to have a lifetime to share with my beautiful sister Maureen.

So, here's to my sister Maureen and my new brother-in-law Gerald. May all your

dreams come true. When times are rough, lean on each other with love."

Martha walked over the Maureen and Clare and returned the clothes she took

when they were skinny dipping in the shark lake.

Then she gave two colas to Gerald, her new brother-in-law.

After the ceremony and reception, all the guests gathered outside waiting for the newlyweds

to depart for their honeymoon.

When suddenly from the bell tower

still in their wedding attire;

Maureen and Gerald made their grand get away.

They zip-lined all the way down to the horse drawn carriage;

eager to make their great escape and start their marriage!

Maureen's older brothers Rob and Kevin who were both horseback riding forest rangers and rode

horseback on patrol:

as their wedding gift they arranged for the zip-line and horse drawn carriage get-a-way

from the get-go!

Not even the other groomsmen or bridesmaids knew of this surprise exit.

To keep this secret hush hush; Gerald didn't even tell all the participates.

Meaning Maureen his new wife which laughed and squealed all the way while

suspended in mid-air!

She threw her wedding bouquet which was caught by her best friend Clare.

Maureen and Gerald kept their honeymoon destination a secret

til they were leaving town. ·

The sign on the back of their little car read:

NEWLYWEDS
HEAVENLY MOUNTAIN BOUND
LAKE TAHOE
... See Ya When We Get Back...DON'T FOLLOW

———

Bells rang, birds chirped and

    Thank Heaven the zip-line worked!

    The newlyweds, Mr. and Mrs. Fitzgerald McGolly drove that day after changing
into traveling clothes to Lake Tahoe; the destination they wanted to reach.
Upon arrival at their hotel they checked in, changed clothes again then had
dinner by candlelight at a restaurant overlooking the beach.
They had a breath taking evening view with huge windows displaying the lake,
few boats by the pier and snow capped mountains exposing a winter wonderland.
To begin their first fine meal together, they interlocked their right arms and drank fruity
fine wine while gazing happily into each other's bright eyes.
That night they consummated their marriage, embracing the marital act by physically,
mentally and spiritually becoming one in union with God.
Both were in the state of grace by going to confession only a few days before the declaration
of their love and devotion to each other during the sacrament of Holy Matrimony.
Years ago, long before they met; each one made a vow to remain chaste until marriage.
Waiting to exercise the act of generation, to be monogamous and faithful to one person
til death do they part.
Only they will know what happened in the heat of passion that wonderful night.
All we know is that devout Catholics (not cafeteria Catholics) have the best sex of any
demographic group on the planet.
It might not be perfect at first but keep practicing on it.
The next morning when they were ready to explore
beyond the honeymoon suite doors;
to check out their natural surroundings of Lake Tahoe,
surrounded on all sides by the Sierra Nevada mountain range covered in snow.
Lake Tahoe is one of the clearest lakes in the world.
You can see on average 72 feet down into its clear cobalt blue waters.
The Washoe Indians called it "The Lake of the Sky".
Mark Twain proclaimed the lake to be "the fairest picture the whole earth affords!"
It was Sunday, so as devout Catholics they went to early morning Mass at
St. Theresa's Catholic Church in South Lake Tahoe, California.
It was lined with stained glass windows depicting Our Lady of Guadalupe,
St. Theresa of the Holy Face and the Child Jesus (also known as the Little Flower),
and beautiful landscapes of the Lake Tahoe.

Mr. and Mrs. McGolly received Holy Communion (the true Body and Blood of Jesus Christ)
into their bodies the first day after embracing the marital act.

God gave us a way to experience sexual pleasure but we must to obedient to God
and do it according to your state in life and His Will.

Some will be called to live a chaste lifestyle for different reasons.

Be obedient to God and leave the consequences up to Him.

The McGolly's were so happy to be joined to God in their marriage,
they lit a candle and said a unified prayer.

Maureen selected a crucifix from the small gift shop (the size of a closet),
and her new husband asked the Catholic priest to bless it.

The priest also gave Mr. Fitzgerald McGolly a special blessing as he was now the head of his
domestic church.

The priest reminded Gerald that his main job as leader of his domestic church and head of the
family was to get his new bride and any future children to Heaven.

The (Mrs.) selected the crucifix
for she is the heart of the family and will beautify the home.

The (Mr.) had the crucifix blessed and received
a special blessing as head of the family and protector of the home.

For both to remember:

> There are three in this marriage now wed
> GOD, ONE MAN AND ONE WOMAN

This crucifix to be placed over their nuptial bed;
then go with them wherever they roam,
wherever they make their home.

To remind them in the days/months/years/decades to come
to be true to the marital promise (in a way pleasing to God);

> in good times and in bad,
> in sickness and in health,
> to love and honor all the days of your life,
> to have and hold from this day forward,
> for better, for worse, for richer, for poorer,
> in sickness and in health,
> until death do us part.

During the actual wedding, after Maureen and Fitzgerald declared their consent to be married,
the priest prayed for God's blessing on the couple and then declared, "What God has joined,
men must not divide." That was the point at which, as a sacrament, the groom and bride
became husband and wife.

On the way out of St. Theresa's Catholic Church, Maureen picked up a large pinecone
lying on the ground and told Gerald she was going to make a Christmas ornament to

remind them of their honeymoon.

Off they drove in their little car (named Nellie) up higher into the mountains.

Being avid skiers, they spent several days skiing in fresh powdery snow

thousands of feet above the alpine Lake Tahoe.

They spent a few opportune times during those days and every night;

in blissful honeymoon mode delight.

Once Gerald looked up while in a supine position

and saw that large pinecone like mistletoe dangling from the ceiling.

Maureen "I told you that pinecone was going to remind us of our honeymoon".

In addition to downhill skiing, a self-guided snowshoe hike in Squaw Valley

and snowmobile adventure added a little spice to activities outside the bedroom.

Friday, February 14th (The Day known for L-o-v-e)

Fritz got up before his beautiful bride and quietly went downstairs;

(their room was located on the third floor) to check out the continental breakfast.

He proceeded outside onto the hotel grounds to prepare his special Valentine's Day caper!

In the fresh fallen white snow he spelled out with his boot prints in gigantic letters:

I LOVE MAUREEN

LOVE, FRITZ

He returned to their honeymoon suite with a powdered doughnut, blueberry muffin and a

two cups of Mexican hot cocoa.

Good old Martha told Gerald (now known as Fritz to his new bride); how Mexican hot cocoa is

like the marriage covenant.

Martha also gave Gerald a small bottle of Tabasco sauce and some ground cinnamon for the road.

Fritz opened the curtains and stated "You've got to see this! Come and look outside".

Maureen rubbed her eyes and slowly emerged from the bed with a blanket wrapped around her.

She was so surprised and happy she gave Fritz the 'You're the BEST HUSBAND EVER REWARD'

complete with all the fringe benefits!

The Mexican hot cocoa was hot and spicy that Valentine's Day.

On the last full day of their honeymoon,

for the grand finale they rode on the Heavenly Mountain Gondola 2.4 miles up

scenic Heavenly Mountain.

They had lunch at the busy lodge,

tried snow tubing for the first time ever, spinning down the hill at a very fast speeds.

Liked it so well, they did it several more times;

it was easy since a conveyer belt was available to take people and their snow tubes up the hill.

Maureen giggled and screamed all the way down the slippery slope.

With her red hair flying, while spinning; she looked like an image in a kaleidoscope.

Due to centrifugal force, Gerald's green stove pipe hat flew off;

while spinning he laughed and a few colorful Irish phrases

echoed on the mountain top.

All in a day's fun!

On the gondola ride down Heavenly Mountain they cuddled

while enjoying the breathtaking scenery with a loving embrace.

The two had the gondola to themselves and held each other close

as they slowly came down the mountain while observing the beautiful lake.

When they reached the little village at the base of Heavenly Mountain,

Fritz had made a reservation for a slow steady pace horse drawn sleigh ride

along the beach of Lake Tahoe.

There was a little daylight left as they bundled up in a blanket for the scenic,

relaxing 30 minute tour.

After returning to their hotel on the beachfront they took a moonlit beach stroll

and then fired up the fire pit and snuggled while stargazing and sipping wine.

It was the last night of their honeymoon they decided to take advantage of the

outdoor hot tub in this winter wonderland.

It was a romantic exciting night!

First getting hot in the hot tub then rolling around the freshly fallen snow;

LAUGHING ALL THE WAY!

Isn't that what you do when you go outside to play?!

Their honeymoon was a super romantic adventure.

A time of their lives they will always remember.

As for that large pinecone;

Maureen decorated it with plain white glue and white glitter

at each pinecone tip; once she returned home.

It hung on their Christmas tree every Advent Season.

When the light from the fireplace hit the pinecone just right,

it cast out sparkles that looked like the stars of that moonlit night.

The next morning was Sunday,

as they were leaving town they attended Holy Mass

at Saint Francis of Assisi Catholic Church in beautiful North Lake Tahoe.

> THE PRAYER OF ST.FRANCIS
> LORD, make me an instrument of your PEACE.
> Where there is hatred...let me sow LOVE.
> Where there is injury...PARDON.
> Where there is discord...UNITY.
> Where there is doubt...FAITH.
> Where there is error...TRUTH.
> Where there is despair...HOPE.
> Where there is sadness...JOY.
> Where there is darkness...LIGHT.

O DIVINE MASTER, grant that I may not so much seek
To be consoled…as TO CONSOLE.
To be understood…as TO UNDERSTAND.
To be loved…as TO LOVE.
For
It is in giving… that we receive.
It is in pardoning… that we are pardoned.
It is in dying… that we are BORN TO ETERNAL LIFE.

★★★★★★★★★★★★★★★★★★★★

This Catholic Church combined a serene and spiritual environment
with some of the most spectacular sights of Lake Tahoe.
Following Holy Mass one of the priest was explaining to a group of
catechumens (people taking classes to come into full communion with the Catholic Church).

CATECHISM OF THE CATHOLIC CHURCH # 1247, 1248, 1249
The Baptism of adults
*Please look up in the CATECHISM OF THE CATHOLIC CHURCH

The Catholic priest was giving a speech to prepare the catechumens for the sacrament of reconciliation:
A priest must have the right words and the right matter in order to perform a sacrament.
Every priest all over the world must say the right words and the right matter must be present
(with a few exceptions under severe circumstances).
In Baptism the right matter is holy water.
In Reconcilation (Confession) the right matter is sorrow and the person asking for forgiveness
must bring the sorrow with him/her. If someone confessed to a sin they were not truly sorry for;
they were never forgiven even if the priest gave absolution (because the right words AND
the right matter were not both present).
You must truly be sorry for your sins in order to be forgiven.
In Confirmation the right matter is a special oil (oil only for Confirmation).
This priest stated that once he accidentally used the wrong holy oil and had to recall all of those
catechumens back using the right oil to confirm them in the Catholic faith.
In Holy Matrimony the right matter is the marriage vow. Remember the priest must state the
right words (the couple can't make their own vows) AND the right matter is the vow the man
and woman state to each other and God. It is the vow that is the right matter in the sacrament
of Holy Matrimony.
On their way home, they discussed the right words/right matter with the sacraments;
it was their very first in depth religious conversation as husband and wife.

It was the first of many wonderful Christ centered conversations they
would have together throughout their lives.

HOMEWARD BOUND:

Maureen and Gerald were still floating in the clouds when they returned home.
They lived with Maureen's parents for awhile to save money to buy a patch of property
on the outskirts of town...the highest hill.
It was their little Heavenly Mound minus the gondola ride;
however they did have zip lines to get down McGolly Hill.
But to get up the hill it was necessary to do that the old fashioned way...
walk, ride horseback or in their little trusty car named Nellie which managed to
putt-putt it's way up the hill.
Not long after the McGolly's moved into their log cabin at the top of the hill;
came Molly, their first bundle of joy,

a bouncing baby girl!

then Mike and Mark,
      then Maryann and Miriam,
            then John and Joseph,
                  then Leo, Patrick and Shawn.
Twelve McGolly's an even dozen,
      all living in the little log cabin.
Now back to the story:
      On Sunday mornings the McGolly clan attended Holy Mass.
Saturday mornings the school age children were at Catechism class.
According to Mr. McGolly, praying was their glue.
The family that prays together, stays together too.
Tuesday evenings after school and work,
Mr. McGolly read next Sunday's gospel reading.
Every member of the family then had to choose a word, phrase or idea from that spiritual feeding.
Dad read it again and then thrice;
just in case someone didn't hear it all after he read it twice.
Mike and Mark seem to have selective hearing.
Molly says that since there's not much between their ears, the echo must make it confusing.
Neither Mike nor Mark found her comment amusing.
The whole family, each and every person was to participate.
Discussing the gospel reading sometimes led to a debate.
Once the babies start talking this tradition could take all night.

(LUCK OF THE IRISH)

Right now it only took about 20 minutes to everyone's delight.
They always made sure Jesus had a chair.

24

Even though they couldn't see Him; surely He was seated there.

Nightly, Mom made sure everyone recited their prayers.

The Our Father, Hail Mary and Glory Be

then they rounded it out with Guardian Angel prayer to watch over thee.

GUARDIAN ANGEL PRAYER

Angel of God	★	Ever this day
My guardian dear	★	Be at my side
To Whom His love	★	To light and guard
Commits me here	★	To rule and guide. Amen.

Dad would dip his thumb in holy water and make the sign of the cross on each child's forehead.

He blessed them all in the name of the Father, Son and Holy Spirit

before they hopped into bed.

The girls had a pet raccoon

in their bedroom.

Probably the worst idea ever to have a nocturnal animal next to your bed.

Bandit was awake all night licking his paws and wanting to be fed.

Molly preferred Bandit to the boys pet, Sly, the snake.

Sly the snake had escaped!

Between Bingo the dog and Alley the cat and the triplets;

that snake didn't stand a chance;

or maybe Mom caught it and made snake kabobs or mystery stew.

Since snake taste a lot like chicken...

then no one knew!

The thrifty queen was also a great cook; Bonepetite!

Whether she was preparing snake kabobs or pickled pig feet.

Although there have been many unusual dinners,

Holidays are always traditional winners.

> Thanksgiving traditional turkey.
>
> Christmas traditional turkey.
>
> New Year's Day traditional ham.
>
> Easter traditional lamb.
>
> Groundhog's Day traditional groundhog.
>
> Fourth of July traditional hamburgers and hot dogs.
>
> April Fool's Day non-traditional mystery meat.
>
> Valentine's Day traditional something sweet to eat.
>
> Chinese New Year traditional Chinese food to go.
>
> Traditional Mexican food on Cinco-de-Mayo.

Earth Day traditional vegian.
Carrots, potatoes, tomatoes and lettuce fresh from the garden;
including the triplet's favorite, pureed fresh green beans.
Fridays during Lent traditional seafood from the creek fresh trout;
or from the pond fresh bass, the kind with the big mouth.

Most holiday dinners were delicious and pleasing but regular days it was fate...
what would end up on your plate.

(LUCK OF THE IRISH)
Most of it tasted great!

Molly spent some of her spare time in the kitchen, feeding the triplets in their high chairs;
what a mess.
In addition she liked to help Mom and Grandma bake pies, cookies and cakes...mmmmm
they were the best.
Molly was on the move as a general rule.
She was also extremely resourceful.
'Necessity is the father of invention': was her favorite cliche'.
Molly preferred this phrase to 'Beggars can't be choosers' or
'Waa! Waa! Waa! You're acting like the triplets',
when she didn't get her way.
They only had one bathroom in the house and waiting in line got old.
So, Miss Resourceful built a portable outhouse that rolled.
Also, by the spring water she rigged together an outdoor shower stall.
Using a pulley system with buckets and a shower curtain for privacy: instead of a wall.
Her necessary inventions worked well in the Spring, Summer and Autumn seasons...
but when winter blew in she just stayed inside and constipated within reason.
Molly used wood from Dad's woodwork shop;
to make the shower stall, outhouse including the roof on top.
Putting the outhouse on wheels was a stroke of genius.
Until Mike and Mark rode it all the way down the hill
and hit the mailman just going about his postal business.

(LUCK OF THE IRISH)

The offensive outhouse odor kept the dogs away
and the mailman completed his appointed rounds early that day.
So the mailman didn't file a complaint with the police chief for tampering with the U.S. Mail.
In return Molly and her twin brothers were able to stay out of jail!
Digging the new hole for the rolling outhouse was fun:
covering up the old one was not.
Crumpled up white phone book pages sometimes served as toilet paper;

26

the yellow pages as wallpaper.

It really had a bathroom library feel;

more like the book mobile since it was on wheels.

Every time Dad chopped down a tree he planted at least two in its place.

'REDUCE, REUSE, RECYCLE AND REPLACE'

These words printed plainly on a wooden plaque,

on the entrance to his wood work shack.

Most evening Dad would shout out "I'm going to work in the wood shed."

This was after the kids did homework and all the little ones were fed and in bed.

Mom would lovingly shout back "Good, build us a bigger log cabin

with quarters for maids and nannies about 6 or 7".

Dad built two great tree houses, one for the boys and one for the girls.

Maryann and Miriam played house all day long;

their tree house had a bakery and dance studio so they could twirl.

They boys used their tree house as a fort and sometimes as a deer hold;

not to shoot deer but just to stay out of the cold.

The McGolly's used pulley systems for everything from a dog run to

mail delivery from the bottom of the hill.

The mailman would use a clothespin to attach the letters to a reel:

then give a tug on the line which rang a little bell.

Sometimes the bills and important papers would get lost

and as a result the electricity would get cut off.

(LUCK OF THE IRISH)

The McGolly's had energy from flowing water in the creek, solar power from solar panels

and wind power from the wind mills.

So, even if their credit score took a dive;

they had plenty of food and energy to stay healthy, happy and alive!

No matter how well planned out your life may be;

sometimes unforeseen events cause plan A

not to be as good as plan B.

Then it's Mexican hot chocolate all over again,

sometimes you lose and sometimes you win!

Life is going to throw you curve balls, it happens to everyone.

So will you strike out or hit the ball out of the park and leisurely around the bases run?

Striking out may be the best call,

if it is the only way to follow God's law.

Making the big money or getting all the glory is not worth selling your soul.

Catholics (once Catholic always Catholic) put God first and leave the consequences to Him.

Once given the fullness of the Christian faith (Catholic religion), you will be accountable to God.

We must follow all of the 10 Commandments.

The 10 Commandments are the only part of the Bible God wrote Himself.

••

A reading from the gospel according to Mark (Mark 12:28-34)

And one of the scribes came up and heard them disputing with one another, and seeing that he answered them well, asked him, "Which commandment is the first of all?" Jesus answered, "The first is, 'Hear, O Israel: The Lord our God, The Lord is one; and you shall love the Lord your God

with all your heart,

and with all your soul,

and with all your mind,

and with all your strength.'

The second is this, 'You shall love your neighbor as yourself.' There is no other commandment greater than these." And the scribe said to him, "You are right, Teacher; you have truly said that he is one, and there is no other but he; and to love him with all the heart, and with all the understanding, and with all the strength, and to love one's neighbor as oneself, is much more than all whole burnt offerings and sacrifices." And when Jesus saw that he answered wisely, he said to him, "You are not far from the kingdom of God." And after that no one dared to ask him any question.

••

Author Note: Every Catholic should get a copy of An Examination of Conscience and review the mortal and venial sins against each of the COMMANDMENTS. The first Commandment:

I am the Lord your God. You shall not have strange gods before me.

The following are mortal sins against the first Commandment: Involvement in occult practices, e.g., witchcraft, Ouija boards, séances, palm reading, tarot cards, hypnotism, divination, astrology, black magic, sorcery, etc.; Involvement in or adherence to New Age or Eastern philosophies, atheism or agnosticism, Apostasy (leaving the Church), Adherence to a schismatic group, Putting faith in superstition, e.g., horoscopes, good luck charms, etc., Joining the Masons or other secret society, Receiving Holy Communion in the state of mortal sin, Receiving the Sacraments of Confirmation or Matrimony while in the state of mortal sin, Willful participation in illicit (non-emergency) 'General Absolution' services, Being married by a Justice of the Peace or by a minister of another denomination (without dispensation), Involvement in false or pagan worship, Willful denying the Faith of the Catholic Church, Despair of God's grace or mercy, Presumption (committing a mortal sin with the idea that you can just go to confession), Hatred of God, Simony (buying or selling spiritual things), Failure to receive Holy Communion at least once per year (if possible, during the Easter Season), Desecration of the Holy Eucharist.

The following are venial sins against the first Commandment: Failure to pray on a daily basis, Not trying to love God with my whole mind, heart, soul and strength, Entertaining doubts against the Faith, Failing to seek out or learn the teachings of the Church, Indifference or ingratitude to God, Lukewarmness in the relationship with God, Acedia (spiritual sloth), Putting other things or people before God, e.g., TV, radio, sports, hobbies, etc., Attachment to human respect or affection, i.e., caring more about what others think than what God thinks in order to fit in or be liked, Not trusting God, Failure to fulfill the duties of one's state in life, Playing Dungeons and Dragons or similar games, Tempting God, Being angry at God, Failure to support the work of the Church monetarily and/or with time and ability, Not taking part in the work of evangelization, Being willfully distracted at Mass or in prayer, Putting off confession needlessly, Refusing or denying the mercy of God, Failure to pray when tempted, Failure to examine one's conscience daily, Giving into depression, self-pity or self-deprecating thoughts.

••

Author Note: There are possibly many more ways to be involved in occult practices now since the world seems to be pushing a satanic agenda. If you are playing magic games on the internet or dressing up and pretending to be witches or other characters honoring magic, you could be in great danger. Beware when you start to honor these kinds of characters when you are neglecting the Lord your God. You are inviting the evil one into your household and this is very dangerous to you and your children. Parents that are dabbling in the occult such as fortune telling, tarot cards etc... You have opened the doors to satan and your children are in great danger. Knock off anything that has to do with magic even if you think it is harmless. Your children being possessed by an evil demon is not harmless...especially when you yourself are the one who opened the door to evil. Your children need to be formed properly in the Catholic faith. Get your children into religious education classes now. As for yourself, go to confession and repent for drifting so far away from the TRUTH of the Catholic faith. Do not despair nor become despondent; God has an ocean of mercy. However, you alone are the one who has to ask for forgiveness with true sorrow and have a firm conviction to change your ways. Also, do not encourage others to sin against God. You must throw away the material things related to the occult like: throw away cards, internet games, books, movies, costumes or other articles used in games as not to encourage others to play these (seeming innocent but evil) games. Even if you lose a lot of money by throwing these items away and not putting them on the internet for sale; it is best for these items never to be used again. The great deceiver has deceived us all and it is time to WAKE UP! Once you have ridded yourself and your family of these evil practices, make positive changes. Go to a musical concert, park, movie, read the Bible or other good books that will nourish the soul. The world is full of wonderful, exciting beautiful hobbies, ways to physically exercise, types of art and music, try volunteering (corporal and spiritual works of mercy are very good for the soul)... explore things that nourish the soul and will someday lead you and your family to Heaven.

I'm a nurse at a hospital and I have a story to share about a little boy about 4 years old. A volunteer from a local Catholic Church came to the hospital several times a week to bring the True Body of Jesus in the appearance of bread to the Catholic patients and their families (if they have had their first Holy Communion and hopefully are in the state of grace). One day Liz (name changed) came to the pediatric department with a startled look on her face. She had just visited the Pediatric Intensive Care Unit (in a separate building; joined to the Pediatric Unit by a long hallway) and she seemed frightened. This was an elderly woman with a lot of energy and a bubbly personality who could and would talk to anyone. She was used to going in and out of hospital rooms and dealing with many situations for years. That day was different! The father (who was an older man) was sitting in a Pediatric Intensive Care Unit room with his 4 year old son and Liz was talking to him. Liz was carrying the ciborium (a covered cup for holding the consecrated wafers of the Eucharist); she reached over to rub the little boy's head and she was thrown across the room. She immediately came to the Pediatric department because she knew the nurses very well; for she had been bringing the Body of Jesus (in the form of bread) to the Catholic nurses on Sundays for many years. That was not the first time she had visited that little boy and his family. The little boy had been very ill and spent a couple of weeks in the hospital. Liz remembered another time she visited the child; she gave him a plastic rosary. She started talking to the parents or maybe the grandmother; she looked over at the little boy and he was trying to crush/squeeze the rosary in his hands. Liz felt this was a strange occurance. I personally thought she was over exaggerating the events. After all Liz was elderly and it wouldn't take much to push her and maybe in her mind she 'went flying across the room'. As far as the little boy trying to crush the rosary; well he's a little boy that doesn't have any idea what the rosary stands for and boys will be boys. Liz contacted a Deacon at the Catholic Church that she knew and informed him of the event. Later Liz told us that the grandmother of that little boy goes to her Catholic Church. The grandmother told Liz that her grandson had been telling family members that he talks to satan. When the grandmother tries to get the parents to look into the matter, she is shut out of the little boy's life. I'm not sure what happened to the little boy, but I know the grandmother is praying and trying her best to help her grandson.

I told a woman whom I consider very holy (due to her work, lifestyle choices and prayer life) about this little boy and possible demonic possession. Her first response was "What's the mother into?"

Meaning if the mother is practicing some type of involvement in occult practices (witchcraft, Ouija boards, séances, palm reading, tarot cards, hypnotism, divination, astrology, black magic, sorcery, etc…); then she has opened up her house to satan. Beware of anything you do in your house that invites satan in; you and your children will be in great danger. This warning includes what you watch on television, the music you and your children listen to, the clothes you wear, tattoos permanently stained into your skin etc…. If you are honoring satan then he is your father. If you are promoting evil and ignoring your Heavenly Father, what sort of judgment do you think is waiting for you and all those you have influenced…like your children! Common sense should tell you to honor your Father in Heaven and stay away from anything that takes you away from your Father in Heaven. I believe Liz's story…and want to warn everyone to stay clear away from any source of sacrilege!

●●

There is no way to transition gracefully back to the story after such a stern warning, but here goes…

Now back to the McGolly family pulley systems.

They would fish with many hooks and string the pulley gadget across the creek,

an hour later they had enough fish to eat for a week.

Fish tacos, fish croquettes, fish sandwiches, grilled, baked, fried fish even fish pies.

They had so much fish it was coming out of their eyes.

Mike and Mark would make fish faces and the other twins would laugh.

At least until Mother would say "Boys, it's time to take your bath."

By the way, they also used the pulley system to fetch water from the spring.

The fresh spring water was used to cook, drink, bathe and clean.

The older kids used the pulley zip lines to breeze through the trees.

Not too far from the ground just in case they fell and scrapped their knees.

Molly, Maryann and Miriam loved singing while bathing in the shower.

When the three of them sang together they were a trio.

Their combined voices sounded much better than the other trio crying:

Shawn, Patrick and Leo.

The angelic vocal cords from Miriam and Maryann made them a dynamic duo singing a duet.

If they had one more girl the trio would be a quartet.

For now the three sang to their heart's content,

while they were showering to get clean by getting wet.

Maryann and Miriam loved to sing their songs in rounds.

So their voices were like echoing sounds.

Their favorite song: Row, Row, Row Your Boat

Row, row, row your boat, gently down the stream.

Merrily, merrily, merrily, merrily life is but a dream.

Sometimes Molly would sing solo.

She could hit the high notes, so she sang soprano.

A hush came over the whole hill.

Everyone and everything became calm;

when Molly sang 'AVE MARIA' her favorite song.

If music soothes the savage beast,

this song seemed to produce peace;

all tension ceased.

Mother would often place a request;

'BATTLE HYMN OF THE REPUBLIC' she loved the best.

Mine eyes have seen the glory of the coming of the Lord;

He is trampling out the vintage where the grapes of wrath are stored;

He hath loosed the fateful lightning of His terrible swift sword;

　　　His truth is marching on

　　　　(Refrain)

Glory! Glory! Hallelujah!　　　Glory! Glory! Hallelujah!

Glory! Glory! Hallelujah!　　　His truth is marching on.

I have seen Him in the watchfires of a hundred circling camps;

They have builded Him an altar in the evening dews and damps;

I can read His righteous sentence by the dim and flaring lamps;

　　　His day is marching on. Refrain

I have read a fiery Gospel writ in burnished rows of steel;

As ye deal with my contempters, so with you my grace shall deal;

Let the "Mother of the Savior" crush the serpent with Her heel;

　　　Since God is marching on. Refrain

He has sounded forth the trumpet that shall never call retreat;

He is sifting out the hearts of men before his judgement seat.

O be swift, my soul, to answer him; be jubilant, my feet!

　　　Our God is marching on. Refrain

In the beauty of the lilies, Christ was born across the sea;

With a glory in His bosom that transfigures you and me.

As He died to make men holy, let us die to make men free.

　　　His truth is marching on. Refrain

••

Even the boys joined in singing during the Refrain.

It was like the hill was alive when this song was sang.

Maureen McGolly once heard or perhaps she had a dream that this song

is the Virgin Mary's favorite song.

Since she loves Mary so much, maybe that's why she chose it as her favorite song as well.

It's a powerful song, listen to the words and upon them dwell.

Are you living your life on a path to Heaven or Hell!?

The battle has already on, which side are you on?

All confirmed Catholics are soldiers for Christ

and must be ready to defend Christ and His Church with their life.

••

　　　Mom would say "Those who work hard or play hard;

either take a shower or sleep outside in the yard."

Once Mike and Mark tried sleeping outside at night,

they refused to take their showers and smelled ripe!

Both took the quickest showers ever after the very first coyote howl;
almost forgot to dry off with a towel.
Mom didn't say a word, you know she only smiled at night;
that night she smiled til daylight.
The McGolly's needed a shower or bath at the end of the day.
Most of their time was spent outside for work and play.
Little of their time was spent in front of the television;
due to the fact at the top of the hill on the outskirts of town
they got poor television reception.
Molly loved swinging on the zip lines through the trees like Jane and Tarzan;
playing manhunt when it got dark and kick the can.
She and her siblings played leap frog while in the pond or creek.
It was so much fun playing outside they didn't want to go inside to eat or sleep.
Even playing hide and seek was a blast,
or watching for shooting stars while lying on a blanket in the grass.
Spending rainy days on the big covered porch was fun too.
They played board games like Chutes and Ladders and Monopoly
and card games like Go Fish, Old Maid and Juice Rummy.
However, the all time favorite McGolly game was Bingo.
They loved it so much, they named their dog Bingo.
B-I-N-G-O   B-I-N-G-O   B-I-N-G-O and Bingo was his name O!
Everyone who played had to bring something worth winning.
If you didn't, you got banished and had to sit in the kitchen.
Good stuff included a cool rock found on the hill
or something they made in the woodshop or on the pottery wheel.
Maybe a fresh piece of fruit from one of the trees.
Miriam and/or Maryann sometimes brought jars of honey from the honeybees.
Since honey is so yummy and sweet,
that was a really good treat!
Solitary activities were also popular like painting, reading a book or writing a poem.
Or playing a practical joke on your twin when they're least expecting one;
then being thankful they were not conjoined.
They took turns playing the piano unless two would play chopsticks together.
Checkers by the fireplace, another twosome activity during rainy weather.
Dad occasionally would teach the older kids his woodworking craft.
Mom would show the children how to bake cookies or tell a joke and make them laugh.
Grandma McFrugal taught Molly how to sew and beginning crochet.
Molly and Grandma would rock back and forth in the rocking chairs knitting away all day.
So, this was the home life of Molly McGolly;
who was part of a large Irish Catholic family.

To the fullest they lived their faith and took care of God's beautiful green earth,

almost from the moment of their birth.

Reduce- Reuse-Recycle-Repent

but not in this order...get the hint!

God first in every decision.

Most children know right from wrong by the age of three.

Make sure your exposing your children only to what God would want the innocent to hear or see.

Parents you are your children's first teachers,

show them how to love by example: Start by loving each other.

A husband as head of the family is to love, honor and cherish his wife.

The first time a husband looks at his wife with distain or strife,

he starts replacing love, honor and cherish with hate and/or unforgiveness.

Left unchecked, meaning not going to confession on a regular bases;

in time hate and/or unforgiveness can overtake love, honor and cherish.

So for heaven sake!

Go to confession before it's too late!

Husbands don't be so proud to admit sometimes you might need help with your small domestic church.

Your wife and children are relying on you for guidance to get them to Heaven

and to feel secure here on earth.

Husbands as head of the family you should be looking up instead of giving up!

Half the men in this country have already failed.

Husbands you get one wife, you can't give her up and take up with another;

for that is not the vow you gave to God and each other.

Divorce is an unresolved conflict and the death of a marriage; part of the culture of death.

What God has put together, no human power can dissolve.

Men are you battle ready?

Do the hard work required to weather the storm so you can come out on the other side;

your ship (your soul and the souls of your family) sailing toward the horizon.

Remember you're teaching your children by example and they're watching your every move.

They too will have storms to weather; what will they have learned from you!?

Of course sometimes no matter what you do things will still fall through the cracks.

Put God first and leave the consequences to Him and you will have no regrets.

Natural Family Planning (N.F.P.) is a way to open up the lines of communication in holy matrimony.

Here are a few other ways to get you and your family to Heaven:

1). Be a good example by word and deed; Go to confession at least once a month.
2). Go to Holy Mass every Sunday and Holy Days of Obligation (and listen).
3). Learn about Natural Family Planning even if your wife is not interested at first (maybe with good Christ centered conversations you will be able to share what you have learned).

4). Join a men's group at the Catholic Church (this is where you will find encouragement to live a faithful Catholic life). Remember no one there is perfect either...encourage each other to live as Catholics ought!

5). Pray, pray, pray. Find time in your day to grow in your faith.

6). Stay away from the porn trap. What a man does when no one is looking shows his true character.

7). Follow All the Commandments (they are not negotiable).

8). Love your holy matrimony sacramental wife...your whole life (til death do you part).

9). Make sure all of your children are receiving proper catechism classes and the sacraments. Make sure all of your children are confirmed in the Catholic faith (remember to be a good example).

10). Talk to all of your children about living a chaste life style until they are married. Tell them about the benefits of a holy matrimony marriage (age appropriate and remember each child is different). Do this several times throughout their lives so they will be properly prepared to resist temptations as they arise. Please do this in a grace filled way; in other words pray about these Christ centered conversations ahead of time.

*Feel free to change the order of the above suggestions as long as you do all of them.

■■

WRONG IS WRONG EVEN IF EVERYONE IS DOING IT
RIGHT IS RIGHT EVEN IF NO ONE IS DOING IT

■■

Women: Here are a few suggestions to grow in holiness. Remember the woman is the heart of the household.

1). Go to confession at least once a month. Confession is good for the soul. Air your dirty laundry including what you're watching on television, computer and cell phone, and what you're wearing out in public (cover up your cleavage and other parts of your body that ought not be exposed).

2). Love your holy matrimony husband with all his virtues and shortcomings. No one is perfect, but with love and God (Father/Son/Holy Spirit) the relationship can be strengthened and grow in holiness.

3). Go to Holy Mass every Sunday and Holy Days of Obligation (and listen).

4). Your body is the temple of the Holy Spirit so take care of your body. This includes not using any form of contraception other than Natural Family Planning (N.F.P.) in a holy matrimony marriage and only for a good reason.

5). Be forgiving.

6). Perform charitable acts with love.

7). Part from female forms of pornography: This includes elicit books, magazines, movies, romance novels, soap operas on television (the daytime and nighttime versions). Men are lured by visual stimulation and women are lured by emotions and relationships. If you don't think men should be looking at porn behind closed doors then women should not be watching soap operas or reading illicit romance novels or watching television shows or movies that lead women to think in sinful ways.

8). Select books, movies, television shows, music, games that will nourish your soul. Refuse to watch or listen to movies/television shows or music that encourage mortal sin (lust, fornication, adultery, divorce and re-marriage without annulment, homosexual acts, birth control (other than N.F.P.), abortion, euthanasia, murder, sacrilege etc…). If you would not feel comfortable with Jesus Christ sitting right next to you while you're watching a movie, television show or computer or cell phone activity then you shouldn't be doing it.

9). Be a good example in word and deed and in all your choices…including how you dress.

10). Smile more and remember God loves you.

Prayer: TO THE BLESSED VIRGIN from a booklet PIETA page # 17

My Queen, my Mother, I give myself entirely to Thee, and to show my devotion to Thee, I consecrate to Thee this day, my eyes, my ears, my mouth, my heart, my whole being without reserve. Wherefore good Mother as I am thine own, keep me, guard me, as thy property and possession. Amen.

"An indulgence of 500 days"

*Author note: Of course you actually have to do this all day. I challenge every man or woman to live this prayer for a full day. Everything you do, watch, hear and say matters.

★★★

Men are you battle ready.

Men, you are the head of your households. It is up to you to get your holy matrimony sacramental wife and any children and yourself to Heaven. It is very difficult for women and children to be good and feel safe if the father of the household doesn't put God (Father/Son/Holy Spirit) first. Men, take this responsibility seriously. Remember when you were confirmed as a soldier of Christ. On your Confirmation Day you received the seven gifts of the Holy Spirit. Men, you are already armed for battle!

All confirmed Catholics are soldiers of Christ. We are an army ready to defend Jesus Christ and His Church with our lives. Keep close to Jesus with the sacraments. Go to confession frequently. Jesus taught Saint Faustina (according to her diary) that He would speak through the Priest in the confessional, even though she could see and talk to Jesus directly herself. Jesus did this to teach us that He is truly in the confessional and will speak through the Priest for us too. Pray before you enter the confessional for TRUTH.

Scripture: John 6: 52-59

The Jews then disputed among themselves, saying, "How can this man give us his flesh to eat?" So Jesus said to them, "Truly, truly, I say to you, unless you eat the flesh of the Son of man and drink his blood, you have no life in you; he who eats my flesh and drinks my blood has eternal life, and I will raise him up at the last day. For my flesh is food indeed, and my blood is drink indeed. He who eats my flesh and drinks my blood abides in me, and I in him. As the living Father sent me, and I live because of the Father, so he who eats me will live because of me. This is the bread which came down from heaven, not such as the fathers ate and died; he who eats this bread will live forever." This he said in the synagogue, as he taught at Caper'na-um.

∙∙

The Catholic Church is the Universal Church founded by Jesus Christ Himself and His apostles.

Scripture John 20:19-23

Jesus Appears to the Disciples

On the evening of that day, the first day of the week, the doors being shut where the disciples were, for fear of the Jews, Jesus came and stood among them and said to them, "Peace be with you." When he had said this, he showed them his hands and his side. Then the disciples were glad when they saw the Lord. Jesus said to them again, "Peace be with you. As the Father has sent me, even so I send you." And when he had said this, he breathed on them, and said to them, "Receive the Holy Spirit. If you forgive the sins of any, they are forgiven; if you retain the sins of any, they are retained."

∙∙

Remember God gave all of us the 10 Commandments and sent His only Son, Jesus (The Way, the Truth and the Life) to show us how to live. Since the Catholic Church was founded by Jesus Christ Himself and His apostles and set up the way Jesus wanted His Church with the sacraments to keep us close to Him, it is the fullness of the faith. The fullness of the faith is a beautiful gift and as Catholics we are blessed to have the TRUTH. Catholics have been given the TRUTH and the fullness of the faith and are held to a higher level than our protestant brothers and sisters. Protestants have been given only partial truth. That is why Protestants should be encouraged to come into full communion with the Catholic Church. Once they are converted they can receive the True Body and Blood of Jesus Christ, and have the benefit of confession to have sins forgiven etc... They bring much devotion and love for Jesus with them, as they grow even closer to Jesus Christ and the fullness of the faith. A Catholic who changes to a protestant religion is in the state of mortal sin called apostasy (leaving the Church). Once you have the TRUTH and the fullness of the faith there is no reason to leave except to do your will over God's Will. The Catholic Church tells you what to think. There is only one objective TRUTH, anything else is choosing your will over God's Will.

Let's look at birth control. The Protestants once believed the same as the Catholics on the subject of birth control until 1930's at the Lambeth Conference. One of the protestant religions approved some form of birth control and that opened the flood gates to many other birth control methods. This in turn has led to promiscuity of many cultures and we have ended up with a world of immorality on a level only 50+ years ago would have never been imagined. This one deviation has led to (lust, fornication, adultery, no-fault divorce, divorce, single parenthood leading to poverty, poverty, abortion, suicide, higher prison population (many don't have a father to help raise them), decline in mental health, and many more bad results. However, people refuse to look at the facts and return to God's laws. Let's bring back the virtue of chastity (for your state in life). No birth control (except Natural Family Planning in a holy matrimony marriage and only for a good reason). Let's foster good marriage practices and keep families together.

If only Catholics would live their faith fully, this would be a better world. When two cultures are mingled; the morality of that society tends to drop to the lowest denominator. As Catholics we can not deviate on any mortal sin. Catholics must live their faith fully and not fall for the ways of the world (secular culture). Once Catholic, always Catholic. We have been given the TRUTH and our Father in Heaven expects us to live it. Catholics, on Judgment Day you will not be able to say 'I didn't know lust or fornication was a mortal sin or I didn't know birth control (other than Natural Family Planning) was a mortal sin...because all Catholics know better (even YOU). So Catholics: It's time to step up to the plate, put your best foot forward and hit this one out of the park. Catholics have the TRUTH but many think they can pick and choose what to do on matters of morality. These Catholics are sometimes called cafeteria Catholics but the more accurate name would be damned Catholics. Mortal sin is the only thing that separates us from God and many of these Catholics refuse to repent. They love their sin/sins more than they do God (Father/Son/Holy Spirit). God has an ocean of mercy to forgive each and every one of us, but you have to ask for forgiveness with true sorrow. Wake Up Catholics and go through your conversion back to God's grace. Depending on how far you have strayed, that is how far you of free will must come back. You can do it! It will be hard to change habits but don't become despondent nor go into despair. Ask Mother Mary and your favorite saints to help you! Increase your prayer life, read the Bible, GO TO CONFESSION!

If you are having trouble forgiving someone who has betrayed or hurt you; try praying for your enemies. Here's a tip that will make it much easier to pray for your enemies: WHEN YOU PRAY FOR YOUR ENEMIES YOU ARE REALLY PRAYING FOR YOURSELF. Why? Through your continued prayers, in time your enemy/enemies have a better chance of converting to God's Will for them in their lives; which is better for you and others. If they are already dead then daily prayers for them will help you eventually to forgive them. Also, it seems that the more you pray for those you have a hard time dealing with, much less wanting to spend any of your valuable time praying for them; in time you will honestly start loving them and wanting them to eventually go to Heaven. There is a peace that comes over those who truly are praying for their enemies in a way pleasing to God. Try praying for your enemy/enemies everyday; keep it up and in time see what happens. You may have to spend some time trying to figure out how they got that way or start replacing negative memories of them with positive/happy times spent together. Your arch enemy may never admit they did anything wrong and they might not want your forgiveness; pray for them anyway. Your prayers will help you forgive them and you will have more peace in life.

SCRIPTURE: Luke 16:18 Marriage indissoluble

'Every one who divorces his wife and marries another commits adultery, and he who marries a woman divorced from her husband commits adultery.

••

SCRIPTURE: Matthew 14: 3-12

For Herod had seized John and bound him and put him in prison, for the sake of Hero'di-as, his brother Phillip's wife; because John said to him, "It is not lawful for you to have her." And though he wanted to put him to death, he feared the people, because they hold him to be a prophet. But when Herod's birthday came, the daughter of Hero'di-as danced before the company, and pleased Herod, so that he promised with an oath to give her whatever she might ask. Prompted by her mother, she said, "Give me the head of John the Baptist here on a platter." And the king was sorry; but because of his oaths and his guests he commanded it to be given; he sent and had John beheaded in the prison, and his head was brought on a platter and given to the girl, and she brought it to her mother. And his disciples came and took the body and buried it; and they went and told Jesus.

••

Author note: John the Baptist didn't change his mind and say it was okay for Herod to be with Hero'di-as. John the Baptist was beheaded (BECAME A MARTYR) for standing for the TRUTH. Look how far many cultures have deviated from the TRUTH, including the United States of America. We now live in a culture that seems to say you have a right to live your life as you choose and leave God out of it. Perhaps that statement is too harsh. Let me try again. We now live in a culture that seems to say you have a right to live your life as you choose and not as you should. There is only one objective TRUTH and you will find it in the Magisterium of the Catholic Church because it was founded by Jesus Christ Himself and set up the way He wanted it with the sacraments to keep us close to Him. One of these sacraments is Holy Matrimony.

So' let's get back to the basics of the Catholic faith and live out your vows in a way pleasing to God. How?

1). Do a virtues checklist on yourself and make the changes necessary to be a good mate. The virtues you do not possess will be the ways you will hurt your spouse in a long relationship (marriage).
2). Prior to marriage do a virtues checklist on your future spouse. The virtues they do not possess will be the ways they will hurt you in a long relationship.
3). If married and going through a difficult period (any length of time short or long), pray. If you're already praying, then pray more. If you're already praying, going to Holy Mass and in the state of grace; then try fasting. People have forgotten prayer and fasting can suspend natural laws and ward off wars.

Difficulties in marriage can sometimes feel like a war. A friend of mine told me she was very unhappy in her marriage for several years. Everyone she confided; encouraged her to get a divorce (this included her father, friends and close coworkers). No one encouraged her to work through these very difficult circumstances (husband lost his job, husband faced a drug addiction brought on by difficulty trying to find a job, her health compromised by brain tumor and resulting stroke, living far away from family and other issues). She had a strong Catholic Christian faith and decided to start fasting once a week (from 6am-6pm every Friday/ having only bread and water during this time period/after 6pm she would eat a normal dinner). She looked right at me and with conviction stated "It worked!" I asked her how long did she fast before she started seeing results and she told me "about a year". To me this did not seem like very long because I too had been in an unhappy marriage for many years. The point to this story is that it never occurred to me to fast. So before falling for the ways of the world which leads to the destruction of family values; try prayer and fasting. She and her husband celebrated their 25th wedding anniversary by renewing their marriage vows in the Catholic Church. A wonderful way to show the youth of today by putting God (Father/Son/Holy Spirit) first; marriages can survive the trials of today. Remember, it is the vow you take to God and your spouse that is the matter in the sacrament of Holy Matrimony. Someday God will ask you about the vow you took in front of Him and your spouse. What will be your answer? Did you live up to the vow in good times and in bad, for richer or poorer, in sickness and in health til death did you part?

Attending weddings is another important decision. A Catholic who attends a wedding that is in contrast to Catholic teaching (such as someone who was married in the Catholic Church procured a civil divorce but did not get an annulment from the Church and marries another is in the state of mortal sin (adultery), married by the Justice of the Peace or another (a non holy union) without the mention of God (Father/Son/Holy Spirit) in the vows, married by minister/ pastor of another denomination without obtaining dispensation from the Catholic Church, homosexual marriage etc...) would be in the state of mortal sin by attending/supporting these unholy unions. If you're invited to a wedding; before you R.S.V.P. ask a few questions and also express your reservations for unholy unions compassionately but truthfully. Someday God will ask you if you knew homosexual acts offend Him. What will be your answer? He will want to know why you led your friend / family member / adult child to commit such acts when you knew it offends Him. Why did you not talk to these people you love and tell them the TRUTH with compassion. When face to face with God; what will be your answer?

Catholics who marry in the Catholic Church attend marriage preparation classes. Part of the reason for these classes is to help the couple foresee any areas of conflict ahead of time and problem solve before they take vows. Unfortunately the Catholic divorce rate is about the same as the general divorce rate (50% or greater). Devout Catholics the divorce rate is about 2-3%. Only about 2-3% of Catholic marriages (sacrament) should be able to get an annulment in the Catholic Church. Yet in the United States many more marriages are being approved for annulment. This discrepancy leaves me puzzled. Perhaps the Catholic Church is giving out too many annulments in the United States... for whatever reason. Maybe the best practice would be to stop making it so easy to get an annulment and make sure these indissoluble holy matrimony unions truly fall within the guidelines for an annulment. As a society we need to reverse 'No fault divorce'. Also as individuals, we need to explore options with our family members/friends/co-workers to keep marriages and families together. Remember, you're probably only getting one side of the story. It can be difficult to bring up reconciliation or working through problems when the other person only wants you to agree with them. They may cut the conversation short, excuse themselves from situations to have to talk to you, make you out to be too righteous. Their reaction may hurt you but as least you put the TRUTH out there for them to think about. What they do with this view point is up to them. Of course if they have not asked for your opinion it might be better to keep it to yourself. If they do want your advice give them the TRUTH with charity as best you can.

Parents, get into practice of giving your children (all ages, even adults) doses of Truth of the Catholic religion their whole life; so it will be natural as issues arise that you need to intervene with love and charity to save their eternal souls. What are the chances that your grown children (now adults) are going to repent with true sorrow for mortal sins in this culture when their own parents are going along with the flow (acting like mortal sin is just fine since so many people are doing it). This means the adult children and the parents are like dead driftwood floating down the river getting ready to go down the waterfall to the abyss of Hell forever! WAKE UP and swim against the current, show that your soul is still alive and well. Encourage chastity until in a holy matrimony marriage; so our culture can clean up this mess we have created by doing our will over God's Will.

••

SCRIPTURE: Matthew 7:1-5 Judging Others
"Judge not, that you be not judged. For with the judgment you pronounce you will be judged, and the measure you give will be the measure you get. Why do you see the speck that is in your brother's eye, but do not notice the log that is in your own eye? Or how can you say to your brother, 'Let me take the speck out of your eye," when there is the log in your own eye? You hypocrite, first take the log out of your own eye, and then you will see clearly to take the speck out of your brother's eye.

••

Author Note: Once you decide to speak the TRUTH and pick up your cross and follow Jesus; get ready for many persecutions. If only people could see that you are standing for TRUTH because you love them. That you love them so much that you are willing to put up with their negative reactions to being told the TRUTH (snares, being told you are being too righteous, being told you are judging them, being told that you lack compassion, being told we don't have to live by those Commandments any more, being told if God didn't want us to use birth control He wouldn't have given us the technology, being told your being to righteous by refusing to give birth control pills to teenagers or anyone, being shunned for defending life by placing a prayer to end abortion on your locker at work. Standing up for TRUTH rarely will make you popular in the secular world even if surrounded by people who claim to be Catholic. So many Catholics are cafeteria Catholics on issues of mortal sin and are refusing to repent because everyone else is doing it. The above Scripture reading: Matthew 7:1-5 was placed next to my locker for my benefit by a co-worker that I spent over a year driving 32 miles one way to sponsor her becoming a Catholic. I am unable to discuss this matter at work for I am waiting for her to open up this topic for conversation. Remember if they don't ask for your opinion, often it is best not to give it. Apparently something I said in the past on issues of morality must have touched a nerve. Most likely she or one of her adult children is/was living in mortal sin. Therefore I'm being too righteous and judging. I find this very common. People will agree with you on matters of morality until you mention something they're doing or someone they love (like an adult child). People in my own family might be doing the same thing and I don't give in and tell them mortal sin is okay; so why would I tell her it's okay to support immorality of people in her family. If a courageous conversation were to begin with this individual; I would try to convey to her I have taken the log out of my own eye. I'm not a hypocrite. I have repented for all of my mortal sins and hopefully most of my venial sins with true sorrow, done my penance and I do not tell people it is alright to commit the same mortal sins or any sins. People seem to think only serial killers and evil dictators are the only ones on a path to hell. When in fact it is us who condemns ourselves to Hell by doing our will over God's Will. Mortal sin is the only thing that separates us from God. So if we die in the state of mortal sin; meaning we never ask for forgiveness with true sorrow; that we have lived our lifestyle in a way unpleasing to God on serious matter and are not sorry... YES GOD ALONE JUDGES; but He did not just throw us out there and say figure it out. Our Loving Father gave us the 10 Commandments and sent His only Son Jesus (The Way, The Truth and The Life) to show us how to live. These 10 Commandments are divided up into mortal and venial sins. It would be good for every soul to review them and also to remember just because everyone is doing it will not hold up on Judgment Day. Pope Francis has challenged all of us to learn the 7 Corporal and the 7 Spiritual Works of Mercy. Here are the 7 Spiritual Works of Mercy: 1). Admonish sinners 2). Instruct the uninformed 3). Counsel the doubtful 4). Comfort the sorrowful 5). Be patient with those in error 6). Forgive offenses 7). Pray for those living and dead.

The first Spiritual Work of Mercy: Admonish sinners, is a difficult task even when trying to be compassionate. Do you love them enough to tell them the TRUTH; knowing most likely they will not take it well? Continue to be a good example in your lifestyle and pray for them. Always be obedient to God and leave the consequences to Him. If no one ever tells them the TRUTH; they could die in the state of mortal sin and be damned to Hell forever.

I recently heard a man state that his devout father when giving him advice on something he probably didn't want to hear; always ended the talk charitably with "Stop what you're doing and come back to the Church" (the Catholic Church). After his father died that statement stuck with him and he did indeed eventually come back to the Catholic Church and is now a deacon (in the Catholic Church).

••

Author Note: I hope and pray the (SEVENTH DAY) of the Novena to the Divine Mercy will give encouragement to those who are leading others to God through TRUTH.

••

So, now let us return to the story of Molly McGolly.

Molly decided this would be the year to teach her classmates to be green;

for them to follow her lead and take care of every living thing.

From the bees that buzz

      to the flowers that was.

You know the circle of life must thrive

      to keep all things alive;

            including us if we want to survive.

To make a good impression on the first day of school;

Molly laid out her clothes the day before to be 'cool'.

You see, every morning she dressed in the dark to conserve electricity.

Some days she chose not to brush her teeth; to save water.

On those days she would chew on a mint sprig from the herb garden.

After the first week of school, Molly just dressed in the dark without coordinating her ensemble.

Sometimes when you're trying to make a point, you have to be original.

The point was to reduce, recycle, reuse and save the PLANET!

For the planet won't be pretty very long if there's nothing on it.

Molly rode her bike to school every day with her brothers Mike and Mark the twins;

that's right, just one bike not three.

Molly sat on the seat and pedaled with a twin brother on each knee.

Mike had the family official bike helmet.

Mark wore Dad's old high school football helmet

and Molly a pot for a plant (today no plant in it).

They lived at the top of the highest of hills

and on good days had two inflated wheels.

You should see them when it's raining with their make shift umbrellas.

It looks like the Wright Brothers coming in for a landing.

Molly's clothes didn't match and sometimes her shoes were in the wrong place.

(LUCK OF THE IRISH) She was too young to wear make-up upon her face.

Instead of having green mint sprigs stuck to their teeth

the other girls in her class preferred to brush theirs.

They dressed at home with the lights on,

so their clothes matched and wore their shoes in pairs.

The more fashionable girls were trying to get handsome Joe's attention.

But he paid no attention to them because Molly was much more interesting.

He would say "You look ridiculous with that flower pot."

In which case she would retort "ridiculous or hot!"

Molly would wear the most unusual outfits.

Stripes with polka dots, pants as sleeves,

sweaters inside out, miniskirts to her knees.

Once she sported a hat that looked like her father's briefs.

From her head to her toes...anything goes!

Would Molly have a bird in her hair

or some dirt from the flower pot there!

Were those freckles on her face or bird droppings?

Did she wear glasses so she could see or so the birds would have a perch?

If she dressed like this for school, what did she wear to church?

The McGolly children were seated at their desks with seconds to spare,

before the tardy bell rang, Molly removed the flower pot from her hair.

Her hair was red and curly whether she brushed it or not;

it always seemed messy and had a few knots.

The kids in her class made fun of her hair

in which she replied "I do it on purpose so the birds can nest there."

"Do you keep it dirty too, so the birds can dig for worms?" chuckled William the water boy.

"Of course I do because Mother Nature is my friend not foe"

Molly softly spoke in her most hospitable southern belle voice so very gentle and low.

William got the hint that Molly was not amused by his statement that was mean.

Molly pondered, well maybe her hair was a little dirty but for a good reason.

However his hair was much too clean.

The water boy washed his hair 3 to 4 times a day, it was always wet;

and he put on clean clothes even more than that.

His family watered their lawn everyday

and twice on Saturday.

From the top of the hill Molly could see his house.

It had the greenist lawn

and ornate water fountain complete with manmade cement pond.

Even when there were city wide drought restrictions,

William's family continued to water their lawn without permission.

So William the water boy and Molly had a difference of opinion;

on the resource of water and when and if it was to be given.

William the water boy seemed to want to waste water.

He would stand at the water fountain at school and hold the release button

while he looked around not taking a sip.

Molly would walk by and remark "Water, water everywhere but not a drop to drink?"

with a frown on her face while raising her lower lip.

She wanted to say "Hey buddy, you have to move your mouth to the water,

I have a dog that is smarter."

Molly knew these actions were unkind and she would have to bring it up during confession with a priest.

So she had to come up with a positive reason why the water boy was such a beast.

Maybe he would grow up to be an elite scuba diver

or make the U.S.A. proud and be a gold medal Olympic swimmer.

Perhaps this was the reason William the water boy was draining the city of every drop of water.

Molly decided to be more tolerate and patient.

She would win William over by being nicer or maybe she would just set him on fire.

So he would have a good reason to use all that water!

Wasting water was a hot button issue;

coupled with her red headed Irish temper too!

Molly was going to have to learn to pick her battles with a calm cool head.

Persuasion is an art achieved by firm kindness and sound advice.

Her advice would sound like this "Stop wasting water" while trying to be nice.

This classmate was going to be a challenge; a thorn in her side.

However, Molly had another classmate who was already on her side.

Sonny was Molly's best friend and they went together everywhere.

He was handicapped and sat in front of Molly in his wheelchair.

Sonny ran the school's Clothes Closet mission;

recycling gently used clothing or blue jeans in any condition.

Later this spring Sonny's mother and the P.T.A. are organizing a school wide garage sale charity event;

to take place on the teacher's parking lot Earth Day April 22nd.

Clothes, furniture, bikes, books and maybe a few of the teacher's cars to be sold;

to raise money for a good cause, they were told.

Sonny and Molly shared a common bond as best friends often do.

They had a homing pigeon named Homer; from one house to the other it flew.

Instead of using electricity by cell phone, texting or E-mail

      by computer or checking a list by some guy named Craig;

Sonny and Molly wrote important messages in secret code tied to the pigeon's leg.

They were making plans to get a Saint Bernard snow dog.

The dog would be able to carry more around its neck in the medicine barrel collar log.

Very cool if you need medical attention, want to share a snack or surprise someone with a jumping frog.

Sonny had bigger dreams; he wanted a horse to deliver his mail by pony express;

that way he could deliver his messages in person on the back of a trained stallion

      like back in the wild, wild west.

But for now, Sonny and Molly became good pen pigeon pals.

Molly wanted to be a good example;

she practiced what she preached and then some.

      Recycle, reduce, reuse or just plain do without.

      Have you ever noticed: People who always want more, more, more;

      never seem to have enough.

People who have almost nothing are thankful for what they've got
especially when times are tough.

The very first day of school Molly made a grand entrance, even though a bit absurd;
she had a nest on her head complete with a mockingbird.

The teacher instructed her to lose the bird hat by placing it on the rack in the back.

Second only to Molly's baby brother triplets this bird craved attention.

That bird talked all day until it was sent to detention.

Then the principal set it free, which seemed prudent;
after all it was a bird and not a student!

On the first day of school in September, Molly brought her teacher a shiny red apple;
and for the rest of the class a basketful.

She encouraged her class to take the apple cores including the seeds
and throw them on good soil on the way home somewhere;
that way in the future there would be more apples to share.

Water boy William spent ten minutes washing his apple before he took a bite.

Molly watched all that wasted water flow down the water fountain pipe.

The color drained from her face as she watched the steady stream disappearing
down, down, down the drain.

Molly had to muster all the strength she had and it was quite a strain.

She bowed her head and said a silent prayer

"Dear Lord, keep me from pulling out all his wet hair."

Down deep in her heart she knew this thought would offend Jesus.

So she bowed her head again and asked Jesus for forgiveness.

That evening Molly painted beautiful posters promoting water conservation.

The next day at school she was allowed to display the posters with the principal's permission.

The school hallway looked like a nature preserve, it was pretty cool!

The posters were all different and very colorful.

Scenes with rivers, streams and trees
and others with flowers, animals and birds and bees.

Each had the words SAVE THE PLANET and CONSERVE WATER.

Molly placed the biggest painting by the water fountain, reaching from the ceiling to the floor.

Even water boy William would find this giant poster impossible to ignore!

The posters had slogans like: Turn off the running water when you brush your teeth;

Use only the water that you need; To use less water take a bath or time your showers.

She also put up a suggestion box to encourage others.

The appropriate suggestions were put into action.

The jokes were posted in the teacher's lounge as a humorous distraction.

Good suggestion: Rain, rain go away, come again another day.

Replace with: RAIN, RAIN YOU ARE OUR FRIEND.
WE NEED YOU TO GROW OUR FOOD AND THE EARTH TO CLEANSE.

Once the suggestion box
                was full of rocks.
Molly knew this foul deed was the work of Mike and Mark her mischievous brothers.
So she took the rocks home and put them in their bunk beds under the covers.
That night when they hopped into bed and felt the rocky lumps;
Molly leisurely strolled by and stated "You two are lucky Dad doesn't know or you guys might
                have sore rumps.
Water conservation is a serious affair, we should all care".
The two boys just looked at each other with bewildered stares.
They couldn't tell on Molly or they too would be in trouble.
So they pulled back their bed covers and cleaned up the rubble.
Mark stated "Sometimes you win and sometimes you lose."
Mike finished "It's more fun to win, you get less bruised."
So the school year started off with a bang!
She wanted to save the earth and every living thang!
Every school day she arrived on the bike before the first bell rang.
After school she and her twin brothers returned home the same way,
                after the last bell clanged.
Coasting the bike downhill to school was easy;
after school pedaling uphill made Molly's breathing a bit wheezy.
Mother McGolly would say "Offer your suffering for the poor souls in Purgatory
                and you will receive graces".
This phrase was shortened to "offer it up" and stated frequently and in many places.
Sometimes Molly had the twins take turns pushing the bike uphill;
while she sat comfortably on the seat to steer the front wheel.
She would say to her very competitive brothers "Who has the biggest muscles
since your both getting so strong?"
Instantly it was as if a rocket was strapped to the back fender
                as Molly whistled merrily along!
Molly didn't really care why they were so competitive,
                as long as it worked to her advantage.
                In October, once again Molly tried to lead by example.
She wanted to take care of the earth and it's beautiful animals and people.
October 4th the Catholic Church celebrates the
                Feast Day of Saint Francis of Assisi (The Peace Saint).
He is also known as the patron saint of environmentalist.
In celebration of St. Francis of Assisi Feast Day was the blessing of the animals.
All pets needed to be in cages or leashed.
Baggies for accidents were provided and also water and dog treats.
The Church bulletin stated: Invite your friends; even the two legged variety.

Event starts 8am sharp and is over at 8:30.
The McGolly family brought Alley the cat, Bingo the dog, Bandit the raccoon
      and the youngest milk cow Muffy.
Sonny brought Homer the homing pigeon and one of his sheep named Fluffy
      which looked extra puffy.
There were lots of cats, dogs, birds and guinea pigs
      but the most unusual pet was a monkey.
The Monks had a pet monkey named Monk.
Soon after the monkey received his blessing he got away and climbed a tree that had a trunk.
The monks laughed and remained calm
      as one of the monks held a banana in his palm.
Down came Monk ready to eat … the desired monkey treat.
Monk the monkey didn't need a leash he jumped from one monk to the other
      on their backs, but mostly their shoulders.
Now, Mike and Mark wanted a monkey and began their monkey search.
While Molly refocused on her mission to save the earth;
      This all happened October 4th at the Catholic Church.
      The next day at school Molly gave water boy William a tall cool glass of water
before he got into the water fountain line.
She greeted him with a pleasant smile and he took the gesture fine.
Molly thought maybe he was changing his water wasting way;
until the very next day.
William the water boy gave Molly a bottle of shampoo and a new hair brush set.
He gave the gift with a smile and she thanked him; so they were both politically correct.
Molly pondered; one step forward and two steps back;
the water boy was not going to be an easy nut to crack.
Next time she gave him a glass of water she was going to pour it over his head;
but on second thought he might like that so she decided not to instead.
She must continue to be nice; as the saying goes:
      'You catch more flies with honey than vinegar.'
However, Molly wasn't trying to catch flies, she was trying to conserve water.
She decided to branch out and try a new strategy.
Molly wanted to reach out to more people in the school and community.
Instead of spending so much time trying to convert the water boy;
why not reach out to more people to become save the earth green with joy!
Recycle, reduce and reuse; it was time to refocus on the goal.
October was a good month to promote the Clothes Closet as school.
Sonny and Molly worked together and made scarecrows with the recycled clothing.
They placed them by the pickup and drop off point for students every morning.
The signs read: Donate clothes your children have out grown

or swap clothing, remember your kids are still growing.

Molly and her twin brothers were the Clothes Closet's best customers.

Mike and Mark posed as live manikins with the scarecrows; just to ruffle Molly's feathers.

This caused a donation collection boom,

      so Sonny and Molly joined the charade with her goofy brothers.

She even added a couple of live crows on her shoulders.

Molly made her Halloween costume by recycling clothing found in a trunk in the attic.

She conserved materials, money and even gas not having to drive to the mall like a shop-a-holic.

The more popular girls purchased their ready-made costumes at the party store.

They were no match for Molly as she entered the classroom door.

Molly had a vintage Victorian red velvet dress full of ruffles and lace;

white gloves, hair up puffy in a bun with a gold crown and powder white face.

Red ruby lips, short black strap up boots;

she even had classical music playing from underneath her wire bustle caboose.

Who would have ever expected Molly to dress better on Halloween

than she did any other day of the year?

Handsome Joe certainly didn't, he almost fell out of the chair!

The popular girls were impressed but a bit jealous.

A few spiteful remarks surfaced such as: Molly must have eaten a bushel of cherries from

      the family cherry trees to get her lips that color;

        AND The McGolly family must have been recycling their clothes since the Victorian Era.

Molly also helped her younger brothers and sisters with their Halloween hand-made costumes.

Mike and Mark were pirates (pillage and plunder).

Maryann and Miriam dressed as gypsies (the world to wander).

John and Joseph were disguised as ghosts draped with white sheets.

They kept taking off the sheets and stepping on them leaving dark spots.

Molly said they were Dalmatians instead of ghost tots.

She decorated bio degradable brown paper grocery bags to use while candy collecting;

not brand new plastic trick or treat bags which will end up in a landfill for a thousand years,

starting the next morning.

The older twins had another use for the brown paper bags.

Mike and Mark made stink bombs by filling the bags with who knows what;

better not to ask or you might throw up!

They catapulted these bags into people's yards that did not give our candy, money

      or good baseball cards.

According to Mike and Mark those people deserved what they got,

because they were suppose to give out candy or watch out!

Their house could get toilet papered, egged or become a stink bomb recipient.

After all it's All Hallows Eve and the ghoals are disobedient!

Not to mention their most likely on a sugar high.

So don't turn off your lights and try to hide,

and mistakenly think your house is off limits;

because your house isn't going anywhere and it's a pretty big target!

The McGolly's celebrated October 31st All Hallows Eve (also known as Halloween or All Saints Eve);

not out of superstition but just out of fun.

They dressed up in costumes going door to door collecting candy while on the run.

At the end of the night, Mom shouted from the bottom of the stairs

"Kids, get in bed and say your prayers; The Our Father, Hail Mary and Glory Be and the Guardian Angel prayer to watch over thee and while your at it, say a prayer for me!"

It's not an easy task getting children to sleep after eating so much processed glucose.

That night Mother McGolly didn't smile at all;

> her facial expression looked like a scary ghost.

The triplets bawled, and both sets of boy twins brawled;

> Maryann and Miriam had tummy aches all night long.

Mother McGolly declared "No trick or treating next year,

> I'm going to cut October 31st right out of the calendar."

Now, Halloween or All Saints Eve is celebrated October 31st.

Which means All Saints Day is celebrated November 1st.

All Saints Day is a Holy Day of Obligation.

This means it is mandatory to go to Holy Mass no matter what day of the week it falls on.

Catholics consider the saints our older brothers and sisters who went straight to Heaven

> when they died.

The saints were in the state of grace which means no mortal sin (at the time of death) and were not held down by pride.

They put God's will first and the 1st Commandment they did abide.

Some of the saints lived their whole lives in accordance with God's will (like Saint Therese of the Child Jesus and the Holy Face; who was told by her confessor she had never committed a mortal sin); and others only after a great conversion (like Mary Magdalene and Saint Augustine) of free will, dramatically changed their life styles.

Putting God's will first above your own will involves many self sacrificing trials.

The saints proved it can be done and are our great examples.

Many of the saints were martyrs too;

> they gave the ultimate sacrifice...their very lives.

JESUS IS LORD IS THE TRUTH

If you die a martyr defending Jesus and His Church, you immediately go to Heaven like the saints.

Believe it or not, there is an up side to dying for Mother Church (the Catholic Church)...no Purgatory!

Remember while in your death agony that Jesus is right beside you.

Song: Be Not Afraid

Part of song: Be not afraid, I go before you always. Come, follow Me and I will lead you home.

After dying a martyr's death, your reward will be instant.

You will be in Heaven and see the beatific vision;

no more suffering and no more pain;

only love and joy forever are gained.

Red martyrs are killed defending the faith whether eaten by lions in a coliseum

or by spilling of their blood by other forms of violence being done to them.

Martyrs bring many souls to the Christian faith.

People want to know about what was important enough to give their lives for...and the

answer is Jesus Christ and His Church.

Christians are not to retaliate back with violence.

Violence only begets more violence.

Remember Jesus stopped Peter (upon this rock I will build My Church) after cutting off

a roman soldier's ear in the Garden of Gethsemane.

Jesus then healed the soldier's ear before they put Him in chains and led Him to be condemned.

Jesus said to Peter something like "No, violence is never the answer".

It's not a tooth for a tooth but rather turn the other cheek.

Live by the sword, die by the sword;

  pain and suffering all around.

Violence is a vicious circle with no end to be found.

Consult a priest on matters of self defense

  or when fighting back is justified like Saint Joan of Arc.

So Christians, up your prayer life and start fasting on a regular bases.

I heard or had a dream that when they lined up all the Christians who were killed by lions

in the coliseum; they all had smiles on their faces.

Their sacrifice merited an immediate reward.

The martyrs were instantly in Heaven with their Lord.

Saint Philomena was a child red martyr; about 12 or 13 years of age.

Saint Philomena was a child princess and traveled with her parents to ask for protection

for their small kingdom from a powerful ruler.

This ruler wanted to marry Philomena but she refused.

Philomena had vowed to remain a virgin giving her whole life to Jesus

and never wavered from her conviction.

Her parents pleaded with her stating that she was too young to make such an oath

and by marrying this ruler her life would be spared and the whole kingdom would be protected!

Young Philomena would not waver in her pledge to Jesus.

The ruler first had flaming arrows shot at Philomena; which turned in mid-air

killing all the archers.

The ruler then had Philomena thrown off a bridge into raging waters chained to an anchor.

She was miraculously freed from the anchor and survived!

Next, the ruler had her thrown into a dungeon where she died on a cold floor.

Mother Mary and two angels appeared to Philomena letting her know she didn't have much longer to suffer; about five days later Philomena died.

Saint Philomena, powerful with God, pray for us!

Saint Philomena is one of the patron saints of "hopeless" and "impossible" causes, like St. Jude and St. Rita.

Saint Philomena is known to be especially powerful in cases involving

> conversion of sinners,
>
> return to the Sacraments,
>
> expectant mothers,
>
> destitute mothers,
>
> problems with children,
>
> unhappiness in the home,
>
> sterility,
>
> priest and their work,
>
> help for the sick,
>
> the missions,
>
> real estate,
>
> money problems,
>
> food for the poor and
>
> mental illness.

Saint Philomena's devotees have discovered, no case, of whatever matter, is too trivial or too unimportant to concern her.

Saint Philomena never gave up her virginity or her vow to Jesus.

Author Note:

> Virginity is a virtue which God holds in high regard.
>
> The entire Holy Family (Jesus, Mary and Joseph) were/are virgins.
>
> Philomena was a child red martyr.
>
> Others may be called to be white martyrs for their faith.
>
> They may not be called to die a physical death but their sufferings will be great.
>
> Persecutions come in many forms living and defending the Catholic faith.
>
> Perhaps you won't get the promotion at your job; or maybe you will get fired upholding God's laws.

When the government dictates everyone must pay into a healthcare system that forces us to contribute to birth control (other than N.F.P.), abortion, euthanasia, sterilization; all against our religion and in violation to our nation's constitutional first amendment rights; what are we good Catholics to do?!

Let's consider following our conscience and living according to God's laws and the TRUTH of the Catholic Church. Be obedient to God and leave the consequences to Him (good or seemingly bad; but may well end up being for our own good). Since our government is forcing us to go against our religious convictions and the government is very wrong to do this, the only way to combat this great injustice in a peaceful way is to continue to fight in the courts, attempting to wear down the opponents and return to God's laws; reverse Roe vs Wade (stop murdering our children); change health care to include our religious rights (not to pay into a system that supports abortion, euthanasia, birth control(other than N.F.P. in a holy marriage and only for a good reason according to God's laws (Father/Son/Holy Spirit), do away with no fault divorce (take responsibility for our actions & change to a society who supports keeping families together in a way pleasing to God (Father/Son/Holy Spirit).

The other way to win the battle against these forces of evil would be on the home front and very well may include becoming a white (or perhaps a red) martyr for the Catholic faith. Remember you were armed for battle when you were confirmed in the Catholic faith and became a soldier for Christ. At some point we as Catholics may have to walk away from health insurance. We may have to return to pay as you go, and will limit the healthcare we will be able to receive. Major heart surgeries and chemotherapy (these life sustaining elective options) will be difficult for most of us to pay out of pocket. We will possibly have shorter life spans or maybe we will take on healthier life habits and be better to our bodies in the process. Perhaps knowing we can't get the more expensive medications or procedures might encourage us to start treating our bodies like they are temples of the Holy Spirit. Remember: Natural conception to natural death. We must consider if we are willing to take on these consequences since our health care system is forcing us to go against God's Will. Several states have already allowed euthanasia, and with an aging population I fear more states will follow pushing these death sentences. Abortion and euthanasia are ways to kill the people we should love the most. The great deceiver has deceived us all! We will need to bring our aging family members, or other members of our family who may need physical or financial help into our households with love. What a great opportunity to practice the corporal and spiritual works of mercy. In this age of I want what I want and I want it now; reaching out to help our family will take an avalanche of kindness. Other than raising our children, most of us have never had to serve others in this way. Not that long ago, having several generations in one household was the norm. Abortion and euthanasia are mortal sins. If we are forced to pay into these forms of murder and suicide; we must ponder if perhaps we have already sold our souls to the evil one. Catholics at some point we are to walk away from a healthcare system forcing us into supporting mortal sin. God's fifth Commandment: Thou shalt not kill. It seems to me that it would be so simple to have an option in our country's health care system available for those of us who are against paying for birth control, abortion, euthanasia because of our religious convictions to have a separate account. If this option does not open; we as Catholics and like minded peoples will have to go without health insurance. We as employers will not be able to offer health insurance to our employees or for ourselves. Sometimes I think that it might come down to carrying a health insurance card or an identification card that includes health care (either via our country or world) that might be the sign you are owned by the anti Christ. Instead of being a chip in your forehead or a tattoo on your right wrist, the sign is if you of free will have given into evil by paying into a system that encourages/pays for mortal sins. I'm starting to think that only heroic devout Catholics are going to make it past the purification. By this I mean Catholics can't be part of the frozen chosen; you as a confirmed Catholic are required to show your loyalty to God by words and action. You are soldiers of Christ and must defend Jesus and His Church even with your own life. Those Catholics paying into our current healthcare system but not having an abortion or taking birth control themselves are still spreading evil by paying into a system that delivers these services to others. Pretending this isn't affecting our world (including our loved ones very close to us) is a deception. Remember that when mingling two cultures together, the society tends of fall to the lowest denominator. However, we as Catholics are expected to rise above the difficulties and obey our Father in Heaven. We as Catholics should always strive to be in the state of grace at all times; if we fall then we repent with true sorrow, pick ourselves up and continue down the path of rocks and thorns til we someday will cross over to the other side and are in paradise forever. The way to Heaven is narrow. You must be let into Heaven, you can not get there on your own. Yes, we're all a bit confused because social morality has changed so fast; but God has not changed and never will. So, Catholics and like minded peoples (Protestants, Jews, Muslins etc…) of the world; it's time to make that decision (individually and of free will) and if we are not offered a separate health care option truly respecting our religious liberties then cancel your insurance or next time your insurance options come up…cancel your healthcare insurance. The action being not paying into a government system that forces you to go against God. The government is making it illegal not to have healthcare insurance and is offering a form of healthcare. This sounded like a good idea at first but it makes people pay into a system that goes against God on mortal sin/s (birth control, abortion and possibly soon to come euthanasia). If we refuse to have health insurance on the grounds of immorality according to our religion; will we be fined/ refused care at doctor offices or hospitals/thrown into jail like criminals/shot and killed for going against the government???? Once government takes a higher place in our society than God; we are in great danger. Guess what? We are in great danger! It is time we all stand up for the TRUTH and get back to honoring God by living the 10 Commandments and the teaching of Jesus Christ. When we withdraw from God then He can't protect us. When we choose to honor another way and separate ourselves from God of 'free will' then God steps back. We will pay the consequences of our own actions (or inaction). I am currently under a health care plan and hoping the courts can resolve these dilemmas soon. If not; I have a decision to make. Also I'm older and it is becoming increasingly more difficult to do my job, but in order to pay for health care I must continue to work. I may just have to quit my job and pay as I go for healthcare. Will I be fined/refused healthcare/thrown into jail for electing to pay as I go for healthcare. If the government wants me to pay into a healthcare system; it must not force me to go against my religious convictions and be affordable. This does not seem like a difficult task to me; so why are they taking so long to come up with a reasonable solution. I don't really want to give up healthcare insurance but I would much rather go to Heaven someday than Hell for doing nothing to stop so much mortal sin from spreading across the world. If I give up healthcare insurance, this will mean my resources will be limited and possibly someday might have to suffer as a white or red martyr for Jesus and His Church. By the way if having a healthcare card/ identification card (that includes national or world health care forcing us to go against God) turns out to be the sign of the anti-Christ or if it actually is a computer chip in the forehead or tattoo on right wrist; then making the sign of the cross with holy water when we Catholics enter the Catholic Church will remain an invisible sign that we belong to Christ. We will dip our right hand in the holy water and bring it to our forehead; the rest of the holy water will touch our clothing. Remember I said that choosing to not have healthcare insurance that forces us to go against our faith is an individual decision of free will; we must know that not all Catholics will choose to cancel their healthcare insurance (stating they themselves do not go against the teachings of the church or maybe they are cafeteria Catholics and are on a path to Hell because they agree with the government on issues of morality). We as Catholic Christians must be charitable and kind to those who do not think or act as we do. Maybe someday soon the cafeteria Catholics, through our example or what the Priests are teaching from the pulpit will change their minds; not just on healthcare but on morality and our life choices in general. We want everyone to feel welcome in the Catholic Church. Remember, Jesus came to save sinners.

If every family will work together and come up with a solution to aid their elderly loved ones; nursing homes can be for those who have no one to care for them. This way our nation can steer away from euthanasia. Families should attempt to live in close proximity to be able to share the responsibility. Mother Teresa showed us how to treat the elderly, dying and disabled; with love and dignity for every human life (no euthanasia). Maybe Catholic doctors can hang a sign on their doors (Natural Conception to Natural Death) this would let Catholics and other like minded people know they are welcome. Let's get back to love God first (meaning doing God's Will over ours) and our neighbor second. We need to love each other; not kill the people we should love the most! Redemptive suffering has great rewards. Chastity until after married in a holy matrimony marriage also has great rewards. Before closing on the subject healthcare that goes against our Catholic religion; I would like to state that Natural Family Planning (N.F.P.) has another benefit! A way for women to reduce their chances of certain kinds of cancers is to stay away from birth control pills/patches/injections. According to the World Health Organization, the birth control pill is listed as a poison along with asbestos and radon. N.F.P. has no physical side effects, it is natural. Birth control pills, injections and patches are listed as group 1 carcinogens (substances that produce cancer) by the World Health Organization.

••

Remember confirmed Catholics: You were given the seven gifts of the Holy Spirit at your Confirmation.

The seven gifts of the Holy Spirit are: Wisdom, Understanding, Counsel, Piety, Fortitude, Knowledge and Fear of the Lord.

The twelve fruits of the Holy Spirit are: Charity, Joy, Peace, Patience, Kindness, Goodness, Forbearance, Mildness, Faith, Modesty, Self restraint, Chastity.

Catholics, while I'm on my soapbox; I have something else to boldly state: Once Catholic always Catholic. You've received the Truth of Catholic teaching and will be held to it; makes no difference whether or not you agree with it. Truth is Truth and does not change even if you and many people in the world agree with you. Stop allowing yourself to be deceived! WAKE UP! Get out the mustard and spice things up! When I was in Sterrett Alabama to be present during the apparitions of the Virgin Mary on one of my many trips; I blindly opened a Bible and asked the Holy Spirit to select a meaningful scripture passage for me. I opened the Bible and my pointer finger of my right hand landed on the passage about having the faith of a tiny mustard seed and allowing it to grow. I was insulted because at that time I felt I was living a pretty good life. Although the truth was that I was still a cafeteria Catholic and had just begun my conversion back to the Truth of the Catholic faith. Trying to sneak around and hold unto the ways of the world just won't work on God; even if you think you're getting away with it. After all, everyone else is doing it, right! Wrong. Mustard is bitter. Just like tasting mustard for the first time, it can wake up your taste buds! Well, that scripture passage was bitter for me. I wanted to select another passage but you're suppose to go with the first one. I still rejected the meaning of that Bible verse, but guess what? It turns out that it was very fitting for my soul was still rejecting some of the Truths of our faith. God means what He tells us.

Remember a mustard seed, the smallest seed of all the garden plants grows into a large bush with bright yellow flowers that the birds from the sky can see and go to rest on their journey. However the mustard seed can only grow well, if planted in full sunlight. If we have a tiny spark of faith in us, we too can grow spiritually with the light of Jesus Christ to lead the Way. Be that mustard seed. Take that spark of faith buried underneath a lifestyle of doing your own will and join it to Jesus on the cross; because there will be suffering once you decide to follow Jesus. There is an inner joy and peace knowing you are right with God. Nurture that tiny seed of faith until it blossoms and grows into a soul willing to do all that God asks of you…even if called upon to be a white or red martyr for the Catholic Church (the Truth of Catholic Church guided by the Holy Spirit). This may mean refusing to pay into a healthcare system that allows others to participate in mortal sin/s (birth control, abortion, euthanasia). Now would be a good time to say a heartfelt prayer for our elected leaders to pass a healthcare insurance plan that will not make us go against our God. God over nation.

I recently learned that the phrase 'Separation of Church and state' is not found in the documents of 'The Constitution of the United States of America' or the 'Bill of Rights'. Instead it is in a letter written by Thomas Jefferson to a Baptist congregation; ensuring they will always have the right to believe as they wish free, from government interference. The original intent of this phrase 'Separation of Church and state' was to protect our religious liberties, not stomp them out. Somehow this phrase has been twisted by those with an agenda to promote the exact opposite. So if you are under attack and someone tries to harass you into silence; remind them of the true intent of the phrase 'Separation of Church and state'. What IS in the 'Bill of Rights' is religious liberty!

Now let me tell you what this tiny mustard seed did once she realized she was still a cafeteria Catholic. I had to change. I had to start telling the truth. I had to come clean and stop acting like my mortal sin/s which I had repented for, did my penance and no longer engaged or promoted…but they still had repercussions. We Catholics know that on Judgment Day we will also see how our lives (virtues and vices) played out to future generations. What was our influence to our children, spouses, families, friends, co-workers, neighbors, strangers, enemies and anyone else we encountered during our trial here on earth. I realized the concept of sins carrying over from one generation to the next; the sin/s of the father continue to affect future generations because of the father's influence to his own family. I needed to talk to my grown children about the facts of life (the spiritual life). I needed to explain to my adult children about mortal sins that the secular world has normalized but gravely offend God. Boy was I scared. I knew the best course of action was to do this one on one with each of my children and with charity. However, before I knew it, my son who is an aerospace and mechanical engineer was moving off to Seattle Washington for a job. All of his furniture/belongings/truck/motorcycle were on the way to Washington, so my daughter brought him to my house. I had no choice but to 'evangelize' my own children at the same time. We (my ex-husband according to civil law) and myself raised our children in the Catholic religion with the Sacraments. So when I'm referring to evangelizing; I mean state the facts that fornication, living together outside of marriage (with benefits), practicing birth control (in any form, since neither of my children are married), homosexual acts are all mortal sins even if everyone seems to disregard these truths. I was shaking from head to toe; my voice was cracking and my knees were knocking. This had to be done and time was up. I made a nice breakfast and cornered them into an area where they couldn't get away from me. They knew something was up and I'm pretty sure they knew what it was since my conversion was visible. Somehow I stated my business, hopefully with compassion but also sincerity. I don't want my children that I love with all my heart to remain deceived because I didn't do my parental duty and instruct them towards the TRUTH of the Catholic faith. God puts no one in Hell, we do it to ourselves by choosing our will over God's on serious/mortal sin (like lust, fornication, birth control, homosexual acts etc…). The ways of the world are pulling most of us in the wrong direction…downward. I want my beautiful children to live in a world that encourages and nurtures a culture of life; this would include keeping families together. Natural conception to natural death. I gave my son a Bible with an inscription on the inside front cover. My daughter looked overwhelmed and went out for jog around the neighborhood. They both looked at me like I was a religious fanatic. This needed to be done even if it didn't turn out so great but I have peace inside knowing I did it. When are you going to do it? Go ahead and laugh, make fun of me, but this little mustard seed grew a little that day.

Men; as head of your household, are you living your Catholic faith; ALL OF IT!? No picking and choosing of the Commandments. Catholics do not have the excuse of not knowing the TRUTH. They do of course have free will and have the choice of whether to live the fullness of the faith. However, when it comes down to it, on Judgment Day, you will not have the excuse I didn't know better. All Catholics (men, women and children) should aspire to be devout Catholics. I often wonder if to make it past the purification, Catholics will need to be heroic devout Catholics. Rationalization of the unTRUTH leads to cafeteria Catholics (most of which have at least one mortal sin they are not asking for forgiveness). That means that mortal sin/sins remain an eternal sin and therefore eternal punishment. Eternal mortal sin=Eternal punishment. This means you of free will have chosen to separate yourself from God by doing your will over God's will. You may think you are a good person (and maybe you are); but you may be making bad decisions. Evil dictators and serial killers (who do not repent with true sorrow for mortal sins before they die) are not the only ones who will be separated from God forever. Catholics have been given the fullness of the Christian faith and therefore have a responsibility to live accordingly. So, cafeteria Catholics here is your wake up call. Your Father in Heaven loves you and wants you with Him. He created you and wants you with Him in Heaven. OBEY your Father in Heaven...Obey God's 10 Commandments. The Ten Commandments -the only part of the Bible GOD WROTE HIMSELF ON STONE TABLETS. God stated His business! So husbands, and fathers have you stated your business? Are you leading your domestic church/ family in a way pleasing to God (Father/Son/Holy Spirit)? Are you leading by good example and defending your wife, children and all who dwell within your household from dangerous outside influences/evils? What's on your television; in every room? What are your children looking at on the computer, cell phone etc...? Who are your friends and the friends of your children? What television shows and movies are you watching, what music are you listening to, what concerts do you go to, what are you looking at on the computer, what are you doing on your cell phone?????? How do you spend your spare time? Do you have a happy marriage or should you be working to make it better? Maybe it's time to take the whole family camping (turn off the cell phones/ no TV etc...) and have some old fashion family conversations. Bring back dinner around the family dining room table; no television. Fathers, let's talk a little about defense. While your children are young, go to church every Sunday and Holy Days of Obligation, read bible stories and other children stories with good morals, play with your children, help them patiently with their homework (not all children are good students even if their parents were; they may have other virtues, so be kind and patient), give them a father's blessing every night before bedtime, love honor and cherish their mother (your wife), make sure all of your children are getting good religious education classes and become soldiers of Christ with the sacrament of Confirmation. In other words lay a good foundation for your family. The higher the house you want to build, the deeper the foundation to be laid.

When was the last time you went to confession with a Catholic priest? Think about the confessional as being a tomb and when you leave the tomb a new beginning. When was the last time your wife or children went to confession? Go to confession together so your children can see you; the head of the household; go into the confessional. When your family member is going against God's laws; you as head of the family must intervene as a soldier of Christ; state your business! Sometimes you may have to be stern when needed, but your children should know that you love them.

Who do your wife and children idolize? If Jesus was sitting right next to them would He be pleased or offended? Let's face it; most of what is on television is very offensive to God. What's going on inside your house? Ask your family members who they idolize and why. Listen to their television shows, movies, music lyrics, video games and then explain to them why you don't want them to listen/watch/play these activities if they are against God and leading them in the wrong direction. Fathers you only get a short amount of time to influence your children before they are on their own making their own decisions. Let their friends hang out at your house under proper supervision. Maybe you will be the only good example their friend/friends may have... who knows what's going on at their house. You may be the only hope that child ever experiences. One of the spiritual works of mercy given to St. Faustina is to instruct the uninformed and another to be patient with those in error. So give them a positive role model and as a soldier of Christ lead them to Heaven by your good example. Remember Jesus wants us to love each other so lead others outside your immediate family also. Your children are eventually going to move out and need to know how handle all sorts of situations. Of course Dad's your also going to have to play defense. If your daughter or son is hanging around with unsavory bad influences it's time to intervene; ask more questions and get answers, set rules and curfews, say no and state your business.

Husbands and fathers, it is very hard for women and children to be good if the head of the household is breaking God's laws, and then acts like he has the right to do this and God will have to conform. Men, go to Holy Mass, go to confession with priest on a regular bases (once a month or more), love your holy matrimony wife (love, honor and cherish her), lead by good example (word and lifestyle). Live by God's laws: The Ten Commandments. God does not change. The 10 Commandments remain the same yesterday, today and forever. When parents (father and/or mother) have one or more mortal sin/sins they are not sorry for and have incorporated it into their lifestyle; (examples: birth control other than N.F.P., divorce and remarriage without annulment) these actions can be very confusing for the children. They know that what they are taught in the Catholic Church conflicts with what their parents are living at home. If their parents are going against the teaching of the Church and have no remorse or firm action of amendment to change their lifestyle; then what does this mean to the child/children? They may grow up to do the same mortal sins without remorse or may sin in other ways. The parents might act surprised when their child or children grow up and do things that are against God's laws and the teaching of the Catholic Church. Who taught them, parents you did! What did they learn from you? To follow God's laws or it's okay to pick and choose. Parents don't go into despair nor become despondent. It is time to go to confession and take the wooden spike out of your own eye. REPENT, get back into God's good graces and unburden your soul of mortal sin that you for so long have rationalized. God does not change. That means the hardened sinner must change and finally come to the realization that God means what He says and we (His children) must obey Him. Maybe then your grown children will look at their choices and lifestyles and go through their storms, repent and get back to God's loving embrace. We must get back to a society that puts God first in all our choices; starting in our own lives and in our families. Come back to the Catholic Church, we will meet you where you are at...then it is up to you...free will...to grow in holiness.

Now, I would like for all of us to see how far we have veered off course in less than a hundred years. Our Lady of Fatima (year 1917) said that, in this age, more souls are condemned to Hell through sins of lust than any other sin.

In today's world, many people don't consider lust a mortal sin... but it is! God does not change; only man changes. It seems to me that people also do not see acting on lust as a sin (fornication, adultery, the act of homosexuality etc...); many are no longer asking for forgiveness.

The following comes from a book titled: St. Louis De Montfort's True Devotion

Consecration to Mary

Angelus Press
Part of page 51; WEEK 1: DAY 5-SECOND MEDITATION

Lust

Our Lady of Fatima said that, in this age, more souls are condemned to hell through sins of lust than any other sin. In itself, there is nothing wrong with the sexual appetite. Just as God has attached pleasurable sensations to the act of eating and drinking in order to help self-preservation, so, too, has He attached pleasurable feelings to the act of procreation in order to guarantee the propagation of the human race.

Yet, this pleasure is only allowed within the scope of marriage-whose prime purpose is the procreation of children. Outside of marriage, all such pleasure is forbidden. Not only are extra-marital sexual actions forbidden, but so too is the interior desire for those very things. Did not Our Lord say: "But I say to you, that whosoever shall look on a woman, to lust after her, hath already committed adultery with her is his heart" (Mt. 5:28).

————————————————————————————————————

Author Note: Ask for forgiveness now, while there is still time. Start your conversion before that automobile slams into your car or that bolt of lightning strikes that golf club you're holding or your heart attacks! I don't know about you but during a potentially life threatening event or when I'm experiencing extreme pain; I'm not thinking 'Oh this is a good time to get right with God'. Instead I'm thinking; fight or flight/how to get to safety/how to stop the pain. In other words, the best time to start your conversion is right now, while you can pray, ask for guidance and understanding of obeying your Father who art in Heaven. Do an examination of conscience and go to confession. Go to holy Mass at least weekly and listen.

At some point the period of God's Mercy will end and then will come the Justice of God or you could die before then and have your personnel judgment. You do not want to be in mortal sin and unrepentant for any mortal sin/s upon your death.

(Matthew 23:33) You generation of vipers, how can you (expect to) escape the damnation of hell?

★★

Author Note: Dear Mothers,

Let's talk about our part in the family. Mothers are the heart of the household and should always be growing in their faith. Blessed Mary our Heavenly Mother is our perfect model of all motherhood. At the foot of the cross, Jesus gave His Mother to all of us.

Scripture John 19: 26-27 When Jesus saw His Mother and the disciple whom He loved, He said to His Mother: "Mother, behold, your son."

Then He said to the disciple: "Behold your Mother". And from that hour the disciple gave her into his home. ✱✱✱✱✱✱✱✱✱(end of Scripture passage).

Mothers will also have to be fighters for the faith. She must be strong and often take up spiritual weapons in order to protect her children from the poison of false doctrine or immorality present in our culture. Prayer: All prayer (to God the Father/Son/Holy Spirit) is good. Formal prayers or informal prayers are good and knowing they are good... leads to more prayer! The holy rosary is a beautiful prayer/s and can be said privately in silence or with prayer groups or even while doing the pots and pans. Fasting: on bread and water only, once a week (either 12 hours or 24 hours; if your health permits it). Work towards some type of fasting: maybe no sweets or something you love to eat...depriving yourself of a luxury is good for the soul...offer it up for the poor souls in purgatory or for a special intention (if it is pleasing to God). Fridays no meat (unless you replace not eating meat on Friday with charity for others). Have religious articles around the home and have them blessed by a Priest/s. Place a blessed crucifix in a place of prominence in your house (like at the entrance to your home). I would encourage every Catholic household to have a blessed crucifix on the outside of their house at the front door and the back door; that way the angels will know where you live. Also have plain white wax candles (blessed by Catholic Priest/s) in your house. Have a picture of Divine Mercy Jesus or the Sacred Heart of Jesus in a place of prominence in your house. Sprinkle holy water inside and outside of your house. Put blessed articles on your children (a crucifix/cross, the scapular, necklaces with their favorite saint/s, the Miraculous Medal). Teach your children how to say the rosary by reciting it every night (or some specific time); even if sporadically is better than never. If you don't know how to say the rosary then learn. I was in my 30's before I taught myself how to say the rosary. I said it 3 times a day during that time (for a special intention...to end war) and received sprinkles of joy in my heart that I had never experienced before. These sprinkles of joy (like an orgasm of the heart) happened during the time of literally religiously saying the rosary 3 times a day every day; but not necessarily when I was saying the rosary.

However, I had no doubt whatsoever that I received these signal graces because I devoutly was saying the rosary 3 times a day every day. I no longer have these sprinkles of joy on my heart (not much anyway); maybe that was a way for me to be encouraged to keep praying. Now I just enjoy praying and feel incomplete if I don't pray (to be honest, some days more than others).

Ladies, read the Holy Bible. I like to listen to the daily Holy Mass on E.W.T.N. (Eternal Word Television Network) when I can. This way I hear the word of God and get to hear the homily (which I love). When your children come home from school, plop them down in front of the television with a snack and have them get a daily dose of religion by watching E.W.T.N.

(Eternal Word Television Network/ the Catholic Station). They will learn about their Catholic faith; watch it with them and you too will learn. I love watching the children's programs, I've learned a lot!

Okay ladies, If you are not going to confession with a Catholic Priest, then why not? Whatever you are afraid of is why you need to go. The Priests are usually very nice and will make you feel comfortable; they want you to be there so they can help you. The first time I went back to confession after being gone a long time; I had a list of things to bring up. Somehow, I was in and out before I knew it and only a few things on my list had been addressed. I think that was the way Jesus wanted it; I had something to work on and started returning more frequently. Today I go to confession about once a month. In today's world many of us have gone astray and don't really know how to get back on track. Go to confession and be honest, then listen because the Priest/s is trying to help you...let him. You may have some work to do; that's okay. Remember ladies, you can't forgive your own sins; even the Pope has to go to confession and he does it about once a week. The Catholic Church was founded by Jesus Christ Himself and His apostles and was the only Christian religion for about 1500 years. The Catholic Church is the purist of the Christian religions. Jesus set up the sacrament of confession/reconciliation the day He rose from the dead on the first Easter Sunday. Jesus had to complete His mission and die for our sins as our Savior before He could give His apostles the power to forgive sins. Remember your Father in Heaven loves you. You and everyone else must be obedient to God and follow His commandments. What does the Catholic Church teach on matrimony, birth control, fornication, abortion, divorce and remarriage?

Think about how the world has turned out because many people are not living according to the laws and teaching of Jesus Christ. What kind of example are you setting for your children when you pick and choose which sins to obey and which sins you have justified. Your children know what the Catholic Church teaches on the subject of fornication/divorce and remarriage/ birth control (no birth control other than N.F.P. in a holy matrimony marriage and for a good reason). When their parents are living in mortal sin according to the Catholic Church and dismissing the behavior as fine because everyone else is doing it; this could cause confusion to your children. Please go to confession and get TRUTH before it's too late. Also, your children may do the same sin/s as you or different ones. Where did they learn it? Your actions have consequences. Your influence on other people; also have consequences. On Judgment Day we will see what the consequences of our actions were on other people (even generations). Some of the modern day prophets and at least one noted saint (Saint Padre Pio) have prophesied about an event in which every person on earth (at the same time) will know where they stand with God. I'm not good at research so I encourage those of you who are to find out more about a paper written by St. Padre Pio to the Commission of Heroldsbach. I've read or heard this event called by different names (the Harmless Warning by St. Padre Pio; others have called it The Illumination of the Soul and Judgment in Miniature). St. Padre Pio called it the Harmless Warning only because there will be no lasting effects when the event is over. Some people will die of heart attacks because it will be such a shock to their system. I could go on and on about this event but the point is that when Jesus returns and judges the living and the dead; He could be talking about the spiritual realm other than the physical. If you have a mortal sin/s on your soul you have a dead soul. Jesus has always been more concerned about our souls than our physical bodies. Mortal sin means deadly sin.

★★★

Another book I've read about the end times states that about 90% of the people will be on a path to Hell when God intervenes in ways He's never done before (like the above mentioned event). I need to re-read that book to make sure I didn't dream up the 90% part (the book title: THE END TIMES AS REVEALED TO MARIA VALTORTA). Well if you ask me, we're at the 90% mark and I can prove it! It's very simple. Take a sheet of poster board and at the top write all the mortal sins (according to the Catholic Church) on slanted lines like a graph. Now, on the left side of the page; write your name at the top followed by 50-100 people you are closest to (family, extended family, friends, coworkers, neighbors, other people you are in close contact). Start checking off the mortal sin/s you and the others have never repented for with true sorrow. If someone on your list committed grave sin/s like perhaps they had or paid for an abortion; but have gone to confession and repented with true sorrow/did their penance/does not encourage anyone else to sin as they have; then do not put a check in that spot. God forgives! Do not make up excuses for yourself or the people you love when doing this exercise. Mortal sin is what separates us from God; and we do it to ourselves by choosing to do our will over being obedient to our Father who art in Heaven. If you do this exercise truthfully without rationalizing these sins; you will see how far we as a society have veered off course doing our wills over the 10 Commandments and the teachings of Jesus Christ. Were you paying attention when you read the part about 90% of the people will be on a path to Hell...Do You Know What This Means?! It means the great deceiver has deceived us all. It means God is serious, that He has never changed (something down deep we already know). If we truly are at the 90% mark, then be ready for what is coming soon. I do not think it is a coincidence that the Catholic Church is having an extra ordinary jubilee year; centered around the Mercy of God (this is only the third or fourth extra ordinary jubilee year since Jesus died for our sins over 2000 years ago and the only one focusing on the MERCY of GOD, Dec. 8th 2015-Nov. 20th 2016) right before the year 2017. I recently heard a Priest state that a lot of theologians think the 100 years that God granted satan more power, started the same year our Heavenly Mother appeared to the three shepherd children in Fatima in 1917. He did not say why the theologians thought this and I am not good at research. So, if this is true; then sometime in 2017 the 100 years will be over. I'm praying that God will act immediately because I'm tired of watching so many people offend God and have no remorse or firm purpose of amending their sins. To me, people seem to think if they're alright with their sins and everyone else is doing it; then God will let them into Heaven someday. Everyone seems to have forgotten the one sin God cannot forgive. The sin against the Holy Spirit; if you are not sorry for your sins and are not asking for forgiveness then how can you be forgiven. Eternally mortal sin=eternal damnation. Please review the 3 things required for a sin to be mortal (deadly to the soul). I do however, still have hope that things can change for the better. One of the secrets of Fatima involved a Pope (in white) would be shot and would die; however though prayers Pope John Paul II was shot but did not die. Instead the Catholic Church grew and grew during his reign as Pope. He had a great love for Mary the Mother of God and believed through Her intercession his life was spared. So prayers, fasting and offering up sufferings for the honor and glory of God, do change even predicted events; even if the prediction/s are from Marian apparitions (Fatima or Medjugorje or other places). Why? The Answer is because we still have free will and our actions are not pre-determined. We can of free will get our lives back on track and change to a culture of life and away from a culture of death. Just think of the changes you can make in the current world (or your little corner of the world), if you right now repented with true sorrow for all of your mortal sins and started doing God's Will over yours. Stop watching television shows and movies that show immorality or lead to a culture of death; and start going to Holy Mass at least weekly and Confession with Catholic Priest at least monthly. Would these changes in your life influence any of the people listed on your poster board? Let's hope so! Conversion happens at different rates, but start now before the 100 years is over and God might unleash his wrath or do something (whether good or bad or both) to get our attention! Of course I don't know when the 100 years will be over, but sometime in 2017 is a good guess. Making the necessary changes will be no easier after the Illumination of the Soul than before; so start now to make the transition easier. Striving to always be in the state of grace gives me peace; remember every day is a battle for the soul. Also, the Divine Mercy Jesus image with the words 'Jesus, I Trust in You' gives me peace of mind. Sometimes I follow this thought with; Jesus I have to trust in you because they won't listen to me or the Priests or follow Your Commandments or the teachings of Jesus Christ in the Holy Bible. I'm still trying to figure out where the 10% of people on the right path are. Are they children who have not been corrupted? That same book about end times states that Jesus is having difficulty finding children who have not been corrupted. As a pediatric nurse for 30 something years, I can tell you that I have seen the sinful effects or our society go from what is on television to what these children are living in their own lives. We have very few intact families anymore. The children have parents who are divorced (possibly remarried), never married, foster children (what happened to their biological parents), homosexual parents, single parents, grandparents raising them (what happened to their biological parents). I've been going in and out of these hospital rooms for a long time; and I see what these children are living in their families/what they are allowed to watch on television (few screen influences appropriately); and most families are not raising their children learning about religion. Catholics (once Catholic always Catholic; because once you have been taught the truth then you are expected to live it) it is time to get cleaned up. Go to confession, return to the Catholic Church and start going regularly to holy Mass. Once you are cleaned up then you will be able to take the Body and Blood of Jesus Christ into your body in communion with God. Remember God is merciful. The following is the Closing Prayer to the Divine Mercy Novena and Chaplet:

ETERNAL GOD, IN WHOM MERCY IS ENDLESS, AND THE TREASURY OF COMPASSION INEXHAUSTIBLE, look kindly upon us, and increase Your mercy in us, that in difficulty moments, we might not despair, nor become despondent, but with great confidence, submit ourselves to Your holy will, which is Love and Mercy itself. Amen

★★★★★★★★★★★★★★★★★★★★★★★★★★★★★★★★★★★★

Good News! Jesus Christ came for sinners. Who was the first person Jesus greeted when He rose from the dead on Easter Sunday? Mary Magdalene. Early in the morning; a new beginning! Mary Magdalene was a big sinner who went through the storm to get back into good graces with God. Yes, you may have a spiritual storm to battle; I think we all do. If Mary Magdalene did it; so can you.

★★★★★★★★★★★★★★★★★★★★★★★★★★★★★★★★★★

Author Note:

Ask Mother Mary to help you undo your knots.

Mother Mary leads everyone to Her son Jesus.

She keeps nothing for Herself.

Jesus Christ is the light on the world.

Mother Mary reflects the light of Her Son, like the moon reflects the light of the sun.

Natural conception to natural death.

Jesus loves you so much He suffered and died for your sins.

You (of free will) have to ask for forgiveness with true sorrow to make amends;

to get back into God's good graces again.

Reach out for help if your burden is heavy and you are overwhelmed.

Pray and be obedient to God and leave the consequences to Him.

★★★★★★★★★★★★★★★★★★★★★★★★★★★★★★★★★★★

Mother Teresa of Calcutta taught us much about natural conception to natural death.

She taught natural family planning (N.F.P.) to the poor in India (the only form of contraception approved by the Catholic Church because it is natural).

I've heard that Mother Teresa said "Peace begins in the womb".

She showed us how to treat people who were in their death agony; with love and compassion (no euthanasia) to join our suffering to Jesus on the cross (redemptive suffering).

Mother Teresa also showed us how to deal with each other between conception and death.

Mother Teresa's Prayer "Do It Anyway"

People are often unreasonable, irrational, and self-centered. Forgive them anyway.

If you are kind, people may accuse you of selfish, ulterior motives. Be kind anyway.

If you are successful, you will win some unfaithful friends and some genuine enemies. Succeed anyway.

If you are honest and sincere people may deceive you. Be honest and sincere anyway.

What you spend years creating, others could destroy overnight. Create anyway.

If you find serenity and happiness, some may be jealous. Be happy anyway.

The good you do today, will often be forgotten. Do good anyway.

Give the best you have, and it will never be enough. Give your best anyway.

In the final analysis, it is between you and God. It was never between you and them anyway.

••

Natural conception to natural death.

No in-vitro fertilization, no cloning, no abortion and no euthanasia.

Why are we killing the people we should love the most with all our heart;

our unborn children and the people who lovingly raised us from our very start.

God's fifth commandment clearly states 'THOU SHALT NOT KILL'

We must put a stop to euthanasia pills

and the abortion mills.

Mother Teresa showed us how to care for the sick, severely handicapped and dying.

She did it in one of the poorest places on earth, Calcutta India in the streets

and slums.

If she did it there then we should be able to do it in our comfortable homes for our

loved ones.

Do it with love and charity for our family in their time of need.

By this I mean treat them with love and dignity;

not have them (euthanized) escorted off the premises.

The Golden Rule: Treat others as you would have them do unto you.

At the beginning and the end of life; we all will need to rely on each other.

Parents and grandparents take care of infants and children with great love, joy and

self sacrifice.

Years down the road the tide will reverse;

flip flop...now you will be on the other side.

Who will be taking care of you?

And will they treat you the way you would like to be treated, with love?

Grown children, including nieces and nephews; take care of elderly

family members and those in need with love, great patience

while being truly nice.

Simply stated "as it should be".

Mother Teresa gave the sick and dying love and dignity while they were suffering;

not giving them pills or IV poison to end their life very sudden.

In our death agony we are to join our suffering with Jesus on the cross.

We must atone for all our sins either in purgatory or while here on earth.

Abortion, suicide or assisted suicide is against the 5th COMMANDMENT:

'THOU SHALT NOT KILL'.

Even if you temporarily find it difficult to carry on; remember God loves you and

God will decide when your life is to end.

Life is worth living! You can pray for others and the world; while you're waiting.

Don't let anyone talk you into euthanasia or having an abortion.

Natural conception to natural death.

We must all convert to a culture of life.

Repent with true sorrow for sins committed and receive forgiveness.

Jesus Christ came for sinners.

Jesus is the Way, the Truth and the Life.

Jesus came to show us how to be obedient to our Father in Heaven.

God is merciful!

If you are a parent and have a child who has disappointed you (something unpleasing to God). If that child (any age) realizes they have done something wrong and state they are sorry (with true sorrow) and stop doing the unwanted behavior; would you forgive them?

I would be so happy, just like when the prodigal son returned home.

Well, it's the same with our Father in Heaven. When we are truly sorry for our sins (no matter how serious, how many times etc...) and we ask God to forgive us, have a firm purpose to amend our ways, do our penance and never encourage others to do these sin/s; then our loving Father will forgive us.

God is merciful...but we must ask for forgiveness with true sorrow.

Mother Teresa also said something like: Follow Jesus when carrying your cross, don't try to lead Him.

When Mother Teresa was asked why is Mary so important?

Her answer four words; "No Mary, no Jesus".

★★★★★★★★★★★★★★★★★★★★★★★★★★★★★★★★★

Magnificat (hymn of the Virgin Mary in Luke 1:46-55)

My soul magnifies the Lord, and my spirit rejoices in God my Savior; Because he has regarded the lowliness of His handmaid; for, behold, henceforth all generations shall call me blessed; Because He Who is mighty has done great things for me, and Holy is His Name; And his Mercy is from generation to generation on those who fear Him. He has shown might with His Arm, He has scattered the proud in the conceit of their heart.

He has put down the mighty from their thrones, and has exalted the lowly. He has filled the hungry with good things, and the rich He has sent away empty. He has given help to Israel, His servant, mindful of His Mercy, even as He spoke to our fathers, to Abraham and to his posterity forever. Amen.

A partial indulgence is granted to the faithful,

who piously recite the Canticle of the Magnificat.

Now would be a great time to put down this book and say a heartfelt rosary.

It would also be a good time to reflect that the first three Joyful mysteries of the Holy Rosary revolve around the conception/ life in the womb prior to birth/ and birth of our Savior Jesus Christ. This should be a reminder that life begins at conception.

★★

That was quite the detour, let's get back to Molly McGolly and her family. We were talking about October. All Hallow's Eve, All Saints Day and All Soul's Day (Oct. 31st, Nov. 1st and Nov. 2nd).

Molly's family visited the cemeteries of their beloved on November 2nd to pray for them. Grandpa McFrugal was buried in a small family plot on McFrugal Mountain.

Grandpa McFrugal always said "Bury me in the sunshine so I'll be closer to the light."

His gravestone was away from the big old oak tree with the big old owl with yellow eyes like headlights.

This year the family went at night and carried candles for light.

That big old owl starred right at Molly the whole time and was quite a fright.

The owl stayed perfectly still perched on a branch except it's head which seemed to turn in a complete circle while screeching hoot hoot out of its curved sharp beak.

That was one bird Molly did not want in her hair or on her shoulder.

She was sure, if that bird was on her shoulder; its claws would be carrying her off to be its supper.

Molly would not recommend anyone to go to a graveyard at night because it is too scary; even if you were one of the buried!

Uncle Clement, Molly's father's brother died suddenly when a tree fell on him ...he was a lumberjack.

One minute he was here, the next...whack!

Accidents do happen; so always be in the state of grace.

You never know when your number is up and you'll be leaving this place.

Uncle Clement had gone to confession the week before.

So maybe he wasn't too long in purgatory before hopefully entering the heavenly door.

Molly heard the welcome mat at the gate of Heaven states 'Welcome Good and Faithful Servant.'

But there is a catch. You have to go round back to the servants entrance; for only the truly humble will actually be allowed admittance.

Once inside you forget all your troubles and are in paradise forever.

Uncle Clement was buried at a big old cemetery at the edge of town.

Molly found all the headstones very interesting to read and walk around.

She read the names, date born, date died.

She figured out how long each person had been alive.

One of the headstones had a picture of lady: so you could see her face.

It had the most interesting inscription:

'I once was as You are now

You will be as I am'.

The first time Molly read this block of marble; she thought her heart stopped beating right then and there.

If that statement didn't send a chill up your spine; you must already be buried somewhere.

This lady's picture was in black and white; she appeared to be about 50 years old.

She looked a little like Autie Eme on the Wizard of Oz.

Scared the living daylights out of Molly and made her heart pause!

57 years, one month and seventeen days to be exact.

Birth and death date carved into the marble plaque;

Molly did the math.

When Uncle Clement died, he was only 24.

He was survived by a wife named Clare and a young son named Sonny.

You see, Sonny was Molly's first cousin and very best buddy.

Luck of the Irish:

They visited this cemetery during the day.

So, it wasn't as scary that way.

Molly's mother told her that cemeteries are less frightening as you get older.

When you know and love the people that are buried there, your memories make the visit endearing.

As your heart heals from the loss and pain;

only the love remains.

The loved one's memory is encapsulated in your heart.

You never forget them and eventually the sadness subsides and the grief departs.

Then pick yourself up and live the rest of your natural born life.

Natural conception to natural death.

At the end of All Soul's Day, Molly's father would add to his nightly blessing "You'll not know the day nor the hour God will call you home. So always be in the state of grace";

He stated while giving each of his children a loving embrace.

Then he tucked each of them into bed;

while making the sign of the cross with holy water on their forehead.

For some unknown reason this comforted Molly and she always slept with great peace on the night of November 2nd (or perhaps it was from complete exhaustion).

She knew this life is temporary; her real home would be in Heaven.

When Molly woke up the next morning she was filled with vigor, pep, energy and zeal.

Time to get back to saving the planet, starting at school.

Nothing like visiting two cemeteries to remind you that you're still alive.

Now it's time to help the living survive!

Molly had to evaluate October's save the planet mission as best she could remember.

Then plan her strategy to turn her class green in November.

October turned out to be a pretty good month in Molly's grand scheme.

If it continues like this, not only will her class but the whole city will be green.

Waterboy William and his whole family will need to be relocated someplace they would consider terrific.

Perhaps to an island in the South Pacific.

All that water, they would be so pleased.

Water, water everywhere and a tropical breeze.

This relocation package would be a win, win situation.

No guilt for Molly; she wouldn't even have to bring it up in confession.

Molly was making progress, at least in her mind.

However no big players have switched over to her planet saving side.

If pride goeth before a fall;

she merely stumbled because her pride didn't last long at all.

Out of her class, only she and Sonny had green blood flowing through their veins.

The rest of the class when it came to saving the plant seemed to have zombie like brains.

Molly needed to stir up enthusiasm.

Perhaps November will be the month to get them green earth thriving?!

Fresh baked apple pies were made from scratch by Molly and her mother in early November.

The money raised from the bake sale to be used to insulate the classroom windows before the cold winter.

The cafeteria was filled with the aroma of warm apples and cinnamon.

Everyone loved this freshly baked goodness right out of the oven.

The cafeteria ladies raved "These are the best pies we've ever tasted!"

Molly smiled graciously and stated "The secret is picking the apples off the tree one hour before baking."

Molly handed out the apple pie recipe and hoped others would share their resources as generously.

There was one boy in her class, Ralph who had a newspaper route.

He started bringing in left over newspapers he didn't deliver out.

Ralph put the newspapers in the teacher's lounge.

The teachers used them for class projects and also just to be more informed.

So maybe Molly was getting through to her class, cracking the ice.

At least one person seemed to take the bait, get the hint; to share with others just to be nice.

Ralph's boy scout troop also had a scrap metal drive this month.

Molly organized the cafeteria ladies to recycle the large tin cans they used to prepare lunch.

Those nice ladies would do almost anything for a slice of Molly's homemade apple pie ala mode.

Didn't even need to be heated; they ate the pie cold.

Molly secretly hoped by helping Ralph with his cause, maybe he would reciprocate.

But even if he didn't; helping others just feels good and doesn't need any other payment.

Helping others always feels G R E A T !

Ralph was a true boy scout through and through.

His favorite subject was geography and he loved hiking.

He was always looking at maps and reading National Geographic magazine.

Ralph either had his head in a book or his boots on the ground.

Molly frequently saw him walking or riding his bike all over town.

Of course getting an Eagle bound boy scout to become more green is a pretty soft target.

For the others Molly needed a big event to drive attention to saving the environment.

(Luck of the Irish)

November is the school wide science fair.

She would use this opportunity to dazzle the judges and make everyone stare.

At what you might ask? Her super fantastic science project, not her crazy red hair.

Oh what the heck, why not!!

Molly put on a white lab coat and fixed her hair with flair;

like the absent minded professor.

Her supersonic science fair project was a giant compost heap on the school grounds.

The food in the trash after lunch mixed in the ground by tossing the garbage round and round.

Then she used her homemade fertilizer in the garden to grow a pumpkin patch.

Those pumpkins were almost big enough to take Cinderella to the Ball and back.

Molly proudly displayed her beautiful extra large orange pumpkins next to the compose heap.

To show the product of homemade fertilizer made cheap, cheap, cheap!

Molly won a second place ribbon because the judges were impressed.

Her project was really good but it was not the best.

However, none of the girls from her class got anywhere near the compost heap.

They only saw it as a great big mess and boy did it stink!

Molly's teacher (Miss Kimberly Bailey) placed one of the giant pumpkins on a bookcase by the newly insulated windows.

Looking out the window while admiring her pumpkin, Molly spotted something and she quickly arose.

A short time later she returned to class with a wild turkey; which gobbled as it hobbled on its feet.

Molly thought that turkey better learn to run faster or zip its beak.

In any event Molly couldn't eat a bite of turkey on the day of Thanksgiving.

She was pretty sure her mother was faster than that wild turkey when it was living.

On the home front, November the triplets were all three baptized.

They had holy water poured over their heads and dripping down between their eyes.

For all three: Shawn, Patrick and Leo it was a great big surprise!

Holy water is the matter in the sacrament of Holy Baptism.

★★★★★★★★★★★★★★★★★★★★★★★★★★★

There are 7 sacraments in the Catholic Church. Each one must have the right matter and the right words spoken by the Priest. This is true for every Priest all over the world for we are a united church (some exceptions in special circumstances).

If you walk into a Catholic Church... look around! Every nationality seems to be represented and are all sitting right next to each other. The words to a children's song comes to mind:

> Jesus loves the little children,
> all the little children of the world.
> They are yellow, black and white
> they are precious in His sight.
> Jesus loves the little children of the world.

Remember, we are all God's children. The Catholic Church was founded by Jesus Christ Himself and His chosen apostles. The Catholic Church was the only Christian religion for about 1500 years. Since the Catholic Church is the only Christian religion that has been around since the beginning and was established by Jesus Christ Himself; it would stand to reason why so many nationalities are in His Church (the Catholic Church). Jesus Christ (prior to His Ascension to Heaven) told His apostles and disciples to go to the ends of the earth and spread the good news of salvation and to baptize them in the name of the Father/Son/ and Holy Spirit. The Catholic Church is still reaching to the ends of the earth to spread the good news. At the same time we need to re-evangelize parts of the earth that seem to have forgotten our part in salvation... we need to ask with true sorrow for forgiveness, do our penance and change our ways to God's way. If you are lukewarm in your faith, I urge you to take this passage from St. Faustina's diary to heart (Notebook III, part 1228 (words of Jesus) and part 1229).

Ninth Day (of Divine Mercy Novena)

1228 Today bring to Me souls who have become lukewarm, and immerse them in the abyss of My mercy. These souls wound My Heart most painfully. My soul suffered the most dreadful loathing in the Garden of Olives because of lukewarm souls. They were the reason I cried out: "Father, take this cup away from Me, if it be Your will." For them, the last hope (65) of salvation is to flee to My mercy.

1229 Most Compassionate Jesus, You are Compassion Itself. I bring lukewarm souls into the abode of Your Most Compassionate Heart. In this fire of Your pure love let these tepid souls, who like corpses, filled You with such deep loathing, be once again set aflame. O Most Compassionate Jesus, exercise the omnipotence of Your mercy and draw them into the very ardor of Your love; and bestow upon them the gift of holy love, for nothing is beyond Your power.

Fire and ice cannot be joined;

Either the fire dies, or the ice melts.

But by Your mercy, O God,

You can make up for all that is lacking.

Eternal Father, turn Your merciful gaze upon lukewarm souls, who are nonetheless enfolded in the Most Compassionate Heart of Jesus. Father of Mercy, I beg You by the bitter Passion of Your Son and by His three-hour agony on the Cross: Let them, too, glorify the abyss of Your mercy...

Author Note:

So are you one of the lukewarm souls? What did you think about the part that Jesus said: For them, the last hope (65) of salvation is to flee to My mercy. Does that sound like we can pick and choose which of the Commandments to follow? I'm glad I've gone through my storm to get back into the state of grace (I haven't forgotten everyday is a battle for the soul so I must be ever vigilant). I spent years justifying my actions, thinking since everyone else is doing it then it can't be all that bad. Wrong! If you look at the effects of your mortal sins on others (your influence) you can see how a little bit leads to more... then we end up the world we have today. It seems to me most people are in the state a mortal sin and have no purposeful desire to change their ways. I flee to God frequently to ask for forgiveness for all who are living a life of doing their will over God's Will. However, each soul has free will and must choose for them self. Then I think of the Image of Divine Mercy Jesus and the words at the bottom of this picture 'Jesus I Trust in You'. My next thought is; I have to trust in You Jesus because they won't listen to me. This Image (DIVINE MERCY JESUS) does give me peace and I deep down feel that Jesus knew we would need that image to help us in these times. I guess for most of us (the faithful) our job is to pray, pray and pray & be a good example in our lives by carrying our cross like Jesus did. Hopefully this image (DIVINE MERCY JESUS) will help many who are worried about their loved ones who are obstinate and refusing to do the Will of God. We must continue to pray, pray, pray for the souls on a path to Hell and of course; make sure we are in the state of grace by going through our storm to purify our souls.

WORDS FROM HEAVEN by a Friend of Medjugorje (15th Edition English).

Messages of Our Lady from Medjugorje (A DOCUMENTED RECORD OF THE MESSAGES AND THEIR MEANINGS GIVEN BY OUR LADY IN MEDJUGORJE TO THE SIX VISIONARIES AND TWO INNER LOCUTIONISTS)

by CARITAS OF BIRMINGHAM

Sterrett, Alabama USA

Please get your own copy of this book to read the full messages and their meanings.

CHAPTER 5: THE PLAN OF OUR LADY AGAINST Satan

THE FIRST WEAPON AGAINST SATAN; PRAYER

THE SECOND WEAPON AGAINST SATAN: FASTING

THE THIRD WEAPON AGAINST SATAN: DAILY READING OF THE BIBLE
THE FOURTH WEAPON AGAINST SATAN: CONFESSION
FIFTH WEAPON AGAINST SATAN: THE EUCHARIST

Author Note: The Virgin Mary, under the title 'Queen of Peace' has been appearing everyday for over 35 years to six visionaries since June 24th 1981. Some of the visionaries have received all ten messages and no longer see the apparitions every day, only on special days. Some of the visionaries continue to see the Virgin Mary in apparitions every day. These may not be the only apparitions of the Virgin Mary currently happening…She is our Heavenly Mother and we are all Her children. She told these visionaries that when she stops appearing to them (Medjugorie, Bosnia) that her services will no longer be needed. She usually appears in a gray dress because she came to clean up a mess. On Christmas she has appeared in a gold dress, carrying Baby Jesus. On Christmas Day (December 25th 2012); Our Lady came with little Jesus in Her arms and She did not give a message, but little Jesus began to speak and said: "I am your peace, live my commandments."

The secrets will be released to the Catholic Priest/s assigned to these visionaries 10 days before they happen; the secrets will be released to whoever wants to know 3 days before they happen. All I can say is to be ready. I started my conversion many years ago when I went to Sterrett Alabama to be present during an apparition of the Virgin Mary. One of the visionaries from Medjugorie Bosnia came to Caritas of Birmingham in Sterrett Alabama. Mother Mary appears to the visionaries where ever they happen to be; even if travelling in an airplane. So my childhood dream came true, I was present during an apparition of the Virgin Mary. Since my first visit to Caritas of Birmingham many years ago, I have returned many times during Marija's (one of the visionaries) visits. I love being present during the apparitions. All I can say is stop kidding yourself by thinking God has changed. God is the same, only man has changed. We must obey our Father in Heaven and live all the Commandments and the teachings of Jesus Christ. There is a peace to being reconciled with God, deep down inside. Of course everyday is a battle for the soul, so I must remain ever vigilant. Use the weapons against satan listed above to help you in your conversion or to keep you on the right track.

I encourage everyone to get a copy of this book and incorporate the teaching into your lifestyle.

Now back to the topic of lukewarm sinners: For the lukewarm sinners, I have another question: What is Purgatory for? Purgatory is for souls who are sorry for their sins and have something to pay off (a purification); Hell is for those who refuse to repent for serious/mortal sin/s. People who laugh while stating "Oh, I know I'm going to Purgatory"; I seriously doubt are going to Purgatory. If you were truly sorry for your sins you would not be laughing about them or continuing to commit them (including encouraging others to sin against God with their mortal sins). How can you be forgiven for something (serious sin) you are not sorry for? How can God give you His mercy if you do not want it? There is only one sin in which God cannot forgive; it is the sin against the Holy Spirit (If you are not asking for forgiveness with true sorrow then you can not be forgiven).

••

Author Note:

Catholics, we are held to a higher standard than others because we have been given the TRUTH. So don't let the ways of the world dilute your faith and become lukewarm. This scripture passage should help you to have the courage to change your ways or become humble enough to do God's Will instead of your own will.

Luke 12:47-48

'The servant who knows what his master wants, but has not even started to carry out those wishes, will receive very many stokes of the lash. The one who did not know, but deserves to be beaten for what he has done, will receive fewer strokes. When a man has had a great deal given him, a great deal will be demanded of him; when a man has had a great deal given him on trust, even more will be expected of him.

★★

Author Note:

Here's a question for everyone. WHAT IS THE ONE SIN GOD CANNOT FORGIVE?

It is called the sin against the Holy Spirit. I know two ways to sin against the Holy Spirit; but it is the same sin!

1). Eternal Despair- People who will not ask God with true sorrow to forgive them because they think their sin/sins are so bad that God could never forgive them. Instead they choose to stay away from God. God does not like anyone to despair because He loves you even when you don't love yourself. God has an ocean of mercy and is waiting for you to ask for forgiveness. Do not despair. God is waiting for you with open arms!

Divine Mercy Closing Prayer:

Eternal God, in whom mercy is endless and the treasury of compassion inexhaustible, look kindly upon us and increase Your mercy in us, that in difficult moments we might not despair nor become despondent, but with great confidence submit ourselves to Your Holy Will, which is Love and Mercy itself.

2). Eternal Obstinacy-This is the category most of the people I know and love with all my heart seem to stagnate. All they need to do is start moving towards the light but they will not budge. They have justified everything (mortal sin/s they have done in the past or are continuing to do or by encouragement are leading others to serious sin) and seem to think they have license to do so. They have been taught the truth but reject it. They have been corrupted by outside influences. In any event they will not ask God for forgiveness. They of free will have become rock hard sinners by rationalizing their sin/sins. These are people (cafeteria Catholics etc...) that know the 10 Commandments and the teachings of Jesus Christ in the gospels, the teachings of Mother Church (Catholic Church) but are obstinate and choose to do their will over God's.

Note the word eternal is in front of both ways to sin against the Holy Spirit. Both 1). Eternal despair and 2). Eternal obstinacy are ways of not asking for forgiveness with true sorrow. God cannot forgive you of your sins if you do not ask for forgiveness with true sorrow. That means those sins remain eternal sin/sins. You cannot get into Heaven with an eternal mortal sin on your soul. Eternal serious/mortal sin = Eternal damnation. We separate ourselves from God by doing our will over God's Will. God puts nobody in Hell; we do it to ourselves by choosing our will over God's (on serious issues). God gets to decide what the serious/grave/deadly sins are, not you! The Catholic Church tells us what to think. Catholics have a right to do what they ought to do, not what they want to do.

None of us knows how God will judge; only God judges. However I would point out that God didn't just throw us out there and say "figure it out". Our Father in Heaven gave us 10 Commandments (the only part of the Bible God the Father wrote Himself on stone tablets) and sent His only Son (Jesus) to show us the Way the Truth and the Life. I feel most (if not all) people who are expecting God to conform are going to be very surprised to learn everything we learned in catechism class when we were young is the truth and that God's Will has not changed to the ways of the world. I have not seen a revised list of the Commandments on stone tablets because there isn't one! God has not changed only man has changed. All cafeteria Catholics know this... so why are you still asleep?! Wake Up to a new day and walk out of the tomb to the resurrection of your soul. Pray that the Holy Spirit will enliven the gifts given to you at your Confirmation and ask for your bishop slap to remind you that you are a soldier of Christ.

★★★

Let nothing disturb thee;
Let nothing dismay thee;
All things pass;
God never changes.   St. Teresa of Avila (Doctor of the Church)

★★

Now back to the McGolly Family.
Earlier that morning before the triplets were to be baptized;
Mother McGolly shared a story with her oldest set of twins.
She told them the story of their baptism through the memory of her maternal lens.
As Mom recollected deep down in the recesses of her mind;
she recalled the moment holy water was poured over Mike and Mark's heads
and in between their eyes.
She stated Mark's eyes were opened wide
and Mike was so surprised he cried.
There are seven sacraments in the Catholic Church.

Each sacrament must have the right matter and the right words spoken by the priest;

for we are a united Church all over the world.

The right matter in Holy Baptism in holy water.

Except for Jesus and His Mother Mary,

we are all born with original sin ever since Adam and Eve

were cast out of the Garden of Eden.

Adam and Eve ate the fruit from the tree of good and evil,

which was the one thing that was forbidden.

Jesus is the second Person in the Holy Trinity (Father/Son/Holy Spirit). Jesus is the God Man. He was like us in every way except sin. Jesus was not born with original sin because He is God (the Second person in the Holy Trinity). Mary's womb was the vessel which held the God Man and could not be stained by sin. So Mary was born without original sin. Mary is known as the Immaculate Conception because She was born without original sin.

The day of our physical birth is the birth of our flesh.

The day of our baptism is the birth in the Spirit.

We receive the gifts of the Holy Spirit and our soul is ignited.

Our soul shines, it is pure, cleansed it is bright lighted!

In the ritual of baptism, God through the Church bestows a precious gift upon the infant,

a sharing in the divine life of the Risen Christ in that instant.

The babies: Shawn, Patrick and Leo were cleansed from sin;

ushered into God's kingdom,

incorporated into the Church

and the door to heaven and everlasting life open to them.

Now, if they die after baptism and are in the state of grace;

they can go to heaven and see the beatific vision.

Baptism is only the beginning, the sowing of a seed to be nurtured.

The life of Jesus within the child must be weaved...

until at an older, more mature age can say "Yes, I do believe."

During the holy sacrament of baptism the parents profess they will train the child in "the practice of the Catholic faith" and bring the infant up "to keep God's Commandments as Christ taught us, by loving God and our neighbor".

The godparents agree if the parents are unable to fulfill this sacred promise to God, then they will take over.

The parents are reminded they are their children's first teachers in the ways of the faith.

The parents ask God to help them be the best of teachers, bearing witness to the faith by what they say and do.

This means in practice that whenever as parents you believe, pray, love, correct, forgive, go to Church, go to confession on a regular bases, help neighbors or those in need or in any way live as faithful Christians, you are nurturing the seed of Jesus' life within your child's heart.

After Father O'Malley poured water over the third red headed head;

very few people in the congregation could hear what was said,

since all three mouths of the babes were loud, loud, LOUD!

Mark took this golden opportunity to play a practical joke on his twin brother.

While all eyes were on the crying triplets by the baptismal font.

Mark chose the re-in-act the day he and his twin Mike were baptized.

So, he thought; it's now or never and decided why not!

Mark took out a concealed water toy and squirted Mike on his forehead with accurate pin point precision.

This action turned out to be a pretty poor, very unwise decision.

Although most people couldn't hear Mike's yelp, they all had 20/20 vision.

Especially Mother McGolly who had eyes in the back of her head.

Also including those sitting in the first 3 pews and every single person in the balcony seats overhead.

If anyone missed the 'in your face water drenching' they could view it on the video camera recording;

since the whole event was captured start to finish with Father O'Malley's permission.

Now, poor Mark instead of water would have his whole life flash before his eyes

...you see, poor Mark was probably going to die.

(Luck of the Irish)

Both Mike and Mark had to wait until Holy Mass ended before Mark could get a head start and run.

Mark prayed his twin Mike had a little time to cool off, decompress, let off a little steam and then some.

Close to the end of Holy Mass after the last blessing,

Mark disappeared before the priest left the building;

which is frowned upon in the Catholic religion.

Mark chose to walk home instead of riding in the car.

He only walked a few miles, through town, 3 pastures and up the hill...not too far.

He was moving quickly especially for a boy on the run known as a fugitive;

trying to stay at least one step ahead of his twin so he had a much better chance to live.

Of course the guilty eventually have to face the music...serve time for the crime.

Since all sins must be atoned either here on earth, your particular judgment or at the end of time.

The great escape only lasted until Mark got home.

How long can a 7 year old hide in the barn or continue to rome?

Answer: Until his stomach starts to growl

or the coyotes start to howl!

Mom and Dad lectured him on the reverence of Holy Mass and the sanctity of a Holy Sacrament to be taken very seriously.

Mark had to apologize to his parents, twin brother and Father O'Malley.

Punishment from Mom and Dad; for the next two weeks he had barn duty.

Cleaning up and feeding the barn animals including the chicken coop/hen house, gathering the eggs, milking Daisy and Muffy the cows, taking care of the goat/sheep/horse/rooster/chickens/pig, putting out fresh hay and removing the old. All he could hear when he went to sleep at night was:' Cock-a-doodle doo, moo moo moo. Nay, baa baa, peep peep peep, oink oink and little lamb bleaps.

He fed the horse and cows hay, the rooster and chickens chicken feed, the goat apple cores and peels and tin cans. He fed Big Mac the pig anything and everything except chickens/horse/cows. Yes, he tried to feed the goat to the pig but Mark couldn't catch the goat; because the —goat ate the rope he needed to catch the goat.

To pass the time in his barnyard prison, Mark would sing songs.

Silly songs, happy and sad songs,

sometimes he would sing songs with words that were wrong.

Some musical selections were upbeat like...'I've been working on the railroad all the live long day. I've been working on the railroad just to pass the time away. Do you hear the whistle blowing...'

and sometimes he sang the blues... 'Be not afraid, I go before you always. Come follow me and I will lead you home.'

Many times he sang religious songs so beautifully, but he usually made sure no one but the animals heard him. Once, when it was starting to get dark outside; Mark was in the loft shoveling fresh hay below. He saw the first star of the night sky and knelt down looking out the large loft window and began to sing to Mary his Heavenly Mother 'Hail, Queen of Heaven, The Ocean Star' (Adoremus Hymnal 539). He was unaware that his parents and grandma were all sitting on the porch in rocking chairs with sleeping babies in their arms; and heard every word he sang. They all continued to rock the babies in silence and never said a word. That was one of those precious moments in life you want to cherish as long as possible.

Mike came to the barn everyday for 2 weeks holding a fully loaded water toy but never squirted a single drop...hum why?!

Mark just looked at Mike and said "Go head, make my day";

but Mike just walked away.

On the last day of barnyard duty; Mom made homemade ice cream and Molly baked a fresh apple pie.

Upon feeding the last of the animals with sweat on his brow;

Mark left the barn through the red barn doors after bidding farewell to that cantankerous cow.

A full bucket of water came crashing down on Mark's full body from above.

His twin Mike yelled out "Now we're even Bub!"

The chase was on! Mark caught up to Mike and they wrestled all over the hill top;

from the top to the bottom and from the bottom to the top.

The strange thing was they were laughing the whole time until it was time to stop.

They were back to being best buds; although exhausted, and mighty hungry.

They ate their ice cream and apple pie in the barn since they were so smelly.

(Luck of the Irish): The animals had all recently been fed so Mike and Mark didn't have to share their food.

Except for that big fat pig named Big Mac which followed them around oinking and was extremely rude.

Before long Mike and Mark were wrestling with that big fat pig in the mud filled pig pen.

Which one was going to win?

Mike yelled "That last bite of pie is mine;

its not for swine!

Not only did they eat in the barn they had to sleep in the loft.

Mike and Mark smelled pretty rank even after a shower the mud would not come off.

Some people might say making the twins sleep outside of the house was wrong.

These people must not have a sense of smell for pig infested mud is a smell that is STRONG!

This pungent odor is worse than the triplets diaper pail in the sun on the hottest day of the year.

Mike and Mark slept on opposite sides of the loft and not next to each other.

The next day they somehow were de-skunked;

more showers, soap, prayers and the pungent pig smell shrunk.

Molly thought her brothers smelled like regular boys again.

Mike and Mark had clean flesh, clean skin.

The triplets had been baptized and had clean souls.

Molly had clean skin and a clean soul.

She went to monthly confession and did her penance.

That evening she took a soapy shower with a final cleaning rinse.

Molly went to sleep with a clear conscience.

She would sleep well that night

even if she died before daylight;

because with God she was alright.

Final Note: A few months later Mark had his very first confession in preparation for his First Holy Communion.

The priest in the confessional was Father O'Malley;

who was very patient and kind while he listened to Mark confess his sins for which he was truly sorry.

Mark asked for forgiveness because he had offended God by playing a practical joke during a holy sacrament.

Mark was truly sorry for planning and executing this untimely incident.

Mark was absolved for his sins and did his penance.

When he completed this task his soul was as shiny as the day he and his twin were baptized...

with all that water dripping between his eyes.

For Mark's penance did he have to say 1 Our Father and 2 Hail Mary's or do something nice for the triplets or help his parents? We will never know because what is said in the confessional stays in the confessional. That information is between Jesus who speaks through the priest and the sorrowful penitent.

November was a month to Remember

but now it's time to plan the strategy for December.

Molly wanted the old light bulbs in her classroom to be replaced with eco-smart florescent ones.

These new light bulbs and panels use less energy and longer they will run.

She bargained with her classmates; with the first big snow everyone could bring their sleds to her house at the top of the hill.

Sliding all the way down was an exhilarating thrill!

In exchange Molly got them to fill up old jars with spare change they found at their homes and in their cars.

The spare change round up was a huge success!

Molly encouraged her class to tell their families eco-smart florescent light bulbs were the best.

Another class project in December was a school wide tradition.

Each class chose a live pine tree on the school grounds and to decorate it was the mission.

The winners were chosen on the last day of school before winter break and directly after the announcements by the principal.

In single file each class walked obediently to their pine tree; it was more organized than the monthly fire drill.

Molly's class entry was very earth friendly; pinecones slathered with peanut butter and birdseeds, accompanied with large red satin bows.

It was met with the wow factor and bird chirping echoes.

You see, during the judging, lots of colorful birds appeared and started eating the birdseeds.

Red cardinals, bluebirds, blue jays, yellow & black orioles and white doves;

even a couple of vultures circling from above.

However her class tree only came in second place.

They were out gunned by the first graders who each had a halo on their heads and smiling toothless faces.

The first graders played the angelic card and took first place.

Their room mothers put live poinsettia plants still in their buckets all over the pine tree,

and a garland of large handmade paper snowflakes covered with glitter lightly blowing in the breeze.

First graders are really cute and they were singing the angel song:

'Angels we have heard on high

sweetly sing a lull-a-bye...

G l o r i a ...(insert words to song here).

Mark and Mike (Molly's brothers) class, strapped a water hose straight to the top of their class tree.

During judging it was like a water fountain WHOA!

Decorations were rain boots and raincoats every color of the rainbow.

Everyone in their class was standing under their tree with umbrellas.

They won honorable mention and most original.

Waterboy William liked this tree a lot!

Molly did not.

Earlier that day, each class had their Christmas party, which started shortly after lunch.

Singing, games, gift exchange and all sorts of desserts like cupcakes, cookies and punch.

Molly spiked the punch with a few fresh sprigs of peppermint

... just to give it a little kick.

She wandered what her classmates would do if she served Mexican hot chocolate.

Molly envisioned Waterboy William following a sip of this spicy hot cocoa with every drop of water available in the state.

So, she sat back sipping her punch with peppermint and a sigh of relief.

This year Molly made Christmas gifts for everyone in her class;

by recycling tin cans, paper boxes, containers of both plastic and glass.

Most of her time was spent on Sonny's gift: a new birdhouse for their homing pigeon Homer.

Dad helped Molly in his woodwork shop construct the biggest birdhouse ever.

It had a huge porch which wrapped around all four sides.

The big windows and porch were all screened with a place to stay warm inside.

It was part birdhouse and part bird cage too.

The pigeon travelled back and forth from Molly's to Sonny's and vice versa it flew.

So, Homer the homing pigeon would have a nice place to call home.

If Homer gets to comfortable then Sonny and Molly just might have to use the phone.

On the day of the school Christmas party; Sonny was so surprised!

He was overcome with emotion to receive such a great gift so personalized.

After he was able to breath and he regained his composure;

Sonny gave Molly her gift which was hidden behind his wheelchair.

It was a gemstone in the rough he ran over with his wheelchair one day.

Sonny put it in his rock polisher until the true color was portrayed.

It literally turned out to be the greenest green he ever did see!

Sonny immediately thought of his cousin Molly.

He took the emerald and encircled it in a thin gold wire.

Then Sonny (with permission from his mother) dangled it from an old chain necklace he found in the jewelry box of his mother.

A beautiful rare find from something he ran over with his wheelchair tire.

Molly and Sonny loved their gifts from each other so much; it didn't matter what they ended up with from the class gift exchange.

Girls brought a wrapped gift for a girl.

Boys brought a wrapped gift for a boy.

Then drew numbers to see what gift with any luck they would take home and enjoy.

Molly got a fingernail polish set; surely from one of the girls in the Miss Priss trio.

Sonny landed an archery set with a suction cup arrow.

Sonny liked his gift and thought he may have found an exciting new hobby.

Molly (to her surprise) liked painting her nails; it made her feel pretty not snobby.

Now, it was time to hand out her recycled gifts to her classmates.

For the three divas; recovered boxes with wallpaper samples to put their many trinkets.

Ralph received a bunch of rocks from Molly's rock collection;

most of which came from her BINGO winnings.

For handsome Joe the class stud;

Molly selected a pair of her Dad's old green socks which she cleaned and darned.

These 2 socks were mismatched

and colorfully patched.

Thinking handsome Joe would just toss them aside; Molly decided to make them as ridiculous as possible.

To Molly's delight he put them on because he thought they were cool!?

He even rolled up his pants to his knees

so everyone could see;

followed by an Irish jig then he asked Molly to dance.

Together they did a silly river dance prance.

Handsome Joe liked his gift even though Molly did leave one giant hole,

for his right big toe!

To her other classmates she gave pen holders to the writers,

pot holders to those who liked to bake.

Molly made so much pottery at the pottery wheel

that one day she got dizzy and felt a little faint.

She also cleaned up a few paint brushes; tied together with a ribbon for Shelly who loved to paint.

What to give Waterboy William was her biggest dilemma.

Surely there was something else he loved other than wasting water.

Molly went to his house, knocked on the door and talked to his Mama.

She found out that he loved dill pickles, lions and his favorite game was checkers.

Molly gave Waterboy William homemade sliced dill pickles from the root cellar

in a recycled glass jar;

along with a brass lion door knocker she obtained at an estate sale with Dad back in September.

Dad had purchased a beautiful antique crystal chandelier.

He bought it to be a surprise when the new addition to the log cabin was complete for his beloved Dear.

Molly was sworn to secrecy...shhh...that was a secret hard to keep

but Molly too wanted Mom to be surprised so she didn't speak a peep!

Dad hid the chandelier in his work shop.

He rewired the chandelier and polished the brass from bottom to top.

Molly's job was to clean every crystal until they twinkled like the stars at night.

They kept their secret well concealed to keep it shiny and sparkling bright.

The duo couldn't wait to see Mom's reaction; they were sure she would smile all night.

Maureen McGolly might smile all day too if the sparkling chandelier was in her sight;

hanging high in her new dining room like a high flying kite.

Now back to the class Christmas party...

Waterboy William was very puzzled and astonished,

he even displayed water coming from his eyes.

"How did you know I like dill pickles and lions?" he asked in a state of shock.

"A little birdie told me, you know they can talk" replied Molly as she began to walk.

She actually had a red cardinal hopping around on her head.

William regained his composure and thought...

a red bird on a red headed head...how absurd!

Birds can't talk, at least not with words.

For the teacher Ms. Kimberly Bailey, Molly found a little white snow bunny

shivering alone out in the snow;

around the bunny's soft furry neck she placed a big red bow.

The teacher fell in love with her new pet and named it Bunny Wunny.

So, everyone seemed to like their recycled gifts especially Sonny!

Molly was sure the whole class was turning towards saving the planet.

They were finally after half the school year becoming aware of the global crisis.

From eco-smart light bulbs,

handmade recycled gifts,

peanut butter and birdseed pinecone bird feeders

on a natural outdoor real pine tree.

Yep, that did it!

Mission accomplished

Molly could let her hair down

Relax

No more worries

The planet was safe

Not only that but...

(Luck of the Irish); IT WAS WINTER BREAK!

The McGolly's always had a wonderful Christmas full of spiritual enlightenment;
celebrating the birth of our Savior the little babe Jesus on Christmas Eve night.

This year Maryann and Miriam at 4 years of age wanted to have a live nativity scene.

They invited all their relatives and pre-school Catechism classmates to attend who believe.

All of the immediate family supported the twin girls in this endeavor.

Mother and Grandma made hot apple cider and homemade cookies with strawberry and cherry preserves from jars in the root cellar.

Maryann and Miriam took turns being the Virgin Mary holding the baby Jesus.

The triplets were swapped out depending upon which one was behaving best,
wrapped in swaddling clothes and cloth diapers;
lying in a hay filled manger.

Joseph played by either Mark or Mike and Mary played by either Maryann or Miriam;
stood by the manger in a mock stable built by their father.

Earlier that day, Mom and Dad went to the hardware store to get supplies needed to make the stable and sand needed for the uphill walkway.

Mr. McGolly purchased wood, nails, sand and fresh hay.

Mrs. McGolly purchased miniature clay animals (donkeys and cows) to give to all the children as party favors and also selected a few paint chips for the future new nursery.

She narrowed the color selection down to either Chantilly lace or soft buttercup; which was a shade yellower than the other.

Molly and the older twin boys (Mike and Mark) prepared the walkway from the bottom of the hill up to the log cabin house on top.

They filled brown paper bags with sand and tea light candles.

After sunset the candles were lit and their guests started to arrive.

Dad had a small wood fire by the nativity scene to illuminate the Holy Family.

No candles or flashlights were needed at the top of the hill;
once their eyes adjusted to the natural light provided by the moon which tonight was full.

Their dairy cows (Daisy and Muffy) served as the ox (swapped out depending upon which one was behaving best) for nativity scene; they had to borrow a donkey from a neighbor.

Mark and Mike tied a carrot to a bamboo shoot ahead of the donkey to lead the stubborn animal uphill; which took a lot of time and labor.

Molly thought a better idea would be to have Mark and Mike switch out playing the part of the stubborn donkey.

But she kept this thought to herself
because she still needed their help.

Sonny brought his two twin baby lambs from his house for he was one of the shepherds with the younger boy twins John and Joseph.

The guests huddled in small groups outside or warmed up by the fireplace inside cozy and nice.

Then the angelic voices of the McGolly girls sang beautiful songs for the baby Jesus Christ.

Molly led the tribute by singing 'Ave Maria' a soprano solo;

even the stars seemed to twinkle more as to say "bravo".

The duet of Maryann and Miriam sang several songs in unison.

It was their idea to have the live nativity scene,

so they took center stage and began to sing, sing, sing!

They were accompanied by Sonny on his trumpet,

every musical note from that brass horn seemed to ascend

from his soul deep down inside of him.

First song: 'O Come All Ye Faithful'

Second song: 'Away In a Manger'

Third song: 'What Child Is This'

For the finale all 3 McGolly girls sang 'Little Drummer Boy';

accompanied by Sonny and his trumpet and the little boy twins John and Joseph with their toy drums.

Since the twins were only 2 years old, the rum-pa-pa-pums

were a little hard on most of the guests eardrums.

The immediate family was accustomed to all the noise

from these two very active little boys.

BUT WAIT...the musical portion of the evenings events were not over!

Literally from out of the blue, Mike and Mark gave their Christmas gifts to their little sisters by singing to Christ a tribute.

Most people (including Molly) were so surprised because they didn't know the boys could sing so well.

Sonny knew since he was at every rehearsal since practice sessions were at his house...but he wasn't going to tell!

Apparently while Molly and Dad were busy building a great bird house and restoring an old chandelier;

Mark and Mike were having voice lessons while Sonny practiced his horn and guitar.

Sonny practiced until his fingers had blisters;

it was all worth it to see the looks on the faces of the McGolly twin sisters.

The boys sang:

Song one: 'Silent Night' with Sonny's guitar

Song two: 'Hark the Herald Angels Sing' with Sonny's brass horn

Song three: 'Glory Be to the New Born King' with Sonny's trumpet

You would think things couldn't get any better for Maryann and Miriam but then it did!

Sonny surprised Miriam and Maryann by giving them his two little lambs.

The little girls named their new pets Chantilly and Buttercup because one lamb was a shade yellower than the other.

Twin girls with twin lambs and serenaded by their twin brothers;

a live nativity scene, surprise Christmas gifts, this Christmas was one to remember.

Everyone knelt and prayed the family rosary; the joyful mysteries.

It was time to thank God for all they had received especially

Baby Jesus our Savior!

The Joyful Mysteries of the Holy Rosary:

1). ANNUNCIATION (Luke 1, 28-31)

And coming in, he said to her, "Greetings, favored one! The Lord is with you." "and behold, you will conceive in your womb and bear a son, and you shall name Him Jesus".

2). VISITATION (Luke 1, 41-42)

When Elizabeth heard Mary's greeting, the baby leaped in her womb; and Elizabeth was filled with the Holy Spirit. And she cried out with a loud voice and said, "Blessed are you among women, and blessed is the fruit of your womb!"

3). BIRTH OF JESUS (Luke 2, 7)

And she gave birth to her firstborn son; and she wrapped Him in cloths, and laid Him in a manger, because there was no room for them in the inn.

4). PRESENTATION IN THE TEMPLE (Luke 2, 22-23)

And when the days for their purification according to the law of Moses were completed, they brought Him up to Jerusalem to present Him to the Lord as it is written in the Law of the Lord, "every firstborn male that opens the womb shall be called holy to the Lord"

5). FINDING THE CHILD JESUS (Luke 2, 49-51)

And He said to them, "Why is it that you were looking for Me? Did you not know that I had to be in My Father's house?" And He went down with them and came to Nazareth, and He continued in subjection to them; and His mother treasured all these things in her heart.

Father, Mother and Grandma took turns reading the corresponding scripture readings for the Joyful Mysteries of the Holy Rosary.

Traditionally in the McGolly household, during the third joyful mystery of the holy rosary: Whoever had the little ceramic baby Jesus would place it in the manger underneath their Christmas tree. This year with the live nativity scene which of the triplets would get to be placed in the manger like the newborn King?

Leo (first born triplet) like a lion was a cryin

Shawn (third born triplet) was too tired...with a yawn

Patrick (second born triplet) was happy and smiling; could be because he was the last baby fed.

Apparently if you have a full stomach, it doesn't matter if you have a manger full of straw for a bed.

Who says the middle triplet never gets any attention;

for this Christmas Eve, Patrick was King and the other 2 got honorable mention.

Before the family loaded up in the van to go to midnight Mass, they had an hour or so to rest.

Dad ordered Molly and Mark to watch the campfire until it was completely out.

When you live in a log cabin you can't be too careful with an active fire about.

Mike and Sonny were in the barn with Maryann and Miriam teaching the girls how to bottle feed the little lambs.

Mike decided to tell the nativity story to the animals in the barn, since the shepherds found baby Jesus in a stable.

His version included animal sounds but for the most part corresponded
with the Holy Bible.

Mike and Sonny started a conversation about how the shepherds probably helped the holy family by supplying wool/sheepskin blankets to keep baby Jesus and Mary warm and sheep milk to feed baby Jesus and Mary. After all Joseph and Mary only had what they could load on the donkey for all their needs.

At midnight the McGolly family was at the Catholic Church for midnight Mass.

They even brought all the triplets who were all asleep at last.

From the scripture readings to Father O'Malley's homily
to the choir singing in great harmony;
the midnight Christmas Mass was beautiful,
part lively and part tranquil.

After Mass was over they walked outside with hopes of seeing the bright star of Bethlehem;
no, they did not but there was a clear sky and many twinkling stars above them.

The highlight of every Catholic Mass celebrated everyday in every Catholic Church is the Holy Eucharist.

Once the priest blesses the bread and wine it is changed into the real Body and Blood of our Lord Jesus Christ.

The Holy Eucharist is the source and summit of the Catholic religion.

•••

Scripture Passage (Luke 22, 14-23): The Institution of the Lord's Supper

And when the hour came, he sat at table, and the apostles with him. And he said to them, "I have earnestly desired to eat this Passover with you before I suffer; for I tell you I shall not eat it until it is fulfilled in the kingdom of God." And he took a cup, and when he had given thanks he said, "Take this, and divide it among yourselves; for I tell you that from now on I shall not drink of the fruit of the vine until the kingdom of God comes." And he took bread, and when he had given thanks he broke it and gave it to them, saying, "This is my body which is given for you. Do this in remembrance of me." And likewise the cup after supper, saying, "This cup which is poured out for you is the new covenant in my blood. But behold the hand of him who betrays me is with me on the table. For the Son of man goes as it has been determined; but woe to that man by whom he is betrayed!" And they began to question one another, which of them it was that would do this.

•••

Scripture Passage (Matthew 26: 26-29): The Institution of the Lord's Supper

Now as they were eating, Jesus took bread, and blessed, and broke it, and gave it to the disciples and said, "Take, eat; this is my body." And he took a cup, and when he had given thanks he gave it to them, saying, "Drink of it, all of you: for this is my blood of the covenant, which is poured out for many for the forgiveness of sins. I tell you I shall not drink again of this fruit of the vine until that day when I drink it new with you in my Father's kingdom."

••

Now, back to the McGolly family:

Santa would be coming down the chimney tonight;

since the sky looked clear he and his reindeer should have a good flight.

They returned home, got Dad's nightly blessing

then fell asleep without undressing.

The next morning (CHRISTMAS DAY) Mr. and Mrs. McGolly could hear the pitter patter of little feet;

followed shortly by what sounded like a stampede.

Molly, Mike and Mark, Miriam and Maryann all ran to the Christmas tree.

Was the ceramic baby Jesus (missing one arm) in the manger where He was supposed to be?!

Whomever took baby Jesus the year before must place Him back in the manger.

Their usual tradition was: Whoever took the baby Jesus from their family nativity scene the year before; during the family midnight rosary (the joyful mysteries) would be the one to put baby Jesus in the manger at the stroke of midnight Christmas Eve the following year. This year the live nativity scene changed their usual pattern; but it was well worth it! In previous years, the ceramic baby Jesus was placed in the manger at midnight during the recitation of the rosary and about fifteen minutes later someone had already taken Him for safe keeping until next year.

This was usually the work of Molly's very competitive brothers (Mark and Mike); each one wanted the title of most times placing the ceramic infant Jesus in the manager. In addition to the live nativity scene; this year there was another twist. There were two identical ceramic baby Jesus's this year; even down to the missing arm which had broken off through the years. One in the manger and one in Mark's hand. Mark practically cried saying "I've had this one all year, that one is an imposter."

His twin Mike purchased the other ceramic baby Jesus at the hardware store.

Just so he could say he put Jesus in the manger more times than his twin brother.

Mark and Mike were very competitive;

sometimes to the point that Mom needed a sedative.

So which one actually gets to count this year?

The one who put the imposter baby Jesus in the manger first;

or should it always be the original, no substitutes like an original birth.

If Mom wasn't a responsible adult she would have started that day with

Scotch and water (without the water) or

Gin and tonic (without the tonic).

When attempting to settle your children's disputes

no matter how minutiae;

sometimes it is better to stay out of it, let them work it out, pretend you can't hear them,

threaten to tell their father,

it was to late to cancel Santa Claus Christmas!

You would think after 10 lively children, Mrs. McGolly would be a pro.

Mr. McGolly rationalized that after 2 kids the parents are outnumbered and lose control.

Running the McGolly household was not like a well oiled machine.

It was more like riding a bicycle built for two; petal, petal, petal...and continue to proceed.

Keep putting one foot in front of the other until someday they and their children will

reach their final reward.

Graduation day, when they can throw them out the door!

Just kidding, they all remain our children until the roles are reversed.

Someday those children might be taking care of their parents are other family members;

hopefully with love and joy as they were raised.

But right now Mom had one more card up her sleeve,

She simply asked "What did Santa leave?"

All her children looked around but there were no toys;

not for girls and not for boys!

Soon they were looking in every room,

under their beds and even where Grandma kept the broom.

They checked the porch...no toys to be had;

Oh boy! Oh boy! They must have been really bad!

When Molly yelled "I found them, I found the toys, there in the barn up in the loft.

I guess Santa put them up high to keep the animals off".

Molly wondered if Santa did that before the family went to bed.

She thought that with her brain which was under her hair that was red.

Maybe this year instead of toys for Christmas they were getting farm animals instead.

Now it was time to see what Santa brought;

starting with the tiny tots.

For the triplets mobiles to go over their cribs

and a teddy bear for each and baby bibs.

John and Joseph got toddler trikes.

A pair of new bicycles and helmets for Mark and Mike.

Miriam and Maryann each got a brand new dolly.

Molly a zip line and pulley system with riding seat,

mock green alligator skin purse and a new board game called monopoly.

Molly loved her zip line seat

and thought it was really neat!

However this year for Christmas she got a fingernail paint set and now a purse?!

What was going on in the universe!

Yes, Molly knew she was the oldest,

and eventually would have to check off growing up off her bucket list.

She recently had her first boy girl dance; an Irish jig with handsome Joe.

But she wanted her childhood to go slow.

Molly still played dolls with her younger sisters,

and romped in the woods with her brothers until her feet had blisters.

She would rather zip line through the trees or swing from the barn rafters on rope;

Molly wasn't ready to grow up yet… Nope, Nope, Nope.

So, she and her brothers swang from the barn rafters on Christmas Day

and landed in the soft hay;

while wearing her church clothes (from midnight Mass) showing her maturity level.

Molly didn't want to grow up; she was a rebel.

The children that Christmas morning ate very little breakfast

because they were playing with their toys,

swinging from the rafters and making lots of noise.

Christmas dinner was a feast;

turkey with dressing and giblet gravy, sweet potatoes with apples and pecans.

Green beans, yellow squash casserole and Grandma's homemade rolls

which weren't on the table very long before they were gone.

Pies galore: apple pie, pumpkin pie, cherry pie, pecan pie.

The adults drank wine made right on the premises;

from grapes harvested in their very own vineyard.

The McGolly's had fun making the wine labels:

Woodcrafter's Wine by Dad,

Firey Red's Campfire Wine by Mom,

France Dance Wine by Grandma

Dad stored in the wine cellar a bottle for each of his children from the year they

were born; to be opened some special day after they turn 21.

For Molly this date would be the 12th of never.

She preferred her bottle to remain corked and tucked deep down in the cellar.

She didn't want to grow up, not now...not ever!

Dad always said "The best wine is yet to come, if we are always willing to Love, Love, Love".

Before the Christmas feast, the relatives arrived by plane, train and automobile.

Some by horses and Sonny by his wheelchair wheels.

Sonny got a Saint Bernard dog for Christmas named Ollie.

Ollie came with a medicine barrel collar which held a harmonica;

a new musical instrument to master which was easy to carry on-the-go.

Sonny already had one tune he could play;

Doh-Rey-Me-Fa-So-La-Te-Doh.

He just slowly moved his lips across the harmonica, then in reverse; easy breezy for a trumpet player.

Now, trying to teach Ollie a few tricks might require much more labor.

Responding to commands like fetch, rollover, sit or play dead didn't work on Ollie.

How was Sonny to get this giant dog to be a mail carrier from his house to Molly's.

Saint Bernard's are suppose to be paramedics, traveling great distances in frozen cold weather and blinding snow blizzards;

transporting those in peril to safety on dog sleds.

At least that is what Sonny wanted his dog Ollie to do, come the first big snow.

No big emergency needed, Sonny just wanted a ride to where he wanted to go.

After the wonderful Christmas feast in which all the aunts and uncles embellished;

by bringing more desserts, entrees and trimmings, including Aunt Martha's Copper Coins Relish.

It was made of marinated carrots and was Grandma's favorite relish dish.

Aunt Martha gave every family a jar for Christmas and Grandma her own which she cherished.

Aunt Martha's Copper Coins Relish (Marinated Carrots):

1 pound carrots peeled and thinly sliced

½ Cup sugar

½ Cup salad oil

½ Cup white vinegar

1 Tbsp. prepared mustard

1 (10 ¾ ounce can) tomato soup, undiluted

1 medium onion, thinly sliced

1 Cup green bell peppers, chopped

1 teaspoon Worcestershire sauce

1). In a sauce pan, cover carrots with water and bring to a boil. Boil 1 minute then remove from heat.

2). Add sugar and stir until sugar is dissolved.

3). Add all other ingredients.

4). Try to chill overnight in refrigerator, then serve.

5). Can be stored in refrigerator for a couple of weeks (use common sense).

From Mexican Hot Chocolate to Marinated Carrots, Aunt Martha was always trying to spice things up, rock the boat!

That is probably why she is so active in the Pro-Life Movement. She is very passionate about natural conception to natural death; including everything in between. Why just both ends of the life line, as Catholics and like minded peoples we should also be natural in between. Meaning no artificial forms of contraception (birth control pills, patches, injections; condoms; IUD's or other foreign bodies inserted into vagina for contraception etc...); no in-vitro fertilization (not natural); no artificial insemination (not natural); no surrogate motherhood (not natural); no "selective reduction" of babies in the womb (not natural); no human cloning (not natural); no sperm bank donating (not natural). Only natural family planning for those who have a good reason to hold off having children or for those who want to have children. Natural family planning can help a couple find the most fertile time for a woman to conceive and increase their chances of having children. Also, adoption is a beautiful option for couples who want their family to grow.

Aunt Martha goes to every Pro-Life March in Washington DC on the anniversary of Roe vs Wade, January 22nd, doing her part of reverse the ruling on Roe vs Wade.

Abortion is murder of the most defenseless, human beings on the planet.

If they were big enough (like the people who are taking their life); they would protest having their limbs ripped apart while they are still alive. When Martha was in junior high at a Catholic school; she witnessed a video showing a baby in the womb being ripped apart. The little human being cried like a kitten, screaming as it was being tortured and killed. She knew she would never forget that sight and sound and would do her part in stopping the brutal slaying of her earthly brothers and sisters. As she got older, she started to discover that some of her friends/ co-workers etc... had abortions. For a short while she started to rationalize what these people whom she loved did to their unborn children. Then she remembered the video and screams. Now, she with compassion speaks to anyone who will listen about the dignity of every human life. She also tries to listen to what their objections are to defending these human lives. Starting sometimes with the blunt truth of 96% of abortions are elective abortions.

Only 4 % of abortions are the 'hard' cases. The hard cases for her include (incest, rape, finding out the unborn baby has a physical defect like Down's syndrome or the mother's life is threatened). Martha then breaks these dilemmas down. Research shows that women who have been the victim of incest or rape in time (eventually) get over being the victim (this takes time and physical, mental and spiritual healing) but they can't get over causing someone to be the victim (their unborn child) in many cases. Studies have shown women who are the victims of incest and rape that gave birth to their baby/s; and either kept them or gave them up for adoption have better outcomes because they didn't cause the children to be victims at their hands. The women who aborted their children had difficulty forgiving themselves for causing someone else to be the victim (their unborn child). For these women she recommends a retreat called Rachel's Vineyard or Project Rachel to help them heal spiritually from their abortion/s. If you know someone who is having difficulty after having an abortion please reach out to them and share the retreat information; available also to the father of the aborted baby or grandparents, or aunts/uncles.

Note: For more precise information order a DVD called 'When They Say, You Say' from E.W.T.N. religious catalogue (concerning the subject of abortions and Pro-Life).

Aunt Martha was influenced by Saint Faustina's Diary; one of her favorite lines:

'Patience in adversity gives power to the soul.' (Part 607 page 255, Notebook II)

Martha is very passionate about the dignity of every human life and sometimes it is very hard to be patient. Patience is a virtue she constantly must strive to achieve.

Another one of her favorite lines is taken from a book called 'THE POEM OF THE MAN-GOD' written by Maria Valtorta (from Volume II of V Volumes); page 646:

'Persuasion is achieved by means of firm kindness." This is the first line of a paragraph which goes into much more detail.

She wants to be compassionate to the people she speaks to about abortion but sometimes you can't give them the TRUTH and tell them what they want to hear at the same time.

The Spiritual Works of Mercy:

1). Admonish sinners
2). Instruct the uninformed
3). Counsel the doubtful
4). Comfort the sorrowful
5). Be patient with those in error
6). Forgive offenses
7). Pray for those living and dead

Trying to explain why killing innocent children in their mother's womb is against the Fifth Commandment (Thou Shalt Not Kill) and remain calm with Christians who should know better; can be very disheartening. Admonishing sinners who are using contraceptives, fornicating, committing adultery (have not attempted to get annulment), living together outside of marriage; while trying to appeal to their sense of righteousness and their faith can be a slippery slope. However Martha seems to be good at it! She counsels women considering abortion and gives them encouragement as well as resources to help them in their time of crisis. She also talks to teenagers/women about living a life of chastity until marriage and staying away from birth control. She teaches natural family planning at her Catholic Church (just like Mother Theresa did to the poor in Calcutta India). Children deserve to have a mother and a father. On an individual level, trying to talk to her family and friends about morality is even more difficult. When she gets rejected by their reactions it seems to hurt more because you already love them. However, if you don't tell them the TRUTH...who will?!...they may never repent and change their ways. Silence is the same thing as agreeing with them. The world has turned a blind eye to God's laws. Our own government, what's on television and other forms of multi-media, their own families are also obstacles to overcome. Do you know what the answer is to these problems in our families and society? It's YOU! You might be the only one supporting their decision to choose life. Live Your Catholic Faith Fully. Be obedient to God and leave the consequences to Him. Remember to follow Jesus when carrying your cross/s, don't try to lead him.

Martha reads the Act of Consecration to the Sacred Heart of Jesus to Catholics when she speaks to them.

••

Act of Consecration to the Sacred Heart of Jesus:

Most Sacred Heart of Jesus, I consecrate myself to your Most Sacred Heart. Take possession of my whole being; transform me into yourself. Make my hands your hands, my feet your feet, my heart your heart. Let me see with your eyes, listen with your ears, speak with your lips, love with your heart, understand with your mind, serve with your will, and be dedicated with my whole being. Make me your other self. Most Sacred Heart of Jesus, send me your Holy Spirit to teach me to love you and to live through you, with you, in you and for you.

Come, Holy Spirit, make my body your temple. Come, and abide with me forever. Give me the deepest love for the Sacred Heart of Jesus that I might serve Him with all my heart, soul, mind and strength. Take possession of all my faculties of body and soul. Regulate all my passions, feelings and emotions. Take possession of my intellect, understanding and will; my memory and imagination. O Spirit of Love, give me an abundance of your efficacious graces. Give me the fullness of all the virtues; enrich my faith, strengthen my hope, increase my trust, and inflame my love. Give me the fullness of your sevenfold gifts, fruits and beatitudes. Most Holy Trinity, make my soul your sanctuary. Amen.

••

Now it was time for Dad to give out the gifts he worked on all year in his woodwork shop.
For the triplets a set of wooden drawers that doubled as a diaper changing table.
For the toddlers; John and Joseph, wooden blocks.
Maryann and Miriam; strollers and highchairs for their dolls.
Grandma got a hanging wooden swing for the back porch.
For Mom and Molly, wooden snow skis painted bright colors and varnished.
Mom's skis were red and Molly's were green; Christmas colors!
Dad included snow ski poles purchased from a store.
Mike, Mark and Sonny had to go outside to receive their wooden gifts hidden behind the barn doors.
Mike and Mark had a boat big enough for two
and Sonny also had a boat big enough for two.
Sonny and Molly did almost everything together;
where you found one you found the other.
Unfortunately it was too cold to try out their new boats;
to make sure that they did in fact float.
So the rest of that wonderful Christmas Day, Miriam and Maryann took out their wooden nativity scene from last year and prayed;
and with their new dollies and live baby lambs they played.
Sonny, Molly, Mike and Mark opened up the monopoly game and around the board they raced;
to see which one would come in first place.
John and Joseph played with their new blocks and wooden fire truck from last year by the fireplace.
Dad engineered this fire truck to pump out water by cranking up a special gear...
that was his first mistake.
He also put in a clanging bell and working siren...
that was that was his second mistake.
The noise level was coming through loud and clear;

siren up, siren down, clang, clang, clang over and over.

Then Dad noticed in the fireplace some of the carefully measured cut to order blocks.

That was it...third strike, game over...Dad was about to blow!

Instead he took a deep breath, told his little boys not to put anything into the fire...

they simply didn't know!

Dad thought to himself 'Next year they're getting play-doh'.

He was becoming more patient with the children; all those trips to the confessional were paying off.

He had trained himself to catch his temperament before he exploded and cool off.

It took time and deliberant action for this conversion to unfold.

Firm amendment to change is not easy, it is a difficulty road.

It is the road with rocks and thorns; when you fall, pick yourself back up and continue along the path of righteousness.

This change in behavior (a virtue) led his little boys to want to be around their father.

Many attempts in the past were unsuccessful; but he kept on trying until he was able to change.

In spite of difficulty and opposition remain steadfast in purpose: PERSEVERE, PERSEVERE, PERSEVERE!!!

Until you change the vice into a virtue.

It was like a scene from a Norman Rockwell painting

with about a dozen children playing.

Oh, I almost forgot to mention what Mom got for a Christmas gift for Dad.

It was a heart attack; or that was what he said he would have preferred.

A second hand airplane that could not fly.

Mom got it at a garage sale...it was a really good buy!

The uncles disassembled it and smuggled it in by the pond.

Dad was so busy in his wood work shop with all the noise be was unaware of the con.

Oh, the things at a garage sale you can find.

You just have to have an open mind.

Grandma knitted Dad golf club covers for his new (barely used) golf clubs also purchased at the garage sale for a really good deal!

Now all Dad had to do was learn to play golf and fly a plane.

Dad wondered 'What has happened to the women in his family; have they gone insane?!'

The uncles just looked at him with big Cheshire grins showing all their teeth.

They didn't even try to conceal their laughter for it was just too hilarious.

A few of the uncles had orange and lemon rinds in their mouths from the fruit punch.

This made their smiles look even more cheesy; but not much.

Mom cried, Dad almost died.

The uncles were laughing so hard, rolling on the ground, holding their sides.

Sonny was trying to prepare Ollie for his first medical victim, to no avail.

Ollie just looked at Sonny and wagged his furry tail.

The moral of the tragic tale:

Just because you can buy something at a garage sale

for a good deal;

ask yourself is it something you can really use or are you being a fool.

Sometimes if you buy something for someone on a whim;

it can be a good thing or it might actually kill them.

Heart attacks are serious but it turned out to be a mild anxiety attack.

As soon as he calmed down, they all returned to the house for a snack.

Mom had a mint julep and Dad had a beer.

He thought to himself 'I'm going to have to pay more attention to what goes on around here'.

The women gathered in the kitchen just to gab, catch up on what's new...female companionship...a little girl talk.

The men gathered around the dining room table for a card game, few jokes...male companionship...male bonding...some football talk.

Molly made fancy hats for Mom and Grandma to wear to church.

If you thought Dad had a surprise look on his face when he saw his airplane; that was nothing compared to the stares Mom and Grandma had when they opened their presents!

You would have thought they were about to be attacked by wild Indians or bears.

"Thank you dear. We will wear them to church next Sunday" said Grandma a little bit hesitant.

Mom thought maybe the Kentucky Derby or Halloween would be more appropriate!

Where did Molly get hats with such big rims.

Those hats would provide enough shade for the whole family at the beach.

Think of all the money they could save on beach umbrellas and sunscreen.

Dad smirked and said "I can't wait to see you ladies with your hats at church" as he cast a card away.

Uncle Steve added "Gerald maybe you can give them a ride in your airplane next Sunday".

Dad inquired "Well what did your wives get you guys this year"?

One uncle stated "I really wanted a flying carpet but I got new tires for my car".

Uncle Steve said "I got a pair khaki pants and some underwear; but I had my eye on a suit of armor".

The third uncle stated he got dance lessons again just like last year.

The men waited for the punch line but there was none.

Uncle Robert was as serious as a real heart attack.

He got dance lessons again just like last year but it wasn't so bad because his love life with his wife was re-ignited.

So the guys wanted to see his dance moves so they could make fun of him; but instead he was excited.

Uncle Robert jumped up, put on the music and cleared an area for the impromptu dance floor.

He and the Mrs. danced the fox trot and the most famous dance of all time 'the Tango' like Ginger Rogers and Fred Astaire.

Soon all the men were dancing with their beautiful wives.

Uncle Steve even did the splits like John Travolta while singing to the tune of 'Stayin Alive'.
He ripped the seams of his new khakis and everyone could see his new underwear.
Mike, Mark and Sonny were dancing with Grandma, Sonny's Mom (Clare) and Molly.
Every dance move you could imagine, happened right there on the dance floor in the log cabin; didn't have to look good, just had to be mov'in and a grov'in.
Each couple began with their versions of classical dances like the fox trot, tango, rumba and the Blue Danube waltz.
Then Elvis must have entered the building because everyone was doing the twist.
Soon every dance imaginable made an appearance: Indian War Dance, Clogging, Rock n Roll is here to stay, Hokey-Pokey, the Pony, Batman, the Bump and the 1940's Jive including a walking headstand.
Grandma can do the Can-Can; she learned to dance in France!
She must have gone to Poland too, because she taught her grandchildren the chicken dance.

There were only two forbidden dances:

    1).   The Strip-tease because it is so immoral.
    2).   The Irish River Dance because it was somewhat sacred in the Irish circle.

An Irish jig was permissible!
Marry in the M-Dances: the Mom-Bo, March of the Penguins, Monster Mash and the Mac-a-rina; even the little girls joined in by dancing like a ballerina.
They did the 2 Step, the 4 Step with pep;
add to the mix a few yoga moves and the Bunny Hop;
they just couldn't seem to STOP!
Suddenly they all paused because something happened to their ears;
it was called a slow dance and they were back to dancing in boy/girl pairs.
Dancing cheek to cheek; slowing swaying to the music; love was in the air.
The married couples did not seem to have a single care.
The last dance was a slow one
before most of the guests packed up and went home.
Some of the guests spent the night
then left the next morning at daylight.
It was still winter break when the first big snowfall arrived.
Molly put on her new snow skis and wobbled down the hill.
She fell 3 times but it was still a thrill.
Molly's Mom came weaving back and forth like a professional skier, she even did a few mini jumps and said she was just getting started.
Sonny came with his dog Ollie; this time the medicine barrel collar served as a first aid kit.
It was full of bandages, band aids, antiseptic wipes and a can of bear mace spray.
You can spray a bear with bear mace from 25 feet away.

Molly questionably stated "What bears?"

Sonny answered "Exactly, you can never be too prepared!"

Mark used a splint when he thought he broke his arm;

but the hospital x-ray proved it was a false alarm.

Merely a sprain so back to the hill, for another run.

Broken bones or not; sledding is fun!

Mike hit his head and thought he saw birds circling and tweeting.

Molly told him that was perfectly normal; happens to her almost every morning.

When Molly crashed, her hair was messy, her glasses crooked, and her clothes disshoveled;

she looked pretty much the same, so back to the top of the hill to do it all again,

and again until she was completely exhausted.

Soon, everyone in Molly's class showed up on the hill with their sleds, skis and inter-tubes.

They came to collect on the spare change collection for fluorescent light bulbs.

Sleds, skis, tubes were coming from every which way …zoom, zoom, zoom.

Sonny got in his inter-tube and went sliding down the hill.

The kids in the class and Ollie his dog took turns pulling Sonny back up the hill in his inter-tube.

They had sled races, snowball fights and even made snowmen and snow angels.

The class came together and made a giant snow bear and used millions of pine needles as its fur.

Then Sonny demonstrated how to use his bear mace spray.

There have been no bears spotted in this area til this day.

When they got cold they went inside by the fireplace;

to drink hot chocolate and hot apple cider.

School started a few days later.

The kids showed up to school with new clothes and gadgets they received for Christmas.

So much for the hard work making their homemade gifts, recycling, reuse…blah, blah, blah.

Molly was right back to square one…

Will they ever learn?!

January, the start of a new year.

Molly whispered her New Year's resolution into Sonny's ear.

<u>"I'm going to conform, follow the crowd because peer pressure works. After I gain their onfidence</u>

I'll switch gears and use peer pressure in reverse."

Sonny just sat back and shook his head side to side;

waiting for this new plan of Molly's to collide.

Molly started showing up for school with her red hair clean and combed;

her face was washed and fingernails polished.

Molly's eyebrows were tweezed and her teeth were flossed.

The seams of her clothing were not inside out;

her shoes matched and lips were glossed.

Molly started to dress like them, eat like them; arrived to school in a motorized vehicle.

She learned to text, google, twitter and giggle!

Once she got carried away and dressed like the teacher;

she put her red hair in a bun, wore a sweater and sensible shoes.

If imitation is the most sincere form of flattery; there was no way she could lose.

The teacher loved the new look but the popular girls did not.

I must conform to the majority Molly thought.

At home she was painting her fingernails while watching celebrities on tv.

Then it occurred to her to use some of the new technology to get her class green;

she would devise her new scheme under the radar screen.

Molly used social media to convince the popular girls to carpool.

If you all arrive to school together that would be so cool;

by together she meant in the same motorized vehicle.

She created a plan to save the earth gas.

How many kids can arrive to school in the same car from any class.

Contest: The most kids to arrive or go home in the same car.

The contest would be a blast but she had no prize.

How could she get them to do it; simply because it's the right thing to do in their eyes.

Out with the paints on cut up grocery brown paper bags.

This time instead of water conservation the signs were to conserve energy.

She was able to enlist the help from Sonny and her new friend Shelley.

Shelley might turn out to be a convert to the green side.

She even arranged to pick up a couple of kids on her block for a school ride.

Shelley loved to paint and was willing to use her talent for the cause...

You know...TO SAVE THE PLANET!

The signs read:

Carpool! Carpool! or Ride a Bike or Walk to School (Save Gas)

Turn Off the Light When You Leave a Room (This sign was completely black except for he words)

Wear a Sweater or Long Johns to Keep Warm on Cold Days (Sonny put real sweaters and long johns from the school Clothes Closet on signs to get attention. Whose long johns they used to belong he did not mention).

Keep Thermostat 72 degrees (Winter); 78 degrees (Summer)

Use air-dry button on dishwasher or wash and dry dishes by hand

Unplug Appliances not is use

The signs were creative, colorful, informative, sensible, silly and even made to local news!

Although Molly was making some progress;

she returned back to her old way pretty fast.

The creativity of these signs caused quite a stir.

However Molly had a revelation; If you can't beat them/join them, just wasn't working for her.

So she returned back to her true self.

Sonny patiently waited but he was so happy he sent Ollie to deliver Molly a rose.

Where Sonny got a rose in the middle of winter nobody knows.

Molly thought all the roses ought to be froze.

But Sonny was always amazing in Molly's eyes.

She loved Sonny so much, the rose made her cry.

Molly completed a nine day novena on Joy in Suffering according to St. Therese of the Child Jesus, just the day before.

St. Therese of the Child Jesus was Molly's favorite saint; also known as 'the Little Flower'.

★★

"I will let fall from Heaven...

a Shower of Roses" ST. THERESE

MY NOVENA ROSE PRAYER

O Little Therese of the Child Jesus, please pick for me a rose

from the heavenly gardens and send it to me as a message of love.

O Little Flower of Jesus, ask God today to grant the favors

I now place with confidence in your hands...

(Mention specific requests)

St. Therese, help me to always believe as you did,

in God's great love for me, so that I might imitate your "Little Way" each day. Amen.

★★

Saint Therese of Lisieux wrote a book called "The Story of a Soul": which Molly borrowed from the church library.

The following is part of the information on the back book cover. Written under obedience, the book conveys her secrets of great holiness achieved in ordinary life, teaching the "Little Way of Spiritual Childhood" her elevator to Heaven, as she called it. In the book St. Therese shows us how her "Little Way of love and confidence" comes straight from Sacred Scripture.

No Catholic should be ignorant of the mighty "little" Therese, of her Little Way, or of THE STORY OF A SOUL.

The back cover of this book states

This book belongs in every Catholic home,... and this is the famous book that was instrumental in bringing down the "shower of roses", or favors from Heaven, which St. Therese had promised to send after death.

St. Therese died at only age 24, after a 9 year hidden life as a cloistered Carmelite nun. Millions of copies of THE STORY OF A SOUL were distributed worldwide.

Molly has a prayer card in her Bible with a picture of St. Therese on one side and his prayer on the other side: Prayer to Saint Therese

O Lord, who said:

"Unless you become as a little child,

you shall not enter

into the kingdom of heaven;"
grant us, we pray you,
so to walk in the footsteps
of your blessed Virgin Theresa
with a humble heart,
that we may attain
to everlasting rewards:
who lived and reigned
the world without end. Amen.

Molly also had a small wooden statue of St. Therese of the Child Jesus and the Holy Face;
which was last year's wooden Christmas gift from Dad.
Inscribed into the wooden statue:

> O Little Therese of the Child Jesus,
> please pick for me a rose from the
> heavenly gardens and send it to me
> as a message of love.

So the fact that Molly received a rose the day after she completed novena...
Molly was sure it was sent my Saint Therese from above.
Before St. Therese died she said, "After death, I will drop down from Heaven a shower of roses."
Molly asked Sonny where he got the rose so beautiful.
Sonny said it was lying on the snow by his wheelchair after carpooling home from school.
She told Sonny about the novena, St. Therese and the shower of roses.
Sonny replied "So you think the rose is for encouraging people to carpool to save gas".
"No" replied Molly, "Not just for that. It's January the beginning of a new year. So I prayed the novena 'Joy in Suffering' to become more spiritually enlightened. I went to confession last night on the last day of the novena. I'm in the state of grace and received the Body and Blood of Jesus Christ after completing my penance with a contrite heart (truly sorry for sins) during Holy Mass last evening. The special intention of saying the novena was for others to take better care of the earth. So receiving the rose from you with love which seemed to drop down from Heaven...well it just makes me very happy".
Molly grabbed Sonny's chin with her left hand for her right hand was holding the rose so tight; then she kissed Sonny between his eyes with all her might.
Since she still had red lip gloss on her lips, Sonny had a kiss print on his forehead that could be seen from outer space.
By going to confession and Holy Mass, Molly received much grace.
Sonny decided to go to confession due to Molly's good example;
before the celebration of the Eucharist during the next Saturday evening Vigil.
Sonny knew that Jesus, after His resurrection on Easter Sunday gave the power to forgive sins to His Apostles.

Jesus had to complete His mission and die for our sins first.

He desired for each one of us to ask for forgiveness for our sins; when during His passion and crucifixion He said "I thirst".

Scripture Passage: John 20: 21-23

"He said therefore to them again: Peace be to you. As the Father hath sent me, I also send you. When he had said this, he breathed on them; and he said to them: Receive ye the Holy Ghost. Whose sins you shall forgive, they are forgiven them; and whose sins you shall retain, they are retained."

★★★★★★★★★★★★★★★★★★★★★★★★★★★★★★★★★★★★

Through apostolic succession, the power to forgive and/or retain sins has been handed down through the ages. Only those ordained into the Catholic priesthood have been given this power through God. Not even deacons in the Catholic Church have been given to power to forgive or retain sins.

Sonny remembered a story he heard about a noted Saint (although he couldn't remember which saint); who watched a seminary student for years. This Saint could see the student's guardian angel. For years the guardian angel protected the student while in front of him. After ordination to priesthood; the guardian angel was behind him. Catholic priests are chosen by God to be His representatives on earth. In the confessional (the tomb) Jesus speaks and directs us through His chosen ones; the Catholic priest/s. Sonny refers to the confessional as the tomb because if a person repented with true sorrow for all mortal sins (and venial) and was forgiven... as they walk out of the confessional...they are cleansed, purified and have a new life...resurrected like Jesus on that first Easter Sunday.

So, Sonny prepared himself for confession with an examination of conscience; in other words he reviewed the 10 COMMANDMENTS from a leaflet: An Examination of Conscience (A preparation for the Sacrament of Penance).

Sonny took out a booklet he found in his deceased father's belongings called. CONFESSION ITS FRUITFUL PRACTICE with an Examination of Conscience.

Sonny took this little booklet everywhere with him that week;

even brought it to school to look up a couple of words in the dictionary.

One day he left it at school and his teacher found and read the whole thing.

It made quite an impression,

so she too went to confession.

Miss Kimberly Bailey (Sonny and Molly's public school teacher) was raised Catholic but switched to a Protestant Christian church several years ago.

Catholics are given the fullness of the Christian faith so changing to a protestant church is apostasy. Only in the Catholic Church can you receive the true Body, Blood, Soul and Divinity of Jesus Christ into your body.

When a Catholic leaves the Church for a protestant religion, they are walking away from the fullness of the Christian faith. Only Catholic Priests have the authority given to them by God through apostolic succession to forgive sins. The Catholic Church was founded by Jesus Christ Himself and His chosen apostles. The Holy Bible was compiled by the Catholics led by the Holy Spirit; it didn't just fall out of the sky. It is impossible to be closer to Jesus than to receive His true Body, Blood, Soul and Divinity into your own body (Full Communion with Jesus) in the Blessed Sacrament while in the state of grace.

∎∎

When a Catholic leaves the Catholic Church because they don't agree with the teachings; they are telling God they want to do their will over God's. If someone wants to marry outside the Catholic Church they need to get dispensation from the Catholic Church or once again they are doing their will over God's. Whatever their reason for leaving the Catholic Church; it is usually the Holy Eucharist that brings fallen away Catholics back. Worth repeating: Only in the Catholic Church can you receive the true Body, Blood, Soul and Divinity of Jesus Christ into your body. The Holy Eucharist is the source and summit of the Catholic Church.

Miss Bailey left the Church in search of a more active singles group. She was looking for a potential husband but her dates so far had not yielded a lasting relationship.

After reading this booklet (CONFESSION ITS FRUITFUL PRACTICE) that Sonny left by the class dictionary; Miss Bailey's eyes were opened and spiritually she WOKE UP!

It was page 6-7; The Lax Conscience; that got her undivided attention.

That week Miss Kimberly Bailey went to confession and attended Holy Mass for the first time in years.

She received Holy Communion while in the state of grace and she felt like she was home. While in the Church still kneeling after she received the true Body, Blood, Soul and Divinity of Jesus Christ; she asked God to lead her to a good man if marriage was to be her vocation if life. She even asked St. Anne (Mary's mother) to intercede for her: "Saint Anne, Saint Anne, send me a man". This booklet is 79 pages long and Miss Bailey found every page gripping. She had returned to the fullness of the Christian faith...she was back home in the Catholic Church. She had to humble herself in order to put God first...that is how humble a soul must become. God must increase and (your name here) must decrease. Kimberly felt peace in her heart. There is only objective TRUTH and it is in the Catholic Church. The Catholic Church tells you what to think. You can fight it if you want to but it will not change the TRUTH. Once Catholic, always Catholic... it is in there. Now, like when Jesus ascended into Heaven and the apostles knew they had work to do; well Kimberly also knew she had work to do.

Sonny had a coat drive for the Clothes Closet the second week of January.

Molly earned school bucks for her work collecting coats & setting up for Clothes Closet Extravaganza.

She earned enough school bucks to purchase a ski jacket.

The P.T.A. started a program were students could earn school bucks by helping out around the school or participating in school activities.

They could use these bucks to buy school supplies or Clothes Closet items or assorted perks throughout the school year.

Mike and Mark tried to use school bucks to bribe their way out of detention but somehow ended up doing more time.

They also were disappointed to find out school activities did not include detention
for they would have been school buck millionaires.

Molly got a new ski jacket; she was happy, happy, happy and had no cares.

Sometimes you do acts of charity because it just feels good and is the right thing to do;
and sometimes you do charity and get a ski jack that was barely used. YaHoo!

We can't complete the month of January without mentioning the Super Bowl Pregame Activity:

Pregame activity: The McGolly Football Bowl.

Molly thought it should be called the McGolly Football Roll.

Playing football at the top of a hill has its disadvantages.

The teams were somewhat evenly divided each set of twins were split up according to their ages.

Molly's team had Mark, Maryanne and Joseph and a couple of uncles.

Sonny's team had Mike, Miriam and John and a couple of uncles.

Dad was the umpire
and he declared to be fair.

At the end of the game he added each team's scores together and divided them by two.

So the game ended up a tie with no overtime to do.

Miriam and Maryanne loved that they both won, and the game was through.

Most of their time on the field was spent doing cart wheels and running away from the football.

They both won most valuable day dreamer of their respective teams;

Hooray, Hooray Rah! Rah! Rah!

Molly vowed next year she was going to be the umpire, and that Miriam and Maryanne would be cheerleaders.

Next year the McGolly Football Roll would have a clear team winner...
and the winning team would take NO prisoners!

Molly had a competitive spirit, which she didn't get from her father.

She glanced at her Mom who was holding 2 babies; no competitive spirit there.

Maybe it was one of those genetic things that skip a generation.

She glanced at her Grandma who was holding 2 baby lambs; no competitive spirit there.

Molly thought she must have been left on the doorstep by a band of red headed gypsies.

She solved the mystery,
     by golly she was a competitive gypsy!

Dad put up an antenna on top of the house for better television reception, for the Super Bowl Game.

After the game he would remove the antenna because it attracts thunderbolts when it rained.

During the game they had a clear picture of every football play.

Everyone was cheering for the same team, Hooray! Hooray!

It was a close game so there was a lot of excitement;

at least up to the last few seconds and their team fumbled the ball.

The general consensus was...that it was a bad call...

looks like you can't win them all.

Oh, well at least the food was good.

Chips and dips, bar-be-que ribs and the men drank beer;

Molly was pretty sure it was a keg of root beer.

Grandma made her Healthy Super Bowl Dip, served with Pita Chips

Layers of: Hummus (on the bottom of her Super Bowl); fresh cut Spinach; cut up Artichoke Hearts, Greek Yogurt, chopped Red Pepper, drained can of Black Olives, and Feta Cheese sprinkled on top.

Molly recapped the month of January from a green standpoint.

- ⋆ Recycle and Reuse- 'Coat Drive for Clothes Closet'
- ⋆ Reduce: (saving the planet gas) Carpooling up 200% from last year
- ⋆ Repent: 9 Day Novena for the intention of others to take better care of the earth prayer

January in Review:

- ⋆ If you can't beat them then join them tactic did not work for Molly;
    there was no PEACE living a double life.
- ⋆ Carpool to save gas campaign; Carpooling up 200% from last year.
- ⋆ Conserve energy poster campaign: Started off well but eventually most fell back to their old ways. However she could see some of the kids, teachers, lunchroom ladies and even the principal were wearing sweaters and long johns and that the thermostats were set on the correct settings. The principal had all the light bulbs changed to eco-friendly lighting. So, little by little there were positive changes in the whole school.
- ⋆ Molly received a rose from St. Therese (known also as the Little Flower).
- ⋆ Molly led Sonny by example to go to Confession; which indirectly influenced his teacher Miss Bailey back to the confessional and home to the Catholic Church.
- ⋆ Sonny's January Clothes Closet Winter Coat Drive- Huge success!
- ⋆ McGolly Football Bowl/Roll- From a green standpoint (recycle) they used a football made of pig skin.

Unfortunately Molly's team did not win.

The score was a tie so Molly could not bask in glory and rub it in.

So the New Year started off with a few wins and a few defeats;

time to roll up her long john sleeves.

In the month of February:

Somehow use the LOVE theme

    to turn her whole class green.

February: The Month of Love

Roses are red.

Violets are blue.

What is it going to take to turn Molly's class earth lov'in green.

Green doesn't rhythm but it has a color theme.

This month's earth friendly service project was to recycle used books.

Campaign Slogan: (Books Need New Eyes for a Second LOOK)

For every book you donate you receive a school buck,

then trade your school bucks in for secondhand, barely used books.

Bucks for Books!

Molly reasoned that people still read books even in this technologically advanced society.

She knew they wouldn't give up their E readers but they might part with books they've already read; to give others more variety.

Molly found a subgroup of people who love to read and encourage others;

these people are called teachers.

Each teacher selected a pupil from their class to round up books from the students homes.

This band of bookworms set up a comfortable book area in the cafeteria,

complete with several brightly colored bean bag chairs.

Students had to use school bucks to purchase books.

A school buck was issued for each book donated;

then they could select a book; therefore the books were rotated.

Mike and Mark tried pushing their luck and attempted to swap out their school books like spelling and math.

The librarian was not amused, in fact she seemed to be on the warpath.

Mike and Mark ended up having to separate all the books according to subject matter;

after school and during recess (for a week) they had to perform this new earned chore.

(Luck of the Irish): They found several books of interest and put them aside to swap for their school bucks.

The librarian was happy to see the boys eyes being opened to the love of books.

She gave them school bucks for their chore;

so their punishment turned into a win, win score.

They were able to take home their barely used books that very day to enjoy!

Mike and Mark started spending more time in the library after that day.

Sometimes to get books and other times to help Mrs. Wren the librarian, their new friend.

Helping others just feels good even if there is no reward in the end.

Lots of the kids who didn't like to read found it fun to browse and open books to see what was inside.

If you're going to read a book, February was a good month since it is freezing cold outside.

Another school wide event was the Valentine's Party.

Molly had handmade valentines for her classmates on February 14th Valentine's Day;

they were not store brought or conventional in anyway.

She used woodchips from the chopping block
and scrapes from Dad's wood work shop.

Molly used paints (pink, red and white) to fill in the hearts of each of the engraved mini wooden plaques.

As the finishing touch to reduce the possibility of splinters, each valentine she schlacked.

Once again Molly led by shining example: Reduce, Reuse, Recycle and even Repent.

Occasionally OUCH! came out in different words (like dang or sugar) but the same intent.

Her classmates wouldn't know about this part but Father O'Malley would next time Molly went to confession.

Although Mr. McGolly supervised while Molly was engraving the wood chips with wood burning tools, she occasionally did get hurt; Hazard of the trade/ Goes with the territory/ No pain no gain.

All these crazy clichés came about because someone, somewhere or actually lots of people and lots of places experienced some pain while learning to do something new.

I'm pretty sure they all went to confession too!

(Luck of the Irish): Grandma put aleo vera from one of her healing plants on Molly's small burns.

Molly wounds were gone in no time.

Molly's father believed: A pinch of prevention is worth a pound of cure.

Dad made Molly wear long pants, long sleeves, gloves and even eye googles.

Mike and Mark looked at her and remarked "You forgot your helmet".

In which she replied with a hot wood burning tool in hand "Come over here and say that".

Finally she completed her valentines and handmade valentine mailbox to receive school valentines.

Her mailbox looked like a birdcage;

Oh wait, it was a birdcage.

Molly used an old platter she found in the attic, some wood pieces from the wood shop, grapevines from the grapevines and scrapes of unused chicken wire from the barn;

to construct an odd but beautiful birdcage which she painted pink, red and white and then schlacked the wooden parts; a couple of spots were tied with red yarn.

(Luck of the Irish): Grandma let Molly borrow her two love birds so she didn't have to try to cram a full size chicken in the lovely cage.

The love birds were chirping away: the bird language of love.

Molly had to cover the cage so the birds would be quite, and not make a peep.

Otherwise the principal might come by and throw them out in the street.

Mother McGolly helped Molly bake a cake for the class.

They used the last jar of strawberry preserves which was from the garden last spring.

Two layers of white cake with strawberry preserves in-between then frosted with white icing.

Molly loved the day of Love February 14th!

She thought about giving Handsome Joe a great big kiss with red lipstick on both cheeks;

if she missed she just might hit his lips.

That was a chance she was willing to take.

He won't know what hit him until it was too late!

Handsome Joe was completely taken by surprise;

you could tell by his wide open mouth and eyes.

However Sonny was even more surprised when his valentine arrived.

Molly's Uncle Ivan (from her mother's side of the family) was a horseback riding forest ranger.

He showed up at school in uniform on his horse partner.

When the room mothers showed up and took over the Valentine's party...

freeing Miss Bailey to go to the teacher's lounge for their party.

Upon leaving the lounge and returning to her classroom;

Miss Bailey was shocked to see in the hallway a white horse with a handsome man in uniform standing squarely right before her eyes.

Did someone spike the punch a bunch?!

Miss Bailey's next thought was...Saint Anne you did a great job finding me a man-and the white horse was a nice touch.

A handsome single young man with a job, on a white horse on Valentine's Day is the stuff dreams are made.

Then he spoke "Hee-hee-hee-hee";

I guess the horse felt a little uneasy.

The stud (now I'm talking about the handsome young man) said in his wonderfully deep voice "I'm looking for Ms. Bailey".

"That's me, how may I help you Prince Charming" is what she was thinking but what came out was "Yes"; which was the answer to any question he might ask!!!!!!!!

Ranger Ivan McFrugal stated he was commissioned by Molly McGolly to take Sonny McGolly home from school.

So Sonny was completely surprised with a horseback ride.

Sonny's eyes were triple sized

they were so wide.

Molly walked up to Sonny with a wooden plaque that read:

> Roses are red.
>
> Violets are blue.
>
> You get a Horseback Ride Home from School
>
> Love, Molly

Ranger Ivan, Sonny and the horse rode off down the hallway, out of the school all the way to Sonny's home.

Sonny was singing the tune to 'Happy Trails' as the horse galloped away swishing its tail!

Miss Bailey sat at her desk and sighed and cried;

until Ranger Ivan McFrugal came back to school and gave her a horseback ride.

That evening Sonny sent thank you notes to Molly via homing pigeon and St. Bernard barrel collar.

Completely unnecessary for she could still hear him holler "Molly you are my very best friend"!

She could hear him up the hill and through the wind.

On the McGolly home front, Dad always gave Mother a red rose on Valentine's Day.

This year he painted a big red heart on the water tower with the words:

'I LOVE MAUREEN

MOST BEAUTIFUL WOMAN I EVER SEEN'

This made Molly's Mom smile and laugh.

Then 'Fritz' opened a bottle of champagne.

Oh my, love was in the air.

They (Fritz and Red) danced all the way up the stairs.

The next morning while Mom was still smiling she stated "I love the heart on the water tower but please remove it."

Dad said he used Miriam and Maryann's sidewalk chalk and it would wash away with the first good rain, but his devotion to her would remain.

In February Mom prepared for her annual Catholic Women's Retreat;

Held at a convent, Mom, her sisters and sister-in-laws would meet.

One of Mom's biological sisters (Aunt Carolyn) is a real sister (Nun); her new name is

Sister Mary Valentine (named after the Virgin Mary and St. Valentine).

Sister Mary Valentine lived with the other nuns at the convent.

This year's retreat theme: Catholic Women are Spiritual, Charitable and Beautiful

The beginning of the retreat was a reflection on Mary (Virgin, Mother and Queen),

our model to be spiritual, charitable and beautiful Catholic women;

presented by Sister Mary Valentine.

During the weekend retreat there would be reviews of biblical scripture concerning marriage (God, one man and one woman); marriage not to be redefined and natural conception including natural family planning (the only approved method of contraception because it is natural and not artificial). Natural Family Planning was highlighted on this retreat for women.

Each year during the women's retreat one of the 10 Commandments was highlighted; this year it was the SIXTH COMMANDMENT: You shall not commit adultery

Mortal sins against the 6th Commandment: Adultery, Fornication (intercourse prior to marriage), Masturbation or other impure acts with self, Homosexual acts, Using a contraceptive, Dressing or acting in a manner intended to cause arousal in another (spouses excepted), Kissing or touching another passionately for the purpose of arousal (spouses excepted), Allowing another to kiss or touch you in a sexual manner (spouses excepted), Intentionally causing a sexual climax outside of intercourse, Onanism, i.e. intentional withdrawal and non-vaginal ejaculation, Flagrant immodesty in dress, Bestiality (sexual acts with animals), Oral sex (permitted as foreplay in marriage), Anal sex or other degrading sex practices, Prostitution, Rape, In-vitro fertilization or artificial insemination, Surrogate motherhood, Selective reduction of babies in the womb, Types of fertility testing that involve immoral acts, Involvement in or support of human cloning, Willful divorce or desertion, Incest, Polygamy or polyandry (many wives/husbands), Cohabitation prior to marriage,

Destroying the innocence of another by seducing or introducing them to immorality, Lust in the heart ("if I could I would"), "Swinging" or wife swapping, Transvestism or cross-dressing. Speakers reviewed scriptural passages and read from the Catechism of the Catholic Church on the subjects of marriage, contraception (Part 2370); The fecundity of marriage #2366-2372 The Catechism of the Catholic Church; Part 2366-2372 GET YOURSELF A COPY OF THE CATECHISM OF THE CATHOLIC CHURCH AND READ THESE PARTS!

••

The next part of the program covered Natural Family Planning

The only approved method of contraception is natural family planning because it is natural.

The speaker brought up Mother Teresa of Calcutta who lived and worked with the poorest of the poor in India. Mother Teresa and her sisters taught natural family planning to around 30 thousand people (10 thousand Christians, 10 thousand Hindus and 10 thousand Muslims). Mother Teresa cared for everyone. These people did not (most likely) have access to modern birth control (pills/devices etc...) and were highly motivated because they had good reasons to use natural family planning (poverty, not enough food/shelter/basic necessities). The results were highly effective. Molly's Mom couldn't remember the stats. The team leader actually taught them how to use 3 methods of natural family planning, the basics.

How to Use Natural Family Planning: (3 Ways to Use Natural Family Planning) Natural Family Planning, also known as the rhythm method, is a method of birth control which is acceptable to all religions and cultural backgrounds. On top of this you can learn to use it and not spend more than the cost of a calendar, a thermometer, or your own fingers.

Method 1 of 3: The Calendar Method
*Note: the teacher stated that she started keeping a purse/pocket calendar at a very young age (when she started having periods as a young girl); she would draw a little flower on the dates she started her period and the last day of her period. She suggested that everyone in the class start keeping track of their menstrual periods in this way even if not interested at all in N.F.P. at this time. She also encouraged them to get their daughters to start keeping track of the dates of their menstrual periods. Their Gyn/Ob doctors usually want this information anyway.
*Note: the teacher also stated that if the woman is trying to conceive a child; change step #6 to: Have sex during your fertile phase.

Method 2 of 3: The Temperature Method
Method 3 of 3: The Mucus Method

The team leader reviewed each of the methods and the warnings.

- Be patient. These methods can take a long time to use, however will be worth it, if your religion restricts your use of contraceptives.

The teacher reminded them that the Catholic religion most definitely restricts your use of contraceptives. She stated the Natural Family Planning methods are the only methods of contraception allowed because it is natural and should be used in holy matrimony marriages and only for a good reason. A good reason being if the married couple have financial difficulties (unable to provide food, shelter, necessities of life) or if the woman has advanced in years and now has medical problems making it difficult to carry a child to term. Of course if the woman does conceive a child, she is expected to have and love the child. A selfish reason to use N.F.P. would be to decide you only want 2 children so you can live in a nicer house with 2 nice cars and go on nice vacations and put both children through college. Review your marriage vow which is the matter in the sacrament of Holy Matrimony in the Catholic Church. Also remember the vows were not optional (no picking and choosing) that there are 3 in your marriage (God, one man and one woman). Someday you will stand before God and have to answer for your choices. We of free will must choose to do God's will over our own will and this will include whether we chose to use contraception not in line with the teachings of the Catholic Church. The teacher stated there are many reasons to choose N.F.P. in addition to the moral teachings of the Catholic Church such as: the birth control pill/patch etc... is listed as a carcinogen by the World Health Organization, along with radon and asbestos. You are literally putting a poison into your body every day; just think of what long term use could do to a body. Also the birth control pill/patch can cause an abortion; the sperm and egg can still come together (the pill/patch/injection is not full proof) and if the uterus has been 'thinned out' the conceived child has no place to be implanted and is sloughed out of their mother's womb. This is an abortion because life begins at conception. Therefore if the woman is sexually active, she may be aborting a child/children every month and be unaware. If you just read or heard this information; what are you going to do with it? You can't ignore this shocking truth anymore. Ask your Ob/Gyn physicians, the medical/drug companies why they did not make this information more known to the general public who are relying on their professional opinions/judgments/leadership. The teacher asked at the beginning of her talk for everyone just to listen with an open mind and that there would be no debate. She also stated that at the back of the room there was a table with the information and resources she used for the Natural Family Planning session. The session also included a plea to Ob/Gyn physicians to help women who have fertility issues by using natural methods or methods (sometimes surgery) that are approved by the Catholic Church to cure the underlying problems of fertility. In-vitro fertilization, artificial insemination, "selective reduction" of babies in the womb, what to do with frozen fertilized eggs (conception has occurred), surrogate motherhood, cloning are mortal sins. There are other options available (in line with the teaching of the Catholic Church) and she covered a few then referred to more information available on the table in back of room including a list of physicians to prescribe to God's laws in these matters. Other benefits of N.F.P. include bonding of the married couple and the woman feeling good about her fertility (you have one partner and only a certain amount of time to produce fruit of the womb); she feels loved, honored and cherished if she and her husband together are putting God first in their holy matrimony marriage (whether they are blessed with biological children or not). She also discussed ways to open this conversion up to their husbands in a charitable way. This concept of natural family planning may be over whelming once you start to objectively think about it! Look at how our society is functioning and then look further. Since the introduction of the birth control pill (and other ways of contraception other than N.F.P.); the correlation of the breakup of families, promiscuity, single parent births, sexually transmitted diseases, the young adults don't believe in marriage as a lifelong commitment (even though most of them desire it), depression, suicide, the list goes on...goes hand in hand with the introduction of the birth control pill and other forms of artificial contraception. The teacher showed the graphs to further drum into their heads the truth about artificial contraception. She concluded with a choice to be made: whether to think of natural family planning in a life affirming positive way, which is as God intended or look at the negative effects brought on by those of us doing our will over God's. God's Will always leads to life; doing our will over God's always leads to death (like divorce, break up of families, adultery, sexually transmitted diseases, depression, suicide, abortion, euthanasia, death of conceived human lives (life begins at conception), living together before marriage (with fringe benefits); either ends in split up or greatly increases chance of divorce if they do get married, crime (many people in prison do not have a good father figure in their lives). Choosing God's Way, even if difficult, even if difficult for a long period of time, even if it involves suffering is always best in the end. If you are the first person in your family to change the tide, then so be it. Pray and arm yourself with good resources and like minded people. The back table also had a sign-up sheet for those interested in joining a group at their Catholic Church on Natural Family Planning (any age) or would like more information to give to others on this subject (husbands/friends and family/physicians). The sign- up sheets were on the table with the coffee machine (and all kinds of additives like sugar, special assortment of creamers, cinnamon); this woman must be in marketing as her real job. She also had home family photos, a real table cloth and lovely flowers on this table. She also discussed the many benefits of using Natural Family Planning.

> *Author Note: Verify Natural Family Planning methods for accuracy before using these method s for birth control (whether to increase chances to conceive a child or to hold off having children for a good reason in a Holy matrimony marriage).

She was followed by another speaker who was upbeat and positive. This woman stated she was a cafeteria Catholic on one subject, contraception. One day while reading the Bible she read a scripture passage which stated that God's ways are not burdensome. She immediately thought of one area that she felt was very burdensome, the Catholic view on contraception and birth control. She began to look into this area and her research lead her to believe that the Catholic Church was right. So she talked to husband and they started using Natural Family Planning (the only contraceptive method approved by the church because it is natural). Changing her life in this one way, opened her life to better relationships with her husband and children and to God Almighty. She found that God's Way is not burdensome, it is better! Now she travels once a month to speak to Catholic women about her discovery.

Also they listened to a CD by Professor Janet E. Smith: CONTRACEPTION; WHY NOT (78 minutes) 3 rd Edition

Cracking The Contraceptive Myths
My Catholic Faith Press; www.MyCatholicFaith.org; PO Box 24886; Federal Way, WA 98093
1-866-267-4113

It listed what the birth control pill/devices etc... were expected to achieve when first introduced to society. Enough time has elapsed to see what the ACTUAL effects have produced. What a DIFFERENCE!!! Wow, have we all been deceived! Sound familiar; the great deceiver will deceive us all. The Catechism of the Catholic Church is right! Contraception (other than Natural Family Planning in a holy union and for a good reason) "is intrinsically evil". This CD systematically reveals what these forms of birth control were expected to do (with a list) and then reveals what has actually happened (the real results). Everyone especially Catholics should listen to this CD. I say especially Catholics because a large number of Catholics are using contraceptives even knowing the Catholic teaching (and the fact it is mortal sin which separates a soul from God). This CD is an eye opener. Once you listen to this CD you will wonder why you've never heard these truths before. How have we as a society been kept in the dark for so long. It is time we returned to our natural state and treat our bodies as temples of the Holy Spirit. Suggest to your Priest/s about starting Natural Family Planning classes for everyone to become informed and supportive to couples using N.F.P. Look how our society and the world has changed since contraceptives have been introduced...promiscuity is rampant. Professor Janet E. Smith is a great speaker and delivers cracking the contraceptive myths in an enlightening and informative way.

Following this segment on Natural Family Planning they had quiet time for reflection. They could find a quiet place inside or stroll outside on the beautiful grounds of the convent.

Once the women returned from their alone time in silence, it was lunch time followed by a fashion show. Lunch was catered by a parishioner who owned a restaurant... and it was mouth watering delicious! Best chicken salad, fresh fruit, hot tomato basil soup, assortment of breads and desserts. After lunch they took their seats for the 'Catholic Women are Spiritual, Charitable and Beautiful Fashion Show'. The lights dimmed and the show began. It started with a classical feel with matching music and the models wearing stylish fashions appropriate for all sorts of occasions. Modestly dressed models glided down the center isle to the stage... it was quiet nice.

Then there was a change in the music...from classical to lively?! The teenage girls from the church took over the stage and also became the new models. The clothing styles went from refined to ridiculous. The new announcer described the crazy git ups with flair:

*   This dress has balloon sleeves and a scoop neckline (the sleeves literally were made of full blown up balloons and the young model had a necklace made of ice cream scoops. These scoops were clanging together as she walked the cat walk).

- ⋆ Ladies the next model is wearing a turtle neck sweater and bell bottom pants (she actually was wearing a turtle neck sweater but in addition had toy turtles around her neck; cow bells dangled the bottom of her pants, with every step the bells were clanging).
- ⋆ Mini skirt with Go-Go Boots (The model wore a red and white poke a dot skirt like Minnie Mouse including a mouse tail swinging back and forth as she glided down the cat walk with rollerblades).
- ⋆ Moo Moo Dress (made of cow hide).
- ⋆ Tee-shirt (Tea kettle hat with tea cups on each shoulder and several light brown stains on her white tea shirt.
- ⋆ Bathing Suit (old fashion diver outfit with brass helmet). The announcer stated "Ladies as Catholic Christian women we need to be fashionable but conservative in our beach wear...and you can't get more conservative than this".
- ⋆ After 5 Wear (cocktail dress with rooster feathers especially around the hip area).
- ⋆ Tribute to World Travelers (Can-Can skirt made of colorful cola cans; a must in France).
- ⋆ Tribute to the Movies-Gone with the Wind (Scarlet O'Hara famous green dress made from curtains at old plantation house; the model wore green velvet dress with curtain rods hanging across her shoulders).
- ⋆ Tribute to Sports-Basketball (hoop skirt, model had a basketball hoop with net around her waist).
- ⋆ Grand Finale: Wedding Gown (with long flowing train...she literally had a toy train from engine to caboose trailing behind her).

A little comic relief goes a long way.

They had a short bathroom break and then began the testimonies. Several women from their Catholic church spoke about their spiritual lives (including early life, their families and spiritual upbringing; life events and trials, growing up and life milestones, health, their families and landing at their current spirituality and challenges. Let's face it... life keeps changing and it will continue until our dying day. We: if were still living and breathing are part of the church militant. That means there is an on going battle for our souls every day. So, remain vigilant/ prepare a solid foundation to better able withstand the trials when they surface. Now would be a good time for some of that comic relief but on with the story. There were 3 speakers. If you have a hankerchief, box of Kleenex or mild sedative this would be the time to take it out.

April, gave the first testimony (brave woman). She was about 30 years old, attractive, in great shape, long dark hair and had a super personality with great sense of humor. She would be a hard act to follow. If fact after college she went to Hollywood and landed a job writing for a popular sit-com. This caused her parents simultaneously to go into shock. She met a man and fell in love. They lived together and shared a wild life, Hollywood style for several years. April became pregnant and they had a beautiful baby girl. That's when the trouble started. She just assumed that after the baby they would both settle down. Unfortunately he did not share this life style change. He continued staying out late (or even days at a time) partying and eventually she moved back home (several states away) to raise their child alone. Her parents were there to help her. However she had to re-invent herself in order to get a job and make a living for her daughter and herself. So she decided to become a police officer; causing her parents simultaneously to almost have cardiac arrests. When her daughter was about 5 years old and only days before she was to give her testimony, her ex came back into her life. She recently was working through issues of trying to forgive the ex for betraying her (not living up to responsibilities causing her to deal with the situation alone). She sent him photos of their child, a necklace (with some significance) and a heart felt written letter of forgiveness. He wrote her back and stated he wanted to meet his daughter and bring his fiancée. She agreed to the meeting but it had not happened before her testimony. She truly wanted to forgive him but wasn't sure what this would mean for her and her daughter. This beautiful young woman with the wonderful personality and great sense of humor seemed venerable at this time. She returned back to the Catholic Church after setting adrift for many years. Working through her difficulties, bad choices, good choices, returning to Mother Church and going to confession on a regular bases. At the same time she had a new adventure starting; a new job opportunity using her talent as a gifted writer. Working nights, weekends and the day to day stress of being a police officer was difficult for a single mother (even though her parents were close to help out). She loved the excitement and people she worked with as a police officer but decided to make a career change. So her story ended in a transitional state. What will happen next?! As a writer her testimony seemed to end appropriately...A CLIFF HANGER!

For Molly's mom (who listened to every word attentively), the underlying theme in this young woman's testimony was: when things got tough and she hit rock bottom and needed help... where did she turn... back to God (Father/Son and Holy Spirit) and Holy Mother Church (The Catholic Church). No matter how far you drift, God will always be there to hold your close. Also her family was there to help her in her time of need (virtues of love and charity).

This would be a good time to open up your Bible and read: The Prodigal Son

The son who was welcomed back warmly on his homecoming in repentance (Luke: 15: 11-32).

May, gave the second testimony. Remember these women are from the local parish and are revealing parts of the entire life; this can be intimidating even for the best of speakers. May was born a cradle Catholic in a large family (many brothers and sisters all from the same parents). She appeared to be in her late 50's; who in her twenties started to pick and choose what part of the faith she wanted to live. After all, everyone else was doing the same things she was doing. In fact compared to most of the others her age, she was pretty good by most standards. Especially since the bar in society was set pretty low. This wayward Catholic became a cafeteria Catholic; justifying everything she did and no one was telling her any different. She knew what the Catholic Church taught on social teachings of morality but rationalized her mortal sins away. In her defense she stated the Catholic Church didn't teach why birth control was wrong or how to use Natural Family Planning. If the Catholic Church is expecting people to reject artificial contraception when it is so popular; they need to teach us why it is "intrinsically evil" and how to use N.F.P.

under proper conditions. We as women will need to offer to help the Priest/s and Bishop/s to teach this truth of our Catholic faith. However, the Priest/s need to take the lead because they are the Fathers. Fathers are the head of the household. Fornication before marriage, birth control pills (before and after marriage) and when she decided to stop taking birth control pills, she signed off on her husband to have a vasectomy. May stated she didn't stop taking birth control pills because of morality; she stopped because as a registered nurse she knew the pills (poison) were harmful to her body. She knew even back then that the birth control pills would eventually take its tow on her life. She had rationalized to herself that birth control was okay because she wasn't killing a life that had been started (conception). She didn't know back then that the sperm and egg could still come together and then be sloughed out of the mother's womb because the birth control pill thins out the uterus giving the child (life begins at conception) no place to implant. Both she and her husband were cradle Catholics who had fallen for the ways of the world. They lived as cafeteria Catholics their whole marriage. They had two beautiful healthy children but sadly did not have a happy marriage. She said she regretted everything she did against the social teaching of the Church and wondered if they had lived according to God's laws from the beginning (or started at any time of their marriage); would they still be together and happy. He left her after 23 years of marriage and 2 beautiful children to pursue other women and interest and seems to have no remorse. May on the other hand, grieved for a very long time over the loss of everything she had worked for, that seemed to disappear in a day and she couldn't do anything to stop it. When they leave you and are served divorce papers, you get one month to sign the papers or reject or they go through whether you want them to or not. She stated that no fault divorce needs to be outlawed...it is someone's fault (most likely both parties). She had a dream that she felt was one of her 'God moments' which helped her during this very sad time in her life. She could see herself from behind; as she stared at an adobe type house completely crumbled to the ground. You would think this was a sad dream but it was a joyful beautiful image. Why? Because above the crumbled abode house was the most beautiful clear deep blue sky that reached far above to the heavens. May, knew from this dream that she would be alright. However she still grieved for a lot longer the death of her marriage and the breakup of her family. She said that there truly is a silver lining to every storm cloud. Now for the good news: God can bring good out of what seems to be the worst thing that can happen to you. The only good thing that comes out of divorce is that you have more time to get closer to God. May also stated she felt Mary (our Heavenly Mother) is the one who brought her back to the TRUTH in the Catholic faith. Mary always leads us to her Son Jesus, she keeps nothing for herself.

May never left the Catholic Church but she saw her conversion to be towards the TRUTH in the Catholic Church. No more picking and choosing. Good bye cafeteria Catholic. There is wisdom in listening to God. If people would take a moment and think about what has led us to this culture of death; they would see it's because we are not living the way God intended us to live. We of free will are living as disobedient children of God. We are doing our will over God's Will and rationalizing our behavior. After doing our will over God's Will; our soul has shriveled up and died and we no longer feel guilty or sorry for our sins. No remorse. We seem to be in a fog thinking only serial killers and evil dictators are the only ones going to Hell (if they do not repent with true sorrow before death). May said she saw herself in a pretty good light even when she was in the state of mortal sin. Looking back she wonders how this came about. Remember mortal sin is the only thing that separates us from God. Mortal sin on one thing can separate us from God forever if we do not repent with true sorrow. Divine mercy is available to all. We have a loving God. May revealed that through her conversion to the TRUTH in the Catholic Church she could see why the teachings of the Church are true. She selected to read from the Catechism of the Catholic Church; Part 2385 on the subject of Divorce

> Divorce is immoral also because it introduces disorder into the family and into society. This disorder brings grave harm to the deserted spouse, to children traumatized by the separation of their parents and often torn between them, and because of its contagious effect makes it truly a plague on society.

May, reflected on going to confession sparsely during her marriage and when she did go she didn't bring up the fact she was taking birth control pills or signed off on her husband having a vasectomy. It is a mortal sin; (Telling a lie or withholding a serious sin in confession). She has since repented for these mortal sins and wished she had never done them. Holding back in the confessional was a BIG MISTAKE! She suggests- tell the Priest/s what you are truly sorry for and then what you know to be against the Catholic Church (like birth control pill etc..., fornication, homosexual acts) but are not sorry for at that time. Then be quiet and listen; don't argue with the Priest. He is trying to save your eternal soul. Think about what he says and start your conversion towards the TRUTH...pray for TRUTH. Just because you have no remorse for a sin doesn't mean you are right...it means that your soul is dead. Mortal sin is the only thing that separates us from God.

Forgiving her ex-husband (or husband; however God sees it) was difficult for May. She saw his departure as an unjust betrayal. She did mention that his version was a bit different. However this was her testimony and she was going to tell the truth as she saw it. They were married in the Catholic Church; it was a sacramental marriage and therefore like super glue. Long story short: He left her and she had to find a way to forgive him... hate and/or unforgiveness can keep you out of heaven. Let's face it hate and/or unforgiveness is the definition of divorce. It is an unresolved conflict. Can we get into heaven if we carry unresolved conflicts... a place of peace, happiness and harmony? We have to learn to love even those who hurt us and hope they will forgive us for our offenses to them.

Now... how to forgive. Prayer, prayer and more prayer. At some point May had to admit part of the break down in their marriage was her fault. All she knew was she would not want to sit down and watch her whole married life unfold on a video screen as it actually happened (like you see on the Catholics Come Home commercials on television). The answer was to ask for forgiveness from God for her part of the marriage breakdown, with true sorrow. She did write a letter to her ex-husband (or husband; however God sees it) asking for forgiveness for her part of the marriage breakdown along with photos of the children/family and a couple of gifts. Before she sent these items to him; she told God she would accept whatever response she got with charity. She continues to pray for her and her ex-husband (or husband however God sees it) to see the TRUTH and seek forgiveness from God. Then for her to go and sin no more.

On Valentine's Day, May spent four and a half hours in her soon to be ex's lawyer's office with her husband and his lawyer and her lawyer and a mediator. They originally had a different date but somehow got rescheduled on the only day everyone could be there...Valentine's Day...the day known for love (how ironic). An agreement was reached so there was no court date. Hind sight, May said she would never sign a no fault divorce... she didn't know better at the time.

A few years later, May decided to change a negative view of the day of love (February 14th) to a positive view. She decided to recite the Fifteen Prayers revealed by Our Lord to Saint Bridget of Sweden with 15 Our Fathers and 15 Hail Mary prayers daily for an entire year.

May read from The PIETA PRAYER BOOKLET

As St. Bridget for a long time wanted to know the number of blows our Lord received during His Passion, He one day appeared to her and said: "I received 5,480 blows on My Body. If you wish to honor them in some way, say 15 Our Fathers and 15 Hail Marys with the following Prayers (which He taught her) for a whole year. When the year is up, you will have honored each one of My Wounds."

Our Lord made the following promises to anyone who recited the 15 St. Bridget Prayers for a whole year:

1). I will deliver 15 of his lineage from Purgatory. 2). Fifteen souls of his lineage will be confirmed and preserved in grace. 3). Fifteen sinners of his lineage will be converted. 4). Whoever recites these Prayers will attain the first degree of perfection. 5). Fifteen days before his death I will give him My Precious Body in order that he may escape eternal starvation; I will give him My Precious Blood to drink lest he thirst eternally. 6). Fifteen days before his death he will feel a deep contrition for all his sins and will have a perfect knowledge of them. 7). I will place before him the sign of My Victorious Cross for his help and defense against the attacks of his enemies. 8). Before his death I shall come with My Dearest Beloved Mother. 9). I shall graciously receive his soul, and will lead it into eternal joys. 10). And having led it there I shall give him a special draught from the fountain of My Deity, something I will not do for those who have not recited My Prayers. 11). Let it be known that whoever may have been living in a state of mortal sin for 30 years, but who will recite devoutly, or have the intention to recite these Prayers, the Lord will forgive him all his sins. 12). I shall protect him from strong temptations. 13). I shall preserve and guard his 5 senses. 14). I shall preserve him from a sudden death. 15). His soul will be delivered from eternal death. 16). He will obtain all he asks for from God and the Blessed Virgin. 17). If he has lived all his life doing his own will and he is to die the next day, his life will be prolonged. 18). Every time one recites these Prayers he gains 100 days indulgence. 19). He is assured of being joined to the supreme Choir of Angels. 20). Whoever teaches these Prayers to another, will have continuous joy and merit which will endure eternally. 21). Where these Prayers are being or will be said in the future God is present with His grace.

May stated she recited these prayers for the 15 souls in her lineage that would be delivered from Purgatory, 15 sinners of her lineage that would be confirmed and preserved in grace and 15 sinners of her lineage that would be converted. She started saying these prayers a couple of months before February to get into the practice of saying them every day (some days she had to play catch up and say 2 or 3 sets). February 14th was the official start and completion date. Now when she thinks of February 14th the day known for love...she thinks of the people in her family/lineage that through the prayers given to St. Bridget by Jesus Himself...have been delivered from Purgatory, confirmed and preserved in grace and converted. Valentine's Day is a day known for love. When that year ended, May hoped to receive some kind of a sign...but it was just an ordinary day. However she now had a positive memory for Valentine's Day to add to previous happy memories of the day known for love. Mission accomplished. However, she met a man who on the last day of his year of saying the St. Bridget prayers devoutly; ended up at the Catholic Church in which Jesus gave St. Bridget these prayers. This man did not plan this event (Divine or coincidence?!).

May talked about other events such as taking care of her elderly mother along with one sister to share the blessings and difficulties; lasting about 7 years before their mother's death. She desires to spend more time with her adult children, who live far away. Still working as a registered nurse and looking forward to retirement and new adventures ahead. May wants to become more active as a volunteer at the Church, especially teaching children the religion. She had a great childhood and also wants to spend more time with her siblings and their families.

Molly's mother remembered one part of the testimony that really stuck with her. May stated she was continuing to live out her vow she gave to God on her wedding day. Even though May's husband left her and 'moved on' as the saying goes; May stated she would live a chaste life style the rest of her life (til death do we part). She was doing this because it is the Catholic teaching and to show her children (and everyone else) that marriage vows are sacred in the Catholic Church. However she said she would not want to be reunited with her ex-husband (or husband-depending on how God sees it); she chooses to live a chaste life style with God at the center. Too many of the young people today don't think that marriage is permanent (even though most of them desire it). By choosing to live a chaste life style with God at the center; is her way of showing that sacramental wedding vows are sacred even if the marriage doesn't turn out the way you envisioned. She never filed for annulment because she wasn't asking God to say the marriage should have never taken place. May encouraged others to file for annulment who were civilly divorced before they considered 'moving on'. How else would you know if you are in the state of mortal sin, if you don't fall within the guidelines of an annulment.

June gave the third testimony; a lively woman in her early 40's, fairly short with athletic build and short curly brown hair. Her most striking feature was her exuberant smile coupled with her bubbly personality. Part of her spiritual life testimony covered a change in her personality that occurred after she got married. On her wedding day she had 14 bridesmaids and could have had more. June was very popular and could talk to anyone no matter what the situation. No one would have ever imagined that after having several children, she would have mental illness causing her extreme difficulties. Over time she learned to deal with this chemical imbalance but it is something she still struggles with today (the day of the testimony). God does work through doctors. Medication and counseling helped her but she found that jogging several times a week also helps her feel better. She found she could use less medication as long as she routinely kept jogging. June felt like her husband was a saint by staying with her. She could handle other people, but the person who lives with you sees more of the real pain and suffering. She was very thankful to have such a loving husband. More details were given during her story on this subject but she was carrying her cross and her spouse was helping her through a difficulty that might be a lifelong ordeal. This mental illness was not present on the day they said "I do". She mentioned that she would not blame him if he left her. They are both cradle, devout Catholics. June decided several years ago to sign up for Eucharistic Adoration and their Catholic Church. Her holy hour was on Wednesday from 2–3 pm every week. Her testimony started to revolve around this life changing event. Although she still had her cross to bear, it was easier on the weeks she attended Eucharistic Adoration. She started noticing a difference if she missed a week. "God already knows what I'm wanting" June bluntly stated. So she begins by thanking God for the many gifts in her life and adoring God. Instead of focusing on what you want or think you need; Eucharistic Adoration is about adoring God and being thankful. It just makes you feel better inside down deep. June stated, many times she will just sit in the silence and be open to listen to God. She always feels more peaceful when she leaves and her week just seems to go better even if hectic and full of trials.

June still prays for a cure for her mental illness. She also had other trials in her life. One of her children had medical problems that lasted for many years involving several surgeries. Also when her mother died she was the sibling in the family that took over the care of her elderly father. June continues to go to Eucharistic Adoration religiously because it lifts her soul up for the week ahead. Her family knows exactly where she is on Wednesday from 2–3 pm and they leave her with Jesus at that time because they see how it helps her.

After each testimony there were activities in groups. One group wrote a poem, another group made a poster and a third group did a skit to re-cap each of the women's testimonies. These activities were a lot of fun and offered a bonding experience.

Free time followed the last activity. Dinner was a surprise because the men's club cooked and served the meal and did the dishes and put away the tables and chairs after the meal and vacuumed the floor. None of the women had to lift a finger, except to feed themselves.

There were a few more events but some things are better kept a secret. I will tell you they all had the chance to go to confession before turning in for the night. Air mattresses were available and already blown up for each of them. Each one had their overnight bag, and a chair by their air mattress.

That night while Molly's mother laid there in the semi dark with her eyes wide open. She thought of how blessed she was to have such a good man for her husband like June in her testimony. Then Maureen thought about her sister-in-law Clare who was on the next mattress over. Clare has one child and Sonny was born with a severe disability, spina-bifida. He has been in the hospital several times especially when he was younger and kept having problems with his ventricular shunt. Sonny was doing well presently and no surgeries for the last few years. However he is confined to a wheelchair most of the time. Clare also lost her husband suddenly when a tree fell on him, he was a lumberjack. Although there was much grief and heartache in the beginning (when these events first happened); both Sonny and his mother Clare today are very happy. In fact Clare is the happiest, calmest person Maureen has ever met. Maureen asked Clare why nothing seems to bother or upset her. Clare's response "Because the worse things that can happen have already happened, so nothing frightens me anymore. I'll just deal with it when it happens and adapt; God will help me. Right now I'm living in the present moment and enjoying life".

Clare also said that after her husband Clement died, she became a spiritual daughter of St. Padre Pio. She wanted help for herself and her young son. One of the quotes from Padre Pio tells how he looked after and loved his spiritual family: "Once I take a soul on, I also take on their entire family as my spiritual children." Clare stated there was no registry to become a spiritual child; you ask him and somehow in time you'll just know. Of course his spiritual children do need to learn about his life and how he can intercede for us to God and learn Padre Pio's prayers. Padre Pio is the only Priest in Catholic history to bear the stigmata (the five wounds of Jesus Christ crucified). Padre Pio bore these wounds for 50 years. He was also blessed by God with the gifts of discernment of spirits, prophecy, healing, bilocation and more. He is a powerful intercessor for us before Almighty God.

Padre Pio Counsels on Prayer:

> "Pray with perseverance, trust, and a serene and calm mind."
> "Pray, hope and don't worry. Worry is useless. God is merciful and will hear your prayer."
> "Prayer is the best weapon we have; it is the key that opens God's Heart."
> Maureen wanted to know what kind of signs Clare received from Saint Padre Pio.

Clare answered "Well I can tell you because I believe these are true signs but you might think I'm crazy."

Maureen "I think people of faith all get their 'God moments' and they are different for all of us. If I were to tell you my 'God moments' you would think I'm a little crazy too."

So Clare relaxed on her mattress and quietly revealed the signs from Saint Padre Pio. I think I saw a young Padre Pio when I was at work on two occasions. At the time he appeared to look like a normal person. I didn't know it was Padre Pio until I was watching a 4-disc DVD on Padre Pio

> Padre Pio (The Priest who bore the wounds of Christ) by Fr. Andrew Apostoli, CFR.
> E.W.T.N. Global Catholic Network

Clare began "Before I saw these DVD's I recognized Padre Pio only as an older man. While I was viewing the DVD's they showed him as a young man and I was so surprised. He has a very special look. His ears are close to his head and his mouth is very unique. I saw Padre Pio, he was very close to me, only a few feet away. I smiled at him and he just looked at me; he never spoke. Once I realized who he was (after viewing the videos) I have not seen him since. This happened to me before with Saint Bridget of Sweden". Clare states she recited the prayers given to Saint Bridget by Jesus to honor his wounds, 45 prayers a day (15 prayers given to St. Bridget by Jesus and 15 Our Fathers and 15 Hail Marys) for a full year. During that year she saw St. Bridget on two occasions at her work; she looked like a regular person except she was dressed a little odd. She wore a white sweater that looked like seashells with little white pearls tucked into each of the shells. Both times she appeared with upper management. Clare usually tried to stay away from management and not talk to them. Then one day Clare was looking for a certain book about the lives of the saints. When she found the book and turned it to the section on Saint Bridget of Sweden, Clare stopped in her tracks with eyes opened wide and a little shaken. The picture looked like a woman who came to the desk area twice; both times with upper management. The woman never spoke. Once again, when Clare discovered it was St. Bridget of Sweden; she never saw this woman again. St. Bridget has a very distinctive look also. Clare remarked "Now that I know who they are (St. Bridget and St. Padre Pio) if I see them again; I'm going after them. I want to touch them to see if they're real people or if I'm right! Maybe that's why I've never seen them again...or maybe I just have a very vivid imagination. In my defense, in both cases I was completely surprised...not looking for what I discovered.

Many people say a sign from Padre Pio is the scent of sanctity; some describe this scent as flowery like roses or sweet smelling tobacco. Clare states that a few times she has walked into her house and could smell the scent of sweet smelling tobacco. At first she thought that smell came from an old jacket that belonged to her father (who smoked). However this jacket had been washed many times and even when she put her face/nose right up to the jacket and took a deep breath...there was no tobacco or cigarette smell at all. After viewing the DVD's about Padre Pio and learning about this scent of sanctity, it has not happened again. The scent she smelled was of sweet smelling tobacco, not cigarette smoke.

Well, after a little more girl talk they went to sleep. At least they tried. Molly's mom had such a wonderful time at the retreat, she just laid there on the inflatable mattress and smiled. She had a joy from deep down in her heart that made her happy and relaxed. Of course she usually only smiled at night. For Lent this year Maureen was smiling during the daytime too (it was Lent presently)!

Maureen was starting to drift off to sleep...thinking...we can all make changes in our lives by taking that first step...in the right direction...and then persevering. That's right...(yawn)...turn that ship around (as she rolls over to her back)...and get it back on course. Then (while stretching her arms) hold on tight...while you ride out the storm. After weathering the storm...then comes... the peace...(she fell asleep).

Morning came early the second day of the retreat. Maureen stated "Morning came early today". Clare replied "That's like saying 'I was born at an early age'". They both agreed that they needed coffee (even though they were both tea drinkers), so they followed the crowd to the breakfast area. Today the nuns at the convent prepared a pancake breakfast with bacon, sausage and eggs, fresh fruit and yogurt, juices, hot tea and the best smelling coffee.

After being pampered and fed they had a brief rest time to gather belonging and chat or take a stroll on the beautiful grounds before going to Holy Mass at 10am.

Scripture Reading: JOHN 6:52-59

The Jews then disputed among themselves, saying, "How can this man give us his flesh to eat?" So Jesus said to them. "Truly, truly, I say to you, unless you eat the flesh of the Son of man and drink his blood, you have no life in you; He who eats my flesh and drinks my blood has eternal life, and I will raise him up at the last day. For my flesh is food indeed, and my blood is drink indeed. He who eats my flesh and drinks my blood abides in me, and I in him. As the living Father sent me, and I live because of the Father, so he who eats me will live because of me. This is the bread which came down from heaven, not such as the fathers ate and died; he who eats this bread will live for ever." This he said in the synagogue, as he taught at Capernaum.

★★★★★★★★★★★★★★★★★★★★★★★★★★

After Holy Mass they returned to the retreat area for the closing ceremony. All the volunteers were thanked for their charity. On the right side of the stage was a large framed picture of Our Lady of Guadalupe. On the left side of the stage was a large stained glass window; not bound by walls as of yet; of the Virgin Mary with Child (you could see the unborn Child in her womb).

The stained glass image depicted the Virgin Mary with Child. You could see the unborn Jesus in Mary's womb with rosary beads wrapped around the Christ Child as the umbilical cord. This is a newer version of Mary with Child.

*Author Note: I was watching a television program and heard the story of how this image came about from the woman who was inspired to have it commissioned. She first asked one of her children (son) to sketch a picture of Mary with visible Baby in the womb. He said he could sketch Mary, but he didn't know how to sketch an unborn child in the womb. Later the woman while looking through a book, came across sketches of Leonardo da Vinci (I think it was Leonardo da Vinci) and there was a sketch of an unborn child in the womb. Some time passed and she found an artist to paint the picture...but there was more to come. A friend was unable to fulfill her Eucharistic Adoration hour one week and asked this woman to fill in for her. So she did. It was a different hour than her usual holy hour. While she was praying the bells started to ring, at the very moment she thought of the umbilical cord as Rosary Beads (Divine or coincidence?).

The official story to the stained glass image was read to the women as it was unveiled. This image would soon find its home in the new Youth and Evangelization Center at their Catholic Church. The image of an unborn child in the womb is beautiful. The unveiling of the stained glass picture was followed by the story of Our Lady of Guadalupe and Saint Juan Diego. It started with Juan Diego's story being a convert to the Catholic faith.

Our Lady of Guadalupe-Guadalupe, Mexico (1531) Patroness of the Americas
Feast Day in the USA-December 12th

★★★★★★★★★★★★★★★★★★★★★★★★★★★★★★

Author Note: This painting on Juan Diego's tilma with Our Lady of Guadalupe is not made by human hands. The Virgin Mary in this picture is with Child. I've heard or read somewhere (perhaps a dream) that the purple ribbon/sash that is above Mary's waist was a sign of pregnancy during that time and place. Interestingly the tattered robe they put on Jesus during His passion during the crowning the thorns was purple (the color of majesty/royalty and also the color for martyrs). So, Jesus was draped with the color purple early in life and at the end of His physical life here on earth. I also heard somewhere that the stars on her mantle depict the stars in the sky at the time the picture on the tilma was revealed. In addition, the stars are positioned from above looking down towards the earth. Once again, the painting on Juan Diego's tilma with Our Lady of Guadalupe is not made by human hands. I love that Mary is standing on the moon (the original color was silver, now black). Jesus is the Sun (the Light) and Mary is the moon (she reflects the light of her Son, Jesus). There were 14 people (including all the witnesses present when the tilma was first revealed PLUS a small family group of mother, father, and a group of children; in the center of the Virgin's eyes; you would have to be amazed because this technology was not available back then. Once again, this image of Our Lady of Guadalupe is not of human hands. And was this small family (group of mother, father, and a group of children) actually present during the original unveiling; then what does this mean? Maybe it means we need to work harder and with love to keep our families together (as God intended). Mary is with Child in this picture (gift from Heaven) and the small family in the center of her eyes means something very special to our Mother in Heaven. I've always been drawn to this image of Mary because of all the beautiful colors; but when you realize it is the only image of our blessed Mother that was not made by human hands then it becomes even more special. We need to realize that every human life deserves dignity and that life begins at conception. The joyful mysteries of the rosary highlight the beginning of life (the Annunciation; conception), (the Visitation; growing in the womb with a purpose for Jesus and John the Baptist), (the Nativity; the Birth), (the Presentation; presenting the Child to God), (the Finding of Jesus in the Temple; Child growing up). Natural Conception to Natural Death.

★★★★★★★★★★★★★★★★★★★★★★★★★★★★★★★★★★★★★★★

The Event Leader read the following prayer:

Our Lady of Guadalupe,
Mother of Life,

Cast your maternal gaze in your children, born and unborn.
We are in such need of your protection. The enemies of Life
are strong, but you are infinitely stronger, since God chose you
to "crush the head of the serpent," the devil. As we strive to
overcome evil we remember your words of comfort to St. Juan Diego,
"Am I not here, who am your mother?!"
Therefore, we approach you with great confidence.

Our Lady of Guadalupe,
Mother of Life, Pray for Us!

Following this prayer a family (father, mother and several children) walked on stage and sang a beautiful song 'HERE I AM LORD'. The words and voices encouraged everyone to take what they learned at the retreat and evangelize to their families, friends, coworkers, neighbors and even strangers with new actions, and words.

The finale concluded with gifts for everyone to take home as a remembrance of the CATHOLIC WOMEN ARE SPIRITUAL, CHARITABLE AND BEAUTIFUL RETREAT: 7 Day Plain White Wax Candle in Glass Container with a picture of 'Our Lady of Guadalupe' along with a beautiful fresh rose and a copy of Professor Janet E. Smith's CD (CONTRACEPTION: WHY NOT) to listen to on their way home. Father O'Malley gave them a blessing and also blessed all the candles.

Maureen (Molly's mother) and Clare felt like they were floating on clouds when they strolled out to the parking lot to go home. Maybe they were just plain exhausted with blissful joy.

Molly and Sonny had an interesting time during their catechism class the same week as their mothers retreat. After the scripture readings (the same readings for Holy Mass that week) and reflections; the young catechism teacher read off the corporal and spiritual works of mercy. She wanted each one of them in her class to tell about one of the works of mercy they have done before and one they want to try and why!

The CORPORAL WORKS OF MERCY: Feed the hungry, Give drink to the thirsty, Clothe the naked, Shelter the homeless, Visit the sick, Visit the imprisoned, Bury the dead

The SPIRITUAL WORKS OF MERCY: Admonish the sinner, Instruct the ignorant, Counsel the doubtful, Comfort the sorrowful, Bear wrongs patiently, Forgive offenses, Pray for the living and the dead

The teacher was young (college age) and the class loved having a young nice teacher.

Sonny spoke up first. He runs the Clothes Closet at school which falls in the 'clothe the naked' category. The work of mercy he wanted to try was to 'visit the imprisoned'. Sonny wanted to visit his father's best friend who was in prison. He felt he was old enough and thought his father (who was deceased) would want him to visit his friend.

Cynthia and Loreen are two friends in the class and they wanted to try 'feed the hungry'. Their plan was to join the St. Vincent de Paul Society at the church.

Anna's mother recently joined the Home Makers an organization at the church that gathers used/new items like dishes, pots and pans, furniture, bed linens (in good condition) to help people in need of these items. Anna's mother has physical disabilities; her duty/responsibility was to write thank you letters to all the people/companies that donate items. Anna would help out in any way she could.

Molly stated she did most of the corporal works of mercy almost every day with so many younger brothers and sisters. She stated that with every diaper change she 'clothed the naked' she even visited the imprisoned when her siblings were in time out or barn duty. Molly asked if feed the hungry, give drink to the thirsty, clothe the naked, counts if it refers to her triplet baby brothers. The teacher said "yes, at your age; especially if you do it with a joyful heart without being told to help. I'm sure your parents appreciate your help at home. However as you get older, these things in your own family are expected. Then you might consider branching out to help the needy in the community". Molly chose as her work of mercy to try 'visit the sick'. Her plan was to ask her aunt, Sister Mary Valentine if she could go with her to visit the sick. Molly didn't think her mother could leave the younger kids too often.

Several of the children chose 'Pray for the living and the dead'.

Cory, the class clown, stunned the class when he chose a corporal work of mercy 'Bury the dead'. Everyone laughed, except the teacher. The young teacher replied "Cory, we have parishioners at our church who own a funeral home. Their names are on the back of the church weekly bulletin in the advertisements. Make a phone call and see if they will let you dig a gravesite for someone; I'm sure they will let you help". Now it was Cory's turn to look astonished.

The teacher gave the class two weeks to work on their new corporal or spiritual work of mercy. We will share our experiences with the class at that point.

Cory asked the teacher what new work of mercy she was going to try. This was unexpected and the teacher stopped dead in her tracks and turned towards Cory. For a moment, Cory thought he was going to have to dig her grave. The teacher's face lost all color and she looked somber. She started to explain "I have a friend that I am very worried about. I'm afraid she'll make a very bad decision. So my work of mercy is 'counsel the doubtful' and/ or 'instruct the ignorant'. The teacher just kept talking. Apparently this was something very much on her mind. She continued "When counseling adults I heard a Priest on television say to keep 3 things in mind. 1). Do it individually (not with others around), 2). Do it with charity, in a loving way, not mean spirited, 3). Not every time you see them. Otherwise they will turn around and run when they see you coming. The Priest said about every 3-4 months you could counsel them. The young teacher just kept talking. Admonishing sinners is another area of works of mercy to be handled with care. Let me give you an example to help you understand. What if your parents told you to clean your room; and you usually just hid things in your closet and under your bed and straightened your room. Then one day your older brother or sister said this time you need to really clean your room. They said to take everything out of the closet and from under the bed and really clean your room. You probably wouldn't like that very much. Why? Because #1). They are telling you, you've done something wrong #2). Now you have to change. #3). And it is going to take work. Were they wrong to point out the mistake? Did you need to really clean your room the right way? After the work was done and your room cleaned the proper way, how would you feel? Would you forgive the person who steered you in the right direction eventually? The point is, most people don't like it when they're told they are doing something wrong. But if you love them the words need to be stated, otherwise if they continue an immoral lifestyle or make a bad choice they are in danger. They could end up in Hell unless they are repentant with true sorrow and change their ways. Going along with what everyone else is doing is not a reason to go against God's laws. As Catholics it is our job to always stand up for the truth (God's TRUTH), even if it is unpopular. The person you are worried about most likely won't like being admonished. But if you love them wouldn't it be better if they get mad at you and someday start making their conversion back to God's Will. Wouldn't that be better than saying nothing or agreeing with their bad choice/s and your friend/family member dying in the state of mortal sin and going to Hell. We of course would never know if they repented before they died and God alone judges. This is where 'Praying for the living and dead' helps our brothers and sisters. I'm going to counsel my friend and offer my help as much as I can. I'm also going to pray and fast for her. Sometimes I think the world has forgotten prayers and fasting can suspend natural laws and ward off wars. I love my friend and her eternal soul is important to me. I'm willing to suffer the consequence of her getting mad at me even though I plan to be charitable".

The class started and ended with reciting part of the Divine Mercy Chaplet (given to St. Faustina by Jesus Christ). Father O'Malley at this Catholic Church required every meeting in the church to start and end with part of the Divine Mercy Chaplet. Father O'Malley is a good Sheppard.

February was a short month only 29 days.
Now for the month in review:

1). Recycle, Reuse
   ★ Handmade wooden Valentines for the classmates
   ★ Book Drive (School Bucks for Used Books)
2). Reduce
   ★ Sonny got a horseback ride home (saved gas).
3). Repent
   ★ Molly, Mr. & Mrs. McGolly, Sonny, Sonny's Mom (Clare) and Miss Kimberly Bailey went to confession (and most of the ladies at the retreat).

February's Month in Review seems a little short
until you add in the Love List Report!

Love List Report

1). Budding New Romance: Miss Kimberly Bailey (teacher) and Uncle Ivan
2). Strong, Steady Old Flame Romance: Molly's parents their love still thrivin!
3). First Kiss for Molly:

> In front of her whole class she did smack Handsome Joe right on the lips.
> She used red lipstick to make sure he didn't forget!
> Maybe this kiss didn't count, because he was not a willing participate.
> (Luck of the Irish): Handsome Joe did smile when that valentine was sent!
> (Divine or coincidence).
>
> > Violets are Blue
> > Roses are Red
> > Anything can happen

When the teacher is distracted!

★★★★★★★★★★

Violets are Blue

Molly's hair is Red

Anything can happen when the teacher instead of book learn'in

has LOVE in her head!

★★★★★★★★★★★★★

Happy Valentine's Day! HAPPY VALENTINE'S DAY! Happy Valentine's Day! HAPPY VALENTINE'S DAY

■■

The Month of MARCH, blows in like a lion and goes out like a lamb.

March is a very green month and a month for the Irish.

Molly started off by giving hot baked potatoes from the school garden as a special lunch dish.

These potatoes were fortified with the compost fertilizer, then dug up, washed and individually wrapped in foil.

Molly arrived to school early and with Uncle Ivan's assistance (and big man muscles) dug a dirt pit.

She put as many potatoes in 2 large dutch ovens that would fit.

In the dirt hole she put a couple of bricks, lit a wooden log on fire inside the pit.

Once good and hot, they placed the cast iron dutch ovens with lids in dirt hole oven;

and by 'they' she meant Uncle Ivan.

Those cast iron dutch ovens are heavy even without anything inside of them.

Next step, cover the pit with dampened berlap material (it should be wet).

More bricks needed to keep material from falling into dirt pit.

She threw a few shovels full of dirt on top of the earth oven.

These bricks surrounding the hot pit also served as a barrier warning to others;

along with a posted sign (Go around this hot pit in the ground).

Uncle Ivan was to stand guard,

and all safety precautions were upheld.

After all, this hot pit was on the children's playground.

A couple of hours later the baked potatoes were uncovered.

Molly knew it might be a lot easier to cook in a traditional kitchen oven

but she wanted her class to know it was possible to cook food in a dirt pit (no electricity needed).

The baked potatoes were served with all the fixins;

whatever they wanted to mix in.

Fresh homemade butter and sour cream compliments of Muffy and Daisy the dairy cows, onions, bacon bits, chives and/or cheese.

They could add to their personal baked potato whatever they pleased!

She gave the two biggest potatoes to the teacher and Uncle Ivan.

Everyone else got mid-sized potatoes except she saved the smallest one for Waterboy William.

Molly didn't want to give Waterboy William any reason to waste water by stating "My mouth is hot from eating that hot potato".

So Molly tampered with the hall water fountain, which caused the water to flow slow.

She did provide beverages to start the month of March off right.

After drinking her green drink, their teeth were no longer white.

Green tea with green mint strigs and a few green shamrocks.

Everyone liked the green drink until they began to talk.

Molly quickly borrowed Uncle Ivan's cell phone and had every one smile for the photo.

Everyone in her class had green things in their teeth, but they did not know!

(Luck of the Irish) Molly was finally getting all of her classmates to turn green;

starting with their smiles...now let's see what the rest of March will bring!

Maybe this didn't count since they were not willing participates.

Oh well, they were all happy and smiling and their breaths smelled like mints.

A week later at religion class, it was time the share their new corporal and spiritual works of mercy experiences with each other.

(Sonny's tale): Sonny's mother was extremely reluctant to let Sonny go to the prison, but he insisted. So Sonny and his mother began their trips. Sonny and his father's best friend got along very well from the very beginning. Sonny's Mom just wanted the visits over as quickly as possible. After the second visit, Sonny contacted Jay Walker's family to encourage them to start visiting him more often and to start making plans for Jay's release in six months. Where will Jay live? Who can help him get a job with a prison record?! People in Jay's family and Sonny's family pitched in to help prepare for his homecoming and more visits to cheer him up and give him renewed hope.

(Cory's tale): Cory, got to help dig a lady's gravesite the day before she was to be buried. He was given a shovel and dug for an hour and a half before the big heavy machinery moved in and completed digging down deep into the earth. The next day Cory had his mother drive by the gravesite to see the people who came to the funeral. He was sad and surprised to see only two people at the gravesite. Cory jumped out of the car and went up to the two people (a man and a woman) and asked why more people weren't there. He asked if the lady was so old that most of her friends and family were already dead. The man and woman stated "No, she wasn't that old". The reason they suspected people didn't show up for her funeral was because she told a lot of them that they were in danger of going to Hell if they didn't change their ways. The two people were the woman's daughter and son and apparently they weren't too happy with her when she died either. Cory's eyes were wide open and he began to speak in the deceased lady's defense "Was she cruel to them when she was admonishing them or did she counsel them with charity? The daughter said "She wasn't cruel, but she was direct." Cory asked "Well were they in the state of mortal sin?" The man and the woman didn't say anything. Cory continued "If she was telling them the truth with charity, that wasn't wrong just because they didn't like hearing it. Catholics are always to stand up for the truth. If she didn't say anything and no one else ever told them; they could all end up in Hell forever". Just then it started sprinkling and a beautiful rainbow covered the sky. The man shook his head no and said "Telling people they are on a path to Hell if they don't change their ways, wasn't any of her business" just then there was a crack of thunder which rumbled for a little while. Cory asked the deceased woman's children if he could sing her a song. Cory had a beautiful voice and sang 'I am the Bread of Life...and I will raise you up and I will raise you up and I will raise you up on the last day'. The woman had tears running down her face and thanked and hugged Cory with joy. The man seemed to be remembering earlier days with his mother; maybe she wasn't completely crazy...some love started to surface. Cory's mom caught up to him and after the song, she apologized for the inconvenience and shuffled Cory back to the car.

The teacher was in shock and wondered what these people were thinking...What a strange turn of events for this little boy to pop up and defend their mother and then sing a beautiful song for her...completely unexpected. (Divine or coincidence).

The young teacher's next thought was 'I wonder if I'll be excommunicated from the Catholic Church because of this little experiment with the corporal and spiritual works of mercy'. These first two tales were a bit on the wild side.

(Luck of the Teacher who might get excommunicated): The rest of the class had good results and normal stories; at least until it was Molly's turn.

(Molly's tale) On the home front Molly prepared for her corporal work of mercy 'visit the sick'. Mom along with Miriam and Maryann dropped Molly off at the convent with Sister Mary Valentine (Molly's aunt). Mom's old car 'Nellie', the original vehicle in which Molly's parents had when they first got married only held up to five passengers unlike the other family vehicle the mini bus. Occasionally this little car couldn't make it up McGolly hill so all the passengers had to get out and push the little car up the hill.

Molly spent the day with Sister Mary Valentine (alias Aunt Carolyn) visiting the sick. They started at the hospital, then to the homebound and finally to the nursing home with hospice. Sister Mary Valentine brought the blessed Hosts (the True Body of Jesus Christ in a golden container). She would say "This is the Body of Christ" and the recipient would say "Amen" before they consumed the Host. In the Catholic Church (and only in the Catholic Church) once the priest has blessed the bread and wine it changes into the TRUE BODY and BLOOD of Jesus Christ.

★★★★★★★★★★★★★★★★★★★★★★★★★★★★★★★★★★

A person should be in the state of grace before receiving the TRUE BODY and BLOOD of Jesus Christ. If you are in the state of mortal sin you are dominated by satan and to take the Body and Blood of Jesus into your body while in the state of mortal sin forces Jesus to be imprisoned in a body that is dominated by satan until the Host has dissolved. Since it is only mortal sin that separates us from God then it only takes one mortal sin to separate us from God (review the 3 things needed in unison for a sin to mortal/grave/deadly to the soul). Remember God is love and mercy. God has an ocean of mercy to give to each one of us. However we (of free will) must ask for forgiveness with true sorrow to receive forgiveness. If it's been awhile since you've gone to confession (with Catholic Priest) and you are unsure if you're in the state of grace or state of mortal sin; you can fold your arms in front of your heart and receive a blessing (but not the True Body and Blood of Jesus Christ). As soon as possible go to confession and repent for sins you are truly sorry for and discuss what you know (or believe) to be against the Catholic Church's view but you are not sorry. Then listen to the Priest, try not to argue for he is trying to save your soul. Remember you will only be forgiven for what you are truly sorry for even when the Priest states that your sins are absolved. You may have work to do before your soul is in the state of grace. Conversion may take time. You may even fall again but never despair nor become despondent. Get back up and try again...all of Heaven is rooting for you! However YOU must do the hard work to get back into God's good graces. Nobody can push you up the hill (like 'Nellie' Mom's little car); you have to of free will do it yourself. You have to change to God's Will; that is how humble you must become.

I heard a story that went something like this: There once was a holy man who had lots of responsibilities who prayed to God to give him more patience. This man no sooner left the tabernacle where he was praying and was immediately bombarded with several problems. So he returned to the tabernacle later that day and asked God why he wasn't helping him have more patience. God answered "What do you mean. Today I've given you many opportunities to practice patience". In other words: If someone wants the virtue of patience they themselves have to change their own behavior of free will...it's not magic. Conversion is usually a process. You must come up with a plan. The plan in this man's case would be to train himself to behave differently in stressful situations. Even if he loses control at the beginning (his usual behavior) to try to calm himself half way through and in time catch his rage earlier and earlier until he of free will (and perseverance) displays the virtue of patience and becomes more like Jesus and Mary.

So whatever your pet sins are, make a plan to change your behavior. Lust is a mortal sin; your plan may include the following: Stop watching television programs/movies/video games/ computer/music etc...that encourages lust/fornication/adultery/homosexual acts/birth control/ abortion etc...; put your computer in an area where everyone can see what you are watching; ask yourself if Jesus was sitting right next to you, would he be offended at what you are watching or listening to?; remove yourself from situations that may cause you to sin (like drinking alcohol with a certain group of friends; it might be time to find new friends); find good television/movie/ books/art/music/hobbies/ways to exercise or enjoy nature that is also pleasing to God; also there are certain prayers that can help you (ask your Priest what prayers might help). If you have no plan and no firm purpose of amendment; how are you planning on ridding your soul of your mortal sin/s. It's not magic, the change must come from your thoughts and actions. Confession is a great way to make yourself accountable for sins...the veil comes off when you go to confession...you can't keep justifying/rationalizing your sins. If you find yourself saying the same thing over and over again in confession; it's time to come up with a new plan.

Now back to the McGolly Home Front:

Sister Mary Valentine and Molly continued to dispense the blessed Hosts along with prayers at the nursing home. Molly wandered off and found herself at the bedside of a dying man. She asked if she could pray for him and he nodded yes. After arranging a chair next to the suffering man, she held his hand and began praying the Divine Mercy Chaplet for his soul.

★★★★★★★★★★★★★★★★★★★★★★★★★★★★★★★

Sister Mary Valentine and Molly returned the remaining blessed Hosts in golden container to the holy tabernacle at the Catholic Church. Molly lit a candle for the dying man and said another prayer for him. Shortly after Molly completed this prayer her ride home showed up.

Mom, Miriam and Maryann arrived in 'Nellie' the little car. Mother decided to try a shortcut home and they got lost. When trying to turn the car around on a muddy country road, the little car got stuck. Soon all four tires were spinning round and round and they were going nowhere. All four passengers got out of the car, knee deep in mud and tried with all their might to move the car. They were covered head to toe in sticky mud when they finally arrived home that evening. Stunned at their arrival home, Dad asked "Did ya win first place in the mud derby?" Mike and Mark sarcastically reminded them of a certain home rule. Mike started "Those who work hard or play hard...". Mark completed this rule "then they either take a shower or sleep outside in the yard." Molly just looked at her mother and asked "Is this how you get rewarded for doing good deeds (referring to her corporal work of mercy)? Stuck in the mud, walking miles home and then ridiculed in your own home?!" Mom just looked at her with big loving eyes and a semi-smile and answered her question "Yes. Your reward for a life well lived in service to God will be in Heaven. So, offer up all suffering you endure for the poor souls in Purgatory." Now Grandma McFrugal was feeding all three triplets in their highchairs in the kitchen. The babies were covered with pureed green beans and carrots. Grandma said "I've never seen a bigger mess." When suddenly the babies (Shawn, Patrick and Leo) simultaneously stopped eating and babbling and stared in one direction, behind Grandma. Grandma slowly turned around and saw Maureen, Molly, Miriam and Maryann standing there covered from head to toe in mud. When Grandma was able to speak she simply stated "I stand corrected." Grandma continued "I knew this would happen someday! Maureen, you literally took the road strewn with thorns and rocks, apparently there was a mud slide along the way." Molly interjected "Isn't the road strewn with thorns and rocks suppose to lead to paradise?" Mom "That's in the next life too dear; you have to get to the end of the road and when you pass over to the other side at the end of your NATURAL life, then you're in paradise and forget all your worries." Miriam was tired and hungry and made a statement from a child's viewpoint "Mom, maybe there aren't any poor souls left in Purgatory after all the suffering we went through today." Maryann became even more dramatic, putting the back of her right hand to her forehead stating "I've never walked so far covered in mud, wearing my church shoes, my feet are soooo sore, nobody stopped to help us, I guess they didn't want to get mud in their cars, I'm hungry, tired, the cell phone didn't work, feed me!!!" Miriam completed Maryann's miserable moaning "yeah and to make it worse at the end of all that, we had to walk up the hill to get home." Mother McGolly calmly or perhaps due to complete exhaustion with all the energy and compassion she could muster up said "and Jesus too had to carry His heavy cross up the hill". Miriam and Maryann said together "I love Jesus". Grandma fed them, then off to the outdoor shower stalls for a warm shower. Dad turned to Mom and quietly asked her "Do you ever get tired of being so patient and righteous?" Maureen semi smiled and said "Shut up" and walked towards the shower stall. Dad and Grandma chuckled. They were all 4 tired and hungry but managed to sing one song while washings their cares away: 'The Beatitudes Song'.

THE EIGHT BEATITUDES OF JESUS:

"Blessed are the poor in spirit, for theirs is the kingdom of heaven.
Blessed are they who mourn, for they shall be comforted.
Blessed are the meek, for they shall inherit the earth.
Blessed are they who hunger and thirst for righteousness, for they shall be satisfied.
Blessed are the merciful, for they shall obtain mercy.
Blessed are the pure of heart, for they shall see God.
Blessed are the peacemakers, for they shall be called children of God.

★★★★★★★★★★★★★★★★★★★★★★★★★★★★★★★★★

The outdoor shower refreshed their bodies along with dinner and a good night's sleep.
They ate like there was no tomorrow and slept like the dead;
after they removed all the mud from between their toes and the top of their red headed heads.
Dad and a few uncles went to retrieve the little car.
They towed it back home and washed 'Nellie', but Dad decided that little car was beyond repair.
'Nellie' had travelled her last leg and must be retired.
In true McGolly fashion the little car was recycled.
Dad had a plan to incorporate the metal into the new master bedroom in the log cabin addition.
The car would be melted and formed into posts and beams and make the house stronger.
Now the new master bedroom would also be a storm shelter.
If that didn't work, there was always the root cellar.
Molly's young catechism teacher was so pleased with their works of mercy; she gave each one of her students a Divine Mercy Novena and Chaplet leaflet.
Molly was saying her first 9 day Novena (Divine Mercy Novena) for her twin brothers Mark and Mike who would be making their first Holy Communion the 2nd Sunday of March. She started two days ago and would complete the novena next Sunday the very day her brothers would be receiving their First Holy Communion. Mark and Mike would be receiving the true Body and Blood of Jesus Christ for the first time during Holy Mass. The intention of the nine day novena was for her brothers to really understand that it is truly Christ (bread changed into His Body and wine changed into His Blood) after the blessing from the Priest in a process called transubstantiation. When they take Christ's Body and Blood into their body, the two become one/together in communion with each other. The entire Catholic religion centers upon this mystery of the Holy Eucharist. This is why it is so important to be in the state of grace before receiving Holy Communion (each and every time). If you are in the state of mortal sin when receiving Jesus into your body; you are forcing Jesus to be trapped in a body dominated by satan until the Host dissolves.

Molly prayed that her brothers Mark and Mike would never, their whole lives (however long or short) become lukewarm in their faith. Her parents and grandparents were good devout Catholics and Molly prayed that all of her brothers and sisters would continue to follow in their footsteps. She hoped someday they could all be together forever in Heaven.

In Saint Faustina's Diary (Notebook III Part # 1228) Jesus told Saint Faustina:

(Part 1228) Today bring to Me souls who have become lukewarm, and immerse them in the abyss of My mercy. These souls wound My Heart most painfully. My soul suffered the most dreadful loathing in the Garden of Olives because of lukewarm souls. They were the reason I cried out: "Father, take this cup away from Me, if it be Your will." For them, the last hope (65) of salvation is to flee to My mercy.

(Part 1229) Saint Faustina writes:

Most Compassionate Jesus, You are Compassion Itself. I bring lukewarm souls into the abode of Your Most Compassionate Heart. In this fire of Your pure love let these tepid souls, who like corpses, filled You with such deep loathing, be once again set aflame. O Most Compassionate Jesus, exercise the omnipotence of Your mercy and draw them into the very ardor of Your love; and bestow upon them the gift of holy love, for nothing is beyond Your power.

(Part 1588) Notebook V; Today I heard the words: In the Old Covenant I sent prophets wielding thunderbolts to My People. Today I am sending you with My mercy to the people of the whole world. I do not want to punish aching mankind, but I desire to heal it, pressing it to My Merciful Heart. I use punishment when they themselves force Me to do so; My hand is reluctant to take hold of the sword of justice. Before the Day of Justice I am sending the Day of Mercy.

(Part 1605) "You are the secretary of My mercy; I have chosen you for that office in this and the next life"

(Part 1567)... "to make known to souls the great mercy that I have for them, and to exhort them to trust in the bottomless depth of My mercy"

★★★★★★★★★★★★★★★★★★★★★★★★★★★★

In the McGolly home over the fireplace hangs a large framed image of Divine Mercy Jesus with the signature "Jesus I Trust in You". Underneath the picture Mother McGolly placed all the blessed candles from all the sacraments of the family. Starting with the candle from the Holy Matrimony Marriage of Mr. and Mrs. Fitzgerald Paul McGolly and including all the children's Baptismal candles and Molly's first Holy Communion candle. Soon, Mark and Mike's first Holy Communion candles will be placed on the mantle. Next to the wedding candle sits the little crystal candle holder with the blue candle (used as the something blue on the bride) given to Maureen from Mother Mary; on the McGolly's wedding day.

★★★★★★★★★★★★★★★★★★★★★★★★★★★★

March Green Project at School

The school was getting a brand new roof due to leaking too much when it rained. Sonny and Molly started a petition to use the old roof to make a new flat top for the playground. They found information on the internet on turning your old roof into a road and pave the way to a better future. Well, if you can make a road you can make a flat top playground turf.

Molly and Sonny called an emergency meeting to recycle the school roof. Sonny, Molly, Shelley (the girl to loves to paint), Ralph (the Boy Scout) and Molly's brothers Mark and Mike had a mission. They brought every brown paper grocery bag they could find to Molly's house. Mark and Mike cut the sides of the bags off and placed a hole in the bottom of the bags (big enough for someone's head to go through). Shelley, Sonny, Ralph and Molly wrote in bright BOLD words (RECYCLE THE ROOF) on the front of these make shift vests; and on the back (MAKE US A PLAYGROUND TURF). Their plan was to put these eco friendly homemade vests on every kid that would let them; especially as they were going home to their parents. It worked! The P.T.A. called an emergency meeting the very next day. They voted unanimously to use the old school roof along with old jogging shoes and tires to construct a playground turf for their children. A couple of the wealthier parents fronted the money needed to get this project started since the roof was about to be removed in a few days. The P.T.A. voted to use the money from next month's School Wide Garage Sale to pay for the new flat top (made of recycled materials). The P.T.A. parents and teachers also agreed to show up as volunteers to work where ever needed. Once the flat top was completed, the parents and teachers painted a basketball court, four square, and hopscotch lines and installed two posts for a net to be used for volley ball. The project was so successful they had enough materials to make a second flat top. The teachers painted the U.S.A. with all the states including the capitols. School is school. The principal and teachers decided; while the kids are running and jumping; they can still learn something! Hooray! Now even if the ground was muddy the kids could still go outside to play during recess. Recycling the roof for a flat top turf was a great idea. And you know what they say about one good turn!? Yes! One good turn deserves another.

So, Molly feeling very green in a good way, volunteered to clean the windows in her classroom using cleaning solution safe for the environment. She mixed vinegar and water together and the windows shined. Spring cleaning, simple, eco friendly and economical (if she would have added holy water it would also be spiritual). She shared her earth friendly cleaning solution mixture with anyone who was interested. Molly even sprayed it into her own mouth to show you could safely drink it. However, vinegar and water is very b-i-t-t-e-r. Every time Molly sprayed it in her mouth the janitor would offer her a drink of water and a hard butterscotch candy from his shirt pocket.

The very first time Molly sprayed this mixture into her mouth she was instantly mentally transported to her last religion class. Her young catechism teacher taught the class about the last 7 statements of Jesus during His passion and death. Molly remembered that Jesus before His last statement 'Father, into your hands I commit My Spirit.' (Look up Luke 23:46). Jesus drank vinegar and gall. While Jesus was hanging on the cross His second to the last statement He made was "I, thirst". The catechism teacher thought Jesus refused what was being offered to the criminals to anesthetize their pain. He (Jesus) did accept the vinegar and gall. Gall possibly being the blood, sweat and grime from the Roman soldiers arms for they were using vinegar to cleanse the 'gall' from their bodies. The young teacher questioned the class..." What did Jesus say in the Garden of Olives/Gethsemane during His agony in the garden? The answer "Father, if you are willing, take this cup away from me. Nevertheless, let your will be done, not mine." (Luke 22:42, 43). The teacher with great devotion to Jesus thanked Him for suffering and dying for our sins. Then she concluded: "Jesus loved His Father, so much that Jesus did His Father's Will over His own... Jesus suffered and died that our sins might be forgiven". In between the last statements of Jesus Christ "I thirst" and "Father into your hands I commit my spirit"; Jesus drank vinegar and gall. The vinegar could be very bad wine... the cup Jesus wanted taken away from Him. Jesus did suffer and before He died for the salvation of our souls He drank the vinegar and gall. Molly silently thanked Jesus for His sacrifice and then added more water to the vinegar mixture to water it down a little more. She reflected on the passion and death of our Savior while continuing to clean the windows in silence.

★★★★★★★★★★★★★★★★★★★★★

The Fifteen Prayers revealed by Our Lord to Saint Bridget of Sweden (to honor His Wounds)

(Prayer # 7) O Jesus! Inexhaustible Fountain of compassion, Who by a profound gesture of Love, said from the Cross: "I thirst!" suffered from the thirst for the salvation of the human race. I beg of Thee, O my Savior, to inflame in our hearts the desire to tend toward perfection in all our acts; and to extinguish in us the concupiscence of the flesh and the ardor of worldly desires. Amen.

(Prayer # 8) O Jesus! Sweetness of hearts, delight of the spirit, by the bitterness of the vinegar and gall which thou didst taste on the Cross for Love of us, grant us the grace to receive worthily Thy Precious Body and Blood during our life and at the hour of our death, that they may serve as a remedy and consolation for our souls. Amen.

★★★★★★★★★★★★★★★★★★★★★

Every March, Grandma and Grandpa McGolly (Dad's parents) came from the old country of Ireland for a visit. This year was especially significant because Mark and Mike were celebrating their first Holy Communion. Molly's oldest twin brothers had been preparing for this sacrament the whole school year in catechism class. They would be making their first confession in the confessional with a Catholic Priest a few days before the ceremony. After they individually have confessed their sins with a contrite heart (meaning they are truly sorry for their sins) and have received pardon and completed their penance (given to each by the Catholic Priest), then they are reconciled with God and are prepared to receive Holy Communion. In the state of grace they may receive the TRUE BODY and BLOOD of Jesus Christ (The Holy Eucharist) during Holy Mass.

For first Holy Communion all the girls usually wear white dresses with white veils on their heads. The boys wear black suits or nice clothes (the best of what they have or can borrow). It is up to the parents/family/whoever has custody to be sure the children continue to go to confession (with Catholic Priest) at least once a year (during Lent, before Easter) but hopefully much more often (like once a month) until the child becomes a soldier of Christ in the sacrament of Confirmation (usually in their teenage years).

Godparents, stand guard! Godparents may need to step up to the challenge of rearing the child in their religious education and moral teaching if the parents are unable or choose not to perform their duties. Even if separated by distance...strive to enrich your Godchild by sending good Catholic books and inspiring letters, E-mails through out the years. Also Godparents be sure to pray, pray, pray, every day, every day, every day for your Godchild/Godchildren. Also pray, pray, pray for their parents to live Godly lives every day. The family that prays together, stays together.

When the child becomes a soldier of Christ known as the sacrament of Confirmation; they are taking on the responsibility to uphold the Catholic faith even if called to be a white or red martyr. Years ago and even today in some countries, after the Catholic Bishop puts a special oil on your forehead and gives you the sacramental blessing he would 'seal the deal' by slapping you on the cheek. This slap was to signify that someday you may be called upon to die a martyr's death upholding the TRUTH of the Catholic faith. This is what it means to be a soldier of Christ. SO WAKE UP CATHOLICS! Shrinking violets need to blossom into Veronicas (Veronica boldly supported Jesus during His passion by wiping His face with her veil and she was rewarded with Jesus face print on her veil. Veronica stood up against the crowd to help Jesus, she didn't just sit back and watch like a lot of people are doing today). Shrinking violets need to blossom into Veronicas; Cafeteria Catholics (damned Catholics) need to clear their tables and set up the banquet table; Walking zombies need to go to confession with Catholic Priest to resurrect their souls. Jesus was always more concerned for peoples souls over their physical bodies; He never said they were dead unless their soul was dead (in the state of mortal sin). So, go to confession and repent with a contrite heart so your soul can be resurrected. Jesus is waiting for you.

★Author Note: I heard, read or dreamt that Our Heavenly Mother's favorite song is 'The Battle
      Hymn of the Republic'. My eyes have seen the glory of the coming of the Lord
      He has spoken through the prophets and the grapes of wrath restored
      HIS TRUTH KEEPS MARCHING ON
So I ask you "Are you battle ready"?

★★★

Back to the McGolly Home Front;

The aunts, uncles and cousins were gathered at the log cabin for Grandma and Grandpa McGolly to arrive. The lumberjack uncles were at the house almost every day, ever since the logs were delivered for the addition to the house. The major structural formation of the log cabin lodge was in place including the massive logs and roof. Nellie, the little car had been melted and formed into metal posts and beams to strengthen the new master bedroom. Although the shell was completed, much work needed to be done on the inside (like sheetrock on the walls). Dad and the uncles worked very hard to get as much as possible done before their parents arrived from Ireland.

The whole hill seemed to be alive with jubilation. Grandma & Grandpa gave out gifts from the old country to all of their children and grandchildren. Most were Celtic rosaries and crucifixes. In addition, Mark and Mike got bagpipes and their first kilts. Grandpa McGolly stated every devout Catholic house should have a blessed crucifix (with Jesus crucified on it) affixed to the outside of the front and back doors, to show the angels where you live. So, two crucifixes were nailed to the front and back door of the log cabin lodge and two more to Grandma McFrugal's little house attached by a covered walkway to the bigger house. As you can see a few major changes have been made since the original plans were drawn up. Grandpa McGolly wanted to make sure his children were living the fullness of the Catholic faith as devout Catholics and not cafeteria Catholics. He asked each one of his children individually if they were going to Holy Mass every Sunday and Holy Days of obligation. Grandpa also looked at each one of his children in the eyes with love and compassion and asked when they last went to confession with a Catholic Priest. He knew he couldn't make them go to confession but he could bring it to their attention how important it is to him and for their eternal souls. Grandpa McGolly made this a priority every year during Lent at Easter time. Grandpa McFrugal also did this to each of his children when he was alive. Molly overheard Grandpa McGolly tell her father "Always be obedient to God and leave the consequences to Him, even if you're standing alone. We're all sinners and sometimes we fall but our Heavenly Father is always ready to receive and forgive our offenses if we ask with true sorrow. Our Father's (in Heaven) love is everlasting and unchanging. You are the head of your domestic church; lean on Jesus when times get rough. Being a soldier of Christ is not easy but it has eternal rewards." Then Grandpa McGolly dipped his right thumb in the holy water font and gave his fatherly blessing to his son, Fitzgerald Paul McGolly (Molly's dad).

Grandma McGolly had a least one grandchild in her arms almost the whole time singing Irish lullabyes. She had a beautiful voice. Molly got a break from helping with the little kids while the grandparents, aunts and uncles were there. So, Molly spent the extra time swinging through the trees on her zip line seat and fishing with Sonny in his rowboat on the pond.

The Sunday before Saint Patrick's Day
Marcus Fitzgerald McGolly (Mark) and
Michael Paul McGolly (Mike)
Made their first Holy Communion at 9am at the Catholic Church.

Mark and Mike were also allowed to ring the tower bells for the first time (at least the first time with permission). The uncles surprised the boys by putting up a zip line from the tower to the ground...like when their parents were just married. Two years ago when Sonny and Molly made their first Holy Communion; they both got a bird as a gift from the aunts and uncles. Molly's bird flew away but to this day Sonny continues to share his bird with his best friend Molly. Good old Homer the homing pigeon flies back and forth between the two carrying messages and keeping them close to each other.

Following Mark and Mike's first Holy Communion Mass, the whole McGolly and McFrugal clans congregated on McGolly Hill. All the kids changed from their church clothes to play clothes; except Maryann and Miriam because they wanted to wear their new dress shoes (with no mud) just a little longer.

For lunch, most of the heavy cooking was done the day before since Sunday is a day for worship of the Lord and rest/relaxation. Dad and the other men did flip hamburgers on the outdoor grill. Mike and Mark's favorite meal was served (hamburgers, potato salad, coleslaw, potato chips, soda pop and homemade brownies with pecans from John and Joseph's birthday trees).

While the younger kids were being cared for by the women; Grandpa and the other men (including Father O'Malley) took turns zip lining through the trees on Molly's zip line seat. Grandma McGolly just shook her head from side to side and said "Will they ever grow up?" A short while later Grandma McGolly and Grandma McFrugal were both zip lining through the trees and down the hill. Sonny and Molly were in Sonny's rowboat with their fishing poles and Mike and Mark were in their rowboat also fishing. Mark remarked when he and his brother both caught a fish "Maybe someday we'll be fishers of men like the apostles." Mike and Mark were calmly discussing becoming Catholic Priests as their future vocations. Sonny looked at Molly while over hearing the conversation "Maybe we should send a message to Cory and tell him to bring his shovel...cause one or both of us might go into shock and die." Everything seemed backwards. The adults were acting like children and the practical jokers were acting like rational human beings planning responsible futures. However, Sonny and Molly were in the middle of the pond without access to Homer the homing pigeon or Ollie the Saint Bernard dog with barrel collar or cell phone (which neither of them owned). So, they continued to fish and enjoy the scenery. Sonny and Molly each caught two fish; Mike and Mark caught 153.

Maryann and Miriam had changed into play shoes and were leading a band of cousins about their age, setting traps to catch a leprechaun. Next week was St. Patrick's Day and they planned to be ready. They were going to keep their leprechaun in their tree house after he gave them a pot of gold. A doll bed was already set up to receive their future leprechaun...they just needed the last piece of the puzzle.

The next week both the McGolly and McFrugal clans re-emerged on McGolly Hill to celebrate St. Patrick's Day. The day started with Irish green pancakes and an Irish morning prayer...

for today the Irish would have THE PARTY OF THE YEAR!

As the sun rose with a green hue Grandma McGolly was already in the kitchen flipping her famous green shamrock shaped pancakes and green eggs for the crack of dawn breakfast. She also made blood pudding but the kids preferred the pancakes. Coffee with Irish crème and clear liquid gold juice (also known as apple juice) were the beverages of choice. Grandma McGolly stated "I couldn't come up with a green colored beverage so gold juice will have to do." Aunt Rosie walked into the kitchen and casually added to the conversation "Margaritas are green". Grandma McFrugal (Rosie's mother) looked at her with a curious look "Don't make me Bishop slap you." They all laughed, but there was an element of truth to the statement. Aunt Rosie was kind of known as the family 'lush'. She always seemed to have an alcoholic beverage in her hand, more so than anyone else. It started out as a joke but pretty soon took on a life of its own. Aunt Rosie would meet with her friends after work and on weekends to drink and party. Soon she was missing Mass on Sundays because she 'had other things to do' like recover from a hangover.

She was able to catch herself before she lost control and chose to change her lifestyle. She didn't like being known as the family 'lush' and after awhile of denying she had a problem; broke down and asked her brothers and sisters for help. First she tried just having one drink with her friends; but she was unable in that environment. Next she tried to meet with her friends in alcohol free environments, sometimes lunches, movies but this only lasted a short time because it was easier to just meet them in the usual places while drinking and partying. She returned to weekly Holy Mass and confession. She received spiritual guidance and came up with a plan to counteract her addiction to alcohol. Aunt Rosie started showing up on McGolly Hill to be around her family and help out with the log cabin lodge project. She also took up a new hobby to occupy her time; horseback riding with her brothers. She even went on a Caribbean vacation so she could ride a horse along the beach. To be with people her own age, she joined a singles group for young adults at a Catholic Church. It wasn't the closest Catholic Church but it was worth traveling a little further to be with like minded young adults. Rosie found she still had to stand vigilant because some of the 'singles' seemed to need more work on their souls then she did. Most of her new friends were actively working on becoming closer to God. Her peace was with God. Coming back home to the Catholic Church with her family, new practices (staying away from people and places that encourage alcohol, meeting new friends, new hobbies, prayer, fasting, Bible study, Holy Mass at least weekly, confession with Catholic Priest at least monthly); she felt so much better. Her peace was with God. Her family knew that this was a road strew with rocks and thorns but offered their support with love and charity to help her persevere, persevere, persevere. Love and charity go along way. You know what else goes a long way according to Aunt Rosie? Confession! The veil comes off and you have to face your problems. She goes to confession at least monthly to keep on the right track and it just feels good to be close to God.

Rosie's Catholic Church had a healing Mass four times a year, about every 3 months on the Thursday before first Friday of that month. She attended by herself the first time and later would take her nephew Sonny or anyone else who desired physical, mental or spiritual healing.

Scripture Passage: Mark 14:36

"Abba, Father, all things are possible to you,
Take this cup away from me, but not what I will but what you will."

The Healing Mass proceeded something like this:

INTRODUCTORY RITES:
* Entrance Song: Precious Lord, Take My Hand
* Exorcism of Salt
* Blessing of Salt
* Sprinkling with Holy Water (in silence)(by Priest)
* Opening Collect

LITURGY OF THE WORD

* 1ˢᵗ Reading: Acts of the Apostles 4:8-12

Then Peter, filled with the Holy Spirit, said to them, "Rulers of the people and elders, If we are being examined today concerning a good deed done to a cripple, by what means this man has been healed, be it known to you all, and to all the people of Israel, that by the name of Jesus Christ of Nazareth, whom you crucified, whom God raised from the dead, by him this man is standing before you well. This is the stone which was rejected by you builders, but which has become the head of the corner. And there is salvation in no one else, for there is no other name under heaven given among men by which we must be saved."

* Responsorial Psalm (Psalm 118: Let Us Rejoice)
* Gospel Acclamation
* Gospel (A Reading from the Holy Gospel, according to Mark

> Mark 4: 35-41): Jesus Stills a Storm
>
> On that day, when evening had come, he said to them, "Let us go across to the other side." And leaving the crowd, they took him with them, just as he was, in the boat. And other boats were with him. And a great storm of wind arose, and the waves beat into the boat, so that the boat was already filling. But he was in the stern, asleep on the cushion; and they woke him and said to him, "Teacher, do you not care if we perish?" And he awoke and rebuked the wind, and said to the sea, "Peace! Be still!" And the wind ceased, and there was a great calm. He said to them, "Why are you afraid? Have you no faith? And they were filled with awe, and said to one another, "Who then is this, that even wind and sea obey him?"

* Homily
* Intercessions for the Sick
* Exorcism of the Oil
* Blessing of the Oil

LITURGY OF THE EUCHARIST

* Preparation Song: How Can I Keep From Singing
* Preparation of the Altar and the Gifts
* Prayer over the offerings
* Preface Dialogue
* Holy, Holy, Holy/Santo, Santo, Santo
* Eucharistic Prayer III
* Memorial Acclamation
* Great Amen

COMMUNION RITE

* Lord's Prayer
* Sign of Peace
* Lamb of God

* HOLY COMMUNION
    Communion Hymn: All Is Well With My Soul
* Prayer after COMMUNION

CONCLUDING RITE

* Final Blessing and Dismissal
* Transition (from communal prayer to individual prayer for the sick and suffering
    whether mentally, physically or spiritually),
    the laying on of hands and anointing with blessed oil,
    let us invoke the intercession of the Virgin Mary,
    Mother of Christ (our Healer and Savior).
* Concluding Hymn: Hail Mary/Ave Maria

Rosie felt much peace during and after the Healing Mass. She asked for healing of her alcohol addiction during the Mass and the laying on of hands and anointing with blessed oil. Rosie stayed for Eucharistic Adoration which started immediately after the healing Mass and continued into the next day which was 1st Friday of the month (honoring the Sacred Heart of Jesus). She stayed for 2 hours following the healing Mass and returned the next morning for 1st Friday of the month Mass(honoring the Sacred Heart of Jesus).

All those that attended the healing service were able to take some of the blessed salt/oil/ and Holy water home with them. Rosie joined the Single Catholic Group as well as Alcoholics Anonymous through her Catholic Church. One of her new friends who was in both groups like herself was Ozzie. Ozzie had previously lived an active homosexual lifestyle but converted to living a chaste lifestyle and found peace in the teachings of the Catholic Church. Truth is Truth, and it works for those who have homosexual tendencies too. God loves all of His children and knows what is best for all of us. God's ways are not burdensome. She felt comfortable asking Ozzie about his conversion. Rosie explained to Ozzie that she had a co-worker/friend who was living an active homosexual lifestyle and she wanted to know what to say to him if the opportunity presented itself. Ozzie encouraged her to tell the truth if he asked for her opinion and to be genuinely caring. He also said to have this conversation one to one, the information has a better chance of being received without defense or her getting fired for being 'intolerate'.

He also warned her that he probably would not take this well and he could retaliate in different ways. Putting the Truth out there is the best thing she could do if she truly cares for him, but it could come with severe consequences. He said that an old friend from high school was the first person outside of his family that tried to explain why he shouldn't act on his homosexual tendencies…he didn't talk to her again for a year. However that one conversation in which his friend displayed real love and concern for him opened up his heart and mind and he eventually made his way back home to the Catholic Church. When the Priest in the confessional told him about a program called COURAGE for those who have homosexual tendencies, he once again was a reluctant to seek help. Prayers led him to the conversion process and he stated that he was reaching peace in his soul and the Catholic Church was the only place he could find it. He said that he had to go to different Catholic Church for the COURAGE meetings because not every church has a group. He thought about starting a group at their church…but right now he was working on his issues. One more piece of advice from Ozzie was to look for common ground for their friendship to grow…and maybe that opportunity will open up to talk to her co-worker/friend with genuine concern and love.

THEN ONE DAY IT HAPPENED! Rosie invited her co-worker/friend named Jim to her Catholic Singles Group outing that month. Jim was kind of a thrill seeker and that month they were going to the Zoo and some of the group were going to zip-line through the trees over the wild animals below. Jim wanted to do this activity, so he agreed to meet her at the Zoo. He came in his own car in case he was ambushed by a bunch of 'Rightous Catholics'. Jim was raised Catholic but left the Church in his early 20's due to his conflict with his homosexual lifestyle. There were about 20 people that showed up for the Zoo event. Other than the beginning which started with a heartfelt prayer and any special intentions voiced by a few; the rest of the outing was full of fun and fellowship. Jim was pleasantly surprised to find these young people were alive with their faith (some more than others) and trying to live Godly lives in this great big messed up world. He was accepted as he was but he knew if he started to go to the Catholic Church his life was going to change. Jim had a decision to make; he could start his conversion now, or procrastinate a while or shut the door.

Jim chose to pray about it. Good choice! Jim heard Rosie say "Say your rosary every day" and that was the avenue he chose to take. He also recently heard that prisoners who say their rosary every day, seem to handle their incarcerations better.

If it works for them under those conditions then maybe it will work for him too.

Ozzie zip-lined over the wild animals at the Zoo twice and came back another day with his old friend from high school and her family. She was an adventure seeker back in high school; that was their common bond. They were back to being very good friends again.

Now back to the McGolly household on Saint Patrick's Day

Grandma McGolly made breakfast, Grandpa McGolly read the real story of Saint Patrick to his grandchildren in the family room.

★★★

THE SAINT PATRICK STORY

St. Patrick as a young boy (about 14 years old), was captured during a raiding party and taken to Ireland as a slave to herd and tend sheep. Ireland at this time was a land of Druids and pagans (no Christians). He learned the language and customs of the people who held him.

During his captivity in Ireland, he turned to God in prayer. St. Patrick wrote "The love of God and his fear grew in me more and more, as did the faith, and my soul was rosed, so that, in a single day, I have said as many as a hundred prayers and in the night, nearly the same." "I prayed in the woods and on the mountain, even before dawn. I felt no hurt from the snow or ice or rain."

Patrick's captivity lasted until he was twenty. He escaped after having a dream from God, telling him to leave Ireland by going to the coast. There he found some sailors who reunited him with his family back in Britian.

In another dream the people of Ireland were calling out to him "We beg you, holy youth, to come and walk among us once more." St. Patrick became a priest and later ordained a bishop. He was sent to take the Gospel to Ireland, converting many to Christianity. Kings, their families and whole kingdoms converted to Christianity when hearing Patrick's message. For 40 years Patrick preached and converted all of Ireland. After years of living in poverty, traveling and enduring much suffering Patrick died March 17, in the year 461. His feast day is March 17th.

St. Patrick taught them about the Blessed Trinity by showing them how the shamrock had three leaves yet was one plant. (One God in 3 persons; Father/ Son/ Holy Spirit). He also built Catholic Churches and schools everywhere in Ireland.

★★

Grandpa closed the book, "So what did ya learn from the true story of St. Patrick". Mike "It seemed like all the hardships of his life were preparing him to do the work of God". Mark "I guess that God can turn even bad into good". Grandpa added with a smile "We should all help each other to strive towards sainthood and to be in the state of grace. All of you children should help each other throughout your lives with love; to continue to do God's Will. There are so many ways to know, love and serve the Lord; and it will different for each of you. Live by the 10 Commandments." Grandpa McGolly gave each of his grandchildren a blessing by dipping his right hand in the holy water font and making the sign of the cross on their foreheads.

After an Irish breakfast, all the children went outside to play. Miriam and Maryann and the leprechaun posse set out with a rope and baby carriage to bring back their leprechaun. No fishing today, instead the older kids went on horseback rides and completed working on their kites in the barn. Molly and the gang were jumping off the loft into what was left of the heaps of straw. Inside the house the triplets were learning how to crawl. Dad and the uncles were playing their bagpipes dressed in their kilts. Mom and the Grandmas and aunts were dancing the River Dance in their Irish dresses and green leotards on the long front porch. So Mike and Mark put on their new kilts and had their first bagpipe lesson and Molly was learning to river Dance. Not Miriam and Maryann, they were hunting for a leprechaun because it was St. Patrick's Day...their very last chance!

This St. Patrick's Day fell during a weekday so Father O'Reilly and Father O'Mally were both able to have lunch Irish style on McGolly Hill. First they blessed the new log cabin lodge and the crucifixes on the doors, including Grandma McFrugal's little house. The Priests blessed each member of the McGolly and McFrugal families. Then a blessing was said before the traditional St. Patrick's Day Feast.

> Bless us oh Lord for these thee gifts
> for which we are about to receive
> from Thee bounty
> Through Christ our Lord   AMEN

Menu:
Blood sausage, Corned Beef and Cabbage
Food fit for a king or a savage.
Roasted carrots and potatoes
garnished with radishes carved to look like a rose.
Homemade rye bread and fresh churned butter, slathered on top of each slice.
Many Irish cakes and pastries for dessert; remember variety is the spice of life.
All washed down their food shoots
to their stomachs with a keg of Irish apple juice.
The ladies drank tea and the younguns drank milk.
Plenty to drink whether they were wearing diapers, priest collar, green dresses with leotards or kilts.

A celebratory toast was made with wine they made from grapes grown on the land.
Molly's dad raised his wine glass in his right hand
"May we Irish always remember the example of St. Patrick, who always by his word and deed did God's Will. We are truly thankful for the food and drink and friends and family to share our blessings. Amen".

Then everyone lifted their wine glass, milk bottle or tea cup and graciously thanked God for their many blessings.

The bottle of wine was labeled [KITE FLYING WINE]. Sonny reminded everyone of the annual kite flying contest at the top of the hill by the big wooden cross. March blows in like a lion and goes out like a lamb. So March is the perfect month for kite flying. Every St. Pat's Day when it stopped raining and the wind was blowing, up to the hilltop to see which kite flew the highest. Sonny and Molly worked together and named their entry (Saint Michael the Archangel) their slogan 'St. Michael defend us in battle'. Dad helped John & Joseph with their first kite since

Miriam and Maryann were too busy this year to be bothered. They named their kite (Dalmatian). Dad mistakenly left the barn for a minute and when he returned John and Joseph had walked all over the kite with muddy shoes. Dad wanted to name the kite (The Day of the Mud) to remind them of the day of the mud. However John and Joseph liked (Dalmatian) better. The Priests had an entry this year named (Miracle in the Sky); actually the teenagers at the Church made it. Uncle Kevin and Uncle Rob (Green Thing) made with light weight tree branches. Aunt Rosie had a little extra time lately so she entered for the first time (Dove with Olive Branch); the tail of the kite was made of green material and looked like an olive branch in the dove's beak when it was floating in the breeze. Uncle Steve and Aunt Rachael live on flat land so they named their entry (Groundhog), Dad's brothers (Luke, Matthew and Thomas) entered one entry this year instead of three (Gerald's Airplane); they could hardly fly it because they were laughing so hard. For weeks while Gerald was at work in town; his brothers (the lumberjacks) brought in parts of an airplane to be reassembled in between loads of massive logs. This old retired airplane was a gift from his wife Maureen. Uncle Ivan and his new girlfriend Miss Kimberly Bailey (Molly and Sonny's teacher) rode horses to the top of the hill; no entry they just wanted to observe. So, we have the serious contenders and those that think the contest is one big joke. Which entry will win?!

An hour later they had a victor…Aunt Rosie surprised them all (especially herself) when (Dove with Olive Branch) soared the highest. Second place (Saint Michael the Archangel). Third place (Gerald's Airplane). The uncles told Gerald "At least the kite can fly". The Priests had everyone laughing saying the reason their kite didn't win was they forgot to bless it." Aunt Rosie received her grand prize which was a beautiful green (different shades) afghan knitted by Grandma McFrugal (Rosie's mother). Rosie was so happy she started crying and hugging her mother.

Then back down the hill to the house for the evening fish fry. They needed to do something with all the fish Mark and Mike caught last week. Bagpipes and Celtic music and dancing were in full swing. Uncles Rob and Kevin used their kite (Green Thing) as kindling for the fire. They have never placed in the kite flying contest. Next year their going to name their kite (Bonfire Kindling) or maybe (Bars of Gold) and make it so heavy it can't get off the ground. If you're going to come in last place…you might as well do it right.

Mom started looking for Miriam and Maryann after the fish fry dinner. She had been so busy chasing after the crawling triplets that she didn't notice the little girls were gone. Mom and Grandma McGolly stayed at the house during the kite flying contest, watching from the porch while rocking the triplets. Mom thought Miriam and Maryann were with everyone else at the top of the hill. Dad was busy keeping up with John and Joseph and trying to fly their kite. He thought someone else was watching Maryann and Miriam. They usually were so easy to watch. Pretty soon, they all realized the last time anyone saw the twin girls was before the kite flying contest. It was almost dark and the little 4 year old girls were lost out looking for a leprechaun! Miriam and Maryann were missing. They were not in the house, the barn, their tree house or anywhere on McGolly Hill. The women took care of all the children and the men formed a posse including the McFrugal rangers with their horses. Police on the ground and in a helicopter from above, all searching for the little twin girls. This story was on the evening news. Even the prisoners heard about the lost McGolly girls. Jay Walker (Sonny's friend) felt he needed to do something to help these little girls; the only thing he could do from prison was pray for their safe return. Jay knelt down on his knees and prayed the Divine Mercy Chaplet (Sonny had taught him last week) and asked Jesus to help the little lost girls. Two other inmates knelt beside him and prayed with him. Many more of the prisoners and workers at the prison also silently prayed for the safe return of the little 4 year old girls lost while trying to catch a leprechaun.

It was dark outside, about 4 hours later at almost midnight...Grandpa McGolly came out of the woods carrying both of his little granddaughters, one in each arm. He found them asleep by a log. Maryann said "Grandpa, we prayed like Saint Patrick a hundred prayers that someone would save us, and you did." The little girls had a few scratches and bug bites but they were in good condition. Miriam said "I don't want a leprechaun anymore, I just want to go home." Mom and Dad hugged Miriam and Maryann, fed and bathed them before tucking each into bed. Dad gave them his nightly blessing and Mother stayed with them until they fell sound asleep. All of the adults knew things could have turned out very differently, so they gathered around the fireplace and offered prayers of thanksgiving for keeping the little ones safe. Sonny's mother (Clare) called the prison to tell Jay Walker the little girls were found and are safe. The next few days the adults watched over the children like shepherds; loving attention and lots of head counts.

This year the last day of March was going to be Easter Sunday. Following holy Mass, Molly and her family would go to Aunt Rachael and Uncle Steve's house for Easter; as was their usual custom. Grandma and Grandpa McGolly departed for their daughter Rachael and son in law's home on Good Friday.

Mark and Mike planned a holy surprise for everyone on Good Friday (the day Jesus suffered and died for our sins). The boys constructed 14 small crosses from scrapes of wood in Dad's wood work shop (with permission). Starting from the bottom of the hill they strategically placed the wooden crosses (with Roman numerals) standing in the ground, up the hill ending at the large Big wooden Cross. Several years ago, Dad cleared an area and placed a large standing wooden cross in the ground and made several unmovable benches facing the cross. This was a special place for outdoor prayers and being close to nature. Grandma McFrugal and Grandma & Grandpa McGolly, Mom and Dad, Aunt Clare, Molly and Sonny (Dad put Sonny in a wheelbarrow; making it easier to get him up the hill), Miriam and Maryann, John and Joseph, the triplets (Leo, Patrick and Shawn carried by grandparents) and Ollie (Sonny's dog) followed Mike and Mark up the hill; stopping at each Station of the Cross. Mark and Mike recited the 14 Stations of the Cross at each cross along the path. When they reached the 12th Station of the Cross (Jesus Dies on the Cross); they asked that everyone look down at their feet. Mike and Mark had not planned the bloodstone to be there...but noticed when they were placing the crosses after it had recently rained...the bloodstone color was much redder when wet. Molly thought of all the times she had gone up and down this trail and never even noticed the bloodstone; in fact she had never heard of bloodstone. Of all the rocks in her bingo winning, not one was a bloodstone.

A SHORT WAY OF THE CROSS as used by
The Franciscan Fathers on their Missions

(First Station): Jesus Condemned to Death

O Jesus! So meek and uncomplaining, teach me resignation in trials.

(Second Station): Jesus Carries His Cross

My Jesus, the Cross should be mine, not Thine; my sins crucified Thee.

(Third Station): Our Lord Falls the First Time

O Jesus! By this first fall, never let me fall into mortal sin.

(Fourth Station): Jesus Meets His Mother

O Jesus! May no human tie, however dear, keep me from following the road of the Cross.

(Fifth Station): Simon the Cyrenean Helps Jesus Carry His Cross

Simon unwillingly assisted Thee; may I with patience suffer all for Thee.

(Sixth Station): Veronica Wipes the Face of Jesus

O Jesus! Thou didst imprint Thy sacred features upon Veronica's veil; stamp them also indelibly upon my heart.

(Seventh Station): The Second Fall of Jesus

By Thy second fall, preserve me, dear Lord, from relapse into sin.

(Eighth Station): Jesus Consoles the Women of Jerusalem

My greatest consolation would be to hear Thee say: "Many sins are forgiven thee, because thou hast loved much."

(Ninth Station): Third Fall of Jesus

O Jesus! When weary upon life's long journey, be Thou my strength and my perseverance.

(Tenth Station): Jesus Stripped of His Garments

My soul has been robbed of its robe of innocence; clothe me, dear Jesus, with the garb of penance and contrition.

(Eleventh Station): Jesus Nailed to the Cross

Thou didst forgive Thy enemies; my God, teach me to forgive injuries and FORGET them.

(Twelfth Station): Jesus Dies on the Cross

Thou are dying, my Jesus, but Thy Sacred Heart still throbs with love for Thy sinful children.

(Thirteenth Station): Jesus Taken Down from the Cross

Receive me into Thy arms, O Sorrowful Mother; and obtain for me perfect contrition for my sins.

(Fourteenth Station): Jesus Laid in the Sepulchre

When I receive Thee into my heart in Holy Communion, O Jesus, make it a fit abiding place for Thy adorable Body.

Amen.

"Jesus, Mary, I Love You, Save Souls."

Most of the family members were very quiet while making this spiritual trek. Truly they were contemplating the sorrowful passion and death of our Savior who died for love of us. Once the family completed the 14 Stations of the Cross they continued their serene prayerful state by saying the Holy Rosary. They recited the sorrowful mysteries:

(First Sorrowful Mystery): THE AGONY IN THE GARDEN

Kneeling down, He began to pray, father if it be your will, take this cup from Me, yet not My will but yours be done. In his anguish He prayed even more intensely, and His sweat became like drops of blood falling to the ground. (Luke 22:42, 44)

SPIRITUAL FRUIT: God's Will be done

(Second Sorrowful Mystery): THE SCOURGING AT THE PILLAR

Pilate released Barabbas to them. Jesus, however, he first had scourged; then he handed Him over to be crucified. (Matthew 27:26)

SPIRITUAL FRUIT: Mortification of the Senses

(Third Sorrowful Mystery): THE CROWNING WITH THORNS

Weaving a crown of thorns they fixed it on His head, and placed a reed in His right hand. To make fun of Him they knelt before Him saying: "Hail-, King of the Jews.' They spat on Him, and took the reed and kept striking Him on the head. (Matthew 27:29, 30)

SPIRITUAL FRUIT: Reign of Christ in our heart

(Fourth Sorrowful Mystery): THE CARRYING OF THE CROSS

When the soldiers had finished mocking Him, ...they led Him away to crucify Him..On the way they laid hold of a certain Simon of Cyrene, coming from the country, and upon him they laid the cross to bear it after Jesus. (Matthew 27:31; Luke 23:26)

SPIRITUAL FRUIT: Patient bearing of trials

(Fifth Sorrowful Mystery): THE CRUCIFIXION

When they came to the place called the Skull, they crucified Him. Jesus said, Father, forgive them, for they do not know what they are doing"...There was darkness over the whole land until the ninth hour and Jesus cried out with a loud voice, Father, into your hands I commend My spirit." (Luke 23:33, 34, 44, 46)

SPIRITUAL FRUIT: Pardoning of Injuries

DIVINE MERCY PUBLICATIONS; P.O. Box 26531, Tamarac, FL 33320, USA

★★★★★★★★★★★★★★★★★★★★★★★★★★★★★★★★★★★★★★

As they sat on the benches or knelt before the big wooden cross contemplating what our Savior did for us on Good Friday; they were truly sorrowful for their sins and thankful to Jesus for His saving passion and death on the Cross.

Later that day, Grandma and Grandpa McGolly packed up and went to stay with Aunt Rachael (their daughter) and Uncle Steve (their son-in-law) and their family, about a 2 hours drive from McGolly Hill.

Saturday Morning (day before Easter Sunday), Grandma McFrugal set up for Easter egg coloring with her grandchildren. She had regular Easter egg coloring and her special silk tie Easter egg coloring. Grandma collected men's silk ties from garage sales and thrift shops throughout the year. Then set cut them into squares big enough to cover an egg. Each egg was tightly wrapped with a silk square and then wrapped again with a thin layer of white gauze. In the enamel pot went the material covered eggs and covered with water and some vinegar to help set the color. She boiled the eggs, just like regular hard boiled eggs. The eggs were removed from the water and cooled. Once cooled they would be placed in the refrigerator, still in their material coverings. On Easter morning they would remove the material to their colorfully patterned eggs.

While coloring the eggs, Molly's dad mentioned the Easter Bunny sometimes brings live bunnies in Easter baskets. Molly's mom stopped wrapping an egg and looked at Dad and stated her business "If the Easter Bunny leaves any live bunnies around here, we'll be having rabbit stew for dinner." Needless to say, none of the McGolly children had a live bunny in their basket the next morning for Easter. Only the chocolate variety Easter bunnies for the McGolly children. They did however get live ducklings. A special treat was left in the barn Easter morning; a mother duck and seven baby ducklings in a large box. Mom's eyes were about to pop out of her head like a baby duck out of an egg. Dad whispered something into Mom's ear, which seemed to calm her anger. Apparently he got the ducks from the pond and he would return them immediately. First they had to catch the ducklings which turned out to be a fiasco. The ducks were running in every direction all over the barn with people chasing them. The ducks feathers were flying, ducks jumping on their backs while the kids were crawling on the ground trying to grab the little fluffy cute birdies. Except for the triplets, each of the children had a duckling in their hands...to the pond...for the great release!

They worked up quite an appetite. So, back to the house for a breakfast of brightly colored hard boiled eggs, chocolate bunny rabbits and candy from their Easter baskets. Then they got dressed in their 'Sunday's best'. The girls took quick bathes and put on their new Easter dresses. Mike and Mark looked handsome wearing their first Holy Communion suits; their ties were not made of silk so they were still in one piece. The McGolly family looked presentable for church with only a few scattered feathers on their clothes.

Easter Sunday Mass was beautiful with Easter lilies all around the altar. More people were present than usual...lots more! Maryann asked why so many more people were at church today, as innocently as a dove. Mom gave her little innocent daughter the truth "Well sweetheart, for different reasons many people don't love God enough to put Him first in their lives. Otherwise they would make the changes to be here every Sunday and Holy Days of Obligation. We as Christians are to love each of them where they are in their faith journey and help bring them closer to God and the state of grace." Maryann asked "How can I help?" Mom looked at her lovingly smiling (remember Mom started smiling during the daytime for Lent this year) "Smile at them and be kind." Molly was listening and told Maryann "I'll teach you and Miriam about the Corporal and Spiritual works of mercy that our Pope wants all of us to know. That way you'll know other ways to help people and lead them to Heaven." Dad joined in the conversation, since they had to park so far away from the Catholic Church due to the volume of parishioners today; "Pray, pray, and pray for the people to love God above all and to do God's Will. Prayers help." Miriam said excitedly "Our church teacher taught us a prayer! Maryann do you remember it?! Then in unison they stopped walking and put their white gloved hands in prayer mode while still holding their Easter purses, closed their eyes and sweetly prayed "Jesus and Mary, I love You, Save Souls".

The McGolly family usually filled an entire pew. Today they were standing in the back of the church on purpose to be charitable to the Easter/Christmas Catholics; in hopes that the visitors would become regular members of the Body of Christ and His Church. Miriam and Maryann smiled at everybody who past by them. All the people seemed to respond well and smiled back.

Easter Sunday of the Resurrection of the Lord (Readings: Acts 10:34, 37-43/ Col 3:1-4)

The homily centered around the fact that Jesus Christ chose a meal in which every human being is familiar; to become the Source and Summit of the Catholic Church. We must eat His Body and drink His Blood to be in communion with our Lord while in the state of grace (no mortal sin). Jesus is food for our bodies and our souls. Jesus asked us to remember the sacrifice He made for us. This is my Body which will be given up for you so that sins may be forgiven... (Liturgy of the Eucharist).

Mr. and Mrs. McGolly, Grandma McFrugal, Molly, Mark and Mike received the true Body and Blood of Jesus Christ into their bodies during Holy Mass. Maryann, Miriam, John and Joseph received a blessing by criss crossing their hands over their hearts when touched on their foreheads as they approached the altar. The triplets also received a blessing on their foreheads. After the final blessing by the priest and the last hymn (They Will Know We are Christians by Our Love) and AFTER the priest left the Catholic Church; the McGolly's filed outside to greet their friends and welcome visitors. Then they piled into the minibus and returned home, changed clothes and off to Aunt Rachael's and Uncle Steve's house to see Grandma and Grandpa McGolly and other relatives for Easter! Grandma McFrugal, after Holy Mass went to one of her other children's house to spend time with Uncle Rob (her son) and his wife Belle and their children (Bobby & Belle and babies), Kevin, Martha (and her children), Sister Mary Valentine, Ivan and Rosie.

Aunt Rachael was Dad's sister, her married name was Donavan. Aunt Rachael, Uncle Steve and their seven children (the Donavan's) lived in a large flat house (one story) with a long flat driveway on flat land with a large flat lake. The McGolly children loved visiting their relatives on flat land because it was so different from the hill.

The boys rode their cousin's bicycles up and down the flat driveway (easier to have races), the girls played hopscotch and drew pictures on the flat driveway with colored chalk from their Easter baskets. Dad brought his golf clubs to play golf on flat land (at home the golf balls often rolled down the hill). Molly helped the adult women hide Easter eggs in the large flat front yard for the Easter egg hunt for the little kids.

Brightly colored plastic eggs filled with all kinds of candy and religious trinkets (like wooden rosary beads, holy cards with the risen Jesus on them, ceramic holy angels). Dad made the wooden rosary beads (anything wooden was usually made by Dad) and the ceramic angels were made by Mom and Grandma (made from bits of clay from the pottery wheel; Molly painted these beautiful angels when her siblings weren't looking). Aunt Rachael handed out the gathering baskets (different from their own Easter baskets); reused each year and then BAM! the Easter egg hunt began. Mike and Mark collected several eggs and then started to steer the younger kids. Maryann and Miriam were having the time of their lives, John and Joseph didn't know what to do! Everyone was yelling at them to get the eggs, so they did. In fact when the hunt was over and eggs were being counted to see who won the grand prize; John and Joseph both had authentic robin eggs in their baskets. John had one robin egg and Joseph had two. Molly returned to the front yard to search for a fallen nest and sure enough she found it. She placed the nest and all three robin eggs in a shoebox to take home to McGolly Hill; she wanted to keep them warm and see if they would hatch into little birdies (she loved birds). One of the Donavan boys ended up with the grand prize which was a new fishing pole. However, Molly felt like she won the grand prize with the robin eggs and nest.

Following the traditional Easter egg hunt, they headed inside the house for the Easter Feast. The women congregated in the kitchen putting the finishing touches on the meal (it was Sunday; so most of the heavy cooking was done the day before/remember Sunday is the day for the Lord and rest / relaxation). The menu included baked ham, sweet potatoes with marshmallows on top (and apples from Molly's birthday tree), deviled eggs (three different varieties), green beans, macaroni and cheese and red jello with cherries from Miriam and Maryann's birthday trees and pecans from Joseph and John's birthday trees. Mom made her special red jello twice a year (Christmas and Easter). Grandma McGolly made her homemade rolls and rye bread and Aunt Rachael made an Easter cake that looked like a bunny. Aunt Rachael was a cake decorator... a really good one. The tiered plate center piece was placed in the middle of the main table with the beautiful silk dyed Easter eggs exposed (this was a tradition because the eggs were so pretty and festive). Sonny and his mother (who are also McGolly's) were always at Aunt Rachael and Uncle Steve's at Easter too.

Another Easter tradition (depending on the weather) was the leisurely ride on the large flat pontoon boat on the large flat lake. This year Mom and Aunt Rachael elected to forgo the boat ride and stay home with the triplets and children under 4 years old (they were afraid that one of them might fall or crawl off the boat). Everyone else put on their lifejackets and boarded the 'Nightengale's Retreat'. Uncle Steve named the boat after his lovely bride, Rachael. Rachael's father (Grandpa McGolly) gave each of his children a pet name when they were growing up and he named Rachael 'Nightengale' for her beautiful voice.

The boys gathered as many small flat rocks as they could find. They had their own tradition...the rock skipping contest (this was not exclusive to just Easter time; it was anytime they were on the lake on the boat). Uncle Steve held the all time record of 14 skips with one throw. It was the last day of March and almost no wind, the lake was very flat (a perfect day to break Uncle Steve's record). The boat had a large slide but the lake water was too cold to go swimming. Uncle Steve told them the only way anyone was going swimming today was if they broke his rock skipping record. Then he would personally throw them overboard and they could 'swim with the fishes'. Of course this was fuel for the fire to Mike and Mark; they wanted to get into the lake...cold or not! Uncle Steve had a great sense of humor and was just kidding; but this spurred the boys on to break the record. Sonny won the contest with 12 skips...not good enough to break the record. Although he didn't have the use of his legs due to his disability, he did have great strength of his upper body. Every day, all day long he had to lift himself in and out of his wheelchair or anywhere he wanted to go. Sonny was able to flick the rocks with more power enabling him almost break the record at a very young age. Uncle Steve was starting to sweat, thinking his rock skipping record was in jeopardy (just kidding). Uncle Steve told Sonny to bring his wetsuit next time in case he gets to 'swim with the fishes'; cause he wasn't kidding about being thrown in the lake. Sonny asked "What's my prize for winning today's contest". Uncle Steve let Sonny drive the boat back to the pier and gave Sonny $ 5 from his wallet. Sonny loved driving the boat! While the boys were being competitive the older girl cousins and Molly sketched, read books and/or painted their fingernails while lying on a comforter nice and relaxed. Miriam and Maryann and their group of cousins had a head standing contest on a moving boat, colored in their new coloring books from Easter bunny and took turns being held by Grandma or Grandpa McGolly while taking in the beautiful scenery of the great outdoors. Dad and the cousin (8 years old) who won the fishing pole were fishing. Molly's dad caught a good size fish and the boy cousin caught a crucifix. No one knows how that crucifix got in the middle of the lake but to catch a crucifix (with Jesus Christ crucified on it) on Easter Sunday is amazing no matter how you look at it (Divine or coincidence).

They returned to the flat house after being on a flat boat on a flat lake after a flat rock skipping contest to have left over food from the Easter feast and watch a movie on the large flat screen television. The Donavan's watched more television than the McGolly's on the hill but their privileges were greatly censored. They were not allowed to watch anything that promotes an immoral lifestyle or that leads to the culture of death. These rules also apply to the family when they leave the premises (yes, including the parents). Too much (almost everything) in today's secular culture being shown on television and other forms of multi- media is corrupting even the adults. People have been desensitized to evil because it is pumped into social media on such a scale they don't even flinch when it's right in front of them. Most adults don't even make an attempt to guard their children from such evil (and they should be guarding their children from corruption of sin and evil in all its forms).

Author note: I've been a pediatric nurse for over 30 years and I can tell you the evil has gone from what is on television to what the children are raised with in their own families. I see very few intact family units anymore; meaning father, mother and their children (from original marriage). 50% of children are born to unwed (single) mothers (where are the fathers and why aren't they committed to the woman who is bearing their child/children, why aren't they keeping their family together including til death do they part from their spouse), parents are divorced and then remarried to someone else (making things very confusing to children) or never married in the first place. The children's relatives are 'living together in sin' but no one acknowledges these sins as sins anymore (fornication, adultery (if no annulment), birth control (other than Natural Family Planning in a holy marriage and only for a good reason), living in sin (not married), homosexual acts) and to top it off the parents (or whoever has custody) aren't raising these children in the faith. So, where are the children getting any kind of truth? We are not to go into despair nor become despondent but we are to return to doing God's Will over our will. This will be difficult for those who of free will have veered soooo far from the path to Heaven. Remember God never changed...it was you who chose to do things your way... while being led by the popular secular culture. If you're Catholic (once Catholic always Catholic; because you have been given the TRUTH whether you like it or not makes no difference) you will be held to the truth. We as Catholics are held to a higher standard BECAUSE we have been given the TRUTH. TRUTH is TRUTH and can't be changed to fit your desires. Remember the Virgin Mary (Our Heavenly Mother and Queen of Heaven) told the 3 shepherd children of Fatima that in 1917 that the biggest reason souls were going to Hell at that time was because of lust. Mortal sins have not changed, which means lust is still a mortal sin.

★★★★★★★★★★★★★★★★★★★★★★★★★★★★★★★★★★

Author Note: The statement: 'Russia will already have spread her errors throughout the world, provoking wars and persecutions against the Church'; notice it states errors not error. I usually think communism as the error/s spread provoking wars and persecutions. Recently while watching television I learned that there was another great error in Russia: In 1917 Russia legalized abortion. The same year the Virgin Mary (Our Heavenly Mother) appeared to the 3 shepherd children of Fatima Portugal. Abortion is an error which has been spread throughout the world, provoking wars (on the UNBORN) and persecutions against the Church. I sometimes (most of the time) think that abortion and euthanasia is the Third World War (or at least a big part). We are killing the people we should love the most (our unborn children) and the people who lovingly raised us (parents, aunt & uncles and grandparents). Oh sure, the third world war could include other nations, if we can kill our loved ones we can certainly kill people we don't know. The Great Deceiver has deceived us all. We can change on an individual level and not wait for our national leaders to do the right thing. If there is not a candidate on the voting ballot that is PRO-LIFE... then what is a good Catholic to do? As a Catholic it is mortal sin under the fifth Commandment (You shall not kill) to knowingly vote for someone who is pro-abortion. Pro-Choice is pro murder of conceived children. If someone says they are Pro-Life if they agree with stopping abortions at 20 weeks of gestation; they are not Pro-Life because life begins at conception. However, stopping abortions at 20 weeks of gestation is better than being Pro-Choice; we can work on abolishing abortion after this candidate is voted into office. Starting at halting abortions at 20 weeks gestation is a good start!

DIARY OF AN UNBORN BABY

Day 1: Fertilization: all human chromosomes are present, and a unique life begins.

Day 6: The embryo begins implanting in the uterus.

Day 22: The heart begins to beat with the child's own blood, often with a different blood type than the mother's.

Week 5: Eyes, legs, and hands begin to develop.

Week 6: Brain waves are detectable. The mouth and lips are present, and fingers are forming.

Week 7: Eyelids and toes form. The baby now has a distinct nose and is kicking and swimming.

Week 8: Every organ is in place; bones, fingerprints begin to form.

Weeks 9 & 10: Teeth begin to form, fingernails develop; baby can turn head and frown.

Week 17: Baby can have dream (REM) sleep.

Look how many human beings have died through abortions just here in the U.S.A. (somewhere around 58 million; and these are the ones who go to abortion clinics). Think of all the human beings that have been aborted from the woman taking birth control pills/ patches/ injections/IUD's or other abortifacient devices. The sperm and the egg can still come together but the uterus has been thinned out, giving the fertilizer egg (conception-the beginning of life) no place to implant and the human being is sloughed out of his or her mother's body. I think the great deceiver has had a lot of help from pharmaceutical companies trying to conceal information (the potential to kill conceived children, the effects on the bodies of women like blood clots, difficulties in trying to conceive children later after taking contraceptives and the correlation of cancers etc...). Now think of how many souls are in jeopardy of going to Hell for killing these conceived children (each aborted child had a mother and a father, plus the people who talked the woman into having the abortion like parent/s, boyfriend, husband, counselor, person who performed the abortion, person who assisted in the abortion act and whoever took the money). God loves all of his children, including those who had an abortion/s or led someone to have an abortion but you must repent for your actions. For spiritual healing please call Project Rachael or Rachael's Vineyard or a Catholic priest. For All Catholics know it is wrong to use any form of birth control (other than Natural Family Planning in a holy marriage and only for a good reason); it is condemned by the Catholic Church for good reason. Just look how the world has turned out, look at the errors that been spread throughout the world. Many Catholics are in the state of mortal sin for using contraceptives yet for some reason they have justified their thoughts/

actions and think this doesn't apply to them or their loved ones. They are mistaken if they think they can leave the Catholic Church, which teaches the TRUTH. TRUTH is TRUTH and does not change. You will still be held to the TRUTH. So, stay with the TRUTH in the Catholic Church and come up with an alternative that leads to light and a culture of life. You know what would really help our society/culture? To return to living a chaste life style prior to marriage. Chastity, chastity, chastity. Let's teach our children about the benefits of the virtue of chastity. We must repent for our mistakes and not pass them on to our children. Chastity, chastity, chastity is so much better than trying to pick up the pieces when your child suffers a broken heart after giving themselves completely to another and then finding out they were used; contracted a venereal disease (many different outcomes including sterility); pregnant from a hookup (no real relationship); pregnant but the father offers to pay for an abortion (a deep hurt to the mother); pregnant the very first time with someone who is not going to stick around and help them raise this baby the list is much longer. Living a chaste life style until in a committed relationship (holy matrimony Sacramental marriage) greatly increases the likelihood of a lasting relationship. Let's promote a culture of love and life long happiness with God at the center. There are many wounds to living a promiscuous life style (heterosexual or homosexual). Promiscuous meaning sex outside of married relationship of male and female (no fornication, no living together before marriage, no birth control (other than N.F.P.); chastity for your state in life. Come home to the Catholic Church and find ways to achieve what you really want...a loving, lasting relationship pleasing to God and support to help keep families strong.

You know, you have a choice as to what you're watching, reading, music you're listening to, sexual acts etc.... Divine Mercy is available to everyone and even more so for those who are in most need of it!

Sometimes, I wonder why God has not directly intervened more in these times of such brazen impiety (lack of reverence for God). One day while listening to a C.D. from LIGHTHOUSE CATHOLIC MEDIA titled: FATIMA Living the Message (Fr. Jason Brooks, L.C.), I received part of the answer. I recommend everyone to listen to the full C.D. for more information and better understanding of the message.

He stated that on October 13th 1884, Pope Leo the 13th at the foot of the altar, heard a conversation between God and satan; one voice kind and gentle and the other voice guttural and harsh. During the conversation God granted satan 75-100 years of more power over those who will hand themselves over to him (satan). Please refer to the C.D. for more information about this conversation.

Author Note: To me this means power over those who have at least one mortal sin. Remember mortal sin (unrepented) means your soul is dead. Also mortal sin (unrepented) means your father is satan.

I have heard of the 100 years of satan being granted more power a few times in my life (by my mother) and even on television (E.W.T.N.) by Mother Angelica (at least once) and by a Priest more recently on Women of Grace (E.W.T.N.) who made reference that some theologians think this 100 years in which satan was granted more power by God, started the same year as our Lady (the Virgin Mary; our Heavenly Mother and Queen of Heaven) appeared in Fatima Portugal to the 3 shepherd children in 1917. This means (if that is true) sometime in 2017 the 100 years will be over.

Pope Leo the 13th immediately following the conversation went directly to his office and composed the SAINT MICHAEL PRAYER, to be said after every low Mass.

PRAYER TO SAINT MICHAEL

St. Michael the Archangel, defend us in the day of Battle: be our safeguard against the wickedness and snares of the devil. May God rebuke him, we humbly pray, and do Thou, O Prince of the Heavenly Host, by the power of God, cast into hell, satan and all the other evil spirits, who prowl through the world, seeking the ruin of souls.

Sometimes I look forward to this time (when the 100 years is over) and hope and pray God acts swiftly to get our attention and help us to come back to God's Will; mainly because I feel sorry for the children/teenagers who have not been given the TRUTH by their elders (parents and grandparents). I plan to finish this book in the extraordinary Julilee Year of Mercy (Dec. 8th 2015-Nov. 20th 2016). This is only the 3rd or 4th extraordinary Jubilee year since Jesus died for our sins over 2000 years ago. I believe that I (at this time because every day is a battle for the soul) am in the state of grace. I have repented for all of my mortal sins (and venial sins); done my penances and have changed my ways and have a firm purpose of amendment to stay away from sin and for the most part don't have any desire to commit sins. Of course I still have much difficulty with patience in general and difficulty in patience with people who won't wake up to the TRUTH (which has never changed); I would like to Bishop slap these people to WAKE them UP (which is not charitable and I am not a Bishop and most likely wouldn't work). Also, television programs that God would approve of are difficult to find, and turning the multi-media devices off completely is challenging (easier with practice). So, you see I have much to work on. I go to confession monthly and might be going bi-monthly soon. You, see if you confess your mortal sins (ALL of them with true sorrow) and receive pardon; do your penance and are in the state of grace then you can go through the 'Holy Doors' designated in every diocese of the Catholic Church (in most countries) and focus on the mercy of God and say prayers for our pope (Pope Francis) and obtain the plenary indulgence. I understand this plenary indulgence (when in the state of grace) is to remove the stains of sins. Even after the soul has been given absolution the stain may still remain on the soul (meaning you still may go to Purgatory). The plenary indulgence (if I am correct) removes the stains. You still must go to confession with a Catholic Priest to be absolved of mortal sins.

Also, I am still paying into a healthcare plan through my employer that allows birth control in different forms and possibly abortion (I'm afraid to ask). I don't feel comfortable paying into this plan even though I myself am not using it for these purposes. If our government doesn't come up with a solution (like having 2 healthcare systems to choose: one for people who do not want birth control, abortions, or euthanasia on their plan at all. These 2 healthcare systems must be completely separate and not cross at any point. This is such a simple solution); then at some point Catholics and like minded people (people that are morally against birth control, abortion and euthanasia) will need to drop 'intrinsically evil' healthcare plans like a hot potato. No one wants to go without healthcare but our eternal souls are more important. I hope I'm not in the state of mortal sin for paying into my healthcare plan, knowing some of the collective monies go to immoral practices and procedures. Commonsense tells me this is wrong, so come on elected officials-DO YOUR JOB! We the people are relying on you! Someday you will be standing before God as will I.

One more thought: I wonder if when the 100 years that satan has been granted more power over those who have handed themselves over to him (by mortal sin) is over…will all these very hardened sinners be much easier to convert back to God's Will over theirs. This thought gives me GREAT HOPE!

★★

"Jesus Christ is the face of the Father's mercy." –Pope Francis   Year of Mercy

A Plenary Indulgence for The Jubilee Year of Mercy

"To experience and obtain the indulgence, the faithful are called to make a brief pilgrimage to the Holy Door, open in every Cathedral or in the churches designated by the Diocesan Bishop"…It is important that this moment be linked, first and foremost, to the Sacrament of Reconciliation and to the celebration of the Holy Eucharist with a reflection on mercy. It will be necessary to accompany these celebrations with the profession of faith and with prayer for me and for the intentions that I bear in my heart for the good of the Church and of the entire world. – Pope Francis"

INSTRUCTIONS

The Faithful wishing to obtain a plenary indulgence, either for themselves or for the soul of one who is deceased, asked to perform the following pious deed:

* ★ Be in the state of grace having gone to the Sacrament of Penance and confessed their sins;
* ★ Have the interior disposition of complete detachment from sin, even venial sin;
* ★ Receive the Holy Eucharist
* ★ Make a Profession of Faith
* ★ Pray for the intentions of the Pope

Notes

Ideally, one ought go to confession, receive Communion and perform the indulgence works all on the same day, but this is not always possible, therefore it is sufficient that these Sacraments and Prayers be carried out within several days (within 21 days) before or after entering through the Holy Door to obtain the indulgence.

The prayers for the Pope's intentions are left to the choice of the faithful, but an "Our Father", a "Hail Mary" and "Glory Be" are customary.

One Sacramental Confession suffices for several plenary indulgences, but a separate Holy Communion and a separate prayer for the Holy Father's intentions are required for each plenary indulgence.

The sick and the homebound may obtain the indulgence by prayerfully uniting their sufferings to the Redemptive Suffering of Christ and fulfilling the other conditions which they are able to perform.

Indulgences can always be applied either to oneself or to the souls of the deceased.

How often can I obtain the plenary indulgence: Once daily.

★the above information taken from a sheet of paper I picked up at the Holy Door in St. Petersburg Florida Cathedral of St. Jude the Apostle; 5815 5ᵗʰ Ave. North; St. Petersburg Florida 33710

★★★★★★★★★★★★★★★★★★★★★★★★★★★★★

I had gone to Sacramental Confession 14 days before passing through the Holy Doors, but everything else I did that day. I didn't read the above information on requirements until I got in my car to return home. I didn't know about the prayers for the Pope's intentions; so I got out of my car and went back in the Cathedral through the Holy Door and said the prayers for my beloved Pope Francis. In my defense, I do pray for Pope Francis (God's vicar on earth) every day as part of my morning routine.

I stated earlier that I might start going to Sacramental Confession (twice a month) because now I know about obtaining this plenary indulgence for the souls of the deceased. I did it for myself and now I want to do it as a spiritual work of mercy for others (Spiritual Work of Mercy-Pray for the Living and the Dead). I plan to obtain plenary indulgences for members of my family who are deceased and also for 2 deceased friends of my daughter and a deceased friend of my brother (who helped me move several times in college and I am still thankful for his help) and others during this extra ordinary Jubilee year (The Year of Mercy). I hope many other people will take advantage of this special time of mercy but remember the last day of this Year of Mercy is Nov. 20ᵗʰ 2016. I also plan to repeat the plenary indulgence requirements again before the end of Year of Mercy for myself to clean up any possible new stains. I don't know about you but I don't want to spend any more time in Purgatory than I have to. However if I make it to Purgatory I will be very happy to be there; because everyone in Purgatory eventually ends up in Heaven.

★★★★★★★★★★★★★★★★★★★★★★★★★★★★★

The Donavan's and McGolly's (including Sonny and his Mom) all decided on a movie. After the family friendly movie and popcorn; everyone spread throughout the flat house and soon were sound asleep. Molly found a place to keep the robin eggs warm, she was going to attempt to hatch them at home.

The next morning after breakfast, it was time to say farewell to their grandparents. Sonny, Mark and Mike played a song on their bagpipes which sounded pretty bad (except for Sonny who had two more years experience) but what did they except. Molly, Maryann and Miriam sang an Irish song 'My Bonnie lies over the ocean. My Bonnie lies over the sea. My Bonnie lies over the ocean...So bring back My Bonnie to me. Bring back, Bring back, Bring back my Bonnie to me, to me. Bring back, Bring back, Bring back my Bonnie to me'. The older girl cousins did a River Dance, while their brothers played their bagpipes and fiddles (sounded great)! For the finale, Aunt Rachael played her harp and sang like a nightingale. Aunt Rachael had the most musical talent of anyone in the whole family.

Grandpa McGolly concluded the farewell festivities by saying a prayer for protection for the whole family:

> St. Michael Prayer:
> Saint Michael the Archangel, defend us in battle, be our defense against the wickedness and snares of the devil; may God rebuke him, we humbly pray and do thou, O Prince of the heavenly host, by the power of God, thrust into hell Satan and all the evil spirits who prowl through the world seeking the ruin of souls. Amen.

Many hugs and kisses before Uncle Steve drove Grandma and Grandpa to the airport.

Uncle Steve returned home and told his wife Rachael, that her parents used this 'opportunity' in the car ride to airport to invite him to convert to the Catholic faith. Grandpa explained to Steve that the Catholic Church was founded by Jesus Christ Himself and His chosen apostles. Jesus and His chosen apostles set up the Catholic Church the way Jesus wanted it with the 7 sacraments to keep us close to Him. He said the Catholic Church was the only Christian religion for about 1500 years, before the break aways. Grandpa stated his business very plainly. He also said the Holy Bible was compiled by the Catholics guided by the Holy Spirit; and that the Catholic Bible has several more books than the Protestants. Grandpa didn't know why the books were removed by the Protestants. No other Christian religion can make the claim that their church was founded by Jesus Christ or that they put the Holy Bible together guided by the Holy Spirit. While Grandpa was stating his business by means of firm kindness, Grandma McGolly was silently praying the rosary; hoping her son-in-law would be open to conversion to the TRUTH in the Catholic faith. Grandpa stated that even the word Protestant means protest. What are the Protestants protesting against? The Catholic Church is the fullness of the Christian religion because it comes directly from the source, Jesus Christ Himself and His chosen apostles.

Grandpa continued to state his business; as Uncle Steve drove the car pretending not a word had been spoken "Therefore the Catholic religion is the truest most pure form of all the Christian religions. Some people might not like the TRUTH of the Catholic Church but it is the TRUTH and TRUTH does not change." Grandpa McGolly continued "Even if 100% of humans took a vote and told God He had to change to our way...God would not change. We are to be obedient to our Father who art in Heaven and the TRUTH is in the Catholic Church founded by Jesus Christ Himself. Priests are called to a higher calling and MUST obey the Will of God. TRUTH is in the Magisterium of the Catholic Church. Most Protestants and a great number of Catholics don't know the Bible was compiled by the Catholics over time guided by the Holy Spirit...not dropped out the sky. I think most Catholics do know this but for some reason don't seem to realize the importance. If they truly believed this they would never leave the Catholic Church. The Catholic Bible has more books than the Protestants. Why did the Protestants dispose of some of them? The secular world think that the Bishops and Cardinals and Pope of the Catholic Church can change doctrine like congress can make amendments to the constitution of the United States or the supreme court changing laws. The Catholic clergy all the way up to His vicar on earth (the Pope); answer to a higher authority, GOD! The word of God in the Holy Bible, traditions of the Catholic Church and the TRUTH cannot be changed. Doctrine does not change in the Catholic Church. Our Father in Heaven knows what we need and we must be obedient to God's Will. I've heard people say that if the first founders of the Protestant religions were to come back today and visit their churches, that they would not recognize them. Why? They made their changes, but did not foresee that the people that led their church after they died would in turn do the same thing...change things as they wanted...each new leader changing to their will or breaking away again and starting a new branch. Today there are over 2000 different Christian religions. Which one do you think is the truest most pure Christian religion, the one founded by Jesus Christ Himself and His chosen apostles and led by God's vicar on earth (the Pope) with the sacraments to keep us close to Him, or the break aways. Protestants have partial truth and if they live by the Commandments and the teachings of the Gospels, that is a great start; however they could get much closer to Jesus in Communion; taking the True Body and Blood of Jesus into their body (if in the state of grace). The Catholic faith has been around longer than the other Christian religions and has not changed doctrine. A Catholic cannot leave the Catholic faith for a Protestant faith because they would be going from the fullness of the Christian religion to partial truth. That is why it is a mortal sin for a Catholic to convert to another religion even in one of the Christian denominations. We pray and hope that our fallen away Catholic brothers and sisters will come back home where they belong. We also want our young to continue living the fullness of the faith and pass it on to their children."

★★★

Let nothing disturb you,
Let nothing frighten you,
All things pass away;
God never changes.
Patience obtains all things.
He who has God lacks nothing;
God alone suffices.

St. Teresa of Avila

★★★

Grandma McGolly sat quietly but in loving support of her husband. She was praying silently that her son-in-law whom she loved would accept her husband's words asking for conversion to the fullness of the faith (Catholic religion). She hoped he would embrace this 'opportunity' like Miriam and Maryann accepted her husband's teaching of St. Patrick's story. Her little granddaughters remembered their Grandpa's words when they were lost for hours at night in the woods while they were hunting for a leprechaun.

(Scripture Passage) (Matthew 18:1-4)

True Greatness

At that time the disciples came to Jesus, saying, "Who is the greatest in the kingdom of heaven?" And calling to him a child, he put him in the midst of them, and said, "Truly, I say to you, unless you turn and become like children, you will never enter the kingdom of heaven.

(Scripture Passage) (Mark 10:1-16)

Teaching about Divorce

And he left there and went to the region of Judea and beyond the Jordan, and crowds gathered to him again; and again, as his custom was, he taught them.

And Pharisees came up and in order to test him asked, "Is it lawful for a man to divorce his wife?" He answered them, "What did Moses command you?" They said, "Moses allowed a man to write a certificate of divorce, and to put her away." But Jesus said to them, "For your hardness of heart he wrote you this commandment. But from the beginning of creation, 'God made them male and female.' 'For this reason a man shall leave his father and mother and be joined to his wife, and the two shall become one.' So they are no longer two but one. What therefore God has joined together, let not man put asunder."

And in the house the disciples asked him again about this matter. And he said to them, "Whoever divorces his wife and marries another, commits adultery against her; and if she divorces her husband and marries another, she commits adultery."

Jesus Blesses Little Children

And they were bringing children to him, that he might touch them; and the disciples rebuked them. But when Jesus saw it he was indignant, and said to them, "Let the children come to me, do not hinder them; for to such belongs the kingdom of God. Truly, I say to you, whoever does not receive the kingdom of God like a child shall not enter it." And he took them in his arms and blessed them, laying his hands upon them.

★★★★★★★★★★★★★★★★★★★★★★★★★★★★★★★★★★★★

Grandma knew Steve didn't go to church at all and that conversion would be a big step for him. On the other hand, he had been watching his wife and children and the entire McGolly family for years live their faith in good times and in bad...unwavering faith. When Mr. and Mrs. McGolly's daughter Rachael married Steve, he was a passive Protestant. They were married outside the Catholic Church and Rachael had to get dispensation (approval from the Catholic Church) in other words pastoral counseling and agreement to let Rachael raise the fruitful additions to their family in the Catholic religion. Steve signed the form but left all spiritual teaching up the Rachael. He also attended with Rachael all meetings for preparation for marriage. So Steve never interfered with his wife raising the children in the Catholic faith but he rarely helped. He did attend each child's Baptism ceremonies and occasionally picked them up after Catechism classes...but only if he was going to take them to baseball practice or something he was interested in.

Grandma asked St. Therese of the Child Jesus (also known as the Little Flower) to intercede on her behalf to ask Jesus for Steve's conversion to Catholic faith.

NOVENA ROSE PRAYER

O Little Therese of the Child Jesus, please pick for me a rose from the heavenly gardens and send it to me as a message of love.

O Little Flower of Jesus, ask God today to grant the favors I now place with confidence in your hands... (mention specific requests)

St. Therese, help me to always believe as you did, in God's great love for me, so that I might imitate your "Little Way" each day. Amen.

Rachael never pushed for her husband to convert. She simply lived her faith everyday in good times and in bad times...unwavering (well maybe a little wavering but always ended up back to her deep faith). One of her favorite saints was St. Rita who was married to man who did not live a Christian lifestyle and through many years of tribulations and some joys, he eventually converted. However there were many more tribulations for St. Rita to face even after his conversion (like her husband's death (killed by a rivaling family), the kidnap of her children to be raised by her husband's side of the family (without her), her twin sons death (plague), depression and becoming a beggar eventually bringing the city together after a long raging war between head families, in her later years she had a wound in the middle of her forehead (with a terrible odor). And you thought you had problems... that's why St. Rita is one of the super saints.

Rachael prayed for St. Rita to intercede on her behalf to God several times throughout their marriage. For the first four years of their marriage they were not blessed with children. Steve was very cooperative with learning how to use Natural Family Planning to help them conceive children. Through N.F.P. the couple can determine the woman's fertile period and the best time to embrace the marital act if children are desired. Of course they also knew there was a possibility that they would be unable to have children naturally and were considering adoption or foster parenting of older children. They knew in-vitro fertilization, artificial insemination and surrogate motherhood was out of the question because these ways of conception are unnatural and condemned by the Catholic Church. Now they have a house full of children and a couple of dogs...and they were both very thankful for their fruitful additions to their family (some adopted and some biological and all loved).

Back to the car ride to the airport: Steve got an ear full during that drive to the airport; he had a lot of father-in-law advice to digest. Steve was pretty much trapped in that car and no matter how fast he drove he had to listen to unasked for advice on a subject he didn't feel was appropriate. He was surprised after all these years of him taking his in-laws to the airport and never a single word about conversion...why now? However this was his father-in-law whom he did respect, partially because he was a devout practicing Catholic his entire life. They arrived at the airport and stopped at the drop off area. Steve got out of the car to unload the luggage and bid his in-laws good bye. He did not make any reference to the words spoken by his father-in-law; it was like the conversation never happened. Grandpa McGolly was at the check in counter with their luggage. Steve leaned over to give his mother-in-law one last obligatory hug. She was standing a foot in front of him, looking him firmly straight in the eyes and then stated her business "Steve, the children are getting older and the ways of the world will be tempting them like never before. The world is portraying evil as good and then not allowing people to stand up for their religious beliefs. Rachael has been teaching the faith to the children pretty much on her own until now. She needs your help. Not only does she need your help but you need God's help. Look around at the world, our own government in Ireland and here in the United States of America. We all need God's help and people like you and me need to join forces to promote the Will of God. I never would have believed a pro-dominantly Christian nation like Ireland (Catholic and Protestant) would ever legalize abortion and same sex marriage, but they have. Look at your own country, the United States of America has legalized: no fault divorce, birth control, abortion, euthanasia (in some states) and now same sex marriage. Time and time again in both of our countries Christians are not standing up for Christian values and OUR CHILDREN ARE SUFFERING. If the greatness of a nation is measured by how it treats its young, its old and its marginalized; then the United States is not the greatest nation anymore. It might even be dead last if it continues on its current path. We Christians and like minded peoples need to reclaim our nations so our children can have the freedom to practice our faith in peace. Meaning not just inside the churches but where we work, go to school, shop, health insurance which will not require us to go against our beliefs (meaning no birth control other than N.F.P., no abortion, no euthanasia, no same sex marriage, no paying into a health care system that supports any of these practices). We love you and want the best for our children and grandchildren; which is someday for all of us to be in Heaven together. How are we going to get our children and grandchildren to Heaven when our governments are forcing us to go against our faith and as a result promote immorality and a culture of death. And I'm talking about death of our souls (eternal damnation) from accepting mortal sin as the norm. As parents, you only get a certain amount of time to influence your children; then they grow up and are on their own. You have a few more years before the older ones leave the nest, stretch their wings and fly away. Time is running short while they're still in your house. Having a loving, strong father who puts God first is a powerful influence for a child, and will hopefully continue to influence their decisions their whole life. We're not always going to be here and having a strong spiritual foundation is what they will need to carry on in this life and reach Heaven someday. Steve, you are the head of your household. Make your domestic church in your household a united one. Give your children the best chance they have to stand against the forces of evil and live 'Godly' lives. Become a Catholic. Wake up to the war we are fighting and get on the right side. Strengthen your children with what really matters before that time is up! We want you to feel invited (EVERYONE IS INVITED) to come into full communion with the Catholic Church. We love you Steve." Grandpa arrived at Grandma's side and the 'evangelizers' both walked inside of the airport.

★★★

The first evangelization was when Jesus Christ became the Word Incarnate and lived amongst us. Jesus Christ is the Way, the Truth and the Life. The fullness of the Christian faith is in the Catholic Church. You must take classes to learn about the Catholic faith and accept ALL of the teachings before becoming a confirmed Catholic in the sacrament of Confirmation when you become a soldier of Christ. Jesus Christ came for everyone so EVERYONE IS INVITED TO BECOME A CATHOLIC. Jesus came for all. He is our Savior. Jesus died on the cross for our sins but we must ask for forgiveness with true sorrow in order to receive pardon for our sins. R.C.I.A. classes for adults, catechism classes for children to learn about the Catholic faith before first Holy Communion (including confession/reconciliation). All Catholics need to be in the state of grace according to the Catholic teaching before taking the TRUE Body and Blood of Jesus Christ into their bodies in Holy Communion (otherwise you are committing another sin). If you are in the state of mortal sin (on one thing or more) you enter the church with some (one or more) mortal sins and leave with more if you took the TRUE Body and/ or Blood into your body while in mortal sin (because you are forcing Jesus to be in a body dominated by satan). So for Heaven sake GO TO CONFESSION! Jesus is waiting for you with love. Jesus is patient, but at some point your time will be up. Jesus loves you. Jesus loves you so much He died for you.

★★★★★★★★★★★★★★★★★★★★★★★★★★★★★★★★★★★★

Steve drove back home without turning on the radio. Once home he told his wife Rachael about her parents words to him on the way to the airport. Steve looked at his wife and boldly with great confidence said "I feel like I'm filled with the Holy Spirit and I want to give my family the best chance to live their lives according to God's Will. When my 8 year old son catches a crucifix when fishing and my in-laws try to convert me the same weekend and its Easter weekend...maybe God is trying to tell me something". Steve asked Rachael to help get R.C.I.A information so he can begin the process to become a Catholic who fully lives his faith. He also told her, he loves her but wanted a man in the Catholic Church to be his sponsor. He was going to ask Kevin McFrugal to be his sponsor. Rachael picked up the phone and had Kevin and her husband talk immediately before the Holy Spirit could get away.

Clare and Sonny were still at the Donavan's flat house when Steve stated his intentions to become a Catholic. Clare and Sonny took a side trip on the way home to McGolly Hill to give the good news of Steve's enlightenment. Molly's parents were stunned but very happy. Mr. McGolly led a Divine Mercy chaplet for Steve's soul and intentions to strengthen his family spiritually. Maureen McGolly with heartfelt emotion stated "I'm so happy for Steve and Rachael and their family. With the exception of the first Easter Sunday when Jesus rose from the dead and set up the sacrament of Reconcilation for us with his chosen apostles; this is my favorite Easter."

That night Molly's parents left their bedroom window slightly open to feel the breeze. As they were lying in bed almost asleep, the most beautiful musical notes from nature filled their hearts with joy! A nightingale bird resting high on top of a tree serenaded them for almost half an hour before flying off in the night air. So the month of March ended on a beautiful note in the McGolly house.

MARCH in review: (Repent, Recycle, Reduce, Reuse and Rejoice)

* Shared fresh hot potatoes cooked outdoors in a dirt pit (Reduced electricity).
* Mike and Mark made First Holy Communion and Confession (Repent and Rejoice).
* First family car 'Nellie' melted down and reformed into metal posts and beams to fortify new master bedroom (for storm shelter) in log cabin lodge expansion (Recycle and Reuse).
* Mike and Mark made wooden crosses from scrapes of wood for the Stations of the Cross (Recycle, Reuse and Repent).
* School roof, old athletic shoes and old tires from the community used to make new flat tops for the playground (Recycle and Reuse)
* Molly shined the windows in her school classroom with homemade environmentally safe cleanser (Reduced environmentally unsafe cleanser).
* Everyone in the McGolly and McFrugal and Donavan families (except for Uncle Steve and the children not old enough to go to confession) went to confession during Lent prior to Easter Sunday (Repent). Next year Uncle Steve will too! (Repent and Rejoice!)
* Maryann and Miriam found safe and unharmed (Rejoice).
* Sonny's friend in prison prayed the Divine Mercy Chaplet for the little lost twin girls (Repent).

March was a very spiritually enlightening month and a green month.
Now it's time to plan the green strategy for April.
This year went from the last day of March being Easter Sunday to April 1st April Fool's Day
Molly's mother always woke up her children on April Fool's Day with her silly poem.

Mom's Silly Springtime Poem
Spring has Sprung,
The Grass has Ris,
I Wonder where the Flowers Is?!

April 1st a day for fools.
Off to school went Mark, Mike and Molly,
for a day full of fun and folly!
Forget all logic, forgot all the rules.
Someone, somehow without getting caught,
moved the teacher's desk from its original spot.
It was placed in the middle of the room
and the student's desks surrounded it like a great big cocoon.
Molly's teacher, Miss Bailey entered, smiled and was not upset.

She must have gone out last evening with Uncle Ivan on a date.

The principal stated during morning announcements:

Whoever put Vaseline on the toilet seats in the teacher's lounge this morning,

would be to detention until the last day of school of their 12th year and this was not a warning!

A reward was offered to anyone with information leading to the conviction of the slippery culprit.

The reward was to equal the punishment.

Before the day was over, Mike and Mark confessed:

One did the deed and the other was the lookout.

Turning themselves in was a stroke of genius; at least from their perspective.

If the reward equaled the punishment,

they reasoned that they got away with it!

Until they saw Mr. McGolly (Dad) waiting for them in the principal's office when school let out.

During this April Fools Day morning announcements a commotion stirred that required the Principal's full attention.

When he returned the principal had the following addition:

"Come to claim your pet whoever released a monkey in the teacher's lounge,

There aren't too many places you can get a monkey in this town;

we will be able to track you down."

Again the overhead announcements had an unplanned pause.

The principal returned and cleared his throat; then spoke through clenched jaws

"Whoever released the piglets in the cafeteria please come to my office now.

Lunches will be served in your classrooms with a menu change; peanut butter and jelly sandwiches, bananas and cartoons of milk from a cow."

(Brief pause) He continued "Lord I hope no one brought a cow!

If no one claims the monkey or the piglets,

we will auction them at the Earth Day School Wide Garage Sale on April 22nd.

There will be no second recess until these pranksters have been identified."

Then a list of the usual suspects were to report to the principal's office at once to be interrogated!

Turns out Mike and Mark were guilty of the piglet invasion, no big surprise there.

But the officials were unable to find the monkey's partner in crime; where was he or she...where?!

The principal, vice principal, janitor, and chief of police needed to expand their search;

which ended when they discovered the monks had a monkey at the Catholic Church.

They were unable to contact anyone at the Monastery because the monks were on a Divine Mercy mission.

The investigators needed to know if they took their monkey or did it escape.

Some good pranks were underway that strange day, full of odd happenings and fun.

When the janitor opened his locker located in his large usually locked supply closet; an avalanche of his favorite candy came falling from above. Someone put a brown grocery bag full of butterscotch hard candies above his locker, arranged to release the candies when the door was swung.

How did they get into his closet? Was it time to put in a stronger lock?

But he liked his candies so he decided well...maybe not.

The janitor didn't even report this intrusion,

after all he had a pretty good idea who the candy was from!

Sonny and Molly were good kids and he loved each one.

The lunchroom ladies also had treats drop down when they opened the cabinets that morning.

How did the trickster get in?

The doors and windows to that part of the kitchen were locked.

The piglets could have been released after the doors to the cafeteria were unlocked.

Who could have filled all those brown paper bags without getting caught?

They had a good idea as to who...the question was when and how did they do it?!

This remained a mystery because Molly and Sonny even under pressure didn't crack.

The secret: Do it when the last cafeteria lady left the kitchen BEFORE Spring break.

The P.T.A. had one final meeting about the roof recycling/playground turf project the last evening before Spring break.

Molly and Sonny used this opportunity to set up the brown grocery bag surprises for the janitor and the cafeteria ladies; for all their help throughout the year.

No one paid any attention to them; not their parents, teachers or the principal.

Everyone had one thing on their minds: SPRING BREAK, yea NO SCHOOL!

While Molly and Sonny put into play their April Fool's Day pranks...now who's the FOOL?

That was one April Fool's Day mystery solved but who brought a monkey to school?

Lunch was delivered to each classroom and the smell of bananas and peanut butter drifted into the hall.

The principal made an announcement: "Teachers calmly close the doors to your rooms, the monkey is in the hall."

They could hear the monkey howling

as it was swinging from whatever was hanging down from the ceiling.

Soon one of the monks showed up with a banana for his pet monkey named 'Monk'.

All that 'Monk' wanted was a banana and a shoulder to sit.

Right before the school bell rang to go home, the principal made an announcement:

"Sonny McGolly report immediately to my office."

It seems that Sonny made arrangements to take care of the Monks monkey for a few days, starting early that very morning while they went on a Divine Mercy mission.

Sonny's mom knew he was taking the monkey to school but thought he had the teacher's permission.

(Luck of the Irish) The monk looked at Sonny and said "It's a good thing for you that I'm practicing divine mercy...The Spiritual Work of Mercy: 'Pray for the Living and the Dead'; I'm covering both scenarios."

Sonny's mother appeared to be in shock "Why did...how...why...this isn't a jungle you know!"

Uncle Gerald (Molly's dad) was sitting next to Mike and Mark "All of you boys are in a lot of trouble".

The monk looked at Mike and Mark "See you two boys at Monk Camp this summer. I think we still have space, the chances are probable."

"What's Monk Camp?" asked Mike with a serious look on his face.

"Oh, you'll spend about 3 ½ to 4 hours in prayer every day with manual labor and eat gruel. You'll love it, it's good for the soul" said the monk with Monk on his shoulder. Mark looked like his face had just been sprayed with mace.

"Will the monkey be there?" injected Mark with a boom!

"Yes he will" smiled the monk as he and the monkey 'Monk' left the room.

Sonny was spared Monk Camp because it just happened to fall at the same time a Guitar Camp; his Mom didn't want him to miss this week long music lesson.

However the joke around the McGolly clan was that the monkey 'Monk' had a restraining order against Sonny and he couldn't be within 200 yards of the monkey at any time; he already had enough to bring up at his next confession.

Normally under these conditions Mike and Mark would have worked for a couple of weeks doing barn duty.

Mr. McGolly decided with the log cabin lodge under construction;

he would put the boys to manual labor digging geothermal walls for their just rehabilitation.

Uncle Gerald taught Sonny how to maneuver the leaf blower; Sonny was part of Mr. McGolly's chain gang.

Sonny would clear the ground before Mark and Mike dug the moat that surrounded the log cabin lodge.

Mr. McGolly put in wind powered roof monitors that removed hot air from the attic.

Roof monitors and geothermal wells together should cool the lodge pretty such automatic.

The backup plan was solar panels on the roof;

facing the correct direction for optimal use.

The installation of geothermal wells would allow the lodge to access the free, clean energy from the ground to heat and cool the new and improved home.

Dad didn't come right out and say it, but Mike, Mark and Sonny couldn't have misbehaved at a better moment.

For their ages and weight, Mike and Mark were good strong workers and Sonny was always good with his hands; they got the job done right.

Until Mom yelled out "Hey warden, it's a school night."

Back to the happenings earlier that day at school on April Fool's Day:

Sonny got caught for his April fool's day prank.

Mike and Mark got caught for their April fool's day prank.

Molly thought she got away with re-arranging her class furniture until the teacher said something that made her heart 'sank'.

Miss Kimberly Bailey gave the class a new assignment written on the dry eraser board.

To make up a story using their imagination, where they are the tall tale, super hero or legend.

Then she politely thanked the class for rearranging the room;

and added "This assignment is due tomorrow at noon."

They were allowed to use props and/or costumes to embellish their character's plot;

they must present their stories in front of the class that she taught.

The class waited for her to say "April Fools" but she did not.

Homework on April Fools! Maybe it's not good to play a trick on the teacher...not a good thought.

Molly hoped her classmates would not put 2 and 2 together;

If Mark and Mike arrived early enough to play their pranks before the arrival of the teachers;

then Molly would also have had time to rearrange the desks.

She would be blamed for the homework due the next day... she would be labeled a villain or a pest!

The last bell rang and Molly was eager to depart with her backpack!

Handsome Joe put his foot out and stopped Molly in her tracks.

He calmed stated "Hey Red, noticed this morning you were here early and now you seem to be in a big hurry."

Molly straightened her stance and her glasses and pronounced "I must get home. I have a paper to write."

Handsome Joe concluded "Yeah, thanks for that."

Then he moved his foot and out the door she literally ran.

One more moment and she could have been in Dad's chain gang.

April Fool's Day was suppose to be for fun and folly,

who imposed all these restrictions by golly!

Molly arrived home at the top of the hill and went straight to her room.

She could not help feed the babies, play with the younger twins or do dishes.

Instead she had to come up with a character; Hero or Villian...what ever her wishes!

As she lay there on her bed pondering her dilemma;

she reflected on the whole year while gazing out the window.

First she checked on the robin eggs to see if they hatched yet,

but all three eggs were whole and the shells unbroken still lying in the nest.

Molly tried teaching her fellow classmates to be green conscious,

to live kindly with the earth's resources.

She gave thoughtful gifts, recycled and fresh produce from the earth.

She rode her bike to conserve fossil fuels,

while the others rode in motorized vehicles.

Molly tried compromising her principles;

'If you can't beat them, join them' as the saying goes.

That just means you've failed, brain washed down to their level,

going with the flow even when you can hear the waterfall below.

Let's step back and think:

What would be lost if she gave in and let them win?

What would happen to the beautiful earth if the humans won't recycle, reuse or conserve?

The water will no longer be drinkable,

the air will stink and be unbreathable,

     unhealthy and probably seeable?!

Who wants to see the polluted air?

It would not be pretty and you couldn't see far.

No one would be able to see a rainbow or a harvest moon at night.

If it gets worse we would lose the sunlight.

You wouldn't even know if it was day or night!

Without the sunlight there would be no more flowers;

no fruits, no vegetables except possibly the ones that grow underground like carrots and potatoes.

(Luck of the Irish) Everyone in the McGolly clan loved carrots and potatoes,

so I guess my family would survive;

but we'll miss cabbage and corned beef and other flavors we have become accustomed to and like.

Life will not be rosy without the roses

or clean water to take a refreshing dip or just to sip.

We won't be able to see a sunset or a sunrise.

Without anything to see, will we lose the use of our eyes?

Will we all be hungry, thristy, sad and cold?

There might not be anything left when we grow old.

So she decided not to give up!

There is too much at stake here so she revived her passion.

Patience is a virtue, which she possessed all year.

Molly felt she had done good work by laying out a good foundation;

but now she was full of zeal and passion

for the earth she loved so dear.

Tomorrow she will take no prisoners.

Every man, woman and child would hear:

How we must take care of Mother Nature by her rules;

for if we continue doing things our way...

who knows... what's easiest at the moment just might be leading us to digging our own graves.

     She tried being loving, generous and kind.

     Led by good example all year, every year she was alive.

     Tried things their way but felt wrong inside.

     Prayed, loved them anyway and even cried.

     Tomorrow she was going to give the performance of her life!

     She was going to pretend to be MOTHER NATURE COME ALIVE!

Before Molly fell asleep she thanked God for her mother and father.

Her parents taught her well and she was glad to be their daughter.

She also thanked God for her best friend Sonny;

who she could always count on to make her laugh he was so funny!

Sonny (her very best friend), wheeled himself to school each day in his wheelchair.

No waste of gas and he was getting stronger.

Molly and Sonny communicated by homing pigeon or St. Bernard dog collar;

not using electricity by cellphone or computer.

Sonny wasn't just the founder, he was the President of the Recycled Clothing Store

located in the school basement.

He recycled out grown clothing and saved money for each client.

The sign over the store read:

>   If you want something bigger to wear
>
>   or if you've outgrown your clothes;
>
>   Then step through these doors
>
>   and swap for a fitted shirt and a pair of pants to your toes.
>
>   Come on in We're Your Friend

Molly realized she wasn't alone, Sonny her best friend was earth friendly too.

They were like two peas in a pod, green all the way!

Molly had gone from tears to a smile.

She felt good inside and had a clear conscience.

It was the right thing to do and tomorrow was her big chance.

For with Sonny, they would become the dynamic duo.

Sonny's Recycled Clothing Center located in the school basement

and his mother's P.T.A. School Wide Garage Sale Event, coming up April 22nd;

coupled together with Molly (AKA Mother Nature)...

They will take the school by surprise

and really open up their eyes!

It takes effort, a change always does,

start somewhere, make a plan and build on it as you go.

Everything you say, everything you do matters.

It matters yesterday, today and when you're a blue haired grandparent.

Even if everything good you do your whole life is washed away in a day;

that's okay.

It was good while it lasted and also resonated with others,

then could spread like a ripple in the waters.

Of course people are going to think what they think...

but that doesn't mean to hold back the truth.

The truth is that their actions today have consequences for tomorrow.

>   So be a good scholar
>
>   Be wise with your choices
>
>   Learn from your mistakes
>
>   Be kind to one another
>
>   AND TAKE CARE OF THE EARTH

It's best to deliver this kind of news with charity, and not every time they see you.

However today Molly was going to try something new;

she was going to get up on her soap box and give it to them straight,

not hold back any punches.

Molly's story would be about Mother Nature.

She decided her version of the Mother Nature would reap havic on the people who didn't do their part in taking care of the earth.

Oh what the heck!

She hadn't tried the scare tactic yet.

Nothing ventured, nothing gained.

Let the games begin.

She had less than 24 hours to invent a larger than life myth of pure fiction.

No problem, Molly made up bedtime stories almost every night;

to get Maryann and Miriam to stop talking and not fight.

Molly tossed and turned while in bed;

should she invent a superhero or villain instead?

Today she played a prank and the whole class got homework and it was all her fault!

For pete sakes it was an April's Fools,

wasn't she allowed to break a few rules?

It wasn't her fault nobody in the entire school had a sense of humor!

with the exception of Sonny (her best friend) and Mike and Mark (her twin brothers).

Hero or Villian? Hero or Villian?

as she lay there pondering her dilemma.

Molly arrived at school the next day and saw all around the room props glore.

No one in the class seemed to care about the arrangement of the furniture anymore;

especially since the desks were back in the original order.

Thanks to Handsome Joe, Molly's new knight in shining armor.

For he knew her secret and stayed after school and moved the desks to help her.

The first half of the day was regular school work...boring;

math, English, geography and last but not least spelling.

Then lunch and SHOW TIME!!!

Sonny raised his hand and announced that April 22nd was the Earth Day Event.

He reminded everyone to bring items to be sold at the giant garage sale tent.

The money raised would go for a very good cause,

to pay for the recycled playground turfs and money left over for another good cause however he didn't know what that cause was?!

The school wide garage sale will be held on the teachers parking lot,

allowing the kids to continue to play on the new flat tops.

Theme: REDUCE, REUSE and RECYCLE

EARTH DAY GARAGE SALE

That concluded Sonny's announcement, time to put on his costume for his tale.

While the class was at lunch more props arrived; strange things were all around the room.

These props were elaborate, there was even an Egyptian type coffin for a tomb.

All Molly had was an old floral bed sheet (she wore like a toga), fish net with a couple of starfish dangling and a fresh green ivy to wrap around the crown of her head.

A little birdie came to school with her but it left before lunch;

which was too bad because it would have helped her costume a bunch.

The students prepared for their performance.

Molly briefly wondered if Handsome Joe would be in shining armor as her Knight.

Instead he put on a white lab coat and his character Doctor Wonderful, cured almost everything including cancer.

He did not wear glasses because he also cured eyesight.

The only aliment he didn't cure was too much pride.

Guess it's hard to be humble, when you're Doctor Wonderful!

He called his character Doctor Do Good,

but the girls changed the name because he was such a stud!

The other boys were dragon slayers, kings, or mutant beast.

One was a car that could fly and talk.

Ralph was a super hero made of rocks.

No surprise the divas were Queens and Princesses.

Candy was princess of Candy Land, she handed out candy.

Cleopatra was an Egyptian Princess, she brought a mummy.

Molly wondered 'Where does one get a mummy on such short notice?' Oh well, on with the show.

Dolly, one the divas in the trio was a singing superstar who could tap dance too, she sounded great from her vocal cords to her feet...Bravo!

Sonny could transform into any animal for any situation in his story;

as the animals changed he had a prop, from the most gentle animal to the most gory.

His hat of tricks consisted of a lion's mane, bunny ears, dog mask, whale sounds, skunk atomizer spray, foxtail then he threw out a rubber snake.

Sonny did this just to create an effect... and it worked great.

The boys laughed and the girls screamed!

(Luck of the Irish): The snake was fake.

He called his character Animal Transformer and his pet dog Ollie was his side kick.

Sonny's opening line "I'm more than a dog and pony show" and his closing line "Ladies and Gentlemen, I hear the call of the wild, I must go" and he pretended to clop away like a horse by cupping his hands and hitting them against his cheeks. Since he couldn't actually gallop off like a horse due to his handicap, he improvised which made everybody laugh and clap. His character was a big hit!

Molly's turn was next.

She put on her floral bed sheet like a toga,

then threw the fishnet with starfish over her shoulder.

She wore the fresh green ivy vine inter-twinded like a wreath around her head.

Molly was ready for the performance of a lifetime, to knock them dead.

She took out a perfume atomizer and sprayed a floral scent to create an atmosphere of the great outdoors effect.

The kids with asthma had to move back or their lungs would react.

Molly's story was vivid and unique,

she wrote it in first person then she began to speak.

"I am Mother Nature and I know you all! By the way you treat the earth...

the animals, plants, water, land and air.

I know who cares for the earth and who does not care.

Rabbits, robins, chickens, ducks, alligators, elephants, butterflies;

geekos, whales, dolphins, cats, dogs, giraffes, zebras, turtles and owls so wise.

Canaries that sing, love birds that love, bees that buzz and pelicans that fish;

every one of you must take care of the creatures of this earth, that is my most earnest wish.

By taking care of the earth you're taking care of yourselves and the human species.

If you like eating healthy varieties of fruits and vegetables like carrots, mangos and my delicious green peas;

then stop using so many pesticides to grow these plants or it may cause your bodies to be diseased.

Instead use citronella plants or other natural means to keep insects away and help the plants thrive.

Taking care of the plants and animals will help all of us feel better and survive.

Now, let's talk about the animals from the gorillas that growl to the kittens that meow,

pink flamingoes, bluebirds, parrots in my jungles and all the colors that dazzle and WOW!,

to the spots on my leopards, stripes on tigers and zebras and patterns on my beautiful butterflies wings;

be good to the gifts of nature and all living things.

You may use what you need but don't get too greedy;

if you do the earth will change from having plenty to go around, to becoming very needy.

Use the gifts of wood from the trees to build your homes and to keep warm.

Replace these trees and protect the land that they grow,

for using and not replacing will lead to great sorrow.

Look at the rings on the cross section of wood and you will see how many years that tree received the nourishment from the soil and sunlight from the Sun.

Then take that piece of the tree and start a fire, and all the years of sunlight stored in that wood will be released for your warmth and provide much needed light.

We should all be thankful for all the gifts of nature... be stewards of the earth and treat it right.

What do you do with that plastic jug or aluminum can after you have consumed the beverage of choice?

Do you recycle the materials or throw it away to end up in a landfill destroying the land and wasting the resource.

We can all do better can't we?! Mother Nature had a big smile and her hands high in the air.

All we have to do is change our ways and then we will all have reason to rejoice!

Let me tell you a story. There once lived a little girl who thought only of herself. She turned every light on in the house. Television and computer on 24/7. Most of the time didn't even close the refrigerator door or the oven. She air conditioned the whole outside and everywhere she went had a limousine ride. I, Mother Nature, let her know exactly where she stood on Earth Day. April 22nd is Judgment Day of the green variety. Lightening zapped this girl's house and blew out the circuit breaker and the backup generator. No lights, no television, no computer, no air conditioning and no electricity for the refrigerator. She was hot, hungry and in the dark. The limousine was out of gas, which did not matter because the car was in the garage and without electricity the garage door opener would not budge. So the little girl started to walk to school but she got lost; for she was always looking at the cell phone when being driven around by the limo driver. She walked North, South, East and West, up a mountain, over a bridge and in a big circle. Finally when she sat down on a rock; the rock asked her 'Have you used every resource and are completely drained?' The little girl answered 'Yes' with all her strength that remained. The rock 'Now you know how the earth feels'. She looked up in the sky and saw giant vultures circling around in the air. Were they getting ready to grab her by the shoulders with their claws and carry her off somewhere? If so she needed to do something to prepare! She trembled wondering if they take her even further away and drop her in the ocean. She dived into a giant groundhog tunnel in one swift motion. It was dark, damp and dirt surrounded her on all sides. Crawling through the underground maze, not knowing which way to go; she crawled for hours before she saw light. When she popped her head above ground she saw a terrible sight! In front of her was the (junkyard) land fill. It was full of stuff that could be recycled and had a very stinky smell. She saw stuff that she would want, minus the odor. One man's trash is another man's treasure. The little girl vowed then and there to change her ways. I, 'Mother Nature' will be watching her like a vulture with claws to see if she really does! If this little girl who has been given another chance, returns once again to her bad habits; maybe I'll send a couple of black crows to pluck her eyes out. Don't think I won't, I do not give idol threats. I love all the creatures, everyone is my pet. I love all humans too, but they seem to be the ones causing all the problems. They are the stewards of the earth and need to step up to the plate...we need a home run!"

Some of the birds outside were flying to the window sills.

Molly played along while the birds twitted; some softly and others with high shrills.

"If you're going to tweet don't waste energy on your cell phone.

Turn off your phone and tweet like a bird, instead of using your fingers use your throat in song.

Soon others will join you and the choir will be heard;

make sure what is being sung is in harmony with nature and not what currently is wrong.

Natural conception to natural death.

Nature continually tries to correct itself.

However if we keep blocking nature from correcting itself and don't use natural resources wisely;

then at some point we will run out of materials, clean water and clean air

and eventually it will be too much for our bodies to bare.

The plants, animals and waterways need us to provide also for their care.

If you continue to harm the earth by your selfishness by polluting my clean pure water in the rivers and lakes;

you will not have clean water to wash clothes, clean your houses, for recreation or even to drink.

You will only have polluted water for our bodies to sink.

You all will have no one to blame but yourselves for of 'free will' you have chosen your path.

Change now while there is still some time and you will not have to face my WRATH.

This is a true story, mark my words."

> Molly's tone changed. This was a surprise to hear Molly speak like this. She was usually so nice and friendly no matter what others would do or say about her. Molly brought them all gifts, not just a select few throughout the year...apples, apple pie, pumpkin pie, bird houses and homemade Christmas gifts (personalized) and a live bunny rabbit for the teacher and homemade valentines and baked potatoes for March. She always had a smile and talked to everyone charitably even if they didn't want to hear what she had to say. She loves birds, people, rabbits and worms.
>
> Today what she said shocked them; they sat up straight in their chairs, opened their eyes and began to squirm.
>
> Under the disguise of Mother Nature, she seems to be accusing them of destroying the earth and bringing every living being...
>
> to the point of extinction.

You wouldn't think that being this direct, out spoken, to the point of just plain rude would work... but it did! Later that day the whole school was a buzz about the class scolding. Everyone talked about Molly's rendition of Mother Nature. Molly became popular but maybe not in a good way. Telling people what you really think is not politically correct. She could be spending the rest of her life paying for her comments: like; Of free will you are destroying the earth to the point of extinction. Those are strong words no matter what clothes you are wearing.

Being a leader is not easy or comfortable. Molly decided that doing the right thing is worth the regrets; if in the long run you help people live healthier happier lives and their eternal souls go to Heaven, when previously they were headed in the wrong direction. We are all to treat our bodies as temples of the Holy Spirit and to be stewards of the earth. This means we are to take care of ourselves and the plants, animals, land, air and water ways. Molly's faith in God and her school life were blended together.

Believing in God (Father/Son/Holy Spirit) and taking care of the earth go hand in hand.

Who do you think created the earth and all this land?!

Molly as Mother Nature stood perfectly still and joyfully submitted a question to the stewards of the earth "Have you seen my forests, savannahs, prairies, oceans and plateaus?

Or my ice burgs, natural springs, canyons and volcanoes?

What about my beautiful waterfalls, rivers, brooks and creeks?

Have you tasted my blueberries, blackberries, raspberries and strawberries or my other natural sweet treats?"

Then Mother Nature paused..........

"Who here uses only what they need?

Who here replants trees when they are chopped down?

Who here finds a new home for the creatures that are displaced due to construction?

Who here uses all their resources wisely like conserving electricity, fuel and the food for consumption?

REDUCE, REUSE, RECYCLE

On April 22nd EARTH DAY

You who take good care of the earth will be rewarded!

Those who know what they should be doing but choose not to_ BAM!"

Molly (alias Mother Nature) on the teacher's desk slammed a book down

..."WILL BE IN GREAT DANGER"!

Mother Nature was very animated... when speaking of nature she was full of love and joy;

when speaking of not taking care of the earth or the living plants and animals...

Mother Nature became serious and sometimes a little sad.

She took Bunny Wunny out of her cage and held the bunny close to her heart;

stroking this gentle animal before setting her on the ground to hop around.

Then Molly 'Mother Nature' pretended to be a twister twirling and swirling around the room;

proving that nature is unpredictable and cannot be controlled.

Until once again she was standing at the front of the class;

Molly regained her composure and her breath

then gave a compassionate yet stern warning to all:

"On Earth Day April 22nd the earth will treat you the way you have treated the earth all year.

Those who honor Mother Nature will be given sweet fruits and gifts;

those that have not will fall off cliffs.

Whether people consider you a nice person is not the criteria.

It's whether or not you have taken care of the planet...did ya?

Have you reused, recycled and reduced? OR have you refused?!

Do you take care of the animals, land, water and air?

Indifference also counts; doing nothing can be very harmful.

Do you take care of the babies; treat them with loving care.

For babies need our help now and are our help when they grow up.

Old people are the memory of generations before

and the young are the strength for our future.

We need the old and young and all ages in between for our survival.

Thou shalt not kill is a Commandment; look it up in the Bible.

If you are actively doing your part; you will have a nice earth day.

BUT if you disregard the earth,

> the earth might split wide open and swallow you whole,
> then spit you out the top of a volcano,
> where you land nobody will know!

The choice is yours.

April 22nd is approaching...time is almost up.

Have you been good, bad or indifferent?

Your actions do matter; SO WAKE UP!

Bye for now, I'll see you all on April 22nd."

Molly (alias 'Mother Nature) walked out the door,

her parting words "Feels like rain".

Molly concluded her performance; school was out and the last bell rang.

She quickly ran home to check on the robin eggs and see if the birds had hatched.

Maryann and Miriam were waiting for Molly to get home;

to tell her that two of the three baby birds were out of their shells and chirping.

The third egg never moved for the baby bird did not survive the nest falling.

Nature sometimes can be cruel;

survival of the fittest is the rule.

Mom and Dad just looked at each other when they heard the news of one of the robin eggs did not hatch like the rest.

"So it was John and Joseph who found the robin eggs?" asked Grandma McFrugal in a pondering way.

Molly knew why Grandma asked that question.

John and Joseph were a set of triplets and not twins;

their third triplet died in their mother's womb.

Mother McGolly miscarried little Jeremiah 3 months before John and Joseph were born.

Baby Jeremiah never even took his first breath.

Grandma told Molly, Mike and Mark "Your parents were very sad when they lost their little son Jeremiah. Your father made a small coffin out of pine wood about the size of a breadbox. Your mother made three little decorative pillows for the triplets while she was pregnant, one yellow, one green and one blue. She chose the yellow one for Jeremiah, the color of light. Your Mama placed that little yellow pillow in the casket for Jeremiah to sleep and I (Grandma) knitted a little yellow blanket to cover his tiny little body. We also put a Guardian Angel medallion in with him and this is why. Several days before Jeremiah was miscarried (stillborn) your father had gone on his yearly hunting trip with the men in the family and was not home. Your mother woke up in the middle of the night and saw a tall man with long golden hair standing at the foot of her bed. She didn't move. None of the men in our family have long golden blond hair, they have either curly red or straight brown hair. Your Mama thinks that at that moment Jeremiah died; that was his guardian angel to take him to Heaven. A few days later when your Dad was back from the hunting trip; Jeremiah spontaneously came out of your mother's body. You all know where little Jeremiah is buried, close to the big cross high on the hill."

Mother and Father McGolly have 10 lively children and one at peace in Heaven.

Mother and Father McGolly took the little light blue robin egg to the top of the hill by baby Jeremiah and buried it next to their son.

They hugged each other and said a prayer for their son Jeremiah;

knowing someday they will get to meet him when they go home at the end of their natural lives. Natural conception to natural death.

Molly returned to school the next day after her performance to find she was a huge success.

This was a new role for her; she always came in second or third place or maybe honorable mention but never the spotlight attraction.

She warmed up to it pretty quick, her fifteen minutes of fame had begun.

The other teachers ask Molly to re-in-act her version of 'Mother Nature' for the younger classes again and again.

Molly was the talk of the school.

Kids from all grades pointed to her in the hallway because she was so 'cool'.

They would ask her for advice about surviving Earth Day!

So, she played along: "Mother Nature is coming April 22nd although she has been watching you all year long.

Have you been good to the earth?...

Are you helping the earth give birth?...

Taking care of the earth and giving new birth is Mother Nature's passion.

You can't hide from Mother Nature, she will find you. Where would you hide?

Behind one of her large boulders? Or in one of her caves? Perhaps high a top one of her great oak trees?

There is no place to hide where she can't see.

Do you reduce, reuse and recycle as a rule or are you wasteful?

Have you contributed to air, water or land pollution?

Earth Day is approaching.

Be Ready, cause you'll get just what you deserve.

Will the wind swirl you around like a lovely dance

or will you get a lightening zap to the back of your pants?

Now I must be off to see if the crocuses have not croaked

and that the cherry blossoms have blossomed."

Only a few weeks until Earth Day, some of the kids in her class finally made changes.

The 3 divas planted drought resistant flowers indigenous to the area and patches of citronella to keep unwanted bugs away; on the school grounds in beautiful floral arrangements.

They also started sharing their clothes and accessories instead of buying everything new at the mall.

Ralph the Boy Scout started collecting used newspapers from his paper route on Saturdays.

Clare (Sonny's mother) received a lot more stuff for the school wide garage sale.

The school seemed to be bursting with Earth Day pep.

Handsome Joe just watched and played it cool;

the only visible change he made was to start walking to school.

Waterboy William kept wasting water at the water fountain as if his mouth had a continous drool.

Many more students were walking or riding their bikes to school.

The principal made quite a statement by turning off the intercom and using a megaphone.

He walked up and down the hallway delivering vital school information like "I turned off the intercom and am now using this megaphone to deliver vital school information... to reduce using electricity." He then added "I also rode my bike to school with my helmet. Safety first as the saying goes...if you value your brain and intellect."

The lunchroom ladies conserved electricity as much as possible and declared Friday's fresh fruit and peanut butter and jelly sandwich days.

This was also good for all the Catholics who are not to eat meat on Fridays...an added bonus;

this is called a win win situation, everyone wins Hooray! Hooray!

Each day after school Molly put on her 'Mother Nature' costume with a sign which read:

> One Man's Trash
>
> Is another Man's Treasure
>
> Donate to the School Wide Garage Sale
>
> On April 22nd Come Find Your NEW Treasure with Pleasure!

She would spray the floral perfume as she paraded around the school property.

Most of the time she smiled politely to encourage everyone to be generous

> with their unused stuff.

However if she passed by an adult smoking in their car

she would cough like her lungs were full of black tar.

Molly became very dramatic; choking as if in a dire panic.

Clasping her hands around her throat gasping for air

while rolling around on the hood of their car.

Smoking is not healthy for parents

or anyone else on this planet.

She was the epiphany of what 'Mother Nature' would really do;

even if it embarrassed a few.

At home Molly was making bamboo flutes

with her father's much needed assistance.

She planned to hand out her bamboo flutes to everyone who arrived at school on bikes or walking on their two feet.

This was going to be a surprise on Earth Day morning, while dressed in her 'Mother Nature' costume.

No bamboo flutes for the students

who were 'Mother Nature' resistant!

Molly ran into a group of second grade girls all wearing clear goggles over their eyes.

She asked what the goggles were for and they told her "we don't want crows to pluck out our eyes!"

She explained they had nothing to fear if they were taking care of the planet.

So they took off the goggles and returned them to the science department.

Outside, while making her 'Mother Nature' rounds after school; Molly saw a group of boys with their football pads under their shirts and one with an inflatable life jacket.

Out of curiosity she inquired as to why they were dressed so strangely; which was like the pot calling the kettle black.

Apparently they were from the same class as the girls with goggles and did not want to be grabbed by giant vultures and dropped into the ocean.

But just in case they were prepared. Shoulder pads for the vulture claws or talons and the boy with a life jacket couldn't swim.

Molly in her most calming soothing voice tried to explain about changing whatever they were doing that they thought 'Mother Nature' would not like and take care of the earth.

She suggested that they gather any litter from the school grounds to show their support.

Then she looked at the one with the life jacket and told him to take swimming lessons.

They did as Molly 'Mother Nature' asked
    and gathered the trash.

On the home front, the first Sunday after Easter Sunday was Divine Mercy Sunday.

The McGolly family went to evening Holy Mass on Divine Mercy Sunday.

They all arrived early to line up for confession on Divine Mercy Sunday.

That morning after breakfast the family completed the 9th day of the Divine Mercy Novena in preparation for receiving the extraordinary grace; provided of course if they were old enough to go to Confession.

Preparation for Divine Mercy Sunday started on Good Friday before Easter Sunday; lasting 9 days.

After breakfast around the fireplace with the Image of Divine Mercy Jesus on the mantle; the family gathered calmly to complete the nine day novena.

However the events that led up to this tranquil gathering were completely chaotic and out of control.

Dad and Grandma were in the barn milking the dairy cows (Muffy and Daisy); while Mother McGolly started to make homemade pancakes for breakfast.

One or two or maybe three of the triplets were in their highchairs crying and wanting to be fed.

The rest of the children were all sitting around the kitchen table with Molly at the head.

The kids were talking, laughing, fighting and pretty soon the ring leader 'Molly' had them all pounding with spoons, forks, knives or their bare fists on the table "WE WANT PANCAKES, WE WANT PANCAKES".

Mother McGolly tried to stop the nonsense but the children were not listening to a single word she said.

When Mom picked up a fresh egg and threw it across the room and it landed right in the middle of Molly's forehead.

Molly was stunned as was the rest of the family, all motion and noise ceased.

Dad and Grandma just happened to be walking in the kitchen door at that very moment that chicken grenade was released.

Grandma handed a kitchen towel to Molly and Dad put the containers of fresh milk in the refrigerator.

Grandma took over making the pancakes while Mom grabbed the first and only completed pancake and left the kitchen in order to regain her composure.

Grandma looked at Dad and stated "When Maureen feeds herself first before the children that only means one thing; I know my daughter."

Gerald "What's that?" as he was filling sippy cups and baby bottles with fresh cow nectar.

Grandma stated "She must be pregnant. That's the most plausible explanation".

Gerald was stunned, he looked like a dozen chicken grenades just hit his forehead with spot on precision.

Grandma had to bishop slap Gerald to get his attention.

Dad fed the triplets and then went to find Maureen and give her a glass of fresh milk.

If Grandma was right, Maureen his beautiful bride would need the extra nourishment.

Natural conception to natural death.

★★★★★★★★★★★★★★★★★★★★★★★★★★★

(Author Note☺)

Through Saint Faustina, God imparted 5 new forms of devotion to remind us of God's mercy.

God's mercy is nothing new but mankind seems to be ignoring God's mercy.

Remember, we of free will must ask God for forgiveness with true sorrow in order to be forgiven.

★★★★★★★★★★★★★★★★★★★★★★★★★★★★★★★★★★★

(Author Note); Reminders of the 7 Corporal and 7 Spiritual Works of Mercy:

(Corporal): Feed the hungry, Give drink to the thirsty, Clothe the naked, Shelter the homeless, Visit the sick, Visit the imprisoned, Bury the dead.

(Spiritual): Admonish sinners, Instruct the uninformed, Counsel the doubtful, Comfort the sorrowful, Be patient with those in error, Forgive offenses, Pray for those living and dead.

★★★★★★★★★★★★★★★★★★★★★★★★★★★★★★★★

The McGolly's collectively chose as this year's Act of Mercy: Clothe the Naked

Everyone cleaned out their closets of clothes and toys to give to younger siblings or donate to charity.

Each person also would chose to do an act of mercy on their own:

Molly, Mark and Mike fed the triplets the rest of the day without being told to by Mom or Dad (Feed the hungry).

Grandma McFrugal went to read a book to little John who was in time out for hitting little Joseph (Visit the imprisoned).

Mother and Father McGolly said a rosary together for the family (Pray for those living and dead).

This Divine Mercy Sunday started out with a bang but ended up being a blessing.

★★★★★★★★★★★★★★★★★★★★★★★★★★★★★★★

THE BIG DAY 'APRIL 22ᴺᴰ' EARTH DAY

Molly used the wheelbarrow to deliver her handmade bamboo flute gifts;

she wore her 'Mother Nature' costume like she was a Christmas elf.

The teachers had a surprise of their own, dressed in hiking casual clothes and to school they
walked.

They had to walk because there was no place to park.

A giant tent for the school wide garage sale covered the teacher parking lot.

All teachers and students who walked or rode their bikes received a bamboo flute.

Today if you had a bamboo flute you also had on good hiking shoes or boots.

The teachers further surprised the children by holding classes outside all day

...to celebrate EARTH DAY...YEA!

This surprise was weather pending, so they didn't want to the kids know;

since it had rained four days straight in a row.

The youngest students had class on the large school porch for added protection and shade.

Older students were under the trees or on the shady side of the building where they usually played.

Every class, starting with the youngest was assigned a nature hike time according to the official
schedule.

With advancing ages the hikes were longer and longer, as a rule.

So Molly's class being the oldest students, their hike would start last

but be the longest.

Miss Kimberly Bailey (Molly's teacher) made special arrangements,

for Sonny to ride on a horse with her boyfriend Ivan for the long hike since he was wheelchair
bound and would need some assistance.

Molly gleefully handed out her flutes when she started to notice a few strange occurrences.

Today was different and this is why:

Some of children arriving to school were happy and laughing; birds sang them songs and flew
playfully around them and then back up to the sky.

Some of children arriving to school were unhappy, out of breath and covered with bird poop,

for they were dive bombed and bird dropping landed on them from on high.

Then it occurred to Molly: It wasn't hard to figure out which kids were good to the earth and
which kids spit in 'Mother Nature's' eye.

Molly pondered: Could there be something to her myth.

Maybe 'Mother Nature' is responding to judging each of them for their actions towards the earth.

185

April 22nd also known as EARTH DAY around the world is Judgment Day for the stewards of the earth.

Molly was kind to all the people who rebelled against the earth.

She gave them each one a much needed hug and a cup of refreshing spring water.

Maybe by her compassion next year they might do better.

Soon it was apparent, they needed a first aid station for the real Mother Nature was not so forgiving!

One boy known for throwing rocks at yard dogs behind fences...he was chased by a pack of wild wolves.

He was crying so hard and stated he would never throw rocks at dogs again.

Molly wondered if he would honor his present intentions when the fright was gone.

Would he change his ways and be nice to the dogs...

to hang on and be strong?!

Time will tell if he will have enough resolve,

to change his mean way and be nice to the dogs.

She took out a notebook and a pen,

Molly wrote down the names, addresses and phone numbers of each person with a negative earth day experience, including a brief description.

She would follow up with each one to see if they made their much needed changes

in the next few weeks and months and offer her assistance.

Of course she couldn't do this by herself, she would encourage everyone to help each other;

not to return to their old ways and over time rationalize their behavior.

They must hold each other accountable and monthly bring up all problems

that might lead them back to damaging and committing earth crimes.

Those who are cruel or indifferent to animals, those who waste energy, those that don't recycle, those that refuse to walk or ride a bike to school.

They must all create an atmosphere of working together with hope,

joy and love and bring their community in harmony with the laws of nature.

Another student who never helped her grandmother (who was wheelchair bound) or her younger brother or baby sister; suddenly found herself on a street with no people. No older people coming to get their morning newspaper from their front lawn or swinging on the porch swing sipping coffee. No young babies being pushed in strollers by their parents, taking older children to school. The street was completely void of human beings, cats and dogs, not even a single bird in the air. She instantly found herself abandoned and lonely. She remembered that she had been loving cared for by parents, grandparents, aunts, uncles and other family and friends when she was a baby and was totally dependent for her every need. She also knew someday she too would be old and once again need help of people who love her. She realized how selfish she had lived her life...never helping the old or the young in her own family. A change of heart came over her soul, she wanted and needed to be around others. The first thing she did when she finally arrived at school was volunteer to help at the first aid station. She told Molly her story then rolled up her sleeves "I'm going to turn off my cell phone. E-mails can wait. I'm going to start paying attention to those around me. I'll watch my baby sister while Mom cooks dinner because now I want to be a good big sister. When my little brother sees me I want him to smile. He will know I'm his good pal. He can count on me for whatever he needs. I love him and I aim to please. This also goes for my beautiful Grandma in her wheelchair. I'll take Grandma out for strolls in the good fresh air."

★★★

Author Note: We are to help the young, old and the marginalized. If a nation is to be judged by how it treats its young/old/and marginalized, where would the United States be ranked? We must take care of the unborn and those who are drawing their last natural breaths. The easiest and best way to do this is to live as God intended...so let's bring back morality according to the 10 Commandments and the teachings of Jesus Christ according to the TRUTH in the Catholic Church. No matter how far you of free will have veered off course it's time to do the hard work required to get back in God's good graces. You CAN DO IT! All of Heaven is rooting for you. Persevere, persevere, persevere!!! If you fall just get back up and amend your ways, come up with a better plan, ask for help and prayers, help others. There are many ways to change bad habits into virtues. Take the first step now. No one can do it for you. Persevere, continue in some effort, course of action in spite of difficulty, opposition, be steadfast in purpose and persist! Pep talks can only carry you so far. Make a plan that is pleasing to God and follow through.

When voting, and you feel you have to vote for the candidate that is the lesser of two evils; then break their political views down to the basics. You must get down to the foundation. Where do the candidates stand on issues of life. Supporting life is the most basic of all human rights. Life starts at conception and ends when we draw our last natural breath. Natural Conception to Natural Death. A candidate that states they are pro-choice is pro death of a human being unable to defend itself. Both abortion and euthanasia are forms of murder and/or suicide. God's fifth COMMANDMENT is :Thou Shalt Not Kill. So, vote for the candidate that best supports life. Stopping abortion at 20 weeks of gestation is better than being pro-choice. We can continue to change our laws to conform with the Will of God; meaning to work to ban abortion and euthanasia and get back to chastity for our state in life. Maybe we will be offered a third choice during the election which will not force us to go against our Father in Heaven's 10 COMMANDMENTS.

Remember the 10 COMMANDMENTS (INCLUDING THE FIFTH COM-MANDMENT) is the only part of the Bible God wrote Himself on stone tablets. How did our country reduce its morality to pass laws that go against the FIFTH COMMANDMENT. The answer is that the people are not standing up and defending life as we ought! So get out and vote for the candidate that best defends life, starting at conception. We can straighten out the rest after we get back to basics of our right to life (for our brothers and sisters, unborn children and ourselves).

When we pass the law that forbids abortion at/after 20 weeks of gestation; there will be consequences for those that oppose/break this law. For the women and those that perform (or assist) in these abortions there will be punishment according to the civil law. What would be the sentence for these people under the law, in which they murder their own child or paid/assisted/ performed these murder/s. How much jail time will they serve? In some states there is a death sentence if convicted of murder. Will time served be equal to the usual lifespan of a human being; will they be in jail for about 70 years (per abortion). Whatever the 'time served' sentence is for breaking this law according to civil law is not anything compared to eternal damnation of a mortal sin in which one has of 'free will' separated themselves from God Almighty by doing their will over God's Will. Remember the 5ᵗʰ COMMANDMENT 'Thou Shalt Not Kill'; we should not kill these people. Two wrongs don't make a right.

This next part will be very hard for most people, but the truth needs to be told about abortion. Abortion is the killing of unborn children. I heard Mother Angelica (founder of E.W.T.N. Eternal Word Television Network (Catholic channel)) talk about partial birth abortion on one of her 'Mother Angelica LIVE CLASSICS' shows. I guess I never put 2 and 2 together to understand that partial birth abortion means that as the baby is being born the abortionist uses some instrument to severe the spinal cord from the head (brain) and the baby dies as being born. This was my understanding of partial birth abortion. I also have a friend who once told me that when she was in Catholic School; she saw a video of a baby being aborted and she could hear the unborn baby scream like a kitty cat while it was being torn apart. My friend said she would never forget that sound as long as she lived. The truth is that abortion is messy and is a gruesome crime against innocent unborn children. Life begins at conception. Abortion is a crime against justice.

The act of abortion is hurtful to the mother not only mentally and spiritually but physically; she (herself) is also physically wounded during the actual procedure. As a pediatric nurse, I have on occasion taken care of young girls who following a batched abortion or an infection following an abortion ended up at my hospital. During an abortion the unborn baby is torn apart by a strong vaacum or surgical instruments are used to rip the baby's limbs (arms/legs) and/or head off while removing the body from its mother's womb. In this age of technology they can video record the actions of the unborn child; the fetus tries to get away from the foreign object coming towards it. Does that sound like a clump of tissue or a life trying to survive?

Let's take a minute to do a mental visual: Have you ever been at the edge of a pond and looked into the water to see hundreds of tadpoles all swimming around? These amphibians as frogs and toads are developing outside of their mother. Tadpoles have gills and tails while living in water and as they mature the gills usually are lost and legs develop. Once they have matured they are able to hop around on dry land as a frog or toad. Second question: Have you ever touched the water where tadpoles are swimming around? When I've bent down and touched the water by swimming tadpoles they instantly all swim away in every which direction. They seem to be trying to protect themselves from some sort of a threat to their existence. That is what I would think a developing live child in the mother's womb would do if something was attacking him or her.

After the abortion, they do a body parts check. Lately it has surfaced that baby body parts are being sold by some of the abortion clinics/abortion mills. Every abortion includes a baby being violently killed and they are completely at the mercy of others. Think about if someone or something was coming for you to tear you apart with weapons that cause great pain; no pain relievers to buffer the pain; you didn't do anything to deserve it; you couldn't do anything to stop it; and on top of all that, the people doing it to you were the person/people that should love you the most (your parents/grandparents etc…). I've heard that towards the end of time there would be so many murders/deaths and they would be horrific…more horrific than ever before. To me this sounds like abortion and soon to be, euthanasia (if we don't stop it).

We have all been deceived by the great deceiver (satan). We thought the Third World War would be nations against nations like the first 2 World Wars; but instead it is us against ourselves. However, it is possible the Third World War could include nations against nations. If we can kill the people we should love the most (our unborn children and the people who lovingly raised us); we can kill certainly kill people we don't know. The fact is that abortion kills more people all over the world than anything else. So we have horrific deaths of the unborn and abortion killing more people all over the world than anything else= The Third World War. We didn't see it coming. The great deceiver has deceived us all. The great deceived created a diversion (the first 2 World Wars) and then at the same time started to use our biggest weakness, lust and sins of the flesh to play his final card. Through birth control (many forms) and television/computers, the great deceiver has convinced us that we can pick and choose what are sins and what are not sins. WRONG! Our Father in Heaven gave us 10 COMMANDMENTS and we are to obey them…ALL OF THEM. Contraception runs against the virtue of chastity. Abortion runs against the virtue of justice. We as a society (on the most part) have fallen for the ways of the world; we have fallen for satan's plan. So I ask you: Which side are you on? God's or satan's. Are you going to get into the state of grace and honor your Father in Heaven by changing your ways to God's Will or keep telling God He has to change to your will because everyone else is doing so (satan's plan). The choice is yours because God gave us all 'free will'.

Jesus has His favorites and they are/were little children. What are we doing to God's little ones? I realize there are circumstances to why many women choose (or feel forced) to have an abortion. We must change society to take away all these reasons; starting with chastity for one's station in life. Most abortions are elective; meaning not the hard cases. 96% of abortions are elective because our societies have decided that human life is disposable. At conception all 23 sets of chromosomes at present; there will never be more or less. Conception is the beginning of a human life that God has created. We do not have the right to kill these little children that God has created. I've said before that I think the third World War is us against ourselves (not nations against nations although it could include nations against nations). If we can kill the people we should love the most (our unborn children and the people who lovingly raised us), we most definitely can kill people we've never met. More people are killed through abortion than anything else and it is happening all over the world. If our government does not reverse abortion laws and if our government starts to add more violence and death to our own people by adding euthanasia to its arsenal of weapons against us…your right to life may be next! Oh, they will try to pass it off as being good for us, but it will lead to death (yours) just like abortion of our unborn beautiful children. When government thinks it is over God's Laws, beware. So I ask you: If the greatness of a country is determined on how it treats its young, old and marginalized; where does the United States stand? Second question: What can you do about it that would be pleasing to God our Father in Heaven? Please remember that God loves all of His children (including you) and is waiting with open arms to forgive you. Repent and ask for forgiveness with true sorrow; then go and sin no more. Read the Bible and grow close to Jesus Christ. Catholics go to Confession.

Now let me throw another obstacle in your path to Heaven (alias the road strewn with rocks and thorns). We have given the government some time to figure out health care to serve the citizens of the United States and how have they done in regards to serving the young/old/ and the marginalized? What do you think they plan to do in the near future. Let's start with the young; abortion of the unborn. It is legal in the United States to kill our unborn children on demand. Life starts at conception. Changing the law to protect the unborn at 20 weeks of gestation is not good enough. Life starts at conception. Having an abortion without being repentant is grounds for excommunication in the Catholic Church. In some countries only priests with special permission have the power to forgive this sin in the Catholic Church. Definition of excommunicate: to exclude, by an act of ecclesiastical authority, from the sacraments, rights, and privileges of a church. Our government is forcing us to pay into a healthcare system that offers birth control methods to others. The birth control pill/injection/patches can be abortive; meaning the sperm and egg can still come together (no guarantee that it won't) and if the uterus lining has been thinned out (by the contraceptive), then the fertilized egg (human being) is sloughed out of the uterus causing an abortion. So, any couple who is sexually active using the birth control pill/injection/patch or devices like I.U.D. could be having an abortion/s every month. Using contraception (all forms) is mortal sin. The marital act should be open to love and life...no contraception. If we are helping paying for this sin we in turn are accomplices (going against God's 5th Commandment). In short our government is making us go against God Almighty on mortal sin which is damnable to Hell. Abortion (at any point) and Euthanasia (at any point) are ways to murder people. Natural conception to natural death. The Fifth Commandment: Thou shalt not kill. The only part of the Bible God wrote Himself on stone tablets was the Ten Commandments. What will help is if we return to a nation (the United States) under God, indivisible with liberty and justice for all (including our unborn children and the marginalized). This means to put God first in our nation (the United States). We must repeal unjust laws that are tearing our families apart (like no fault divorce, birth control which is intrinsically evil (other than N.F.P. in holy marriages and for good reasons according to God), abortion, euthanasia and same sex marriages). We have to do our part to help ourselves, our families and our government with charity. We must bring back chastity as the norm; chastity for our state in life. We must return to God and live by the 10 Commandments. Let's bring back prayer in our own lives and in our families. Do you offer thanks to God every time you are about to put something to eat in your mouth?...start doing this today. This is a great way to evangelize to our communities if we do this while at a restaurant or anywhere others can see us pray. Do you think about thanking God for the gifts you do have (like your eyesight, if you can walk, the fact we can worship God in our country (at least for now), the water you have available to drink, bathe, wash clothes (the refugees pushed out of their homes and even their countries don't have this luxury). We must change our ways to living virtuous lives and thanking God for our gifts. Chastity, chastity, chastity for our state in life; this will solve a lot of our problems. Charity through TRUTH. It is high time we stop telling our loved ones, family members, friends, coworkers, neighbors what they want to hear and tell them what they ought to hear. If you made mistakes in your past and lived according to the world instead of God's laws, you can still stand up for the 'TRUTH'. So many people think they can't tell their teenagers/or young adult children or older adult children (individually and with charity) that fornication, birth control, living with someone out of wedlock, homosexual acts, adultery, marrying someone who has been married before without an annulment are mortal sins. They feel it might hurt their feelings and in return might cut them out of their lives. Well, your right! That is most likely what will happen. No one wants to be told anything they do is wrong. I say to give this information to your loved ones with charity, however I'm not sure how to do this. I have yet to figure out how to say "Birth control pills are intrinsically evil and by using contraception you and your spouse/boyfriend are going to Hell" without the recipient of this spectacular advice wanting to haul off and knock me down. How dare I love them enough to tell them the 'TRUTH' and attempt to save their soul. So by not saying anything to them and they continue to do as they please because everyone else is doing it; they will be damned to Hell. Is that what you want? When they throw your past back in your face; with charity tell them you have repented and have changed your ways. Also you wish that you had not offended God in the first place for mortal or venial sins. Let them know that every day is a battle for the soul and you will always have temptations and/or short comings. If there is something that helps you live a virtuous lifestyle share it with them. Persuasion is achieved by means of firm kindness. Perhaps you go to Holy Mass every week, confession with Catholic priest once a month, certain prayers, after much contemplation you have seen how the world has turned out due to your own influence of mortal sin that you yourself rationalized in the past, possibly helping others (through the corporal and spiritual works of mercy), healthy forms of exercise, going for a daily walk, enjoying the beauty of nature, learning something new like playing the piano or maybe get a dog. Most of all, let them know that to get to Heaven they must be humble enough to put God's Will above their will. The way to Heaven is narrow. There is a peace knowing you are in the state of grace. Our hearts are restless til they rest in Thee. Continue to love them no matter what they throw back at you. You don't have to tell them every time you see them or they will run in the other direction. Just let them know where you stand, the rest is up to them (free-will). You do of course have to take the spike out of your own eye before you take the speck out of your brother's.

Let's teach natural family planning (in every gynecologist office and every hospital) instead to encouraging birth control pills and other damnable forms of contraception. Let's work towards natural cures that heal the underlying cause of women's infertility (some may be surgical but can't go against God's laws). In-vitro fertilization, artificial insemination, surrogate mothers etc... are mortal sins...not natural. If we don't change our ways on a personal level, how can we expect our family, friends, co-workers, and government to change?

The hitch I'm referring to is that at some point all good Catholics and like minded people that believe in the 10 Commandments are going to have to stop paying into an insurance plan that goes against our religious beliefs. Why? Because Catholics by paying into a healthcare system that helps others obtain birth control (pills/injections/patches/I.U.D's or other devices/sterilization techniques etc...), in-vitro fertilization, artificial insemination, selective reduction of babies in the womb, abortions, euthanasia etc..., we are supporting these immoral actions (satan's plan). These are mortal sins and we are providing the resources by paying into a health care system that refuses to honor our beliefs and ultimately will damn our loved ones and brothers and sisters in Christ who fall prey to 'the ways of the world' and away from God's Will and plan for our lives. God's Will and plan for our lives is simple: follow the 10 COMMANDMENTS. Stop rationalizing and justifying your actions especially if you have fallen prey to 'the ways of the world'; Catholics won't be able to use that as an excuse because you have been taught the TRUTH. Also walking away from TRUTH will not help. Once Catholic always Catholic; because you have been given the truth. If you do not wake up and repent for all your mortal sins and make a firm amendment to change your ways to God's ways ... you may very well find yourself in Hell. They say you do not want to be a Catholic in Hell, because you will forever know you had everything available to you to keep out but of free will chose to do your will over God's. God does not force us to do His Will; we of free will must choose to be obedient to our Father in Heaven. We must have the faith of a child and accept the Will of our Father in Heaven.

Open your Bible: Matthew 18:1-14

> True Greatness: At that time the disciples came to Jesus, saying, "Who is the greatest in the kingdom of heaven?" And calling to him a child, he put him in the midst of them, and said, "Truly, I say to you, unless you turn and become like children, you will never enter the kingdom of heaven. Whoever humbles himself like this child, he is the greatest in the kingdom of heaven.

> Temptations to Sin: "Whoever receives one such child in my name receives me; but whoever causes one of these little ones who believe in me to sin, it would be better for him to have a great millstone fastened round his neck and to be drowned in the depth of the sea.

> "Woe to the world for temptations to sin! For it is necessary that temptations come, but woe to the man by whom the temptation comes! And if your hand or your foot causes you to sin, cut it off and throw it from you: it is better for you to enter life maimed or lame than with two hands or two feet to be thrown into the eternal fire. And if your eye causes you to sin, pluck it out and throw it from you; it is better for you to enter life with one eye than with two eyes to be thrown into the hell of fire.

The Parable of the Lost Sheep: "See that you do not despise one of these little ones; for I tell you that in heaven their angels always behold the face of my Father who is in heaven. What do you think? If a man has a hundred sheep, and one of them has gone astray, does he not leave the ninety-nine that never went astray. So it is not the will of my Father who is in heaven that one of these little ones should perish.

★★★★★★★★★★★★★

If Jesus lived among us and was alive today, He would not be paying into a healthcare insurance program that goes directly against THE TEN COMMANDMENTS and His teachings. Guess What? Jesus is alive and living among us today. Jesus is in every Catholic, when we take the true Body and Blood of Jesus Christ into our bodies in Holy Communion.

At some point as Catholics we must stop giving to Cesar what belongs to God.

We're all reluctant to give up our healthcare options and do not want to do this. If we do stop paying our premiums on purpose and resign healthcare coverage due to religious beliefs... what then? The government will possibly make it difficult to get needed care. Most of us can't afford major surgeries/procedures, chemotherapy or other major cancer treatments, long stays in hospitals for a variety of reasons. This is why we have healthcare plans in the first place. So what are good Catholics to do? Some say that as long as you yourself (or those on your healthcare plan) are not using the plan for things that go against your beliefs then you should have a clear conscious. I'm not sure God will agree with this assessment.

So, let me throw another rock on your pathway to Heaven, this one is a boulder. What if God decides to show each one of us (all at the same time) where we stand with Him. Some prophet/s call/ed this anticipated event the 'Illumination of the Soul'. Saint Padre Pio called it 'The Harmless Warning' only because there will be no lasting effects when it is over. However some people will die of heart attacks during this event because it will be such a shock to their system. I hope I am getting this information correct; feel free to look it up for yourself to verify. Others call it 'Judgment in Miniature'. I read somewhere that four hours before this event the animals will become silent and moments before everyone's guardian angel will take on a form we can see (guardian angels are pure spirits) and prepare us for the 'Illumination of the Soul', then it will happen. What if during this event we find out that God is very displeased with everyone choosing for themselves what is right and what is wrong. What if we all find out that God is serious about all of the 10 Commandments and the teaching of Jesus Christ; that God has not changed; only man has changed. Furthermore, during this event where each person/soul finds out exactly where they stand with God that we each experience where we are headed in that miniature judgment. You will feel what it is like to go the Hell if that is your miniature judgment. The veil comes off and the TRUTH is exposed, no more rationalization and no way to escape it. Remember mortal sin is the only thing that separates us from God. Therefore it would only take one mortal sin for a soul to be in grave danger of damnation, if the person refused to repent with true sorrow before dying physically. This person/soul would already be dead spiritually if in the state of mortal sin. Refresher: (look up what 3 things are needed at the same time for a sin to be mortal). What if this event happens and everyone that is paying into our healthcare plan that permits others to use birth control pills/patches etc...finds out this is not allowed by God and is mortal sin... and these people experience the spiritual fire of Hell (but afterwards there are no lasting effects)...would you change your ways? Would you walk away from healthcare that forces you to assist others in mortal sin even if this meant you most likely will not be able to afford major surgery/chemotherapy/long hospital stays for any reason? I pray every single person would choose to do God's Will, your eternal soul is at stake. If this happens in your lifetime be thankful that you were given 'the Great Warning' and remember God puts no one in Hell, we do it to ourselves by doing our will over God's. We of free will choose to separate ourselves from God by doing our will over God's. This means choosing to use birth control (other than N.F.P.), not fulfilling the 3rd Commandment (Remember to Keep Holy the Lord's Day), paying for or encouraging others to have an abortion, living together out of wedlock, homosexual acts etc... God loves you and wants you to come home to the TRUTH in the Catholic Church.

Go to confession.

Take full advantage of God's mercy for what comes next is God's justice.

Be the first one in your family to live a virtuous lifestyle. Change right before their very eyes even if you have been considered the black sheep of the family. Your actions may cause others in your family to change. Think about what a good example and great influence you would be to the young impressionable minds in your family, especially if most of your family members are living according to the ways of the world with lax standards and not as God desires.

A SHORT WAY OF THE CROSS: (FOURTH STATION) Jesus Meets His Mother

O Jesus! May no human tie, however dear, keep me from following the road of the Cross.

★★★

Back to the story:

Ricky a little boy who loved to fish but never threw back the little fishes, experienced a fish attack. On his way to school he walked over a bridge and three fish jumped over the bridge from the stream below and slapped him with their fish tails.

Cuts from fish scales to the face, what a disgrace!

Molly made an entry into her notebook.

This little boy was very excited and was telling everyone he would always throw back the little fish from now on and forever. Now he knew what to do. He must follow through.

A sweet first grade girl 'Katie' who loved cats walked outside this morning and on her front lawn was every cat in the neighborhood, shaped into a giant heart.

Katie's toothless grin was priceless when the cat brigade escorted her to school, purring a song for her enjoyment.

All the students and teachers who did not recycle were chased to school by their rolling trash cans; which spewed the resources within all over the town.

Another little boy who played tricks on cats was sprayed by a skunk.

Molly made another entry into her book.

Jennifer who loved to pick flowers by the roots was stung by a bee!

Guess the bees were not to pleazzzed.

Molly made another entry into her book, after she took a pair of tweezers

and removed the stinger.

Ronda and Lori (sisters) helped their elderly neighbor by shoveling the driveway every time it snowed.

They woke up to snow in their front yard; so they played in the cold.

Ronda and Lori were sad when they had to leave their yard and go to school;

until they arrived and saw a sled and a giant snow hill.

Molly's brothers, Mike and Mark were pulling the sled back up the hill after each ride.

They walked up a hill every day and didn't mind helping the others with the snow hill slide.

Mrs. Wren, the librarian who spear headed the used book drive was rewarded by finding several first edition classic books in mint condition at the school wide garage sale.

She also picked up a tube of red lipstick for 25 cents; her grin was priceless.

Smiles are contagious even if they are outrageous!

Oh! Finding treasure at a garage sale is such a thrill;

It's all legal although it seems like a steal.

The biggest occurrence was when Ralph (the Boy Scout) arrived to school on his bicycle from the sky.

Ralph was usually calm, cool and collective.

Today he was excited and wanted everyone to follow him to a new pond he had never seen before today. This morning Ralph woke up and started delivering his newspapers on his bicycle, when he was lifted up into the air. He could see the town from a bird's eye view. For a boy who loves geography this was a dream come true. While he was up, up, up in the air he saw a clear pond and wanted to take the whole class to see it. For the past three straight days it had rained and maybe that was why this spontaneous clear pond appeared. The teacher, Miss Kimberly Bailey, told Ralph when it was their turn to hike he could lead the way. Normally Miss Bailey would have to get the principal's permission and permission slips signed by the parents to go that far off course. She would probably also have to scope out conditions and do a sight test...the list goes on. Oh well, Miss Bailey was in love with her boyfriend Ivan and was much more lenient with her class these days. Rules were made to be broken right? The class was already approved to go on a long hike, why not just make it a little longer, in a different direction. Miss Bailey already arranged for Ivan (a forest ranger) and his horse to carry Sonny for the hike. Safety first even if you are going off the grid. So, the hike began to the miraculous clear pond.

First the class did math, English and history

under the big oak tree.

They needed some nourishment for lunch; a sandwich, carrot sticks, fruit and cookies they munched. Soon it was time for their scheduled hike to uncharted territory to see Ralph's mysterious clear pond. Mums the word, the class had a secret mission. For once they all agreed and that's what they did. Ralph led the way with his walking stick. He appeared like Moses with his staff, except Ralph's staff didn't look like a serpent.

Over the river and through the woods to Ralph's clear pond they would go.

On foot and hoof the class paraded in single file they hiked high and low.

They entered the forest where Miriam and Maryann were lost and continued until they were standing in the middle of a meadow.

At the edge of the meadow and a mountain which was tall,

stood a rock formation and the infamous clear water pond complete with waterfall.

They rejoiced at the sight, one might have thought they had arrived in the land of milk and honey.

The rock formation looked like a giant bunny.

So the class dubbed this place Ralph's Awesome Pond and Bunny Wunny Falls.

Then they took off their shoes and socks

and took turns jumping off Bunny Wunny Falls giant paws.

Cannon balls, belly flops, somersault off the ledge of the rock formation by most of the class.

A perfect 10 dive by Waterboy William;

everywhere he went a rain cloud followed him.

The sky dumped buckets of water on him since his early morning shower.

When he dove into the pond he could only get drier.

They swam butterfly strokes, back strokes, froggie style and like regular folks.

Some other diving styles included pirates walking the plank, dares, Simon says and holding your nose while anything goes.

Miss Bailey and Ivan played Marco-Polo.

Since they were naturally attracted to each other like magnets, one always needed to be on the go.

The whole class seemed to have a great time, although their clothes were dripping.

There was one unspoken rule, no skinny dipping.

No one really wanted to leave but they needed to return to the school grounds before the last bell.

So back the way they came in single file.

Back through the meadow then to the tall trees,

but this time there was a gentle breeze.

CRACK! a large branch fell and landed on Handsome Joe's head,

he was knocked out cold but he was not dead!

That branch knocked him out like Mohammad Ali.

They had to call helicopter paramedics, to arrive quickly!

They were in a remote area away from roads and civilization.

The teacher now could see why she should have obtained the principal's permission.

So a helicopter landed and Handsome Joe was put on a stretcher with a neck brace.

Off to the hospital the hovering helicopter raced.

The force of the wind created by the helicopter blades flattened the meadow grass blades.

A student in Miss Bailey's care was in a compromising position.

She had to stand strong in order to get the rest of the class safely home.

The rest of the class continued on their trek.

They hiked past the meadow and the forest and as they were going over the river across the ridge...

suddenly a huge wave came out of nowhere and carried Waterboy William out to sea!

Later that day it was revealed that Waterboy William's whole family disappeared.

Where oh where could Waterboy William and his whole family be?

Molly thought maybe they were on an Island in the South Pacific,

surrounded by water and life was terrific.

Down deep she knew 'Mother Nature' doesn't reward people for being wasteful;

so Molly decided to be prayerful.

What was left of the class made it back to school.

The school wide garage sale tent was full.

No cars were allowed on school property, the parents had to walk through the tent

to gather their children and any other treasure collected with money they spent.

Sonny was pushing himself in his wheelchair

when 2 white stallions came from who knows where,

Mark was on one and Mike on the other;

carrying a long banner 'School Wide Garage Sale' in both of the horses mouths

while clasping Sonny's wheelchair from behind and pushing him for the ride of his life.

UP, UP, UP the rainbow to the very tip top!

Then the two white stallions stopped.

Sonny and his wheelchair free wheeled all the way down the rainbow

followed by Mark and Mike on the white stallions yelling WHOA and GO!

The trio ended up at McGolly Hill in front of the new log cabin lodge just completed!

Good things happen to those who all year are good to the earth,

who share their resources and think of others first.

Molly was whisked up by a herd of birds on sort of a magic carpet which read 'APRIL 22nd EARTH DAY'

American eagles to Grandma McFrugal's love birds gathered their feathers to make Molly soar HOORAY!

Red cardinals, bluebirds of happiness, blue jays, two tiny newborn robins, sparrows, birds with yellow scissor tails, pelicans, sandpipers and a nightingale,

a dove of peace, black crows but no scary owl!

Sitting right next to Molly was Bunny Wunny and her cottontail;

the rabbit had no wings but used her ears to flap fairly well.

During the flight they soared up and down, under the bridge and over the rainbow.

She waved to Sonny, Mike, Mark and the dual white stallions galloping over the rainbow.

A bunch of low flying wild geese joined in the flight when they descended by

the pond on McGolly Hill.

The birds sat Molly down softly on top of the hill;

by the new log cabin lodge which was completely built.

Around from behind the new log cabin lodge came a loud honking goose.

It was waddling, spreading its wings, honking and scaring some of the children on the loose!

The Holy Spirit is portrayed in many ways, such as:

> Fire, water, 'burning bush' in the story of Moses, 'in the stillness', as 'descending like a dove' in the story of Jesus being baptized in the Jordan River.

For the Irish, a HONKING WILD GOOSE represents the Holy Spirit.

A wild honking goose is very protective of their own. They work together and keep each member of their community out of danger.

Maybe we humans should start protecting our own better, by teaching the 'TRUTH' of our Catholic faith and not standing behind worldly treasure or pleasure.

When migrating, they take turns leading in the V formation, when tired they go to the end of the V line.

Like wild honking geese we should work together in a way pleasing to God.

The squeaky wheel gets the grease,

> maybe this is how it works with wild honking geese.

When was the last time you stood up to help Jesus like Veronica during Christ's passion.

Time is running out; so decide which side you are on.

Yes, the honking wild goose can be annoying but they have the best of intentions.

The Holy Spirit sometimes will speak loud to make His voice known.

The log cabin lodge was done;

on Earth Day and out came the sun.

That evening the moon reflected the sunlight

and millions of stars twinkled bright.

All of the relatives and friends were gathering outside the new improved dwelling.

They were waiting for the whole family for the grand opening.

Dad had Mom blind folded until just the right moment;

off with the blinder followed by the gasp of sheer delight then Mom hugged Dad with all her might.

Dad gave a speech before carrying his beautiful bride over the thresh hole.

Then while still holding his bride he closed the door with the heel of one shoe.

The entire crowd became silent, not knowing what to do.

The door suddenly opened wide

and Mr. and Mrs. McGolly jubilantly shouted "Come on inside!"

The grand tour included a new family room, three more bedrooms including the new master bedroom and new mother-in-law a joining house connected by covered walkway.

Two more indoor bathrooms, good bye outdoor shower stalls (SWEET!)

and a dining room with three long wooden tables, long enough for every family member to have a seat.

Chairs around the long tables were old fashioned kitchen table chairs from practically every garage sale, estate sale and antique shop in the whole state.

The chairs didn't match but who cares, the McGolly's just needed something to sit upon

and heavy enough that 2 year old twins couldn't toss in the fire, referring to Joseph and John.

The walls of the dining room were painted soft buttercup and Chantilly lace.

Above the long wooden tables was an enormous sparkling chandelier.

Mother McGolly was so happy her smile was absolutely radiant from ear to ear.

She was shining more than the chandelier!

Bagpipes and Irish drums were playing, the women were river prancing,

and the men were Irish jig dancing.

One of the men shouted "I'm tired of all the Irish sterotypes,

as soon as I'm finished with this beer I'm going to punch somebody out!"

All the men laughed but there was no fighting.

Lots of food placed on the long wooden tables for lots of eating.

There were children everywhere running, crying, playing and singing.

Grandma gave tours to everyone who came to the house warming.

Mom just kept smiling while sitting with her feet propped up on a chair

just staring at the glimmering chandelier,

from her face fell a silent joyful tear.

Back to the School Wide Garage Sale, almost everything sold like it was gold.

The money collected from the Garage Sale Event,

a very good cause it went.

After reimbursing the parents (who fronted the money) for the recycled playground turfs,

it covered Handsome Joe's medical expenses.

The rest went to the principal's choice.

The school got a great microscope, lots of art supplies and library books;

the teachers, students, parents and librarian rejoiced!

Handsome Joe woke up two days later; the first thing he saw

was a large sign that covered the hospital wall.

'GET WELL' in old socks darned in colorful patches.

When Joe returned to school he was a green lover convert;

he wasn't so tough under that lump on his head and a few other scratches.

Handsome Joe started a car wash on Friday's, free for the teachers; using minimal water and environmentally friendly soap.

Joe wanted to do something for the teachers for all their hard work.

Some of the other kids, like Sonny, Mike and Mark joined him.

Remember: One good turn deserves another.

As for Waterboy William and his family, no one has heard from them til this day.

Old habits are hard to break

just do it for Heaven sake!

Faith life and school life are blended together.

We are to be stewards of the earth and our bodies are temples of the Holy Spirit.

The teachers car wash was getting more popular.

In fact Molly thought that Waterboy William might have approved of this 'green' activity since it involved water.

By putting a little might behind those old rags they transformed the old clunkers into vintage cars with shiny bumpers.

The teacher's parking lot started to look like an antique car rally.

Seriously, the teachers started to buy cars that needed to be refurbished, really!

Model T's, Roadsters, 1950's long convertibles with fins, an old VW van (the kind Scooby Doo and his crew cruise around in).

Molly never dreamt at the beginning of the school year that the teachers would be reusing and recycling old vehicles.

Her teacher, Miss Kimberly Bailey was driving a 1957 red and white chevy.

It had a stick shift and looked quiet heavy.

Molly didn't understand why her teacher bought that car.

If Molly owned it she would hide it in the barn.

The teacher Miss Bailey visited Joe in the hospital every day until he was discharged.

She read him his favorite book, went over his homework and held his hand.

Never again would she take her responsibilities to her students lightly as long as she lived.

In fact she became a quite overprotective.

Just to go to the bathroom across the hall, she issued numbered hall passes.

During recess the class had to stay on the playground turf and she did a head count every 5 minutes.

Not knowing what happened to Waterboy William while in her care,

was a torment down deep she could not bear.

Molly's mother intervened to pull Miss Kimberly Bailey out of her despair.

Divine Mercy Chaplet Closing Prayer (part 950)

> Eternal God, in whom mercy is endless and the treasury of compassion inexhaustible, look kindly upon us and increase Your mercy in us, that in difficult moments we might not despair nor become despondent, but with great confidence submit ourselves to Your Holy Will, which is Love and Mercy itself. (950)

Ever since moving into the log cabin lodge on Earth Day and re-kindling her marital romance; Molly's mother was so happy in a care free manner and seemed to flit, float and dance.

It was like the two of them switched places.

Molly's mother was the hopeless romantic

and Miss Kimberly Bailey was the over burdened parent.

Molly's Mom incorporated several of the Spiritual Works of Mercy:

    Comfort the sorrowful, Be patient with those in error, Forgive offenses

    Maureen McGolly, Molly's mom said prayers for Molly's teacher before the parent/teacher conference.

She charitably forgave Ms. Bailey for putting the whole class in danger by letting them go on a hike unapproved by the school or the parents. Mother McGolly comforted Kimberly by stating it's what we do with our mistakes, that makes us who we are. Everyone makes mistakes. Molly's mother then confided to Kimberly something that had happened to her in the past that very few people knew. Years ago before she was married, she inadvertently did something that caused great harm to someone. She further explained the circumstance, event and how she couldn't undo what happened... but in time was able to forgive herself. Of course the first thing Maureen did was go to confession and ask for forgiveness. She believed God forgave her but had difficulty forgiving herself because the child was suffering. Maureen was driving too fast in a subdivision and hit a child out walking around the neighborhood. The child was in the hospital for months in traction, but fully recovered. She felt terrible and responsible because she was responsible for the injury to the child. Maureen wished she could trade places with the child and suffer for him, but that's not how it works. Since that event, she is very cautious when driving especially in neighborhoods or around children. Maureen was able to forgive herself by doing Corporal and Spiritual Works of Mercy for others. She explained to Kimberly that helping others takes our minds off ourselves and makes us feel good. She asked if Kimberly had gone to confession because it helps to hear your sins/mistakes are forgiven. Mother McGolly could see Kimberly was clearly sorry for her mistake but Jesus gave the power to forgive or retain sins to His chosen apostles and through the ages this power has been handed down to Catholic priests. Not even Catholic deacons have the power to forgive sins.

Scripture Passage (John 20:19-23)
Jesus Appears to the Disciples

> On the evening of that day, the first day of the week, the doors being shut where the disciples were, for fear of the Jews, Jesus came and stood among them and said to them, "Peace be with you." When he had said this, he showed them his hands and his side. Then the disciples were glad when they saw the Lord. Jesus said to them again, "Peace be with you. As the Father has sent me, even so I send you." And when he had said this, he breathed on them, and said to them, "Receive the Holy Spirit. If you forgive the sins of any, they are forgiven; if you retain the sins of any, they are retained."

Miss Kimberly Bailey listened intently, cried and hugged Maureen McGolly.
She took Maureen's advice and went to Confession with a contrite heart,
then she decided to help others and save a life.
Miss Bailey chose to share her home with an unwed pregnant woman. This woman was considering having an abortion because she felt alone, abandoned and had limited financial resources. She was raised as a foster child and had no real family to help her. Lucy had been pregnant under the same circumstance before and had aborted her child. She felt sad inside and did not want to abort this child like her first child. Kimberly's new housemate was a little rough around the edges but was very appreciative to have a home for her and her unborn baby.

Both Lucy and Kimberly contacted pregnancy outreach programs: Respect Life and Heartbeat International (One who needed help and one who wanted to help).

★★★

PROJECT RACHEL   Peace starts here

For confidential help: HopeAfterAbortion.org   888-456-HOPE (888-456-4673)

★★

Corporal and Spiritual works of mercy healed Miss Kimberly Bailey's wounds; she felt good inside helping her new friend. Lucy used Kimberly's car until she was able to save money to get a car of her own. Kimberly borrowed her boyfriend's (Ivan) car, a red and white Chevy since he preferred his horse for transportation. Kimberly's parents had given their house to her when they retired; and they moved out to the country. They sort of adopted Lucy and were excited about helping her with the baby when it is born. Kimberly did save a life because she offered an alternative to abortion of an unborn child. This helped her forgive herself for the disappearance of her student William while under her care, for she had no idea if he were alive or dead. No one in town knew what happened to William or his whole family; it remains a mystery. Apparently Mother Nature is not forgiving if you know right from wrong and never make amends which leads to destroying the earth and every living thing upon it. Kimberly not only shared her home but also her car, food, her parent's, time and energy when needed, became Lucy's sponsor to become a Catholic, and later helped raise the baby (like an aunt). Lucy helped Kimberly grow in many ways also; she taught her how to cook, use mass transient, and how to persevere when things get difficult. They had their differences and disputes but grew to love each other like sisters. If you think about it, we are all sisters and brothers in Christ.

(Author Note): Helping an unwed woman in crisis is a great place to start showing dignity for every human life in our society. However we must deal with the root of the problem. We as a society must bring back chastity. If we really love our brothers and sisters in Christ we should treat everyone with dignity. Men and women should not use each other merely as sexual objects with no true commitment to each other or possible children formed in the union. WAKE UP, HAVING SEXUAL INTERCOURSE IS RELATED TO GETTING PREGNANT. Every act of generation (intercourse) should have love and be open to life, and should not be merely for pleasure. Since the 'act of generation' is where babies come from, then the couple should be in a committed loving relationship prior to the act of generation (holy matrimony). If conception happens (life begins) then the child will be in a supportive loving family and be born into a family offering love and stability. We all thrive better when loved and our basic needs are met. All forms of birth control (except Natural Family Planning) are intrinsically evil. Simply look around at our society; look what birth control has done to destroy our lives and the lives of loved ones. Look how many babies have been killed by their own parents/grandparents because they (the babies) are unwanted due to lax standards. How do we change our society and our souls? We must live chaste lifestyles for our station in life. If you are not married in a holy matrimony marriage, then you should not be having sex. Lust, pre-marital sex (fornication), living together with benefits, using birth control, divorce and re-marriage without annulment is adultery, adultery, homosexual acts are mortal sins for a reason…they lead to the breakdown of society…and death of our souls because we have separated ourselves from God of free will. God our Father wants only what is good for us and He gave us the 10 Commandments and sent His Son Jesus (The Way, the Truth and the Life) to teach us how to live and be our Savior. We still have to ask for forgiveness with true sorrow in order to be saved.

I'm going to use another approach to get the point across. Recently I've heard from a couple of different sources that there are no good people in Heaven. There are only SAINTS IN HEAVEN. Saints do the Will of God. Everyone in Purgatory eventually will go to Heaven and be saints; but first they have to be purified. No one gets into Heaven or Purgatory holding on to their own will and against God's Will on grave/mortal sin (like taking birth control pills, lust, fornication, etc). So all of the people (alias cafeteria Catholics and like minded people) who are rationalizing their sin/s and thinking they will go to Heaven (maybe do some Purgatory) but are still living in the state of mortal sin, better WAKE UP! There are no 'good people' in Heaven only saints who do God's Will. Yes, you can wait until the last minute to ask for forgiveness but that is dangerous territory. How do you know if you will be sorry for your mortal sin/s when your life is about to end if you're not sorry for them right now?

Also, if it were okay to pick and choose what is mortal sin then Jesus would not have had to suffer and die for our sins. His (Jesus) passion and death would have all been in vain if everyone gets to decide what constitutes a serious sin. The Catholic Church tells us what we are to believe and we are to have the faith of a child and live accordingly. The TRUTH is in the Catholic Church. We must stand up for morality to change our society. We must vote with a clear conscience; meaning according to the teachings of the Catholic Church.

★★★

Kimberly Bailey and her boyfriend (Ivan), brought her new housemate (Lucy) to Holy Mass every week. Lucy of free will, decided to take R.C.I.A. classes and next Easter plans to be baptized, and confirmed as a soldier of Christ in the sacraments of Baptism, Reconciliation, Holy Communion (Holy Eucharist) and Confirmation. Kimberly became Lucy's sponsor to become a Catholic. She attends as many classes as possible with Lucy, which is strengthening Kimberly's faith too.

★★

These are mortal sins against the 3rd COMMANDMENT (Remember to keep holy the Lord's Day)

* Missing Mass on Sunday or a Holy Day of Obligation without a serious reason
* Doing unnecessary work on Sunday for a long period of time, i.e., more than several hours
* Intentional failure to fast or abstain on appointed days
* Requiring employees to work on Sunday in non-essential occupations

★★

Author Note: Some people stay away from going to church because they think the people attending are too righteous or the complete opposite, hippocrits. Well the truth is they are all sinners; some more than others. Everyone filling the pews, singing in the choir, passing the basket are all sinners. These sinners are gathered together to hear the word of God and receive graces. What they do with this information is up to them...free will. I like to think that most of the people who attend Mass frequently are listening and in turn are being transformed to be more like Jesus and Mary (who reflects the light of her Son Jesus). The people who are hardened sinners (cafeteria Catholics who refuse to do God's Will over their own wills) are still receiving graces for attending Mass and maybe this will soften their shells and someday will reconcile with God (on God's terms not theirs). Anyone in the state of mortal sin should not take the True Body and Blood of Jesus into their bodies (Holy Communion) because they are forcing Jesus to be a prisoner in a body dominated by satan. They can receive a blessing by folding their arms over their chest. Go to Confession, it's good for the soul.

There is only one sin that God can not forgive. This sin is called the sin against the Holy Spirit and I know of two ways to sin against the Holy Spirit: 1). Eternal Despair. 2). Eternal Obstinacy. In both cases the sinner refuses to ask for forgiveness, making it impossible for God to forgive them. The mercy is available to anyone who asks for mercy. Have you ever tried to forgive someone who has wronged/hurt/or offended you; and they refused to admit they did anything wrong and furthermore did not need or want your forgiveness. You must forgive anyway, consult a priest or read your Bible if you are having difficulty forgiving someone.

The only sin God can not forgive is the sin against the Holy Spirit; it's a two sided coin. One side are the people who don't think God has enough mercy to forgive their sins (for their sins are too great) and so they stay away and don't ask for forgiveness. This is called eternal despair. For these beautiful people whom God loves very much, need to become humble enough to ask God for forgiveness and they will get it (provided that they are truly sorry for their sins and want to be reconciled to God). On the other side of the coin are people who know God's Will (10 Commandments, the teachings of Jesus Christ in the Gospels, the catechism of the Catholic Church) but are obstinate or disobedient to God. These people are not asking for forgiveness and therefore will not receive it. Did you notice that the beginning words of each of the sins against the Holy Spirit are the same, ETERNAL! If you never ask for forgiveness then the mortal sin remains a mortal sin, because you refused of free will to repent. You of free will have decided to do your will over God's. Eternal mortal sin = Eternal damnation. God puts no one in Hell; we do it to ourselves by choosing our will over God's Will. The Ten COMMANDMENTS are not optional, and you know it! Sometimes people describe it as a little voice inside their head telling them they are doing something wrong. After a while that little voice might go away; you have incorporated mortal sin into your lifestyle and are no longer sorry for your sin/s. Your soul has shriveled up and died if you have no guilt for mortal sin (like taking birth control pills/patch/injections/I.U.D.'s or other forms of contraception). Catholics, stop deluding yourselves. There is only one objective TRUTH and it is found in the Catholic Church (the Bride of Jesus). Take a minute and remember that God has never given into popular demand. No vote. Our Father in Heaven loves us and knows what is good for us. Let's review:

1). One third of the angels were casted out of Heaven for turning against God and siding with Lucifer. Lucifer was a name commonly given to Satan, leader of the fallen angels who were expelled from Heaven.

2). Adam and Eve disobeyed God for eating fruit from the tree of the knowledge of good and evil (the one thing forbidden); and casted out of the Garden of Eden.

3). Sodom and Gomorrah; taken from CATHOLIC BIBLE DICTIONARY Scott Hahn General Editor)

Two of the five cities of the plain (with Admah, Zeboiim, and Zoar) in the area of the Dead Sea that were destroyed by God's wrath (Gen 10:19; 19:24-25; Deut 29:23; Wis 10:6). When Lot and Abraham separated, Lot chose the Dead Sea valley as his home and pitched his tent near Sodom (Gen 13:10-13). The five cities took part in a campaign against Chedorlaomer and his Mesopotamian allies but were soundly defeated and capture (Gen 14:8-11). Taken in the victory were Lot and the kings, including Kings Bera of Sodom and Birsha of Gomorrah. They were all rescued, however, by Abram (later Abraham), who set upon the enemy with 318 men of his household and drove them as far as Dan (Gen 14:13-16). The king of Sodom offered Abraham the booty from the war, but he refused (Gen 14:21).

The fate of Sodom and Gomorrah is decided in Gen 18, and their fiery destruction is recounted in Gen 19. Their fate hung on whether any righteous person or family lived within their gates, for the inhabitants of these cities were abominable sinners before the Lord (Gen 18:16-33). Since none but Abram's nephew Lot and his family were undeserving of heaven's wrath, angels were sent to hurry them out of the area before God's justice hammered down in fury (Gen 19:1-24). Once they were out of harm's way, "the LORD rained on Sodom and Gomorrah brimstone and fire from the LORD out of heaven; and he over throw those cities, and all the valley, and all the inhabitants of the cities, and what grew on the ground" (Gen 19:24-25).

Sodom and Gomorrah were among the proverbial examples in Scripture of wickedness, and their destruction showed forth the just anger and judgment of God destined to come on all sinners (Deut 32:32; Isa 1:9, 10; Jer 20:16; 23:14; 49:18; Amos 4:11; Wis 10:6; Lam 4:6; Zeph 2:9). Sodom and Gomorrah also figured in the New Testament as a prophetic image of divine judgment (cf. Luke 17:29-33; 2 Pet 2:6-10) and as an instantly recognizable example of sin and depravity (Matt 10:15; 11:23-24, Luke 10:12; Rev 11:8).

End of Sodom and Gomorrah (taken from CATHOLIC BIBLE DICTIONARY)

★★★★★★★★★★★★★★★

4). THE FLOOD (part taken from CATHOLIC BIBLE DICTIONARY Scott Hahn General Editor)

Also Deluge, the devastating flood recounted in Gen 6-9 that covered the whole land. The Flood was sent by God to destroy every living thing because of the wickedness of man (Gen 6:5). Noah and his family alone were spared as Noah had "found favor in the eyes of the Lord, for he was a righteous man, blameless in his generation" (Gen 6:9). Noah was thus chosen to become the mediator of a second covenant and to participate in the new creation.

1. THE FLOOD NARRATIVE IN GENESIS

At the command of the Lord, Noah constructed an ark 300 by 50 by 30 cubits in size, made of gopher wood (Gen 6:14) and covered with pitch inside and out. (See also Ark.) Two of every type of animal were led into the ark; Noah included seven pairs (Gen 7:2) of clean animals. Once all were aboard—Noah, his family, the animals, and appropriate supplies—a period of seven days passed, after which the rains began and the flood was unleashed upon the earth (Gen 6:11; cf. 2 Kgs 7:2, 19). The rain continued for forty days and forty nights, during which time every living thing died except for the passengers on the ark.

The above four examples should prove that God means what He Commands. God's rules are not meant to be broken. I wonder if when the one hundred years in which satan has been given more power by God is over; will God have to purify the earth again due to the amount of sin. Some theologians think that the 100 years started the same year as the apparitions of the Virgin Mary in Fatima, Portugal in 1917. Why these theologians think so, I am not sure. If they are correct, then sometime in 2017 satan will lose that extra power. Kind of makes one think that perhaps the reason the world is in this state is because we are not putting God first in our lives...as Commanded in the first Commandment. If we are headed for another purification because human beings are refusing to do God's Will; I plan on being on the 'ark'. I believe the way to be on the next 'ark' is to be in the state of grace according to the TRUTH of the Catholic Church. It will not matter where you live on the earth. Criteria will be to be in the state of grace. Your house will need a blessed crucifix (blessed by a Catholic priest) on your front and back doors. In the Old Testament of the Holy Bible, blood from a slaughtered lamb was placed over their door posts to keep the angel of death from their first born males of each family. Jesus Christ crucified is the slain lamb. By putting a blessed crucifix (with Jesus Christ on it) on your front and back doors, will mark your houses for the angels to protect. Don't wait until the last minute. Also have plain white wax candles blessed by a Catholic priest in your house. During the purification these candles will light up and last for the full 3 days and nights. Candles that are not blessed by a Catholic priest will not light up at all. So, don't worry about where you live. Criteria is being in the state of grace (no mortal sins) before the purification. Don't make excuses and start justifying your sins, which is how you got in the state of mortal sin in the first place. No idea when this possibly will happen, because God may choose to do other things first (like the Judgment in Miniature/Illumination of the Soul/Harmless Warning) and follow this up within a year of the Great Miracle to take place in Spain and then the purification. However, if enough of us change our ways to God's way...then we would not have to go through a purification. I very much believe in the power of prayer, we need God! Prayers and fasting can suspend natural laws and ward off wars. Just think if every single Catholic said their rosary every single day, this would be a much better world. Mary, through the 3 shepherd children in Fatima Portugal asked us to pray the rosary every day. Are you saying the rosary every day? Continue to pray, pray, pray and be a good example by word and deed. Speak the TRUTH and be humble enough to put God first in your life. I firmly believe prayers can change ourselves, our families and world for the better. Most of all change your ways to conform to God's Will. Go to confession, Jesus is waiting for you. The time of mercy is upon us, but it will not last forever; next comes God's justice. I wonder what God will do to get our attention when the 100 years is over. Jesus has given us His Mother the Virgin Mary (Queen of Heaven, Our Heavenly Mother, Queen of Peace) in apparitions all over the world. God has also given us so many great saints. The super saints are our older brothers and sisters who have already been through the trials and are our examples to get us to Heaven someday. Our Popes have been so beautiful and amazing. We're all called to be great saints...not just our Popes. What will God do when the 100 years is over to get us back to His Will? Whatever it is, stand up and take notice, heed the warning! Remember each one of us of free will must do the hard work to get ourselves in the state of grace. We are the ones who strayed...not God...God never changed. Only man changed. PERSEVERE, PERSEVERE,

PERSEVERE and help others! Remember all of Heaven is rooting for you! I plan on looking around and finding the people who had good experiences during the Illumination of the Soul and ask for their guidance. I would think these people will be scattered all over the earth like seeds. Seek them out and see how they live their lives. During the Illumination of the Soul we are each to have a perfect understanding of where we stand with God, and a short time to correct our lives. Heed the warning if this happens in our lifetime. If it does, it means we are far away from God and this will be our last chance of reconciliation. The Illumination of the Soul (Judgment in Miniature, Harmless Warning) will only happen once, followed by the Great Miracle in Spain then the purification of the world.

I find the timing of the extra-ordinary Jubilee Year centering on the MERCY of GOD very curious. This is only the third (or fourth depending on which source) extra ordinary Jubilee Year since Jesus died for our salvation over 2000 years ago. The first 2 centered on our redemption but this one: the MERCY of GOD. This is a BIG DEAL CATHOLICS! It started December 8th 2015 (The Immaculate Conception of the Blessed Virgin Mary) and ends November 20th 2016 (Our Lord Jesus Christ, King of the Universe).

I can't help but wonder if this year of MERCY was put in place by Pope John Paul II (now Saint) before he died. I feel he ushered in the Divine Mercy period. The first saint he canonized was Saint Faustina (known today the world over as the "Apostle of The Divine Mercy").

The reason I find the timing so curious is because of the 100ᵗʰ anniversary of the apparitions of the Virgin Mary in Fatima Portugal will be coming up 2017, right after this 'Year of Mercy' ends.

Also, if it is true that the 100 years that satan was given more power will be ending sometime in 2017 then what will God do?

Remember each of us has free will and must choose God's Will over our own will. God has not changed.

Pray for yourselves and your children.

The Fatima Prayer

O my Jesus, forgive us our sins, save us from the fires of hell and lead all souls to heaven, especially those in most need of Thy mercy. Amen

Angel's Prayer At Fatima

"Most Holy Trinity; Father, Son, and Holy Spirit-- I adore Thee profoundly, I offer Thee the most precious body, blood, soul and divinity of Jesus Christ, present in all the tabernacles of the world, in reparation for the outrages, sacrileges, and indifferences whereby He is offended, And through the infinite merits of His Most Sacred Heart and the Immaculate Heart Of Mary, I beg of Thee the conversion of poor sinners."

★★★

The first evangelization was and still to this day and until the very last day will be for everyone.

The first evangelization was when Jesus Christ came as our Savior was born and lived among us. Jesus Christ is the Way, the Truth and the Life. He suffered for our sake, was crucified and was buried. Jesus suffered for our sins so that we could have eternal life. However we must repent with true sorrow for our sins.

The next evangelization will not be for everyone...It will only be for those who will listen!

★★★

Padre Pio's Prayer for Trust and Confidence

O Lord, we ask for a boundless confidence and trust in Your divine mercy, and the courage to accept the crosses and sufferings that bring immense goodness to our souls and that of Your Church.

Help us to love You with a pure and contrite heart, and to humble ourselves beneath Your cross, as we climb the mountain of holiness, carrying our cross that leads to heavenly glory.

May we receive You with great faith and love in Holy Communion, and allow You to act in us, as You desire, for Your greater glory.

O Jesus, most adorable heart and eternal fountain of Divine Love, may our prayer find favor before the Divine Majesty of Your Heavenly Father. Amen.

Saint Pio, pray for us.
Prayer to Saint Padre Pio

Beloved Padre Pio, today I add my prayer to the thousands of prayers offered to you every day by those who love and venerate you. They ask for cures and healings, earthly and spiritual blessings, and peace for body and mind. And because of your friendship with the Lord, God heals those you ask to be healed, and God forgives those you ask to be forgiven.

Through your visible wounds of the Cross, which your bore for 50 years, you were chosen in our time to glorify the Crucified Jesus. As we lovingly recall the wounds that pierced your hands, feet and side, we not only remember the blood you shed in pain, but your smile, and the invisible halo of sweet-smelling flowers that surrounded your presence, the perfume of sanctity.

Saint Pio, may the healings of the sick, the serenity of the troubled, and the loving comfort received by those in pain and despair be a sure sign that you continue to intercede for us and our loved ones before the Lord.

In your kindness, please help me with my own special request. (Here state your petitions.) Each and every day, bless me and my loved ones. Amen.

Prayer to Padre Pio to become a Spiritual Child

Dear Padre Pio, I recall your promise to Jesus, "Lord, I will stand at the gates of heaven until I see all my spiritual children have entered."

Encouraged by your gracious promise, I ask you to accept me as a spiritual child and to intercede for my prayer request... (Here state your petitions.)

Glory be to the Father, and to the Son, and to the Holy Spirit, now and forever. Amen.

★★★

Now back to the McGolly household:

If you thought Mr. McGolly's surprise of the glowing chandelier was the biggest surprise of the year; you were wrong. Are you ready to hear?!

Maybe you should get out the smelling salts and pull up a chair.

Mother McGolly is pregnant, this time with four.

Four new little McGolly's due sometime this year.

First Molly then 2 sets of twins: Mike and Mark, and Maryann and Miriam, then 2 sets of triplets: Jeremiah (died in his mother's womb), John and Joseph and Leo, Patrick and Shawn; and soon a set of guadruplet girls.

Fast forward one year:

The new babies are here.

All little girls named: Cecilia, Faustina, Jacinta and Teresa.

Three born with red hair and one with light white hair and pink eyes.

Cecilia was born blind and an albino.

Maryann and Miriam always had a soft spot for Cecilia, who needed a little more help.

Cecilia became the third amigo, the three were constantly together.

Where ever you found one, you found the others.

This year most of the adult family members began to go to Eucharistic Adoration, starting with Grandma.

The family noticed how much peace Grandma had, especially after returning from spending a hour with our Lord.

Life is always going to throw us curve balls and we as Christians need to accept the good with the challenges.

Eucharistic Adoration is about giving thanks to Jesus in His Presence.

★★★★★★★★★★★★★★★★★★★★★★★★★★★★★★★★★★★★★★

In the chapel of the Catholic Church the McGolly family attended, had a monstrance (a receptacle in which the consecrated Host is exposed for adoration).

Once a week Grandma McFrugal, Fitzgerald McGolly, Maureen McGolly, Clare McGolly (Sonny's mom), Ivan McFrugal, Kevin McFrugal, Robert McFrugal, Belle McFrugal, Rosie McFrugal, Martha McFrugal, Fritz's brothers the lumberjacks (Luke, Matthew and Thomas/ McGolly family men), and Kimberly Bailey (Ivan's new girlfriend) who recently came home to the Catholic Church...all had their own special hour they spent with our Lord, Jesus Christ in Eucharistic Adoration. Each one had their own assigned hour, so Jesus would not be left alone in the chapel. All from seeing the peace Grandma McFrugal received at Eucharistic Adoration.

Eucharistic Adoration is for praising and thanking Jesus. There is something about being thankful to God for the gifts given to us and praising Him. Each person can adore Jesus in their own way, whether praying formal prayers or talking to Jesus as a friend or just sitting in silence and letting God talk to you. How often do we listen to God in silence in this fast pace world?

★★★★★★★★★★★★★★★★★★★★★★★★★★★★★★★★★★★★★★★

Back to the McGolly household:

Cecelia was born blind and an albino.

She always has a big smile and loves music, singing and playing the piano;

much like the saint she was named after; for St. Cecelia is the patron saint of musicians.

★★★★★★★★★★★★★★★★★★★★★★★★★★★★★★★★★★★★★

ST. CECILIA, VIRGIN, MARTYR

- ★ Feast Day: November 22
- ★ Name Meaning: "The Blind One"
- ★ Patron Saint of: Music, Musicians, Composers, Poets, Singers, Organ makers

PRAYER TO ST. CECELIA

Pray for us that we make music in our hearts to God
and manifest our love for Him in our daily deeds.
Amen.

St. Cecilia is regarded as the patroness of Church Music. Canonized a saint in 402 A.D.

★★★

The second born of the quadruplets was named after Saint Faustina. St. Faustina's Mission:

From the Introduction of Saint Maria Faustina Kowalska's Diary (Divine Mercy in My Soul)

2. St Faustina's Mission. In short, her mission consists in reminding us of the immemorial, but seemingly forgotten, truths of our faith about God's merciful love for men, and in conveying to us new forms of devotion to The Divine Mercy, the practice of which is to lead to the revival of the spiritual life in the spirit of Christian trust and mercy.

St. Faustina's Diary, which Jesus Christ ordered her to keep during, the last four years of her life, is a kind of journal in which the author recorded current or retrospective events related primarily to the "encounters of her soul with God.

- a). The Image of the Merciful Jesus
- b). The Feast of the Divine Mercy
- c). The Chaplet of the Divine Mercy
- d). The Hour of Mercy
- e). Spreading the honor of the Divine Mercy.
- f). The Divine Mercy devotion aims at the renewal of religious life.

★★

The third quadruplet was named after the youngest of the 3 shepherd children that the Virgin Mary appeared in Fatima Portugal in 1917, Jacinta.

From documents on FATIMA and Memoirs of Sister Lucia (the oldest of the 3 shepherd children who lived a long life).

Jacinta was the youngest of the 3 shepherd children that the Mother of God entrusted a message of prayer and penance for the modern world. This was required for peace in the world and in the Church. If her requests were not granted evil would continue to spread-leading souls away from God. The message of Our Lady's Immaculate Heart would be the way to God through her Son Jesus Christ.

The body of Jacinta was exhumed, April 30, 1951 and found to be incorrupt. On May 13th 1989 Francisco (Jacinta's brother), and Jacinta were declared venerable by the Holy See, that is, of "heroic virtue."

Jacinta was given a choice: to go to Heaven soon or to remain suffering on earth a while longer to help the suffering souls in Purgatory. Jacinta, a child, had been shown Purgatory and she chose to offer up her suffering for the souls in Purgatory. Jacinta was told by the Mother of God that she would be in two hospitals, have surgery and die alone. Jacinta accepted this suffering for the souls in Purgatory.

★★

The fourth born quadruplet was named after Saint Teresa of Avila (Doctor of Prayer 1515-1582). She is one of the 33 Doctors of the Church; Doctor of Prayer

★★★

It was a great day of jubilation when the four little girls were born. Although one was born with a severe disability they knew their family had plenty of love to go around. Sonny was born without healthy legs but he never let his disability hold him back.

Sonny's belief in God and the love of a thriving family offered him protection and comfort.

He wanted to hold little Cecilia when she first arrived home.

Sonny held her, fed her, watched her and prayed for her; like she was his very own.

The new dining room in the log cabin lodge was quickly turned into a nursery for the new babies. Instead of a mobile over each crib, they all shared one great big shiny glowing chandelier. Little Cecilia harbored an interior light because she always seemed to know......when the chandelier was in full glow.

Maybe she had some sight or perhaps it was the click of the light switch or the footsteps of someone who for the babies cared.

The other senses are heightened when your vision is greatly impaired.

Smell, hearing, taste and touch;

Baby Cecilia appreciated the senses she had very much.

In the McGolly household there was much playing, singing, crying, eating, praying, fighting and forgiving. Mr. and Mrs. Fitzgerald McGolly had 14 lively children and one in Heaven.

In a large family you have many opportunities to practice the 7 Corporal and 7 Spiritual Works of Mercy.

The older brothers and sisters have a responsibility to their younger brothers and sisters;

to practice virtue every day.

The younger children are watching everything that goes on around them; can't get anything past those little ones.

Even if they are blind and without sight, they can hear and feel everything; soaking it up like a sponge.

So parents and older siblings, what is your influence in the lives that surround you in the here and now?!

Are you living a life giving out love or are your responsibilities cramping your style?

The day the four newest members of the McGolly family were brought home,

Father McGolly planted four plum trees in the family orchard on the front lawn.

Four plum trees; one each for Cecelia, Faustina, Jacinta and Teresa.

★★★

LORICA OF SAINT PATRICK

I arise today

Through a mighty strength, the invocation of the Trinity,

Through a belief in the Threeness,

Through confession of the Oneness

Of the Creator of creation.

I arise today

Through the strength of Christ's birth and His baptism,
Through the strength of His crucifixion and His burial,
Through the strength of His resurrection and His ascension,
Through the strength of His descent for the judgment of doom.
I arise today
Through the strength of the love of cherubim, in obedience of angels,
In service of archangels.
In the hope of resurrection to meet with reward,
In the prayers of patriarchs,
In preachings of the apostles,
In faiths of confessors,
In innocence of virgins,
In deeds of righteous men.
I arise today
Through the strength of heaven;
Light of the sun,
Splendor of fire,
Speed of lightning,
Swiftness of the wind,
Depth of the sea,
Stability of the earth,
Firmness of the rock.
I arise today
Through God's strength to pilot me;
God's might to uphold me,
God's wisdom to guide me,
God's eye to look before me,
God's ear to hear me,
God's word to speak for me,
God's hand to guard me,
God's way to lie before me,
God's shield to protect me,
God's hosts to save me
From snares of the devil,
From temptations of vices,
From every one who desires me ill,
Afar and anear,
Alone or in a multitude.
I summon today all these powers between me and evil,
Against every cruel merciless power that opposes my body and soul,

Against incantations of false prophets,
Against black laws of pagandom,
Against false laws of heretics,
Against craft of idolatry,
Against spells of women and smiths and wizards,
Against every knowledge that corrupts man's body and soul.
Christ shield me today
Against poison, against burning,
Against drowning, against wounding,
So that reward may come to me in abundance.
Christ with me, Christ before me, Christ behind me,
Christ in me, Christ beneath me, Christ above me,
Christ on my right, Christ on my left,
Christ when I lie down, Christ when I sit down,
Christ in the heart of every man who thinks of me,
Christ in the mouth of every man who speaks of me,
Christ in the eye that sees me,
Christ in the ear that hears me.
I arise today
Through a mighty strength, the invocation of the Trinity,
Through a belief in the Threeness,
Through a confession of the Oneness
Of the Creator of creation
     Saint Patrick (ca. 377)

★★

Mr. and Mrs. Fitzgerald McGolly were good examples, to always strive to grow in their faith. Mom and Dad decided to show all their children mustard seeds (the smallest of all the seeds) and plant them in the garden in full sunlight. Then they read the parable of the mustard seed (Matthew 13:31-32) spoken by Jesus in the Bible.

He told them another parable: "The kingdom of heaven is like a mustard seed, which a man took and planted in his field. Though it is the smallest of all seeds, yet when it grows, it is the largest of garden plants and becomes a tree, so that the birds come and perch in its branches."

Dad told the children "so even if you have just a little faith, it can grow and flourish like the mustard seed. Always allow your faith and relationship with God to grow."

Mom added "Every time I see a smiley face it reminds me of the mustard seed parable. Just image how much your faith can grow even if it starts out as tiny as the smallest of seeds. Smile, remember God loves you". Mom learned that smiling made her and those around her happier.

So, every time you see a smiley face SMILE! And just like the mustard seed planted in full sunlight think of ways you can grow in holiness and make your soul bright!

The children watched over the tiny mustard seeds through the Spring & Summer, the plants grew and grew and the bright yellow flowers bloomed.

May God Bless You.

★★★★★★★★★★★★★★★★★

Addendum (Supplement to the book).

MINI STORIES OF THE MCGOLLY
AND MCFRUGAL FAMILIES

AUNT MARTHA'S DREAM

Aunt Martha (Maureen's Sister) was married for 20+ years when her husband served her with divorce papers. They had two beautiful children together. She tried humbling herself to keep the marriage together. They had been to marriage counseling twice in the past, which helped for awhile. Martha and her husband were both cradle Catholics and brought up in stable family enviroments. Martha believed that Jesus raised marriage to the level of a sacrament, and she wanted to keep her family together. Someday she will have to answer to God on how she lived out the vow she took to God and her husband. No matter what happens, keep your gaze 'fixed' on Jesus; join our sufferings to Jesus on the cross.

The words that Martha spoke to her sister Maureen on her wedding day "Be obedient to God and leave the consequences to Him" was a motto she held close in her heart. But what do you do when your spouse leaves you and is 'moving on' and you don't get a choice. Her spouse was also leaving the Catholic Church. In time Martha stated she filled out the papers for an annulment, but couldn't bring herself to file because she wasn't asking God to nullify that the marriage should have ever taken place. What she really wanted was for her ex (according to the civil courts which has no bearing on the sacrament of marriage) to be the husband God intended him to be when they first took their vows in the Catholic Church.

Martha wore the same wedding gown as Maureen (Grandma McFrugal's wedding gown) only one year later. They were married in the same Catholic Church (after taking Pre-Cana classes) with the same Priest...but the marriages turned out so differently. One with love and currently bearing much fruit and the other torn apart (with one leaving the Catholic faith and living according to his will and the other living a chaste lifestyle, attempting to grow closer to God).

This meant she could not date or have sexual relationships. Martha was happy with what she had sexually in the past and she too 'moved on' but in a way pleasing to God and not committing mortal sin with her physical body. She from time to time continued to struggle with forgiveness, for in her mind this was an unjust betrayal of a commitment they both took to God. Now, she was to live without her husband and if she did take up with someone else, would be committing adultery. Furthermore she was not allowed to be bitter by the secular/popular culture which encourages promiscuity. Nor by the Catholic Church she loved so much. The Priest encouraged her to love everyone including his 'new wife' (married outside the Catholic Church) and her children from a previous marriage. That piece of advice was actually easier to live, than to be resentful; although she had little exposure to them.

One Priest acted like it would be so easy to get an annulment and stated he would help her if she wanted to pursue that avenue. Probably for a lot of Catholics, this statement would be welcomed but for Martha who truly felt a loss…the death of her marriage and the breakup of her family…not to mention a bad example to their children…this gesture just made her sad.

She felt no fault divorce should be outlawed on a civil level. Also she felt the Catholic Church in the United States makes it too easy to get an annulment and that only 2-3% of Catholic marriages (married in the Catholic Church) should fall within the guidelines of an annulment.

In any event she had to learn to forgive, not only her husband (or ex-husband, however God sees it) but also herself. She had been forgiven by Jesus in the confessional, but she must forgive herself for her part in the break up. How to come to peace with this unresolved conflict… which couldn't be worked out because they were no longer together.

To have peace knowing you have been forgiven does not mean to go forward and fall for the ways of the world. You must continue to live a chaste lifestyle (unless you have been granted an annulment by the Catholic Church). Read Catechism of the Catholic Church #2348 (The various forms of chastity).

MARTHA'S DREAM gave her the peace she was looking for.

The dream… Martha smiles a little every time she refers to the dream that helped her spiritually survive her devastating civil divorce. She could see herself from behind, staring at an abode type one story house that was completely crumbled to the ground. This represented her marriage, family and home which they had built together. Everything she thought she had was destroyed all at once. Although she could only see herself from a back view, she knew she was at peace. The house was completely crumbled but the sky above was the most beautiful color of blue and there were no clouds. The clear blue sky reached high to the heavens above…endless.. Martha had great peace.

When she woke up, she remembered this dream. Martha felt like God was trying to comfort her.

Be obedient to God and leave the consequences to Him.

★★★★★★★★★★★★★★★★★★★★★★★★

UNCLE KEVIN MCFRUGAL'S CONSECRATION TO MARY

Molly's Uncle Kevin made a decision to consecrate himself to the Blessed Virgin Mary. It was a five month process. On the first Saturdays of five consecutive months, he went to Confession and received Holy communion, recited five decades of the Rosary and kept Mary company for fifteen minutes while meditating on the fifteen mysteries of the Rosary with the intention of making reparation to Mary.

At the same time Uncle Kevin completed the five week preparation: St. Louis De Montfort's True Devotion Consecration to Mary.

It was a tragic event that hurled Kevin into seeking a closer relationship to Jesus through His Mother Mary. Joan, a very good friend and fellow forest ranger was murdered by a derelict while out on her regular rounds on horseback performing her daily duties.

Kevin loved his good friend Joan. He worked with her for several years and they had a close bond. He never got mad at God while searching for answers. Why did Joan have to die so young and under these circumstances…at the hands of a human being. All the rangers knew the risks involved in their chosen occupation. However most of them thought the greatest risks would come from nature itself…not murder by a human being. Nothing like this had ever happened, it came as a huge shock! Kevin and the other rangers felt a certain amount of guilt, not being there to save her from the aggressor. If only they could have been close enough to save her. The rangers were almost always on their own (with their horse) during patrols.

We all know that any day could be our last and should always be ready. Joan didn't know when she woke up that morning that it was her last day.

Kevin missed his friend Joan very much and needed something to fill that part of his heart that was aching with pain. Making the consecration to Mary was the answer Kevin was seeking.

Monthly confession was the biggest eye opener for Kevin. He had already confessed and received forgiveness for what he considered the 'big stuff' long before this tragic event. After the third monthly confession, Kevin noticed he was saying the same thing. He knew in order to grow closer to God he would have to come up with a better plan to avoid these reoccurring sins. He learned conversion is a process. In the beginning he would realize he committed an habitual sin… after the fact…then half way while actively committing sin (like anger, laughing at sorted jokes, saying things that were not pleasing to God, watching television shows or listening to music/ lyrics not pleasing to God). Through his conversion he started catching himself before he lost his temper, walking away from conversations that were going in the wrong direction, choosing television programs and movies that did not compromise his religious convictions. All of these deep routed sins (habits) will continue to be areas to work on; however there came a time when

Kevin actually found it hard to think of anything he needed to confess. He did notice that if he started stretching out confessions past a month he would start to slide back into his old ways. So he had to make it a priority to go to monthly confession.

At one point he read a copy of a booklet that listed the 10 Commandments. This booklet separated each of the Commandments according to mortal and venial sins. While examining his conscience he noticed he had several more mortal sins (serious/deadly sins) than he realized. Some of these mortal sins included (Receiving Holy communion in the state of mortal sin: this sin forces Jesus to be a prisoner in a body dominated by satan until the True Body of Jesus in the form of bread (Host) is dissolved in the body; Missing Mass on Sunday or Holy Days of Obligation without a serious reason). Kevin confessed these sins with true sorrow and came up with a new plan to avoid these mortal sins in the future. No more excuses for missing Holy Mass. Simple.

People generally try to rationalize their sins to ease their conscience but what happens is that part of their soul shrivels up or dies and then there is no guilt. These people are in the state of mortal sin and must repent with true sorrow before they can be forgiven. True contrition, true sorrow is required for forgiveness. He also confessed venial sins like (allowing sports or other schedules to dictate the Sunday schedule, fighting with siblings (he didn't always see eye to eye with family members). Patience is a virtue.

Kevin was a nature lover and didn't watch much television. Most of the programs were immoral and promote a culture of death. He spent his free time fishing, riding or taking care of his horse, painting beautiful natural landscapes, bike riding, some hunting and helping his brother-in-law build a log cabin lodge and making more time for God and growing in holiness.

Kevin prayed for his friend Joan every day, in case she was in Purgatory. He had heard somewhere that souls in Purgatory could see those that pray for them and he wanted Joan to know he loved her and had not forgotten her. Kevin knew that Jesus taught us to pray for our enemies also. It's easy to pray for those we love but to pray for the man who killed his friend was much harder. They found the man that took his friend's life, justice was being served and the people were safe. Kevin prayed that the man would repent with true sorrow and know the power of God's love and mercy.

While on his ranger patrols on horseback, Kevin would say a daily rosary. He also continues to go to first Saturday early Mass (to honor Mother Mary) every month and first Friday Mass (to honor the Sacred Heart of Jesus).

In confession God hears our apology, accepts it and forgives us for our trespasses against His Laws. God loves us, we are His children. God knows what is best for us.

Kevin while out on patrol (on horseback) pondered that Jesus would have suffered his passion and death for nothing if we all get to pick and choose what constitutes a sin. There would have been no need to suffer and die on the cross if we through rationalization and choosing, each of us could do as we please. Instead God revealed to us what is expected. God is unyielding in his Commandments but at this same time is also merciful in His forgiveness and love towards all of His children.

In another Christ centered horseback ride, Kevin contemplated on a passage he read in St. Faustina's Diary. He pondered upon Jesus telling St. Faustina the reason He asked His Father in Heaven to take this cup from Him but to do His Father's Will instead of His; was because Jesus knew how many people were going to become lukewarm in their faith. Kevin knew what Jesus thought about people who were lukewarm in their faith---He wanted to vomit them out of His mouth. Kevin wondered if that meant those people would not reap the rewards of His passion and death on the cross. This thought made Kevin just pray for those people even more because he knew a lot of people that were lukewarm in their faith on mortal sins.

Both of these Christ centered horseback ride contemplations came down to the same conclusion: People need to ask for forgiveness with true sorrow in order to be forgiven. The best place to do this is in the confessional.

Maybe what these 'lukewarm in their faith' sinners need is a horse kick to remind them of the TRUTH. God tells us what the Commandments are and we respond by obeying.

Kevin had been horse kicked several times in his life and he remembered everyone because they hurt. He felt like he had been horse kicked when he and another ranger found Joan's body the day she died; while out on patrol doing their daily duties. Be Ready.

★★★★★★★★★★★★★★★★★★★★★★★★★★★

UNCLE IVAN MCFRUGAL PROPSES MARRIAGE TO KIMBERLY BAILEY

Uncle Ivan decided to be romantic and clever when he proposed marriage to his lovely girlfriend Kimberly. Kimberly Bailey was Molly and Sonny's public school teacher last year.

Ivan thought Kimberly might be expecting him to propose to him on his horse, since that was how they met. He wanted to his proposal to be memorable and unexpected. So he made plans to ask for her hand in marriage while floating down the river in a river raft. He had experienced those rapids on that river hundreds of times and felt confident that this was to best course of action. After all, both of them enjoyed nature and were adventurous.

Ivan concealed the wedding ring in his pocket…just waiting for the right moment to pop the question. It was a beautiful day in August…the sun was shining, trees and flowers lined the river banks. As they drifted along the river with the current, they suddenly noticed a rainbow completely encircling the sun. The rainbow was probably due to the mist rising from the rapids on the river. He took the ring out of his shirt pocket. This was the 'moment' Ivan was waiting for; he turned towards Kimberly and somehow got down on one knee and boldly professed his love for her " Kimberly, would you do me the honor of becoming my wife for life".

Kimberly was so happy, her heart was beating so fast, she joyfully stated "I love you Ivan. I would be happy to be your wife for life!"

Then they embraced and kissed. At the very same time they felt the river raft rock back and forth. Ivan managed to put the ring on Kimberly's finger right before they capsized and ended up in the river rapids fighting for dear life. Ivan saved Kimberly and helped her out of the raging river, after clinging to tree branches and fighting the current, spitting out mouths full of river water, they finally were lying on the riverbank completely exhausted. Both had smiles on their faces and once they caught their breaths they rolled around the river bank kissing and hugging each other, laughing and spreading mud on each other. As they looked up they could still see the circle rainbow around the shining sun. Ivan was her Prince Charming (no horse needed). What could have ended up as the shortest engagement ever turned out to be the conception of a lifelong happy marriage.

Ivan took Kimberly home at the end of that MEMORABLE AND UNEXPECTED PROPOSAL. Kimberly entered her house when her roommate, Lucy (while holding her infant son) was stunned and gasped "I see you two travelled the road strewn with rocks and thorns and then took another wrong turn into a mud slide…What happened?! Kimberly smiled "I'M ENGAGED!" as she jumped up and down, showing off her new ring. Lucy joined Kimberly in her excitement. Baby Anthony laughed he liked jumping up and down.

The beginning of their engagement turned out to be much like their marriage; with ups and downs like an amusement park roller coaster ride. Their marriage was wonderful and had a strong foundation; although they seemed to have more twists and turns along their love journey than most couples. However, this lifestyle seemed to suit both of them well.

They took the Pre-Cana classes (for couples getting married in the Catholic Church) and then were married in the Catholic Church. Following their wedding and reception, as they were leaving the Church in full wedding attire...to get into the horse drawn carriage...the sun was shining and it was raining at the same time. Since the sun was shining the rain drops from the sky glistened and appeared like stars shining during the daylight. On top of that there was a big beautiful full rainbow arch in vivid colors. Like I said, their marriage was full of ups (sunshine) and downs (rainfall); somehow most of the time they ended up with a rainbow (it all turned out well).

It was raining but the sun was shining and a glorious full rainbow adorned the sky on their wedding day in April; eight months after the circle rainbow engagement adventure.

One of their rain storms was that they were unable to have biological children of their own. They had lots of nieces and nephews on Ivan's side of the family and Lucy's son on Kimberly's side of the family. Kimberly (sort of) adopted Lucy as her sister and therefore baby Anthony was her nephew. Kimberly also had many children in her life as a school teacher. As a couple, in the summers, they sponsored a summer camp for Catholic children including, swimming, hiking, fishing, horseback riding, zip lines and last but not least mild river rafting. The other aunts and uncles helped out and taught the religious part and did most of the cooking. The Priest/s came every day and joined in the fun.

They knew in-vitro fertilization, artificial insemination were not options because they are not natural and are mortal sins. In time they adopted an infant and then adopted three more children that were in foster care. Lucy helped them with the challenges of adopting children from the foster care system; being herself bounced around in foster care. These children often have emotional issues which take time and patience to work through. Many may be behind in school due to different reasons (depression, no one to help them with homework, perhaps mental or physical problems etc...). All four of their adoptive children came with many problems of every type. Although they had many difficulties; they grew closer to each other and created a strong family unit. This rainstorm produced a full rainbow with much love.

Another rainstorm came many years later when Kimberly was diagnosed with cancer. She underwent her cancer therapies and then went into remission. This was a difficult cross to bear but her husband was very loving, caring and supportive. During her trials with cancer she would ask Mother Mary and some of her favorite saints to be with her when she was alone/depressed/tired/nauseated/scared. Her wonderful husband and family couldn't always be with her. A lot of these difficult times she wanted it quiet but still wanted someone in the room with her. She would hold her rosary and know Mother Mary was with her.

Kimberly also offered all of her suffering to God. Now her suffering had a purpose: to help others. Redemptive suffering is a concept the secular world doesn't seem to grasp. If they understood about redemptive suffering then there would be no euthanasia. Natural conception to natural death.

After going into remission, every year since, Kimberly and her cancer survivor sisters enter boat rowing (team sport) races and do well.

Ivan and Kimberly always seem to have positive outcomes to their trials in life. They trust in Jesus when times are good and seemingly bad. For the most part, everything they thought was a negative turned into a positive. God can turn negatives into positives in time. Patience is a virtue.

Marriage is a lifelong commitment; might as well make the best of it whatever happens.

★★★★★★★★★★★★★★★★★★★★★

THREE NEW SOLDIERS FOR JESUS CHRIST

Easter Sunday Vigil–Celebrated the Eve of Easter Sunday
Saturday 4:30-8:00pm
Sacrament of CONFIRMATION for ★Steve Donavan
★Lucy Jones
★Jay Walker
★and 40 more Soldiers for Jesus Christ
It was Confirmation Day for Steve Donovan, Lucy Jones and Jay Walker.
Lucy was to be baptized, receive first Holy Communion and Confirmation all in the same day.

Soldier of Christ: Steve Donavan	Sponsor: Kevin McFrugal
Lucy Jones	Kimberly (Bailey) McFrugal
Jay Walker	Gerald McGolly

The Catholic Church was packed. There was a large white tent with video screens set up on the grounds for the overflow crowd of parishioners. Most of the the McGolly's and McFrugal's were in attendance minus the quadruplet baby girls who remained at home with Grandma McFrugal and a couple of her church friends to help her with the infants. Baby Anthony (Lucy's son) was being cared for by Kimberly's parents, sitting in the first pew behind all those being confirmed. Lucy wanted her infant son to be close to her when she came fully into the Catholic Church. Three and a half hours is a long time to entertain a baby, but Mr.and Mrs. Bailey did an excellent job. Lucy knew she was a member of the Catholic Church the first day she spoke to the Director of the R.C.I.A. program at the Church office… but today was the first time she would be receiving the TRUE BODY AND BLOOD OF JESUS CHRIST into her body in full communion with Jesus…while in the state of grace. She had been cleansed of all her mortal (and venial) sins during her first confession with a Catholic Priest a few days prior to the Easter Vigil. Lucy's soul was cleansed of the sins of fornication and the abortion and all other confessed mortal sins. Today she became a soldier of Christ. She seemed to radiate love from her entire body. Peace followed her where ever she roamed. Lucy had been moved by the love and kindness shown to her by Kimberly and her parents. They gave her and her little one a place to live and continued to show great love and charity, helping with baby Anthony…and there seems to be no end in sight. Lucy wanted to be like these people who love.

Jay Walker started taking his R.C.I.A. instructions while still in prison and completed the classes after released from jail. Jay was appreciative of Sonny's visits in prison and encouraging others to visit him. Gerald McGolly helped Jay get a job at the Pulley Zip Line Factory. These acts of kindness encouraged Jay to straighten out his life. The love and charity shown to him while in prison opened his heart. This kind of love was foreign to him. Jay felt a deal of gratitude to everyone who helped him. He requested to receive R.C.I.A. instructions when Maryann and Miriam were found in the woods safe and sound; that night Jay started to believe more in the power of prayer. He was never afraid of hard work or suffering but now offered up his suffering for others in need of the graces gained through suffering (redemptive suffering). Jay felt all the prayers said for him during his incarceration led him to a new beginning. Today he would become a Soldier of Christ and he felt ready to defend the faith with his life. Jay went into 'the tomb' also known as the confessional and after a good confession (repenting for all mortal sins including whatever he did that landed him in jail) emerged resurrected…a clean soul. Jay was amazed at the power of confession; it truly gives you a new start. Today he was filled with the Holy Spirit! Jay told his sponsor (Gerald McGolly) that his time in prison made him 'wake up' to the TRUTH of the Catholic faith.

Jay also thanked Gerald for helping him get a job. Things were going well for Jay on the job. He had already been promoted with more responsibilities. Jay was hanging out at the McGolly house helping with the log cabin lodge and getting to know Sonny and his mother Clare better. Jay Walker and Sonny's father (Clement) were best friends years before Clare and Clement were married. After Clement died, Clare focused on being Mom and never dated. That was ten years ago. The sacred wedding vows state 'til death do you part' so Clare could have dated at anytime but she didn't want to. She was happy with what she had; a happy marriage while it lasted and a son she loved very much. She felt God had taken good care of her and Sonny after recovering from the grief of losing her beloved husband Clement so suddenly. Clare and Sonny were part of a large loving family, always someone around to help when needed. Jay Walker had never married. Sonny, Clare and Jay always seemed to have fun together. The three of them enjoyed being around each other. Chances were this relationship was going somewhere. Clare started to think maybe it would be nice to have some more help with Sonny. Sonny was pretty independent but still needed help as all children do (spiritually, mentally and physically).

Steve Donavan, Rachael's husband seemed to be in a state of great peace. His wife and all of his children were sitting behind Mr. and Mrs. Bailey and baby Anthony (Lucy's son). Rachael felt a great sense of relief, now her partner in life (husband) could help her raise their children spiritually, the burden was lifted from her shoulders. Rachael sang one of the songs during the ceremony 'Summons' with her beautiful nightingale voice. Rachael asked Steve during their first Christ centered conversation "What was the main reason you decided to become a Soldier of Christ in the Catholic Church?" Steve responded "I guess watching this family year after year love each other unconditionally and the charity to each other and people outside the family. I want these values to continue with our children and grandchildren. The best way to ensure this happens is to be the best example I can, even at this late stage. Your parents brought these thoughts out into the open during that talk on the way to the airport. That was probably the most uncomfortable talk of my life, and I didn't say anything. I even pretended not to hear it but it was like a bolt of lightening, when the thunder rumbles and just would not go away. I knew I had to do something or I would not have peace. I learned so much in the classes and want to get closer to God. Back when I was a Protestant, they stressed having a personal relationship with Jesus. You can't get any more personal than taking the TRUE BODY AND BLOOD OF JESUS CHRIST into your own body in the state of grace. Jesus is in every Catholic Church in the Tabernacle. I can't wait to start Eucharistic Adoration, I've already signed up for my hour with Jesus Wednesday 6-7pm. I'll be home late for dinner on Wednesdays."

After this beautiful Holy Mass with sacraments there was a reception with cake and punch. Then everyone went home because tomorrow was EASTER SUNDAY.
SOLDIER OF CHRIST: Steve Donavan CONFIRMATION SAINT:Michael the Arch Angel
SOLDIER OF CHRIST: Lucy Jones CONFIRMATION SAINT: Joan of Arc
SOLDIER OF CHRIST: Jay Walker CONFIRMATION SAINT: Saint Joseph

The next day was Easter Sunday and Uncle Steve and Aunt Rachael's flat house had more guests than ever before. The expanded guest list included Lucy and her baby Anthony, Kimberly and her parents, more McFrugal's than usual (like Ivan), Jay Walker and few members of his family. The extra guests were the new soldiers of Christ and their families and/or friends. Food, fun, music, laughter and complete with the cruise on the flatboat 'the Nightingale' including the flat rock skipping contest. This year all the women, with the exception of Clare, stayed at the house to watch the babies and younger children. Clare wanted to be present in case Sonny beat Uncle Steve's rock skipping record. All the men and older kids were all aboard the flatboat. Sonny's throwing arm was in great condition and his flat rock skipped 16 times...A NEW ROCK SKIPPING RECORD ABOARD THE NIGHTINGALE FLATBOAT! As promised Uncle Steve picked up Sonny and threw him into the cold lake. Sonny was prepared ...he had on his scuba wetsuit. Predictable: Yeah, as predicted this year Sonny would beat the rock skipping record.

Predictable: Yeah, Uncle Steve would throw Sonny overboard, as threatened for years.

Predictable: Yeah, Sonny would be prepared and wear his scuba wetsuit.

But wait...then the unexpected happened!

Sonny did not resurface once thrown overboard in a reasonable amount of time!
Uncle Steve had to jump in the cold water to find and save Sonny (no scuba wetsuit, just his birthday suit and casual clothes). Steve made a big splash followed by Jay Walker who also jumped into the cold lake to save Sonny. Sonny swam over from the other side of the flatboat where he was smiling from ear to ear. You see, Sonny could hold his breath for a long time since he was first chair trumpet player in the Middle School band. Sonny and Molly worked together to pull off this caper. You see, Molly was taking a drama class elective in Middle School. Ever since her 'Mother Nature' debut, she thought maybe she had a calling in theatre or public speaking. She practiced her new skills as an actress by dramatically stating "Uncle Steve, Sonny isn't coming up! What's wrong, WHERE IS HE ?!" as she leaned over the railing with eyes wide open practically crying. She was quiet the little actress because Steve and Jay fell for it (literally). Molly was very convincing and might win on Oscar for her performance or be grounded for life. Sonny told Uncle Steve that he couldn't complain, after all he threw Sonny in the cold

lake first. Then Sonny stated "Uncle Steve I think you set a new Nightingale record…THE BIGGEST SPLASH!"

It was a good thing that Steve was still filled with the Holy Spirit and practicing virtues like patience, otherwise this story might have a different ending…like Sonny might be sleeping with the fishes. Jay Walker was also still filled with the Holy Spirit or he might be back in the big house. Molly's dad and Sonny's mom just looked at the two pranksters then Mr. McGolly spoke "Young lady you have barn duty for two weeks". Clare (Sonny's mom) "You too young man".

Back at the flat house everyone was back to celebrating and having a great time. Some of the neighbors started to drop by bringing food and gifts. One of older ladies asked Steve, Lucy and Jay if they got their 'Bishop slap'? None of them knew what she was talking about. Grandma and Grandpa McGolly and Grandma McFrugal remembered getting their 'Bishop slaps' when they were confirmed many years ago. Grandma McGolly gave a short history lesson to explain about the 'Bishop slap'. "Not that many years ago the Bishops were the only ones to confirm Catholics as Soldiers of Christ. The Bishop would go to the different Catholic Churches in his dioceses and personally institute the sacrament of Confirmation. He would bless each catechumen with the special oil on their foreheads and would then slap the person on their cheek to remind them that now they are a Soldier of Christ must be ready to die defending Jesus and His Bride (the Catholic Church). In more recent years, actually decades the Bishops appoint certain Priest/s to perform the duty of confirming catechumens usually at the Easter Vigil Mass (the Eve before Easter Sunday) in many Catholic Churches. So the 'Bishop slap' went away. About the same time in the United States they outlawed paddling children in schools. Perhaps this impacted why the Catholic Church stopped the 'Bishop slap'. I think they should bring back the 'Bishop slap' to remind Catholics that they are to defend the faith with their life, that's what being a Soldier of Christ means. Maybe we Catholics would take our vow to defend Jesus and our faith seriously and stop being 'cafeteria Catholics' if the 'Bishop slap' returned. Rosie jumped into the conversation "I'll slap'em". Her mother (Grandma McGolly) reminded Rosie "You're not a Bishop". Rosie "I don't care, I'll slap them anyway and don't care who they are! Bam, this is from Rosie. Bam, this is from Rosie." Everyone started laughing and the rest of that evening and night was celebrated with love and joy.

The next day Rachael started to ponder about the 'Bishop slap' she never received when she was confirmed in the Catholic faith. She remembered her Confirmation Day fondly. Her mother's best friend was Rachael's sponsor. Her grandmother made her a beautiful turquoise linen dress for her Confirmation. Rachael selected Saint Cecelia as her Confirmation Saint because Cecelia is known as the patron saint for musicians. Rachael sang 'Ave Maria' at her Confirmation with her angelic voice. Her mother's best friend (Maggie) gave her a St. Cecelia necklace as a gift. Rachael still has that necklace and wears it frequently, especially when singing at church. What she didn't get during her Confirmation was a 'Bishop slap'.

Molly's Aunt Rachael secretly wished she would have received a 'Bishop slap' when she was confirmed as a soldier of Christ. Rachael knew it was a strange thing to pray for but she truly wanted a 'Bishop slap'. For about 2-3 months she asked for her 'Bishop slap' everyday for she felt like she missed out on something she should have received and still needed to seal the deal as a soldier of Christ. On the other hand it's an odd request and she didn't really want a Bishop to walk up and slap her. She still wanted her 'Bishop slap'… but in time… kind of forgot about it.

Rachael decided to consecrate herself to Jesus's Sacred Heart, which is a 9 month process. At the same time she signed up for Eucharistic Adoration at her Catholic Church from 10am-11am on first Friday of every month. Her church was starting Eucharistic Adoration for the first time and it would be once a month on first Friday. The very first time her church had Eucharistic Adoration happened to be the first month of her 9 month process to consecrate herself to the Sacred Heart of Jesus. Rachael arrived at 8am for Holy Mass followed by honoring the Sacred Heart of Jesus then she was present from 9am-11:30am for Eucharistic Adoration which she found exhilarating. Adoring Jesus and thanking Jesus is very different than asking for favors and telling Jesus all your problems. There is something to thanking God and letting God know you love Him. She prayed all the formal prayers available (by choice) and talked to God informally and even sat in silence to try to listen to Jesus. God already knew her problems but she did spend some time thinking about those issues too. This experience in Eucharistic Adoration was uplifting. When leaving the church she was walking outside by several white crape myrtles in full bloom on her left side. On her right she was looking at the bell tower, reading words on each side which read as: CHRIST, YESTERDAY, TODAY, FOREVER. Suddenly a gust of wind picked up and a branch from one of the white crape myrtle trees (in full bloom) smacked her across her left cheek. Rachael was so surprised and at the same time knew that she had just received her 'Bishop slap'. Right there at the Catholic Church on Holy ground after receiving the TRUE BODY AND BLOOD OF JESUS during Holy Mass while in the state of grace, starting the 9 month process to consecrate herself of the Sacred Heart of Jesus and going to Eucharistic Adoration for the first time ever. Some people might say it was a coincidence but Rachael knew this was one of her God moments and nothing would ever change her mind.

Later, Rachael reflected as to why she received her 'Bishop slap' on her left cheek instead of her right. She pondered that probably most Bishops (like most people) are right handed. So if a Bishop were standing in front her facing her and slapped her with his right hand, then he would be slapping her on the left cheek.

This happened about one year after she prayed for her 'Bishop slap'. Her slap didn't come from a Bishop, but the fact it came on such a special Holy day in her life…she believed her prayer had been answered…God didn't forget, God was just waiting for the right moment!

★★★★★★★★★★★★★★★★★★★★★★★★★★★★★★

BAPTISM DAY FOR BABY ANTHONY AND THE FOUR MCGOLLY BABY GIRLS

It was a beautiful Sunday in May, when five babies were cleansed from original sin, made Christians and children of God, and heirs of Heaven. Baby Anthony (Lucy's baby boy) and the four quadruplet McGolly baby girls; Cecelia, Faustina, Jacinta and Teresa were baptized in the Spirit. Catholics believe baptism is necessary to salvation, because without it we cannot enter into the kingdom of Heaven.

All the babies were dressed in white to represent purity of the soul. The babies made all kinds of the usual baby noises, cooing, crying (especially when the water was poured over their heads), and one passing gas loud enough to elicit a brief spontaneous communal laugh. Babies will be babies. All in all it was a spiritual joy to be with these young souls and their families while they received the sacrament of Baptism.

Baby:	Godparents:
Anthony	Ivan and Kimberly McFrugal
Cecelia	Steve and Rachel Donavan
Faustina	Robert and Belle McFrugal
Jacinta	Kevin McFrugal and Rosie McGolly
Teresa	Matthew McGolly(Gerald's brother) and Clare McGolly

Following Holy Mass the families of the babies and their Godparents and Priests congregated on McGolly Hill. Baby Anthony's mother (Lucy) and his Godmother Kimberly (Ivan's new bride) made the lunch feast the day before; all that was needed was to heat up the meatballs and sauces and boil the spaghetti noodles before serving the hungry mob. Lucy and Kimberly also brought a large tossed salad and garlic bread. Mother McGolly (Maureen) and Grandma McFrugal were in charge of the desert and beverages. Grandma McGolly wanted to babysit the grandchildren so the others could do kitchen duty. Grandmas will be grandmas. Maureen made three fresh strawberry cakes. Grandma McFrugal frosted the cakes with her fluffy white icing that morning before they attended Holy Mass. Maryann and Miriam loved Grandma's special icing and they called it 'Cloud Icing'. To them it looked like white light fluffy clouds. Little girls will be little girls.

Mom's Strawberry Cake:

1 Box White Cake Mix

1 Box Strawberry Jello

4 Eggs

½ Cup Crisco Oil

½ Cup Water

½ to 1 Cup Mashed Strawberries (drained)

Combine all ingredients, mix well. Bake 2 layers 350 degrees til done.

Cool 10 minutes before removing from pan.

Grandma's Fluffy White Icing

½ Cup White Corn Syrup

¾ Cup Sugar

¼ Cup Water

Cook until spins thread and hard ball stages.

3 egg whites stiff peaks; mix whites constantly until forms stiff peaks.

Before lunch the rest of the family and guests were relaxing and enjoying themselves. Grandpa McGolly and Mark and Mike were attempting to teach Maryann and Miriam how to fish from the water's edge. Grandpa sat in a chair while Mark and Mike did most of the work. Five year olds can barely tie their own shoe laces, casting a line out into the water takes practice and a little skill and patience. Maryann and Miriam seemed to be interested in catching their first fish but they had new play shoes; tennis shoes the kind with shoestrings that needed to be tied. During most of the fishing lesson they admired their bright green tennis shoes which they needed to retie about every 10 minutes. Mike and Mark remained calm since they were just waiting for lunch to be served.

DING-DING-DING the dinner bell clanged and everyone headed toward the log cabin lodge for the meatball extravaganza.

Kimberly and Lucy prepared three kinds of meatballs and sauces.

1). Italian Meatballs with Tomato Based Sauce

2). Swedish Meatballs with Creamy Sauce

3). IRISH Meatballs and Sauce

IRISH Meatballs

Pulse 8 ounces each sliced corned beef and ground beef, 2 slices seeded rye bread, ½ cup grated cheddar and ½ cup chopped chives in a food processor. Form into balls; pan-fry. Simmer in 1 cup each chicken broth and hard cider, and ½ cup mashed potatoes, 20 minutes.

The Priests said the blessing before the meal. Priests will be Priests. The food was delicious and soon everyone was lounging all over the house with full stomachs. After the siesta; Sonny and Molly decided to go fishing in Sonny's little boat. Mike and Mark continued to stay close to Grandpa McGolly on land and fish.

Maryann and Miriam found a large metal type container that looked like a boat. It was big enough for both of them to fit. It must have been left by the workmen when the log cabin lodge was built. It had dried cement on the bottom but it actually floated when they put it in the lake. They didn't have boat paddles or lifejackets but they found a long sturdy wooden stick and decided to take their 'boat' out for a test run. What they didn't notice until it was too late...were the many tiny holes at the bottom of their odd little boat. It seemed that someone had used it for target practice with a BB gun. Lake water started to fill the little makeshift boat. Shortly after the initial departure from land they started screaming. Maryann "Oh no, my new green shoes are getting wet! HELP!". Miram "Who cares about your shoes, were sinking, our boat is filling up with water! HELP! We Can't Swim!!!!" One twin was laughing while still worried about her new green shoes and the other twin panicking because they couldn't swim without lifejackets.

Mike and Mark ran to rescue their little sisters but stopped at the water's edge and started to roll around on the ground laughing so hard and couldn't seem to stop. Boys will be boys.

Once again Grandpa McGolly had to save his little granddaughters. Last year he was the one that found them at night in the woods while they were hunting for leprechauns this year... water rescue. He calmly waded into the cold water, grabbed the sinking 'cement mixer' and pulled them to shore. Miriam and Maryann jumped out of the make shift boat and sprawled out on the ground. One happy to be alive, the other checking out her soggy green tennis shoes.

This adventure landed them in trouble. They knew the rule about asking permission before doing anything out of the ordinary and the rule about wearing a lifejacket. Mike and Mark felt sorry for their little sisters after they stopped laughing. They decided to teach Maryann and Miriam how to swim this summer without lifejackets; it had to be easier than teaching them how to fish. Maryann and Miriam were punished with two days of barn duty...their first time!

Turns out, these two were just as good at barn duty as they were at fishing and steering a boat. They did however, excel at tying their new green shoes. Learning a new skill takes practice and patience for all of us.

Grandpa told both of the Grandmas that taking care of the four infants was a breeze compared to watching after Miriam and Maryann. Neither of the Grandmas disagreed with him.

Maryann and Miriam were not allowed to have a piece of fresh strawberry cake with white cloud icing after dinner that day. This made them very sad and they cried and went to bed.

The next morning Grandpa McGolly served fresh strawberry cake with white cloud icing for breakfast to his two little granddaughters he loved so much...and he helped them with barn duty. Grandpas will be grandpas. Amen.

★★★★★★★★★★★★★★★★★★★★★★★★★

THE COLORED CHALK WAR

Maryann and Miriam were coloring pictures on the sidewalk, fighting over orange colored chalk. Maryann "I need your orange chalk, mine is gone." Miriam "That's your fault, you used all of your orange and I'm not giving you mine, I need it!" Maryann "But I need to color Leo's orange tree oranges and I have to use orange chalk. I'm taking it! You don't need it like I do. You're being selfish. I would share if you needed some of my chalk." Miriam "You can't have my orange chalk, it's mine."

They were standing almost eye to eye facing each other with their hands on their hips. Miriam drew a line down the middle of the sidewalk and said " That is your side and this is mine. Leave my orange chalk alone or I'll mess up your pictures." Maryann "I'll tell Mom and Dad. You'll be in big trouble." Miriam "No I won't! Mom and Dad will be on my side. You still can't use my orange chalk. You used yours up and this is mine."

Molly intervened because she was tired of listening to the constant bickering all morning. Molly "Miriam why don't you share your orange chalk…be charitable…Maryann just needs a little bit. Someday you might want to use something Maryann has, don't you want her to share with you!" Maryann "I'm not sharing with her anything!" Miriam "I'm going to use my orange chalk. It's not my fault she used hers up!"

Molly seeing her mediation skills were not working decided to switch gears. Maryann and Miriam each had their own agendas and were not leaning towards reconciliation. So Molly tried another tactic…she decided to color outside the lines…sometimes plan B is better than plan A. Molly looked at Maryann and said "Use your yellow and red chalk together to make the color orange. When you mix two primary colors (yellow, red, blue) you develop secondary colors like: red and yellow make orange; blue and yellow make green; blue and red make purple. If you mix your green and yellow you can color Patrick's lime tree fruit yellow green. Maryann "So I already have what I need for my sidewalk chalk pictures?" Molly " Yes". Maryann learned something new and put this information into use. She colored the fruit in her sidewalk chalk orchard. The war was over and both sides won.

Mom and Dad were listening to this conversation out of view. They listened to see how their children would resolve their own problems/differences. Dad looked at Mom and stated "Isn't that amazing. The kids can figure it out but adults continue to fight to fulfill their own agenda instead of coloring outside the lines and try to help each other".

Dad continued to explain "Our government is thinking about building a wall to keep Mexicans out of our country, like Miriam drawing a line down the middle of the sidewalk. In the meantime we have a fence and border patrols which have caused much heartache and suffering to the Mexican people who are just trying to survive or help their family members survive because of need of the basic necessities. Also these actions have not worked. Maybe our government should use the money they are planning on building 'the wall' to better use, by helping the Mexican government use the resources they already have in their own country to give their people what they need. We could send specialists in engineering, agriculture, mining, tourism, transportation and trade to 'jump start' a thriving economy with resources they already have in their own 'backyard'. At the same time we could educate some of their top students in our top universities so they can take over the business of handling their own country's resources. This might take ten years but if done well and with respect of the Mexican people we could develop a great friendship between our two nations. We would need the Mexican government to support and PROTECT the Americans and their families who choose to undertake this mission during the building up period. By being charitable to our country's neighbors we will be creating a beautiful friendship between our nations. Of course once the Mexican people are on their own and no longer feel the need to cross the border illegally, we Americans can't expect the Mexican people or their government to be at our disposal. They have their own country, we are just helping them like a good neighbor should. Now, they could pay us back for any money spent, once they are financially sound and that seems reasonable to do so. We however cannot expect to be 'pulling the strings' until all monies are paid back. We are their neighbors, and we are all brothers and sisters in Christ. Let's try a much more charitable approach, spending the same amount of money but getting a much better outcome. We've all heard the tale: Give a man a fish and he'll have food for a day.

Teach a man to fish and he'll have food for the rest of his life.

Same concept; bigger scale."

Mom added "Maryann's yellow and red colored chalk together gave her orange to color her fruit orchard. Good fruit can come from being charitable and helping each other; like Molly teaching Maryann about mixing primary colors to make secondary colors. That piece of information solved a McGolly Hill twin fued. Even though Miriam was not willing to give up her orange chalk; learning a new way to solve the problem has many advantages".

Dad "Our nation could benefit from having a neighbor that is full of natural resources used well. The current plan is wasting our nation's money and is not working. The future possible plan of building a wall will cost us a lot of tax payer dollars that we as a nation will never regain or get anything to help our country. The 'Color outside the lines' approach is charitable and helps people instead of persecuting them for just trying to survive or help their family survive with the basic needs of life. In time the charitable choice will reap great fruit for people living on both sides of the border and foster love between our two countries. Molly just solved a problem using knowledge of mixing primary colors to make secondary colors and some good old fashion common sense." Mom "I must say it's nice to have peace around here after listening to Maryann and Miriam go at it all morning".

Mom and Dad strolled over to the sidewalk to see the colored chalk masterpieces. Maryann's fruit orchard with log cabin lodge at the top of the hill and beautiful blue sky above on one side of the 'border'; and Miriam's chalk picture of Noah's Ark with impending doom clouds overhead with the animals lined up two by two. The big brown boat was full of animals and more loading two by two on the ramp and ground below. On the top of the Ark stood Noah and his family. Standing around and looking at the Ark were the people not allowed on the ark because they loved their sins more than they loved doing God's Will over their wills. Mom pointed to two leprechauns dressed in green with green top hats and asked Miriam "Are those leprechauns?" Miriam stood up and sternly stated with a serious look upon her face "Leprechauns are not allowed on the Ark because they love their pots of gold more than they love God."

★★

Author Note: Now would be a good time to open your Bible and read:
  Scripture Passage: Matthew 6: 24-34
Serving Two Masters

"No one can serve two masters; for either he will hate the one and love the other, or he will be devoted to the one and despise the other. You cannot serve God and mammon."

Do Not Worry

"Therefore I tell you, do not be anxious about your life; what you shall eat or what you shall drink, nor about your body, what you shall put on. Is not life more than food, and the body more than clothing? Look at the birds of the air: they neither sow nor reap nor gather into barns, and yet your heavenly Father feeds them. Are you not of more value than they? And which of you by being anxious can add one cubit to his span of life? And why are you anxious about clothing? Consider the lilies of the field, how they grow; they neither toil nor spin; yet I tell you, even Solomon in all his glory was not arrayed like one of these. But if God so clothes the grass of the field, which today is alive and tomorrow is thrown into the oven, will he not much more clothe you, O men of little faith? Therefore do not be anxious, saying, 'What shall we eat?' or 'What shall we wear?' For the Gentiles seek all these things; and your heavenly Father knows that you need them all. But seek first his kingdom and his righteousness, and all these things shall be yours as well.

"Therefore do not be anxious about tomorrow, for tomorrow will be anxious for itself. Let the day's own trouble be sufficient for the day.

★★★

Dad wondered if Miriam understood the scripture passage which states: God and Money. No one can serve two masters. You will either hate one and love the other or be devoted to one and despise the other. You cannot serve God and mammon.

Or maybe Miriam was still annoyed that the leprechauns would not share their pots of gold with her. In either case Dad stopped wearing his green stove pipe hat that day, except on St. Patrick's Day. Miriam pointed to Noah and his family and explained "They loved God and obeyed the 10 Commandments. They were the only people allowed on the Ark. Over here are the people that loved their sins more than they loved God and they all drowned during the great flood. God means what He says and we must follow all the 10 Commandments!"

This sparked another Christ centered conversation between Mom and Dad. Mom "Although I agree about helping our Mexican neighbors, by helping them help themselves, I still think having immigration laws are good for our country. I think that bringing in Muslims or anyone without screening could open our nation to harm if radical types infiltrate the system. I feel most Muslims are peace loving people but it would only take a small percentage to radicalize many or start a revolt. I would imagine that most Russians in World War II were peace loving people, but a small percentage of radicals (maybe 5%) would force the rest to comply. Either force, political policies or fear would push the peace loving people to react; or they and their families would also be killed. Communism puts the country's government above God. We need our country to return to our Christian roots with a loving Father in Heaven who loves all of His children. If our country would live as our Father in Heaven commands, the 10 Commandments and the teachings of Jesus Christ our Savior, our country would not be in so much turmoil. We still need a screening process." Dad " Yes, we could help all the Christians that are being displaced by bringing them here, if they want. Of course Jesus wants us to spread the good news of salvation to the ends of the earth. So, Catholic and Protestant Christians need to live their faiths fully and we need to go to the ends of the earth and spread the good news of salvation like Jesus wants us to do. They will know we are Christians by our love.

★★★

The Ascension:
Matthew 28:18-20

"All authority in heaven and on earth has been given to me. Go therefore and make disciples of all nations, baptizing them in the name of the Father and of the Son and of the Holy Spirit, teaching them to observe all that I have commanded you; and lo, I am with you always, to the close of the age."

★★★

So if the Christians that choose to stay and live their faith by facing the consequences; we should support them with our prayers and financial support. Those that want to leave and come to the U.S.A. would relieve the burden on the neighboring countries that are flooded with refugees...but is that even possible. Many of the people displaced out of their homes and countries at a moments notice,do not have all the documents they need to verify their identities. If they do have all the documents needed then they can go through the regular immigration process. If we were forced to leave McGolly Hill and our country and didn't have all the documents for all of our children; we would still be able to prove we are Catholics by the knowledge of our faith and stories of our lives. I would hope that the people making the decisions would be reasonable and want to help our family in our time of great need." Mom "The Priest during his homily stated that being hospitable, later always brings a gift. We can be hospitable by bringing the Christians to our nation thereby reducing the refugee population. Also we can help the Muslims that are displaced by donating supplies to have healthy living conditions until they have settlements." Dad "Since so many of our own people are not living according to God's Commandments and the teachings of Jesus Christ coupled with a radicalized Muslim agenda in our country; this could lead to much harm and the end of our country as a Christian nation. Our country was founded on Christian principals and I want it to continue that way. On one hand we as Christians are to help others in need. On the other hand we're having enough trouble protecting our people against our own people who are being radicalized. We can still help the people being displaced, but not by allowing an open door policy, when much harm can result. This might seem intolerant to some but I'm being a realist. The problem is two fold. Number one; We as a country need to return to God's Will and start living our Christian faith in a way pleasing to God our Father in Heaven. We need to knock off this homosexual lifestyle/marriage nonsense. Sex is for procreation and two men or two women cannot naturally conceive a human child. Homosexual acts (whether they consider themselves married or not) is an abomination to God. We need to state the truth about these abominable acts and help our brothers and sisters lovingly live chaste lifestyles for their station in life. We also need to state the truth to our brothers and sisters who are heterosexual and living in ways not pleasing to God; like lust, fornication, living together out of wedlock, divorce and remarriage (to someone else) without annulment, birth control (other than Natural Family Planning in a holy matrimony marriage and only for a good reason according to God). So, our heterosexual brothers and sisters need to knock off their ways and Wake Up to the fact mortal sin is mortal sin and they better get cleaned up before it's too late. Both homosexuals and heterosexuals need to be going to Church on Sundays and Holy Days of Obligation…that is a Commandment…not a suggestion! Our Priests need to stand firm on the truth from the pulpit; they're being too compassionate. I heard that Pope John Paul II was having breakfast with Korean Bishops and they asked "If the ignorant can go to heaven?" He said "Yes, but their Bishops and Priests will go to Hell". Number two: It's probably best to limit Muslims in our nation at this time…until terrorism by radicalized Muslims is no longer a threat. We as Christians must love our Muslim brothers and sisters, like God has loved each of us, but that doesn't mean being foolish and letting down our guard against known evil looking to destroy our country. Just look at what is happening in Europe to England and France and everywhere else in Europe. Radical Muslims seem to be taking over, due to the fact Christians are no longer living according to God's laws (as evident by contraception, the immodest clothing of our women, abortion, the breakdown of the family, homosexual acts being encouraged, euthanasia, lust, movies, television programs that encourage promiscuous behavior, violence and witchcraft). Even if Europe is taken over by radical Muslims doesn't mean we have to let it happen here too. Limiting or halting all Muslims from settling here in the U.S.A. will just slow the progression of a radical Muslim takeover. It would only take about 5% of Muslims to become radicalized to force/coerce the peace loving Muslims to join them; at some point by force. Look at Miriam's colored chalk picture. Only Noah and his family were allowed on the Ark…maybe it makes sense to be diligent and careful for the future of our country by being selective to who we invite into our country. The people on Noah's Ark were the ones who were living as God Commanded. Our own citizens need to put God (Father/

Son/Holy Spirit) first in their lives…the first and greatest of all the Commandments". Mom " We should help our brothers and sisters who are Muslims and displaced from their homes and countries but we still agree a screening process is necessary for the safety of our citizens; just like anyone else who wants to immigrate to this country." Dad "Yes but most likely the ones who have been displaced are not the ones who are radicalized; they are the ones being persecuted. Unfortunately they may have family members or friends that may have been or will be radicalized that would damage our country and Christian way of life. I still feel the strongest defense is a STRONG OFFENSE. The Catholic Christians need to start living their religion fully and rid their souls of all mortal/serious sin/s according to the Magisterium of the Catholic Church; and stop pretending they themselves get to make the rules." Mom " People are resourceful and will find a way to work around this problem. They will know we are Christians by our love and our charity, especially during this difficult period of their lives. I just had a thought that I think would help England from being taken over by radicalized Muslims. Wouldn't it be wonderful if Queen Elizabeth II would become a devout Catholic while she is still Queen of England. She is loved and from what I've seen, she has lived a good life. Queen Elizabeth has taken her duties seriously her whole life, married once and has remained true to her one and only husband, gave birth to several children and took care of her elderly relatives. Her ancestors before Henry the 8th were Catholics…so it's not a stretch for her to return to the Catholic faith. If she did, most likely a lot of her subjects would be open to living their Catholic faith fully or be open to the conversion process also. Someday Queen Elizabeth II might not be her highest title; she could be Saint Elizabeth. My imagination sometimes carries me away, but wouldn't that be a beautiful gift to the world. In the meantime we should send money and help in other ways to relieve the suffering of persecuted Christians and establish communities for healthy living. Also we should pray for all of our brothers and sisters who have been pushed out of their homes and communities and having to deal with great suffering, in many different countries around the world. I'm going to tell God the problem and let God do the heavy lifting. God knows what all of these persecuted people need better than I do. During the next purification (if I'm alive during that time) I want to survive it because God is first and foremost in our lives. The first 3 Commandments are charity for God and the other 7 Commandments are charity for each other." Dad "God bless us all." Mom "Amen to that".

Miriam got back on her knees and continued to work on the sky in the picture. Instead of a beautiful blue sky like her sister Maryann's picture…Miriam was coloring storm clouds with strikes of lightening, ominous and threatening.

Mom and Dad, making sure no little ears were listening, moved a short distance away and started to speak softer. Mom "Sometimes I think we're headed for another purification, this time by fire. The world seems to be turning away from God. If we are not close to God, He withdraws from us. We do it to ourselves by trying to come up with our own answers and devices instead of living according to the word of God (like contraception, abortion and euthanasia)".

Dad agreed "That's why we raise our children and encourage our family, friends, co-workers to go to Holy Mass, be in the state of grace and use the sacraments to keep us close to God. It's also why we don't allow our children or ourselves to watch much television or go to most movies. Saying the family rosary or Divine Mercy Chaplet daily and reading the next Sunday's Gospel reading ahead of time…hopefully will keep our children on the right path once they grow up and leave our home. If we are still alive when the next purification happens, due to the fact people on a large scale are no longer living the faith the way God wants us to…HIS WILL… like during Noah's time… we need to take precautions to make it through the next purification". Mom "Besides being in the state of grace by repenting for all mortal sins and doing penance and changing our ways to God's ways…what precautions are you talking about?"

Just then Molly walked around the corner of the log cabin lodge where she was standing out of sight of her parents "Do you mean having blessed crucifixes (not crosses but crucifixes that have been blessed by a Catholic Priest; if not blessed by a Catholic Priest it is just a piece of wood) on the front and back doors of your house so the angels know which homes to protect. Grandpa McGolly told me having these blessed crucifixes on the houses lets the angels know which houses to protect because Jesus Christ crucified is the slain lamb. In the old Testament the blood of a slain lamb was spread above the door posts so the Angel of Death would pass those homes by and not kill the first born males of those households. Grandpa told me that is why he brought all the crucifixes and had them blessed by Father O'Malley before he gave them away to all of his children. He also said the plain white wax candles blessed by Priest would light up during the Purification and last the whole 3 days. No other lights or candles will light up for the others who chose not to listen. He said the next Evangelization would not be for everyone. It will be only for those who will listen and change their ways to God's way. Everyone will be invited but only those who do the hard work necessary to change to God's Will over their will… will have the chance to make it through the next Purification". Mom lovingly looked at Molly "Does that scare you?" Molly replied "No because the picture of Divine Mercy Jesus over the fireplace says 'JESUS I TRUST IN YOU'. Jesus told Saint Faustina He wanted that picture for us. I love Jesus and Mother Mary. The closing prayer to the Divine Mercy Chaplet/Novena says that mercy is available to everyone. So if everyone knows mercy from God is for everyone and they chose not to ask for mercy or accept it…that's their choice…free will. It's like last year when I was trying so hard to get my classmates to become more 'green', I could only do so much. They had to of free will change their ways to help the earth and all living things…I could not do it for them. I was a good example by word and deed, invited everyone day by day and month by month to physically, mentally and spiritually to convert their ways to include others and the earth. Changing vices into virtues is not always easy but after going through the storm you reach peace, making the difficulties worth it.

Dad "Anything worth wild takes effort. Learning to play a musical instrument, starting a business, getting a college degree, marriage, raising a family, quitting smoking or fighting a drug addiction, working through an illness or physical injury with rehabilitation (for yourself or helping someone), losing weight by changing dietary habits and exercising. With any big decision in life, there will be days that you wonder why you ever took on that challenge. Just take a deep breath, ask God to help you through your trials and persevere, persevere, persevere. If trying to figure out which way to go then choose Jesus, because Jesus is the Way!"

Molly asked her father "Dad, not everyone in my class is Catholic and they don't believe in having crucifixes and they certainly are not going to have a Catholic Priest bless a crucifix or have plain white wax candles blessed by a Catholic Priest, what will happen to them? Will they have a chance to make it through the next Purification?"

Dad "God loves all his children, God will take care of it. We don't know when this will happen. It might not be anytime soon or even in our lifetimes; especially if people change their ways to God's way. Through our examples people may very well change and we will not have to go through a Purification because it would not be needed. Have peace little one knowing you are in the state of grace. Jesus said "My peace I leave you. My peace I give you" when He appeared to the apostles on the day He rose from the dead and set up the sacrament of reconciliation. So, always stay close to Jesus by using the way He set up for us; confession with Catholic Priest. His mercy is for everyone who will ask for it with true sorrow.

Dad smiled and rubbed Molly's curly red hair and said "Jesus I Trust in You. God will take care of it, don't worry". Mom added "Padre Pio a great saint said 'Pray, Hope and Don't Worry'.

Maryann drew a crucifix on the front door of the log cabin on her colored chalk picture saying "Now this house, family, land and animals are protected for the next Purification".

Miriam drew a rainbow to the side of the stormy rain clouds "The people today better wake up and change their ways or the next Purification will be upon the earth soon".

Mom and Dad decided this was a good time to pack everyone in the mini bus and go out for ice cream. A little too much gloom and doom for children or anyone really! Mother and Father McGolly planned to spread a lot of love to their family that day. After ice cream they drove to the park and played, laughed, hugged and sang. Then back home for hot dogs, chips and fresh fruit and fresh milk from the cow. Showers for everyone then to bed, after Dad's nightly blessing.

Dad later told Mom, this time making sure no little ears could hear his statements. He closed the door to their bedroom, looked in the closet and under the bed and said "The coast is clear. It's a good thing we have blessed crucifixes on our front and back doors (exposed to the outside) and on Grandma's little house front and back doors so the angels will protect us and the land and animals as long as we're in the state of grace. Otherwise the log cabin lodge would be a huge bond fire during the Purification. I do plan to talk to Grandpa about less gloom and doom especially with the kids and to stick to the teachings of the Catholic Church." Mom "They will know we are Christians by our love. Of course on the other hand, if the people continue on the wrong path, choosing which Commandments to follow and telling God to change to the ways of the world...well Miriam might be right...the next Purification might be upon the earth soon. In any event, I'm sleeping well tonight because I have nothing to fear. Being in the state of grace gives me great peace. Jesus I Trust in You".

★★★★★★★★★★★★★★★★★★★★★★★★★★

GRANDMA AND MOM MILK THE COWS
WHILE LISTENING TO THE RADIO

"Grandma and I were milking the cows this morning while listening to the radio. We heard a man talking about Isis bought up a whole town only three hour away from Medjugorje in Bosnia and only 2 hours from Serieavo; they're flying their flag there. A journalist tried to interview someone who lived there and was told to go away. The journalist was able to find someone else flying the Isis flag in that town and one of the statements he made was 'When the cross in broken, Islam will rule'. So Grandma and I started discussing how the cross is broken in the U.S.A.; and came to the conclusion that Isis doesn't have to do anything radical to bring us down because we as a nation seem to be doing it to ourselves!" exclaimed Mom as she crawled into bed at the end of an exhausting day. Dad replied "The part about Isis buying up a whole town so close to where the Virgin Mary (Queen of Peace) has been appearing everyday for 34+ years is troubling. A lot of times when the Virgin Mary starts appearing somewhere, means trouble is coming and she is trying to get her children back to God (Father/Son/Holy Spirit). Of course She can't do it for us, we have been given free will and must make the changes ourselves. So how did you and Grandma decide that the cross is broken?". "Well Darling, at first it was random thoughts jumping from one point to the next and it didn't help that Muffy and Daisy were acting up. Neither Grandma or myself could get a good milking rhythm going" Mom said while getting out of bed and sitting at her wooden vanity set that Dad gave her last Valentine's Day while brushing her long red hair. Then she started listing many ways the cross seems to be broken…

"The cross is broken when we have a law 'No fault divorce'. Let's face it, our country is out of control with the number of divorces and the breakdown of the family. It's someone's fault! Once we start keeping track of why our families are breaking up and who's at fault; then we will have a place to start to correct the problem. We need a plan to keep our families happy, healthy, strong and TOGETHER.

The cross is broken when we have so many people committing and attempting to commit suicide. Why are they so broken hearted? If people had a firm grasp on the Catholic faith (the TRUTH) maybe so many would not go into despair. They would know they have a loving Father in Heaven that loves and forgives and can help them in their trials and also gives meaning to their suffering and trials.

The cross is broken when so many of our people are alcoholics and drug addicts. Why are they trying to drown their sorrows?

The cross is broken when we have a law that allows abortion and the unborn infant (the most defenseless human beings) have no rights. Killing the most vunerable in our society is anti Christian because of the fifth Commandment: Thou Shalt Not Kill. A life begins at conception; a unique human being has been created by God.

The cross is broken when our government passes laws or promotes euthanasia. Euthanasia is already legal in some states. The killing of the most vulnerable (the aged, the unborn, the marginalized) in our society is against the fifth Commandment: Thou Shalt Not Kill. There is no such thing as 'mercy killing', that just doesn't make sense. St. Teresa of Calcutta showed us how to give dignity to every human life (Natural Conception to Natural Death). Redemptive suffering has many benefits when handled with love.

The cross is broken when our women are treated as sex objects. We need to change how women are portrayed on television, movies, music, magazines etc…to encourage dignity for all human persons. We need to change our female idols to caring women with good morals instead of self absorbed women/teens wearing revealing clothing and having immoral lifestyles.

The cross is broken when our men are looking at porn behind closed doors and our women are absorbed in books, movies, television shows that encourage women to think in sinful ways; even if the characters are wearing Victorian style clothing.

The cross is broken when our women are dressing so provocatively. Women should dress modestly. Jesus would not approve of what women are wearing today in most places.

The cross is broken when our American culture sees lust and fornication as the norm and no longer strives to live as God commands. Chastity until in a holy matrimony marriage.

The cross is broken when our supreme court (without the states approval) instituted laws approving of abominable marriage/unions. Homosexual acts (whether random or in a relationship) are mortal sins.

The cross is broken when our religious liberties are pushed away and the people are forced to go against their religion like: Obama Care making Catholics and like minded people pay into a mandatory healthcare insurance system (with birth control, abortion etc…these are damn to Hell offenses in the Catholic religion).

The cross is broken when we don't know which bathroom to use!

The cross is broken when our government tries to pass a law forcing surgeons to do sex change operations on children who are gender confused.

The cross is broken when teenagers are on birth control because they are sexually active (mortal sin). Birth control and being sexual active without being married are mortal sins.

The cross is broken when so many couples live together out of wedlock. Fornication is a mortal sin even if the couple plans to get married someday.

The cross is broken when we no longer or rarely see Nativity Scenes at Christmas time.

The cross is broken when our children don't know who Jesus is, but they know the latest kid movie characters or superheroes.

The cross is broken when a family no longer goes to church on Sunday morning routinely.

The cross is broken when football games are more important than honoring God on the Sabbath Day.

The cross is broken when the true meaning of Christmas is not celebrated in our Christian nation.

The cross is broken when our children grow up and leave the Catholic faith.

The cross is broken when our children grow up and have children of their own but don't raise them in the Catholic faith.

The cross is broken when our culture has such relaxed sexual standards.

The cross is broken when our teens and young adults no longer believe in a lifelong marriage.

The cross is broken when our people get married outside of the Catholic Church (without approval of the Catholic Church).

The cross is broken when Catholics think birth control is alright…knowing that birth control is a mortal sin. I saw a recent poll that stated 82% of Catholics think that birth control/contraception is alright. If that is true, it means that at least 82% of Catholics are on a path to Hell. Our Catholic faith has been watered down because of protestant Christians who don't know better. The protestant Christians have only been given partially truth…the fullness of the Christian faith is in the Catholic religion. The protestant Christians believed the same as the Catholics on the subject of birth control until the Lambeth Conference in 1930. One of the protestant faiths approved of some form of birth control and that opened the flood gates for the other protestant religions. The Catholic religion does not change doctrine. If people would open their eyes they would see that the Catholic religion is right. Look what the birth control pill and other forms of contraception have done to our society. The cross is broken.

The cross is broken when Catholics won't go to Holy Mass on Sunday and Holy Days of Obligation. When Catholics choose to have other gods (like sleeping in after playing on Saturday night, going to football games or other activity and neglecting their duty to go to Holy Mass. Catholics and protestant Christians the third Commandment is: Remember to keep the Lord's day.

When the young no longer believe marriage is between one man and one woman for life…the cross is broken.

The cross is broken when people stare constantly at their cell phones and take no time to watch the Catholic/ Christian sites on their phones.

The cross is broken when people won't turn off their cell phones and say the Rosary or Divine Mercy Chaplet".

Dad interrupted Mom and said " Sweetheart, I'd like to get some sleep tonight so jump to the part of how to fix the broken cross." "That part is easy. All we have to do is return to the Sacraments. God developed a way for us to stay close to Him, call the Sacraments. Now all we have to do is use them to bring us back into full communion with Him. We must OBEY God, it's not enough to have faith. I guess my point is that we Catholic Christians and Protestant Christians have created this mess we're in ourselves…the Muslims didn't do it to us…we did it to ourselves. The way for Catholics to fix the cross since it seems to be broken is to live the 10 Commandments and use the Sacraments to keep us close to God" replied Mom. Dad "What if people don't change? asked Dad as he started to drift off to sleep. Mom " Well, then I guess the Muslim religion and ideology could easily take over our country, especially if accelerated by a few radical Muslims. The peace loving Muslims might have to react if forced to; like peaceful Russians during World War II. You know that radio program Grandma and I listened to also said that the Islamic prophet Muhammad was a war lord. 'What's good for Islam is good and what's bad for Islam is bad' is part of the ideology. That bothered me, so I looked on the internet to see if Muslims donate to charities that extend outside of serving their own people. They really don't, I'm not sure what to make of that. What I do think is that until terrorism is no longer a threat in the world, we should not allow Muslims to immigrate to the U.S.A.. The possibility is too great that radical Muslims could come in or peace loving Muslims may be coerced into terrorist activities. However, what I really think is that all Christians should start living their faith fully and these problems would resolve. When we as a society are close to God, then God can help us" Mom softly answered as she got back into bed and turned out the light. Mom reached over to kiss Dad good night and asked "Are you asleep?" Dad's eyes were wide open and he answered "I'm awake now. I may never sleep again after what you just told me. I'll probably still be awake in the morning so I'll go to the barn and milk the cows." Mom smiled and said "Good. I love you too my Darling Fritz".

WATER TOWER SCRIPTURE PASSAGE

A week later, a lady from Grandma's rosary group replenished Maryann and Miriam's colored chalk supply. The lady was impressed with the pictures and wanted them to draw another scene from a Bible story. The little twin girls asked Grandma to read them the story about Jonah and the big fish.

Now would be a good time to open your Bible to the Old Testament and read:

Jonah 1:1–3:10

The twins were inspired, so out with the colored chalks…this time to work together drawing the story of Jonah and the Big Fish. They drew and colored all day with some time out for eating, drinking, potty breaks and jumping rope. Mom and Grandma made a few phone calls and before dinner most of the family and some friends from Grandma's rosary group showed up to see the story of Jonah in sidewalk chalk. Jonah…the ship leaving the dock…the storm…men casting lots…the men throwing Jonah off the ship…the Big Fish swallowing Jonah(for 3 days and 3 nights)…the fish vomiting Jonah out of the belly of the Big Fish on dry land in the city of Nineveh…the people living and working in Nineveh…the king of Nineveh's decree…everyone and their animals wearing sackcloth and fasting…the people of Nineveh rejoicing after 40 days when they were not destroyed…the people continuing to live according to the Will of God and not returning to their evil ways.

Dad fried up some fish caught in their own lake and stream and everyone brought food for a pot luck dinner.

A couple of days later the sidewalk chalk faded away but the little girls wanted everyone to know about Jonah and the Big Fish and the great city of Nineveh changing their evil ways and not being destroyed by God. So Miriam and Maryann talked Mom and Dad into taking their sidewalk chalk and writing the scripture passage Jonah: 1:1–3:10 high atop the McGolly Hill water tower. Now everyone who visited McGolly Hill would know about the conversion of the people to do God's Will. Mom and Dad were more than happy to oblige, because this was a story of people listening to God through a messenger (Jonah) and changing their evil ways to God's ways and not being destroyed…because the whole city repented and asked for forgiveness with true sorrow.

The little girls knew about the true story of Noah and the Ark in which God purified the earth with a great flood due to people resisting the ways of God. They also heard Grandpa McGolly talk about a future Purification if people don't return to God's ways and away from doing their will over God's Will. So Mom and Dad wanted their children to have a positive happy ending Bible story to give hope and encouragement for happy days ahead. This Bible story offers hope and not all gloom and doom like Noah's Ark, so Mom and Dad climbed the high ladder and wrote the scripture passage so everyone could see, with bright orange colored sidewalk chalk. A couple of days later they had to do it again because it faded. Over the next few weeks they made to climb several times due to fading or rain. Mom and Dad decided to lift the ban on the children climbing the water tower; they allowed Molly, Mike and Mark to climb up to the top and do the honors of writing the scripture passage under the parents supervision from the ground floor. Soon the older kids were 'over it' the thrill was gone; they didn't want to make the high climb anymore. About the third week, Mom and Dad made the last climb up the tall wooden ladder with a bucket of paint and 2 paintbrushes. They combined red paint left over from painting the barn and yellow paint left over from the nursery to make the color orange. In bright orange colored paint JONAH: 1:1-3:10 for all to see on McGolly Hill and the town below.

Like I said, they wanted to give hope to their children for a better tomorrow. By hope I mean the majority of the people turning back to God's ways and the earth not being purified because of the free will choices of so many people changing their evil ways back to God's ways. To be more clear: The majority of people returning to chastity for their state in life; no birth control other than Natural Family Planning (N.F.P.) in a holy matrimony marriage and only for a good reason; no fornication; no homosexual acts; no adultery; reverse no fault divorce; get back to a culture of life and stop abortions and euthanasia; learn to love each other the way God wants us to love each other and keep our families together; stop watching and listening to television/movies/music/anything that leads to a culture of death; start living a culture of life with music, television shows/movies, art, exercise in healthy ways, get back to nature and the beauty of the world in which we live and make it a beautiful place to love and raise our children. All ages should have a right to life, natural conception to natural death and should be treated with dignity at every stage of life. Keep the Sabbath day holy by going to church. Clean up our souls by going to confession with Catholic Priest and truly repenting with true sorrow All mortal sins...get into the state of grace.

In the Old Testament Bible story of Jonah and the Big Fish, the king of Nineveh declared with a decree to encourage the people to change their evil ways back to God's ways. That would be so nice if our elected officials would do the same thing. It would make things so much easier. Devout Catholics need to run for office and stand up for the truth before it is too late. Even if it appears to be too late, we still need our devout Catholics to run for office and stand strong... persevere, persevere, persevere. The rest of us should pray for those who lead us and not despair. Jesus I Trust in You.

There can only be one will in a perfect place of peace. Why wouldn't every human being want that 'one will' to be a loving Father who wants the best for all His children...and we are all His little children. We must OBEY all of God's COMMANDMENTS!

Molly remembered her Grandpa McGolly saying there could be a Great Warning called the Illumination of the Soul in which every person on the planet will know where they stand with God...something that has never happened before and will never happen again. Grandpa said that when this happens...if it happens...that people will be such hardened sinners that the

Great Warning will include a sample of where they are going (a Miniature Judgment) and that 90% will be on a path to Hell…so that means 90% will feel what it is like to be in Hell…there will be whaling and screaming all over the earth like never before…however there will be no physical side effects…no physical burns after the Great Warning has past…but some people will die of heart attacks/fright during the Great Warning. Basically, everything that we were taught in Catechism classes when we were children is the Truth and God has not changed. Only man has changed and rationalized their mortal sins. I repeat: GOD HAS NOT CHANGED. Also remember that mortal sin is the only thing that separates us from God; it is not a scale of good and evil that determines your eternity. It's whether you have mortal sin on your soul that you refuse to repent with true sorrow. Those who have been given much (like Catholic teachings); much will be expected. Eternal mortal sin= eternal damnation. Of course only God judges but He did not just throw us out there and say figure it out your selves. No, God gave us the 10 COMMANDMENTS and sent His Son Jesus to show us the way. For Jesus Christ is the Way, the Truth and the Life. If you lose your way lean on Jesus Christ. Catholics have been taught the Truth, so more is expected from Catholics.

Grandpa McGolly said the other difficult part to people being such hardened sinners is that even once they know where they stand with God and feel where they are going (Judgment in Miniature) that only about 20% of the 90% headed for eternal damnation (Hell) will change their ways. The prediction is that 2/3's of the people living at that time will still be on a path to Hell after the Illumination of the Soul and followed up within a year of the Great Miracle (in Spain with many healings). Of course this percentage can change because we all still have free will. Grandpa McGolly did the math and figured out that 2/3's is equal to 66.6%. He for some reason thought that the sign of the anti-Christ was 666. Grandpa wondered if the 2/3's of people who refused to repent and change their ways on all their mortal sins after the Illumination of the Soul and the Great Miracle; were all part of the anti-Christ. Another way to put this is 66.6% of the people which is roughly 2/3's will still have satan as their father and refuse to repent with true sorrow for their serious sin/s. Free will gives each of us the choice to choose God and our Heavenly home…it might not be easy but it gives you an inner peace.

So, you can see why Mother and Father McGolly were more than happy to have the scripture passage of the story of Jonah and the Big Fish JONAH: 1:1-3:10 printed on their water tower to give hope to their children every day. We all need hope. If the majority of the people come back to God's Will, then there will be no need for a Purification. The Old Testament Bible story of Jonah and the Big Fish offers us hope.

Grandpa said that even if we are headed for a Purification; that if you are in the state of grace you can survive; this too is HOPE. If you survive the Purification you will not be disappointed. Once we have the Illumination of the Soul, the choice is up to each person. Who's your father; God our loving Heavenly Father or satan)?

God is serious about His COMMANDMENTS and GOD HAS NOT CHANGED. Only men have changed and rationalized their behaviors. The great deceiver has deceived us all. Grandma and Grandpa McGolly think that the third World War is us against ourselves. We are killing the people we should love the most (our unborn children through abortion and the people who lovingly raised us through euthanasia). Once again the great deceiver has deceived us. After the Illumination of the Soul and the Great Miracle in Spain, WILL COME the PURIFICATION of the earth. Basically the Illumination of the Soul is your judgment unless you rid your soul of all mortal sin by repenting with true sorrow and changing your ways to God's Will. Grandpa said there will be a great many people returning or converting to the TRUTH in the Catholic faith and away from being cafeteria Catholics, etc…. In our Creed, the part that states 'From whence He shall come again to judge the living and the dead" could be two fold. One: Judgment Day at the end of the world (Final judgment including our influences on others will be revealed). Two: Possibly the Illumination of the Soul (a Miniature Judgment). Jesus was always more concerned about the spiritual (soul) realm than the physical. So, let's consider the soul without the physical body. What if Jesus is looking only at the soul verses the body. Jesus never said anyone was dead if they physically died. Jesus only said people were dead if their souls were dead (meaning in the state of mortal sin without repentance). The Illumination of the Soul is judging the living and the dead when referring to the spirit (soul). How many of us are walking around with dead souls, 90% ? Just because everyone is doing it doesn't mean it is okay; it just means they have rationalized their behaviors. When people justify their mortal sins, they no longer feel any remorse. Why? Because their soul has shriveled up and died. In order to resurrect their soul they need to repent (ask forgiveness) with true sorrow. We must ask for forgiveness in order to receive it. Once again because this is worth repeating: The Illumination of the Soul (The Great Warning) could be your judgment unless you change ALL of your evil ways (mortal sin) to God's Will and repent with true sorrow…do not hold back on any of your mortal sins. Mortal sin (serious, grave, mortal sin/s) is the only thing that separates us from God. Your loving Father in Heaven wants you and me and everyone else with Him at home in Heaven. We are living in a difficult age and it seems the evil one has deceived us all.

If the Illumination of the Soul happens in your lifetime, remember God loves you and this was the last resort to get your attention. Get yourself in the state of grace (abSOULutely no mortal sin/s…don't rationalize your sin/s away) then reach out and help others as much as possible…for they too of free will MUST change their ways. You can't do it for them but you can point them in the right direction and show them the way by your free will choices. Persevere, persevere, persevere!!! Do it with joy. People respond better to joy than gloom and doom. If you are in the state of grace, then you will have nothing to fear during the Illumination of the Soul (Judgment in Miniature) or the Purification. So, you should be joyful and sleep peacefully.

Now, I have no idea when the "Illumination of the Soul' will happen; it might not happen for hundreds of years. I'm just saying that it appeared to me that conditions are ripe now and have been for a long time. The conditions being 90% of the people being on a path to Hell because they are doing their will over God's Will on serious/grave issues and seem to have no remorse. If the majority of people would change their ways to God's Ways there will be no need for a Purification. If we do have the 'Illumination of the Soul' that means a Purification is coming. The time of Divine Mercy will be coming to a close and the time for God's Justice will be next. Be Ready!

Also remember you and your family may have to walk away from health care insurance because it pays for people to engage in mortal sin like birth control (other than N.F.P.), abortion and euthanasia. The government does not have the right to go against God because God is above the government and always will be.

Anyway the McGolly parents wanted their children to be reminded every time they looked up to the water tower that our 'free will' choices can save our world. There will be no need for a Purification if the majority of people do God's Will (like the people & including king of Nineveh).

What's on your town's or city's water tower? Maybe someone should take a bucket of bright orange paint and put JONAH : 1:1–3:10 plainly in Giant bold letters and numbers for all to see. Or maybe use orange sidewalk chalk on your sidewalk or driveway to evangelize in your neighborhood for the whole town/city to see: JONAH: 1:1–3:10. If you are fresh out of orange, then combine red and yellow sidewalk chalk to make orange.

There is always hope whether people come back as a majority or if they don't and those that choose God's Will (in everything) can still make it through the Purification and live full lives.

According to Grandpa McGolly about 1/3 of the people will survive the Purification; that number can change because we all have free will. Remember if we are headed for a Purification that the goal is to be in the state of grace to survive. We can make this number/percentage higher if we pray and fast more. This is not the end of the world. Those that survive the Purification can live full lives, including marriage and children etc…However, it will be a different world… and you will not be disappointed. Making the difficult changes and persevering will be worth it. Grandpa McGolly said that possibly the first 3 years after the Purification, we will have little to eat, we will have to build up our food supply by working together with love for our fellow man and of course God will provide what we need. Perhaps start some type of fasting now to condition yourself and 'offer it up' as a sacrifice for Mother Mary's intentions. May God Bless You and Your Family.

Open your Bible and Read Scripture Passage: MATTHEW 6:24-34

This scripture passage is very comforting. God is our Heavenly Father and He will take care of us if we obey His Commandments and love.

★★

KNIGHTS AT THE ROUND TABLE

Mother McGolly called to order the knights at the round table. The dining room table was now the center to plan a strategy to combat evil that was threatening to destroy their families. The men were away on their yearly hunting trip. Except for Maureen (who spear headed this meeting) all the women were sitting around the dining room table each holding a baby in their arms. The three triplet boys (Leo, Patrick and Shawn) were held by Grandma McFrugal, Martha and Kimberly. The quadruplet girl babies (Cecelia, Faustina, Jacinta and Theresa) were each held by their Godmothers (Rachael, Belle, Rosie and Clare). Incidentally, all the quadruplet infant's middle names were their Godmothers names (Cecelia Rachael, Faustina Belle, Jacinta Rosie and Teresa Clare). Baby Anthony was held by his mother (Lucy); his middle name was Ivan (Anthony Ivan) after his Godfather. Mother McGolly (Maureen) began to speak, straight to the point " Ladies, Holy Mother Church (the Catholic Church) through the Sacraments of Baptism and Confirmation, we have been enlisted into the service of the King as Soldiers of Christ and have been strengthen by the Holy Spirit for spiritual battle.

We are in the middle of the Third World War and most people are completely unaware. The great deceiver has deceived us all. Since the first two world wars were nations against nations, most people think the third World War (the deadliest of them all) will also be nations against nations like in the past. We need to take a step back and look at the facts. More human beings are killed through abortion and soon to be euthanasia than by any other form/s of murder. Yes, abortion kills the most innocent and vulnerable in our societies since they are unable to fight for their rights. The great deceiver has deceived us all. Of course, if we can kill the people we should love the most (our unborn children and the people who lovingly raised us), we most certainly can kill people in other nations too. We now live in a culture, all over the world that permits us to kill our unborn children and the people who lovingly raise us, for our own self centered desires. Sex and babies go together. When people try to separate that fact through contraception, they find themselves doing their wills over God's Will. Life begins at conception, when the sperm and egg unite. There are twenty three sets of chromosomes at conception; there will never be more or less throughout each human beings life; a unique life starts.

The Third World War is us against ourselves, we are killing the people we should love the most; our unborn children and the people who lovingly raised us. Abortion and euthanasia are ways to kill human beings. The 5th COMMANDMENT: Thou Shalt NOT Kill. Our government allows the murder of the unborn and in some states euthanasia has raised its ugly head. Euthanasia is killing the people we should love and give dignity to the end of their lives like Mother Teresa of Calcutta showed us how to do.

In Fatima Portugal in 1917, Mother Mary asked us to say our rosary everyday in order for the errors of Russia not to spread all over the world. Ladies let's pick up our weapons and fight evil. They each took a rosary from out of their pocket or from the middle of the round table and prayerfully and united together said the Joyful mysteries of the rosary.

1). The Annunciation
2). The Visitation
3). The Nativity
4). The Presentation
5). Finding Jesus in the Temple

After the rosary, Mother McGolly recited the Prayer to Saint Michael the Archangel to defend us in battle and be our protection against the wickedness and snares of the devil. She proceeded to explain the origins of that prayer "This was the prayer Pope Leo the thirteenth composed in 1884 after hearing a conversation between God and satan near the tabernacle where he just completed celebrating a private Mass in a private Vatican chapel. At the foot of the Altar his face became ashen white for about ten minutes. He heard two voices; one kind and gentle, the other harsh and guttural. The harsh voice of satan said something like 'I can destroy Your Church.' God said something like 'you can then do so.' Satan stated that he would need more time and power. God asked 'How much time and how much power'. Satan wanted 75-100 years and greater power over those who will give themselves over to his service. God granted satan the time and the power. Pope Leo the Thirteenth went directly to his office and composed the Prayer to Saint Michael the Archangel, to be said at every low Mass everywhere."

Maureen continued "I recently heard a Catholic Priest on the Catholic channel state that some theologians think the 100 years started the same year Mother Mary appeared to the 3 children in Fatima, Portugal in 1917. If that is true then, sometime in 2017 the 100 years will be over."

Rosie "Did you know that in 1917 Russia legalized abortion. When Mother Mary said to say the rosary everyday in order to stop Russia from spreading her errors, she must have been referring to abortion as well as communism. Especially when you think of how many people have been killed through abortion. Natural conception to natural death."

Grandma McFrugal " We just said the Joyful Mysteries of the Rosary and the first three mysteries revolve around the conception of Jesus known as the Annunciation, in the womb known as the Visitation where both Jesus and John the Baptist were in their mother's wombs and the Nativity which celebrates the birth of our Savior Jesus Christ. Every time the Joyful mysteries of the rosary are recited, Catholics are reminded that life begins at conception."

Grandma continued "Fifty years ago, no one would have ever believed our world would change so much in such a short period of time. We're all holding babies in our arms with love. Maybe someone should be holding me, now that I'm entering into my twilight years. Our government might want to make me feel like a burden and of no use, then kill me like the unborn children that are being slaughtered everyday because someone decided they're in the way."

Rosie "Mom, we will all hold you with love."

Lucy "You all know I had an abortion several years ago and I still miss my baby. Through the Sacrament of Confession I have been forgiven by God for that mortal sin which I deeply regret. God has forgiven me and through attending a 'Rachel's Vineyard' retreat I found the comfort I needed to forgive myself. I feel great. There is a love and joy deep in my heart that wasn't there before. I want to stop women from making the same mistake I made, starting from going along with the popular culture and thinking that fornication was okay because 'everyone else was doing it'. Fornication leads to unplanned pregnancies even if using contraceptives. If you're in a one sided relationship, the other half isn't there for the long haul, well you're on your own. It is better to wait until in a stable relationship and feel loved and know any possible children will have both a mother and father, as God intended it. Our Father in Heaven knows what is best for us and His Word is in the Bible. Lust and fornication are mortal sins. Although I was in foster care most of my childhood; I was exposed to the teaching of Jesus Christ from time to time. I was tossed around from one foster home to another and felt like no one really wanted me. I now know that I am a daughter of the King and my body is a temple of the Holy Spirit; I should live my life accordingly. I want everyone to know how much they are loved by God and convert their lives to God's Will. Someday I will meet my unborn baby in Heaven, this now (since Confession) gives me comfort instead of shame and sadness. I still choose to keep my abortion unknown, so I would appreciate your discretion in this matter. I feel this is between God and me. I may not even tell my possible future spouse because that just makes my cross his too and will serve no purpose. I realize some people choose to share their experiences in order to help others not make the same mistakes… and I support their decision. I choose not to broadcast my deepest regret…I'm at peace with God and will do my part to lead souls to God in my own way."

Martha "I'm doing my part. I travel to any Catholic Church or anywhere I am welcomed to teach Natural Family Planning. Before I teach them how to use 3 different methods of N.F.P., I share information: 1).I show graphs of direct correlation between the start of the birth control pill and promiscuity/abortion/sexual diseases and other effects to our society over time. As the use of the birth control pill and other contraceptives increased, the negative effects to our society correspond. 2). I list 6-7 expectations of the birth control pill when it first became available to the masses and compare the actual effects…enough time has elapsed so that we can see the true findings…one can see how the birth control pill and other contraceptives are truly intrinsically evil like the Catechism of Catholic Church teaches. Look up # 2370 CATECHISM OF THE CATHOLIC CHURCH. 3). The World Health Organization lists the birth control pill as a class one carcinogen. To think women are actually taking a poison into their own body everyday over a period of years, and don't even contemplate what this is doing to their own body. 4). Side effects of the birth control can include: weight gain, blood clots, liver tumors, breast cancer, strokes etc… 5).Warning that after being on birth control pills over several years that they may not be able to conceive when they decide the time is right. Also in-vitro fertilization and artificial insemination and surrogate motherhood are mortal sins…not natural. They need to consider that frozen fertilized eggs are human beings. Life starts at conception. What are they going to do with the unused frozen fertilized eggs (human beings)? If they unfreeze them and throw them away, that is abortion. If they keep them frozen indefinitely, who will oversee and pay for this service; not to mention these human beings are kept from living their lives. What if your children are used as experiments in these labs without your knowledge. Men who donate their sperms at sperm banks, how do you know if your children are being treated with love or used as experiments? There are many consequences to our actions. What if down the road the couple get a divorce and one wants to either dispose of the conceived human beings that are frozen (killing the child/children) and the other wants the frozen fertilized eggs implanted into the mother or a surrogate mother. There are many things to consider about how in the long run…effects of all should be considered. 6).I talk about how the birth control pill and other forms of contraception can be abortifacient. Meaning the sperm and egg can still come together (conception, the beginning of life has happened) but the utcrus has been thinned out due to the birth control pill/injection or devices and causes the human being to have no place to be implanted and is sloughed out of the body. At this point I share with them that I for a short time took the birth control pill even though I knew the Catholic Church condemns the use of contraceptives. I explained that my spouse and I (both Cradle Catholics) rationalized the use of the birth control pills. Now I look back and wonder if during that time period we might have aborted a child, possibly every month while using the birth control pill as a contraceptive. I wish that the doctor would have explained this in layman terms as to make sure women know what they are doing; killing a human being at the beginning of life is the same as killing a human being at any point in their life. I would not have chosen to take the birth control pill knowing that it was potentially abortifacient to a conceived child. I let them know that I went to confession and confessed to this mortal sin and I do not encourage anyone to take any kind of contraception. I let them know that this is the reason I teach N.F.P. to any Catholic Church or any place I am welcomed. 7). I explain benefits of using N.F.P. such as there are no physical side effects, the spouses who use N.F.P. usually have better communication and the woman feels loved and cherish including her fertility, the divorce rate of couples who use N.F.P. is about 2-3% which is much lower than 50% of cafeteria Catholics. Perhaps treating your body like a temple of the Holy Spirit has its advantages. 8). At conception there are 23 sets of chromosomes; there will never be more or less. This is a unique human being. One has to wonder how science knows that there are 23 sets of chromosomes at conception. It must have been an experiment on a conceived child in the laboratory; in-vitro-fertilization. A child must have been destroyed for science to obtain that piece of information. Life begins at conception."

Kimberly "Some of the women in my family have difficulty conceiving a child. I'm an only child and my parents had me late in life. Since artificial insemination, surrogate motherhood and in-vitro-fertilization are immoral because they are not natural; then Ivan and I may not be able to have biological children."

Lucy "You can adopt. I always wanted someone to adopt me when I was a foster child but no one did."

Belle "I think our culture puts too much pressure on the young or actually adults also, to have sex strictly for pleasure and it doesn't seem to be tied to having babies anymore. We need to somehow bring back a culture of dignity to every human person and stop using each other as objects for pleasure only. I want my children to have loving long lasting secure relationships, keeping their families together when they grow up and I'm long gone. My children are young now but the world around us seems to be closing in and I'm ready to do my part to fight for the spiritual well being of my children and all of humanity. Our culture needs to bring back chastity for your station in life. We should combat the evil of sexual sins from both sides. On one side to try to stop lust, fornication, divorce, adultery, homosexual acts by changing societies perception of current lax standards. On the other side let's bring back chastity. An ounce of prevention is worth a pound of cure. Of course we do this for our own families but how do we spread this concept to our communities."

Grandma "The fathers need to talk to each of their children. A father's presence in the home is greatly underestimated."

Clare " I feel like we have been not only deceived by the great deceiver but we have been deceived by pharmaceutical companies who promote oral/injection contraceptives and/or devices to stop contraception and OB-GYN doctors who will not offer alternatives to infertility other than what is morally unacceptable. Even most Catholic OB-GYN doctors are practicing and prescribing medications that will damn them to Hell; specifically birth control pills/injections/devices/ in-vitro-fertilization/ artificial insemination. I watch Catholic television, Catholic radio and read Catholic books and magazines, even I know that there are other alternatives available for women who have difficulty conceiving, or have heavy periods or severe cramping. If I know about these alternatives then why don't intelligent physicians who have studied for years about the female body know?! Research needs to be focused towards healing the problems of infertility, not in-vitro-fertilization or artificial insemination. The doctors on the Catholic programs have ways of diagnosing the actual problem (lab tests, sonograms etc...). NaProTechnology is the way of the future for OB-GYN physicians who do not want to go to Hell. Kimberly if natural conception turns out to be an issue, you and Ivan might want to find a doctor who practices NaProTechnology."

Lucy "Or adopt a foster child that needs you!"

Clare " In the other direction, people need to be educated about the TRUTH of what the birth control pill is doing to their own bodies and to our society as a whole. We need to educate the public. This is so difficult with the secular world which promotes a culture of death. I wish there was more on television that would promote a culture of life and love according to the 10 COMMANDMENTS and teachings of Jesus Christ. Almost every channel allows fornication, living together out of wedlock, divorce, divorce and remarriage also known as adultery, adultery, lust, homosexual acts and lifestyle, murder, murder and more murder. We as a society need to stop watching these very seductive programs. We are lured by the beautiful people, exotic settings, music and devious plots to watch trash tv that will desensitize the masses to see sin as sin anymore. How do we get the masses to do something more productive and life affirming with their time".

Maureen "In your list of sins on almost every channel, you mentioned lust. Mother Mary told the 3 shepherd children of Fatima Portugal in 1917 that the main reason souls were going to Hell at that time was because of lust. Since God does not change, that means lust remains a mortal sin. In 1917 they did not have the internet, or television or movies or certain music lyrics we have today. The great deceiver has deceived us all; most people don't even see the actions of lust as mortal sins anymore; like fornication, divorce and remarriage to someone else without getting as annulment, adultery, homosexual acts (not the tendency). Makes me wonder what God will do when the 100 years is over that satan has been allotted more power from God. Mother Mary has been appearing all over the world for we are all her children. She wants to bring us (her little children) back to her Son, Jesus Christ. I feel like she has kept us from destroying our world but could do more if we all would pray and fast more to receive the graces we need to save our souls and the world. Praying should be at the top of our strategy since that is what she asked us to do in Fatima Portugal in 1917, praying the rosary every day. Each person should ask for Mother Mary's intercession to help all of us in these times. If we all give all of our prayers to Mother Mary for Her intentions, our prayers will go further. She knows the best way to use these graces to help us all.

Rachael "Last week when I went to confession, I told the Priest that people seem to think I'm too righteous and they just stopped telling me what's going on in their lives or with their families. The Priest told me maybe the people need to hear why certain sins are wrong; to explain how these sins affect them and other people whether directly or indirectly instead of a list of : Thou Shalt Not's. So, I told him that I have never heard a Priest from the pulpit talk about 'Why' the birth control pill or other forms of birth control are morally wrong. I ask why the Fathers of the Catholic Church are not teaching from the pulpit the evils of birth control when almost every Catholic sitting in the pews is using some form of birth control if they are sexually active. I also don't hear anything about lust, fornication, adultery, divorce and remarriage without an annulment, living together whether as a trial or before marriage, homosexual acts and lifestyle during the homilies. Only once in all my years of listening to homilies have I heard a Priest talk about divorce and remarriage without getting an annulment. Since the Priest was suggesting that I should explain the whys, maybe the Priests should explain these concepts to all of us from the pulpit. The Priest compassionately explained that people are in different stages of conversion and to make a blanket statement might cause everyone to get up and leave or just not come back. He also stated that there are many children in the church and it would not be appropriate to bring up certain subjects. He said those subjects were discussed one on one in confession or in groups that meet for certain information/reasons. I felt those were good reasons and that Priest/s have been dealing with these issues for a long time. We need to help our Priest/s. We should ask them what we can do to help or come up with a plan and ask for permission to teach certain topics with their approval. However, I would prefer for the words to come directly from the Priest/s during homilies."

Grandma McFrugal "The Fathers need to talk to their children."

Rachael "The only time I remember a Priest talking about divorce then getting married outside the Catholic Church or a couple living together outside of holy matrimony was on Catholic television during a homily. While I was listening, I got the feeling the Priest was inspired by the Holy Spirit to speak on those topics. I felt that he planned to preach on his prepared speech written in front of him but the Holy Spirit prompted him to go in a completely different direction. Who knows, maybe events in his own life and people very close to him contributed to this shift in his homily. It was one of the best homilies I've ever heard, and I'm a cradle Catholic. He said when people come into the confessional and tell the Priest about their situations, not to get upset with the Priest if he seems mad or upset with them. The Priest isn't mad; he is trying to figure out how to help you. As part of this enthusiastic and heartfelt homily, he said that these people may have to separate from living together or live as brother and sister until the marital issues are resolved. The Priest smiled saying "Now calm down. We're not punishing you, but the truth needs to come out. That is what the annulment process is for. Some of these issues are very complex and we need more information". This Priest seemed to be pleading gently with people to let the Priest/s help them get right with God and each other. His plea was to help the people who have lived according to their own wills and popular culture; to reconcile with God no matter how far off they have strayed. He reminded them that they are the ones who have strayed and they of free will need to do the work required to clean up their mess. "We want to help you but it may take some time and effort to unravel the knots" said the Priest as he peered into the television camera lens. He was trying to be as compassionate and kind as possible…for this information may be difficult to hear. He smiled with kind eyes through most his homily but was stern when needed. The Priest basically said that the Priest/s can help you but you have to do your part too. God is waiting but He won't wait forever. At some point your time will be up, so take this opportunity to reconcile with God and each other."

Rachael continued "Now let me tell you about the timing of this homily and how I feel like it was an immediate answer to a plea from me to God. I had a co-worker, actually she was my boss and her husband left her in a terrible way. In her grief she chose to start internet dating and was pretty aggressive about finding a man. When she found one she liked, she let him move in with her and her 15 year old daughter in a small apartment. I had a few conversations with her about morality since we were both Catholics and I considered her to be my friend and not just a co-worker/boss. We had worked side by side for years. I tried to appeal to her conscience about living together with a man she was not married and the bad example to her 15 year old daughter. I also encouraged her to get an annulment but to this day she remains resistant. These conversations were sporadic but each time, before the shift was over she would take a break and come back with new vigor and seem to be empowered to continue to live her life her way. I knew she must have talked with her 'significant other' and discussed our conversation/s. He in turn must have told her what she wanted to hear and not what she ought to hear.

One day during one of our regular conversations, she spoke about a television sit-com that she thought was so funny. That show promoted divorce and remarriage (without annulment) and homosexual lifestyles. I told her that I don't watch that tv sit-com because I know I would probably like it but it leads to promiscuity in our society. I told her that I don't watch anything that encourages immorality or the culture of death. Those programs have the beautiful people, best actors and the money to make their shows every appealing to the masses but they have an agenda. The agenda is to desensitize people to the evil of sin. At some point the conversation must have turned to her living with her 'significant other' out of wedlock with her teenage daughter when she made the statement "Well at least I'm not out there with everyone." That was how she rationalized her chosen lifestyle…that and watching television sit-coms! In her mind she was with one man and happy. Once again she returned from taking a break with renewed vigor and pep. The new shift was coming on to relieve us of our work responsibilities and she was very loudly promoting that sit-com tv show and laughing as to say to me "I don't care what you think. I'm going to live my life the way I want to and I don't need or want your too righteous opinion!" I got the anvil right on top of my head.

So on my way home, driving in my car I had a very spirited conversation with God. I was adamant about Him letting me know how to handle this situation. I cried loudly, yelled and screamed loudly and beat my fist on the dash board loudly while hopefully driving the speed limit since I'm so righteous and moral. I said "God, I'm trying to help my friend by bringing attention to her immorality…she's Catholic…she knows better…her daughter is being influenced by her actions…what about his family and the influence to his 3 little girls…did she break up his family?!…does she need to get an annulment?…I'm concerned for her eternal soul and I don't know what else to do! Dear God, if I am wrong about trying to lead her back to You then show me…If they are right and I'm wrong then show me. Also Lord show each of them (my friend and her 'significant other') individually if they are wrong.

One thing I haven't shared with all of you is that I really do like this man she is living with out of wedlock. I want him also to be led to truth.

Well, by the time I got home I calmed down. Like most of my prayers, conversations and pleas with God, I didn't expect an immediate response. Most of the time if I get an answer at all, it comes weeks, months, years or I'm still waiting…sometimes the answer is no. My point is that I wasn't expecting an answer so fast. It was a three day weekend before I returned to work which was a good thing because I needed some time to cool off. During that weekend, I heard that homily about divorce and remarriage without an annulment and living together out of holy matrimony. Like I said it was the only time I've ever heard a Priest from the pulpit speak on those subjects and it happened after my adamant conversation with God where I was asking for an immediate response. I got it! Yes, she needs to file for an annulment. Yes, living together out of holy matrimony is either fornication or adultery; both are mortal sins which need to be repented for and addressed.

The same long weekend, my friend/co-worker/boss was in an automobile accident. Directly in front of the Catholic Church, her minivan was completely stopped when she was plowed into by a car from behind. She could see the car coming from behind in the rear view mirror and couldn't do anything to stop the two vehicles from colliding. She suffered with neck discomfort periodically for years after that wreck.

In addition and much to my amazement, her 'significant other' woke up at home from a sound sleep and insisted that she get a Bible and open it up to a certain scripture passage. He never did anything like that before! Timothy 5:12

On Monday when my friend and I returned to work, I found out about her accident and the Bible scripture passage. When I asked what the Bible verse stated, she tried to explain that the verses ahead of it talked about helping widows and orphans. They decided that the meaning behind that passage meant he was to help a relative who was staying with them for a short time. The relative was travelling around without a job and recently became a father. He was not living up to his responsibilities as a father. My friend's 'significant other' tried to help him get a job and become involved in his child's life.

I remembered that we had a condensed version of a Bible in one of the rooms, so I went to get it. It was a light green paperback condensed version, maybe just the New Testament. I turned to 1 Timothy: Chapter 5 Verse 12 which stated (Damnation because you are not living your faith).

When I returned to my friend, things were getting busy and I was unable to show her the direct words from that Bible. Every time I thought about bringing up that subject about the words in that condensed version of that light green Bible, I was never able too because we were too busy at work. Then that light green condensed version of the Bible disappeared. I've never come across another Bible that put those exact words on that Bible verse.

I felt like all three of us got an answer to my plea. I heard the homily on the exact subject I wanted an immediate answer, and I got it. My friend could have died in that car accident without addressing her mortal sins; she was given a warning with time to repent. Her 'significant other' woke up to a warning from God through a Bible verse; something that never happened before to him. The odd thing is that neither she nor he seemed to get the meanings to those events. She did not stop and repent for anything. They both thought the Bible verse meant something else instead of (Damnation because you are not living your faith). It seems to me that if people love their sins more than they love God; they refuse to think they are doing anything wrong even when they know what God commands. He didn't wake up to the scripture passages before Timothy 5:12, only Timothy 5:12. They both rationalized the warning. I was never able to tell her what the scripture passage stated in that condensed green Bible. So, why do you think God gave my friend's 'significant other' that very ominous warning if he didn't understand the meaning. I also was never able to talk to my friend about the homily I heard that weekend. She made it very clear she was not interested in what I thought. They eventually after 3 ½ years of living together went to Las Vegas and were married. She said it was a Christian service with Elvis singing. Her children have grown up and have an assortment of serious sins to which they are unrepentant. Many people are in this situation but in her case, it seems to me that she was the turning point in her family. Her parents had a happy long marriage. Once she decided that living together before marriage and never getting an annulment from her blessed marriage in the Catholic Church was not something she needed to do; well she like many other people turned into a cafeteria Catholic. (Remember satan was granted more power over those who would turn themselves over to him for 75-100 years; and we might be living in that time period). It looks like her children have learned from her example and are selecting for themselves how they want to live their lives. None of her children have married their significant others except for the one in a homosexual relationship. Now his youngest, still in high school tried to move in with her boyfriend. Their children have learned from their example and they still don't get it. When people are this hardened in their serious sins, what will wake them up to the Truth?"

Rosie " Many people have warnings or near death experiences, just because it happened in front of the Catholic Church could be a coincidence. How do you know that they were wrong with interpretation of Timothy 5 :12. Maybe they are right and you are wrong. Just because the dream stated Timothy 5:12 and not the previous chapters, maybe God meant for all of the other chapters to be included also. Maybe they could see beyond what was actually stated in the dream. The homily I have no excuse other than coincidence. The fact all 3 of these separate events happened on the weekend you plead with God for a direct answer, well that could be a coincidence too. As far as her allowing him to move in with her and her teenage daughter and live in sin for 3 ½ years and possibly longer since she refused to look into an annulment. Well, maybe God will just overlook all these things since she is happy."

Rachael " You think that they are fine living their life as they choose while offending God in many ways and not the least bit repentant."

Rosie "Why not, as long as they are happy! Isn't that what the world thinks. Surely God will change for them. Just because they have been disobedient; so what, as long as they are happy. Who cares if by their example all their children are also living in sin and completely unrepentant. Now her whole family is on that road of sand and flowers, music and dancing until they come to the end of that road and fall off into the abyss of Hell. Rachael, I think you're right and you got the answer you requested but your friend and her man are rock hard sinners and can't see the effects of their own sins. Even when all of her children are repeating her sins and adding new ones; in which no one is repentant. Sounds like his children might be starting down the same path. The only good thing is that she is still going to the Catholic Church as a cafeteria Catholic and someday she might decide to go into the confessional and seek help to get into the state of grace. The Catholic Church wants to meet people where they are at, then it is up to the individual to change if they choose to."

Belle "When I was a pediatric nurse at a hospital, I saw what people are allowing their children to watch on television. Most of the parents were not screening what they or their children were watching on television. So, unfortunately I would say most kids have been exposed to all kinds of corruption and the culture of death. I would also say it's not only what they are watching on television, it's what they are living in their own families. It's ironic that in today's culture, the parents might get upset about their children hearing the TRUTH in church about birth control, fornication, homosexuality acts and not protecting their children from the evil that surrounds us in our culture through television and even relationships in our families. Nowadays, parents need to explain to their children about real life circumstances. An example would be: Let's say their aunt is living with her boyfriend and not married. The child might be confused about this situation. The parents should explain that God tells us the best way to live but sometimes people don't do what God tells us. We love them anyway but we do not encourage or approve of their actions. In short: Love the sinner, hate the sin. Instead parents go along with the norm and say nothing acting as if they approve of the sin. This sends mixed messages to the child and they just accept anything they are being taught, even if it is leading them in the wrong direction. Parents need to teach by good example and by explanation if situations of confusion arise. When the parents themselves are picking and choosing 'being cafeteria Catholics', it makes TRUTH even more distorted to the children. My husband and I have chosen to live by the 10 Commandments and the teachings of the Catholic Church. I'm not so sure I want the Priest/s talking about these sensitive topics during Holy Mass with my children hearing about such things. Robert and I try to protect our children from the evils of the world and feel we provide a loving, caring and God fearing home. I feel sorry for the children whose parents are not taking their adult responsibilities seriously and are freely exposing their children to corruption by their examples and what they allow their children to watch and listen too."

Grandma McFrugal "The Priest/s are going to have to come up with a way to teach TRUTH about why birth control is intrinsically evil and has led to the society we have today without harming or exposing our children to the evil. They are our Fathers and must teach us the TRUTH. Martha just mentioned many things that the Priest/s could talk about to explain why birth control is intrinsically evil and still be able to talk about these topics with children present. Maybe the Priest's should strongly urge every adult to attend classes on these sensitive subjects and make these classes easily accessible like directly after Mass. I think people need to hear it from our Fathers the Priests directly to make a bigger impact."

Belle "I remember as a pediatric hospital nurse, I would walk out of the rooms where an unmarried teenager and her sick child were both miserable. The baby with a high fever, vomiting and/or diarrhea, crying, just having had lab work and an IV started. The young mother being completely dependent on help from family because she was unable to financially and in other ways provide for herself and her child. Several times the grandma of the child would be present and I could feel tension in the room; the white elephant 'Daughter you did this to yourself and you're lucky I'm helping you and giving you and the baby a place to live'. Most of the fathers were not in the picture at all. To me these situations were mostly brought about by a promiscuous society that encourages our young to have sex before they are able to handle the consequences. When I walked out of these rooms I would go someplace and have a mini breakdown…cry… then pull myself back together and go back to work. I wondered how I could be so completely against abortion when I could see the misery of the young mother abandoned by the father of the child and having to deal with difficulties of raising a child basically on her own. Then one day I had a revelation TA DAH! The light was turned on and the world made sense again. I was only seeing these young mothers and their sick children during their worst days. If a child is sick enough to be admitted into the hospital for care, believe me, this is one of their worse days. The child is suffering physically before they are taken to the hospital; then we do things that are uncomfortable and the child does not understand why. On top of that, the child and mother have usually been up for 2-3 days before they even think about coming to the hospital.

Pain and suffering, fear of the unknown, exhaustion, possible depression, finances and job security if missing work, while trying to comfort the child…believe me…this is a difficult time. What I'm not seeing is the mother and child on the good days. When a child smiles and hugs their mother…when a child is celebrating their birthday…when a child does or says something so innocent and loving that causes their mother to smile in the most unexpected of moments. Out of the mouths of babes come the most wonderful phrases that make us all happy to be alive. The second part of the revelation is that we ALL have difficult times in our lives. We get sick or have to take care of others in our families that are ill and sometimes are in the hospital. We all have difficult times in our lives and we must all work through them. Once I understood that I was only seeing the difficult times and that these mothers and children have many wonderful adventures awaiting them…well the world was beautiful again! Love makes the world go round. Of course, love means being there for your loved ones in good times and bad. So we need to treat all humans with dignity. Life starts at conception. At the same time we need to encourage a culture of chastity for one's state in life. In other words we need to live our lives in a way pleasing to our Father in Heaven; God knows what is best for us. To be clear; No sex until after married in a holy matrimony marriage. This way provides for better outcomes for the married couple and children. Whatever the situation start to work towards life. Single parents have much to look forward to in life with their children…but they must return to a life of chastity for their station in life. To be clearer; No sex until after married in a holy matrimony marriage. In this very promiscuous culture, don't let the world tell you lust and/or fornication are not a mortal sins. These sins create a culture of death. In fact these sins cause souls to shrivel up and die; unless repented for with true sorrow. Don't let the great deceiver continue to pull you into his snares and traps. These beautiful children that are the products of lust, fornication and adultery are innocent but their biological parents need to repent with true sorrow and have a firm purpose of amendment. They need to reflect on how they got themselves into that situation and come up with a plan to combat it from happening again. Without a good, well thought out plan… meaning chastity until in a holy matrimony marriage…not birth control…the same outcome could and very well may happen again! Wake up! Sex and babies go together! When I think about the young unwed mothers and their children, I wonder what happened to the fathers of these little children. Every 'act of generation' should include love and be open to life. When I say include love I mean be in a Holy matrimony marriage.

Grandma McFrugal "The fathers need to talk to their sons about chastity and the dignity of every human being."

Martha "There was a brief time when I was in college that I started to believe that abortion might be alright depending on the circumstance. I was adamant against abortion until one day one of my very best friends confided to me that she had an abortion when she was a senior in high school. The very first time she had sex, she got pregnant. Her parents decided she should have an abortion. She went to a small school and everyone knew of her predicament. After the abortion her parents sent her off to live with an aunt close to where she would be going to college the next year. I loved my friend. She was raised very protestant and her parents were very involved in their church. My friend and I had several conversations in the past about abortion. I couldn't believe anyone would ever kill an unborn baby and she never budged from her stance that there are different reasons for having an abortion. There always seemed to be something behind her statements, but I was young and didn't have a clue that she was talking about herself. During a holiday when most of the girls in our dorm were away, we were going to go out and get something to eat. For some reason we entered into the abortion discussion as we descended down the stairs of an un-airconditioned hot stairwell to get to the car. As we were stepping down, down, down the stairs she told me she had an abortion and described the circumstances. I was stunned at this new information but found myself being very compassionate. I instantly knew that my statements from the past must have really hurt her. She was such a good friend and I cared for her very much. I also knew her parents and aunt and thought the world of them all. Since I cared for my friend, I started to see things from her point of view. In time I rationalized that maybe I was being too rigid and that maybe abortion might be alright. It was the first time she had sex and was still in high school, how could she go to college and raise a baby…her parents were making the decisions… apparently they didn't want to help raise the child. She was from a well to do family, so finances were not the issue… it was that her parents thought she was to young to have a baby and mess up her life…this unexpected baby would be a burden and mess up all of their plans. They rationalized their actions. I too started to rationalize the reasons for having an abortion because I couldn't imagine my friend going to Hell for this action we were all excusing away. Maybe this is one of the schemes of the great deceiver: If people look innocent or if we like them, then they can't be doing anything seriously wrong…right?! Well the TRUTH is that God does not change, only man changes. Abortion is murder of the unborn. The fifth COMMANDMENTS still stands: Thou Shalt Not Kill. Instead of letting our love for someone blur the TRUTH; we must love them more and help them live God's laws. No one ever said this was going to be easy; especially not Jesus. I should have explained compassionately that I understand she must have had a very difficult time but I believe every human has a right to life. That God created her child just like he created her. The baby was a victim. God would not like it if someone took her life either. God loves both her and her baby. Our loving Father in Heaven loves all of His children and has an ocean of mercy to forgive us for our sins. She should ask for forgiveness with true sorrow and she will get it; only then will she have true peace. Abortion goes against the virtue of justice. To act as though nothing was wrong with ending a life is an injustice that needs to be reconciled. Our God forgives but He wants us to learn from our mistakes and not encourage others to follow in our footsteps and make the same mistakes. My friend's mother counsels women at an abortion clinic into having abortions and as far as I know is still doing so. She remains very active at her protestant church even plays the piano at most of the church services. I couldn't understand how these beautiful people could be so active as Christians and on the other hand kill unborn babies without any remorse. The fact that her mother for years in counseling women into having abortions almost seems like she has unrest deep in her soul with the decision to terminate the life of her grandchild so many years ago. I pray for my friend and her parents (who I love) to repent with true sorrow for going against God's fifth COMMANDMENT; Thou Shalt Not Kill. If they would take some time and think about the life they cut short for their own selfish reasons. If they would reflect that they could have another child or grandchild to love and be in their lives. The life that was terminated was unique; 23 sets of chromosomes from the moment of conception. That life will never be duplicated. Most likely if they would have made the sacrifices needed to support the life of that child (however difficult at the time), they would have loved that child very much. The only way my friend and/or her parents are truly going to have peace is to reconcile with God and ask for forgiveness with true sorrow. Then and only then will they each have the peace they are looking for."

Lucy "Adoption is also an option. Another family could have loved that child very much!"

Martha " I hope and pray my very good friend and her parents will ask for forgiveness with true sorrow. We must reflect on our actions and how they impact others; the abortion killed a human being that had a right to live their own life. God created that child and they did not have the right to terminate its life. We can't dwell on our past mistakes forever; but we must be accountable. They all need to ask for forgiveness with true sorrow before they die. I pray they all become devout Catholics (not cafeteria Catholics) and can go to confession and repent, do penances and get into the state of grace and merit Heaven. I love these people, and feel they are very much misguided on the subject of abortion. Several years have passed and science seems to be proving that life begins at conception. Ultra sounds show the formation of the babies as they grow in the womb; they are not just clumps of tissue. Also unfortunately, abortions prove these are tiny human being and their body parts are sometimes sold for profit. There are 23 sets of chromosomes from the very beginning of life (life begins at conception). I hope that these forms of enlightenment will lead by friend and her beautiful parents to the realization that they have a child and grandchild in Heaven and if they repent with true sorrow and start to love that person, someday soon they will get to meet in Heaven. Going to confession can bring about great peace for long standing wrongs."

Grandma McFrugal "Since we're talking about rights for life, I just want to say I do not want to be euthanized. Now that I'm entering into my twilight years…well maybe someone at this round table should be holding me. I also believe in redemptive suffering and will 'offer up' my suffering for Mother Mary's intentions."

Rosie "Mom, we will all hold you."

Grandma McFrugal " If you knights at the round table will excuse me, I need to get dinner ready for the men who will be returning soon from their hunting trip."

Maureen "First let's summarize the round table meeting and we'll help you Mom. Let's come up with a battle plan and get our marching orders.

BATTLE PLAN:

1). Pray the rosary every day. Let others see your rosary in your hand or hanging from your car rear view mirror. Put bumper stickers on your car 'NEED A WEAPON/PRAY THE ROSARY' next to the bumper sticker that says 'DO YOU FOLLOW JESUS THIS CLOSE'. Make the rosary visible, take it out of your purse and quietly say your rosary while standing in line at the grocery store, while waiting for your children at soccer practice. Try saying more than one rosary a day.

2). Offer our assistance to our Priest/s to teach N.F.P.(Natural Family Planning) or other subjects to teach TRUTH. Offer assistance in other ways such as babysitting while the Priest/s teach the TRUTH on sensitive subjects such as (fornication, why birth control is intrinsically evil, etc…). Put together a video library with TRUTH from Catholic prospective (about sensitive topics) and movies appropriate for the whole family (no immorality or culture of death) for members of the church to check out.

3). Put together packages to give to our OB-GYN Doctors and their partners.

    a). Books on teaching Natural Family Planning to start classes in their offices/hospitals.

    b). Encouragment to find healing/cures for infertility; including books from a Catholic doctor who practices NaProTechnology.

    c). Include facts on how harmful birth control pills/devices are to women.

    d). Homemade goodies so they will want to read above information.

4). Promote Chastity for Your State in Life Campaign

    a). Live it.

    b). Find resources to show to our own children.

    c). Start teaching at young age that God shows us the best way to live by giving us 10 Commandments and the teachings of Jesus Christ in the Gospels. Sometimes people choose not to obey God's way. We still love these people but we do not encourage these sins. Love the sinner, not the sin. When situations are confusing, explain truth to children instead of ignoring it.
Consult a Priest if you yourself are confused.

    d). Be selective of what you and your children watch on television or at the movies or what music including the lyrics to listen to. If any of it is immoral or leads to the culture of death…turn it off.

5). Stand up for TRUTH Campaign

    a). If you are around people who are joking about fornication or laughing about television shows or movie/books that encourage lust, fornication or other indecent subjects do one of the below listed alternatives

      aa). Walk away, maybe they will get the hint.

      bb). Just come out and state lust and fornication are against God. Someday we will be judged by God. God's ways are higher than our ways. God sees anger as murder and lust as adultery. We must obey God. God does not change. Suggest they go to confession with a Catholic Priest before it is too late.

6). Go to confession at least once a month.

7). Hold Grandma with Love.

MARCHING ORDERS:

* Everyone pray the rosary at least once a day for Mother Mary's intentions.
* Fast in some way at least once a week for Mother Mary's intentions.
* Everyone to bring appropriate CD's and family oriented videos for church library.
* Kimberly, Belle, Rosie and Martha to talk with Priest/s and offer their assistance with teaching classes and arranging for babysitting while the Priest/s teach classes on sensitive topics.
* Lucy, Maureen to put together information for OB-GYN doctors (since they most recently had babies, they were most familiar with the doctors).
* Rachael-Put together information packets for chastity for the young and come up with a plan to get information out there. She started a blog and got her teen age daughters and their friends and parents to participate.
* Grandma McFrugal started a rosary group with her church ladies. She also had a talk with the men in the family that very day about talking to all their children on sensitive topics. Yes, every child is different but each one needs to hear from their father certain Truths. She told the fathers to teach their sons to have respect for the women they date, and dignity for all human life. Grandma told them to look into their sons eyes and state their business 'I don't ever want to hear that a son of mine took advantage of a woman for their selfish pleasure'. She strongly advised for the fathers to teach their daughters that they are daughters of the King of Heaven and to act accordingly including who and how they date and how they dress.

This talk given by Grandma McFrugal- took place when the men returned from the yearly hunting trip that very evening. They were all sitting at the Round Table. Grandma led them in saying a full rosary before they had a bite to eat. Then the feast began. Grandma walked over the piano and played a hymn 'Faith of Our Fathers'. The men were hungry and ate in silence for about twenty minutes, wondering what happened while they were gone. Soon the whole family was having a good time. The men were telling their stories and laughing about their hunting adventure. For the women: ONWARD CHRISTIAN SOLDIERS MARCHING AS TO WAR

WITH THE STRENGTH OF JESUS GOING ON BEFORE. There was work to be done and they had a battle plan and marching orders to keep their families strong in the Catholic faith and promote a culture of life. As for tonight, they were going to enjoy their families. That day the 'Round Table' served as the center of nourishment for their souls and physical bodies.

★★★

CONVERSATION IN THE DEER HOLD

    Molly's Dad and his youngest brother Luke went hunting. While sitting in the deer hold high up in a strong sturdy oak tree the two men were silently waiting for a deer sighting. Uncle Luke was reading St. Faustina's Diary; the part that Jesus tells her that we will find out what He (Jesus) was thinking about when He was alone and imprisoned the night before His death. Molly's Uncle Luke pondered what he thought Jesus might be thinking about that long night while alone, abandoned, betrayed, humiliated and naked…thrown down into a cistern/hole in the ground/solitary confinement (whatever type of prison they placed Jesus). Luke wondered if Jesus contemplated about the sins against the Holy Spirit. Luke knew there was part of the Gospel that states that God will not forgive the sins against the Holy Spirit. Luke knew of two ways to sin against the Holy Spirit: 1). Eternal despair 2). To be eternally obstinate (to stand against God, to oppose God, unreasonably determined to have one's own way; not yielding to reason or plea; stubborn, mulish, resisting remedy (not repenting with true sorrow). Luke knew that both of these ways to sin against the Holy Spirit were the same sin: They were not asking of forgiveness and therefore they cannot be forgiven. The only sin God cannot forgive is the sin against the Holy Spirit because the sinner will not ask for forgiveness with true sorrow. If the sinner does not ask for forgiveness then God cannot forgive them. 1). Eternal despair affects souls that think their sins are so great that God could not forgive them. God has an ocean of mercy to forgive even the most hardened sinners but they must ask for forgiveness with true sorrow. 2).Eternally obstinate; these people/souls know the truth (10 COMMANDMENTS and the teachings of Jesus Christ in the Gospels and the teaching of the Catholic Church according to the magisterium (the authority claimed by the Roman Catholic Church, as divinely inspired, to teach true doctrine) but remain obstinate refusing to ask for forgiveness…because they are not sorry. Many of these cafeteria Catholics have decided that God has to change because so many people have rationalized their sins and gone against the Will of God and are relying on their own solutions. These cafeteria Catholics only allow God to be a part of their life as long as God doesn't interfere with what they want to do. They are obstinate and are rock hard sinners…they have not asked for forgiveness and have no intentions to do so. Luke said a few prayers for some of the people he knew in this category; he prayed that these people would return back to God.

    Molly's Uncle Luke's favorite hobby was photography and he developed his own photos in a dark room. He recently heard Mother Angelica on one of her 'Mother Angelica LIVE CLASSICS' programs talk about an encounter she had with God while in a dark room developing film in the silence. She was looking for 2 negatives that were similar but she could not find them. Later she picked up a negative by the sink and discovered it was the 2 negatives on top of each other and looked like the same negative. Mother Angelica stated she heard God speak to her and told her to look at the 2 negatives together; this is what Heaven is like. When our will and God's Will are the same. Then God asked her to slide the negatives apart; this is what Purgatory is like. Uncle Luke pondered that we must atone for all sins until they line up with God's Will. Then God asked Mother Angelica to separate the 2 photo negatives completely; this is what Hell is like. When we are acting on our own and apart from God's Will; we ourselves have separated from God because God's Will does not change. We are acting on our own and apart from God. Mortal sin is the only thing that separates us from God; God decides what is mortal sin, not man. We must be obedient to our Father's Will. Luke said a heartfelt 'Our Father' prayer while deeply contemplating on the words. He also started to think about sins that are taking people/souls away from God like lust, fornication, birth control (other than Natural Family Planning in a Holy matrimony marriage and for a good reason), divorce without getting an annulment and then marrying someone else (adultery), not going to Holy Mass on the Lord's Day or causing others to miss Holy Mass on the Lord's day ect... .

Molly's Dad and her Uncle Luke were hunting on a Sunday. However they both fulfilled their obligation to attend Holy Mass at the Saturday Vigil Mass. They did not cause others to miss Mass on Sunday because they did not stop at gas stations/grocery stores/restaurants or any other place that would require people to work…giving them the excuse not to go to Holy Mass/Church on Sunday. They planned ahead and had all the gas, food and other supplies needed for their hunting day at the little cabin deep in the woods.

Uncle Luke's mind veered back to the dark room and developing photos. If people don't get their will to line up with God's Will on serious sin/s then they have separated themselves from God. God puts no one in Hell, we do it to ourselves by choosing to do our will over God's. All these cafeteria Catholics may very well find themselves in Hell for eternity since they have been taught the truth in the Catholic Church. Once Catholic, always Catholic. God knows what is best for all of His children; we are to be obedient to our Father in Heaven. Cafeteria Catholics need to stop coming up with their own solutions and following the secular culture. There can only be one Will in a perfect place of peace which is in Heaven. Why wouldn't all of us want that one will to be a loving Father who wants the best for all of us. This means we all need to get our wills to line up with God's Will like the 2 film negatives of a beautiful photograph. Luke hoped that today the people he prayed for would hear God's voice and harden not their hearts.

Luke sat quietly and listened for God's voice.

Other topics Luke talked about to God included whether he should ask Lucy Jones out on a date. He saw how happy she was around her baby Anthony and the whole McGolly family. He saw her at least once a week at the Catholic Church because her Holy hour with God during Eucharistic Adoration was 6pm-7pm and his was 7pm-8pm on Thursdays. Luke could see the peace and joy on Lucy's face as she was leaving the Chapel after her Holy hour with Jesus.

Luke was also contemplating whether to return to college to become an architect. He had 2 years of Junior College under his belt before he became a full time lumberjack. On the job site (a forest) he injured his left lower leg and foot; he found it increasing more difficult and painful to work such long hours on his feet all day. He accepted this suffering and offered the pain and suffering up for Mother Mary's intentions. However, he wondered how long he would be able to continue working manual labor all day with his leg and foot in that condition. Luke and Jay Walker both loved working on the log cabin lodge and started to talk about turning this interest into a career. They could design and build homes and other building with geothermal wells, solar energy power and other natural resources found locally. They might even be able to design whole communities if they worked towards becoming architects. Luke felt he was willing to make the sacrifices necessary to obtain this goal with God's help. Everything comes from God, but we are to use what God gives us in a way pleasing to God.

So you see, there were two men in the deer hold that day but the conversation was between Luke and God in the silence.

★★

MOLLY AND THE SILVER ROSE

The Knights of Columbus were taking one of four Silver Roses through North America on its way to The Shrine of Our Lady of Guadalupe in Mexico. This Silver Rose was on display at the Catholic Church and the McGolly family, McFrugal family, Donavan family and Lucy Jones and her baby boy Anthony and Jay Walker were all in attendance for Holy Mass during for this event. The Silver Roses are a symbol of building a civilization of love and a culture of life; they represent keeping babies safe in the sanctuary of their mother's womb. The Knights of Columbus would like for everyone to say a heartfelt 'Hail Mary' prayer every time you see a rose. This way we will be sending a rose garden to Mother Mary to promote life.

Molly saw the lovely Silver Rose on a royal blue pillow and thought it was beautiful. After Mass, Molly went to the Chapel close to the Tabernacle (where Jesus is) and began to pray. She was kneeling next to a silver statue of the Virgin Mary holding Baby Jesus. Molly turned and looked at the statue and noticed for the first time that Mother Mary was holding Baby Jesus and that Baby Jesus was holding a single Silver Rose. This made a major imprint on her mind. Mother Mary and Jesus want all of us to take care of the unborn. Molly pondered what does God want us to do? The answer was clear: 'What ever you do to the least of your brothers, that you do unto Me'.

Molly silently said a heartfelt 'Hail Mary' prayer.

> Hail Mary, full of grace.
> The Lord is with thee.
> Blessed art thou among women, and blessed is the fruit of thy womb, Jesus.
> Holy Mary, Mother of God, pray for us sinners,
> now and at the hour of our death.
>
> Amen

★★

Author Note: I thank everyone who took the time and energy to read this book. Now I have a question for you. WHAT ARE YOU DOING TO PROMOTE A CULTURE OF LIFE? Catholics are you truly living your faith or are you part of the culture of death by living as a cafeteria Catholic (living or promoting mortal sin without remorse). Remember, once Catholic always Catholic. Once given the TRUTH in the Catholic faith (the Church founded by Jesus and His apostles and the only Christian religion for the first 1500 years) you will be held to it. Also remember the Catholics compiled the Holy Bible, guided by the Holy Spirit (it didn't just fall out of the sky). The greatest gifts and treasures are found in the Catholic Church; the True Body and Blood of Jesus Christ to be taken into our bodies (I beg you to be in the state of grace so that you do not force Jesus to be in a body dominated by satan), Jesus Himself is in every Tabernacle found in every Catholic Church all over the world, you can be forgiven for sins (if you are truly sorry for them) by going to confession with a Catholic Priest. Other treasures are: Mother Mary (Queen of Heaven, Our Heavenly Mother, Queen of Peace) and our older brothers and sister the saints (who are our examples to live virtuous lives and help lead us to Heaven). We can ask Mother Mary and the saints to intercede to God on our behalf. We have the sacraments to keep us close to God.

The battle is in progress and your eternal soul is at stake. The world seems to want to fight fire with fire; how is that working?!!!! It's not!! So let's try doing things God's way. Let's all starting praying to God and asking for help. God withdraws from us if we are not close to Him. We do this to ourselves by doing our will over God's Will; our 'free will' choices can separate us from God. When the majority of us have separated ourselves from God (by choosing to be in the state of mortal sin over the state of grace); then we are telling God we do not want or need His love and protection. If we continue down this path of disobedience to God; we may be headed for a Purification of human beings.

Open up your heart and let the sunshine in. Start with yourself and get into the state of grace; go to confession and repent with true sorrow for all mortal sins (and venial sins). Love your neighbor as yourself and stop being self centered. God withdraws from us if we are not close to Him; so get close to God. The sacraments help keep us close to God…so use them. Have your children baptized in the Catholic Church, go to confession (at least once a month), get married in the Catholic Church (and live the vows in a way pleasing to God). The seven sacraments are: Baptism, Eucharist, Confirmation, Reconciliation (Confession), Matrimony, Holy Orders, Anointing of the Sick. We all need to wake up our prayer life. While praying we need to thank God for everything we have been given; everything comes from God. Sometimes I think Hell is a place without sunshine, birds chirping, flowers, flowing rivers, star lit nights or even stormy nights that bring forth clear sun lit mornings …all the things we seem to take for granted. I hope no one enters Hell (a place of no hope) before they figure out that everything came from God. What we desire is peace and peace can only come from being truly in harmony with God's Will. There can only be one will in a perfect place of peace.

Reconciling with God and each other is the ultimate goal. To do this it takes a plan and action. It takes hard work to weather the storm but we know every dark cloud has a silver lining. We should have a better attitude knowing in the end we will feel better and have peace… the peace we always desired but were looking in all the wrong places. So roll up your sleeves and let's all get to work getting our souls in harmony with God. If you haven't been to confession in a great while, you very well may feel like the weight of the world is lifted from your shoulders when you leave the confessional. Change takes a will that wants to change. I have a joke to share: How many psychiatrists does it take to change a light bulb? Answer: One, but the light bulb has to want to change. GET IT!

Let's get close to God by using the sacraments. Cheer up and know that your Father in Heaven loves you and wants you with Him in Heaven forever.

I thank Mother Mary for bringing me back to Jesus Christ (her Son) and the truth in the Catholic Church. I have repented for all my mortal sins, done my penance and try my best to stand up for what is morally right even in the face of opposition. It has not been an easy road but it is very fulfilling. However everyday is a battle for the soul; so I must persevere, persevere, persevere. I highly recommend everyone to say at least one heartfelt rosary a day for Mother Mary's intentions. Mother Mary is your Heavenly Mother also, and she can lead you back to her Son Jesus and His Church (the Catholic Church is the Bride of Jesus) too.

One last request, please ponder:

What are you doing to promote a culture of life and a civilization of love?

★★

Author Note: Today (08/28/2016 Sunday), while I was watching and praying the Rosary with the Priest on E.W.T.N.(Eternal Word Television Network) from Lourdes, France (at the site of the Virgin Mary's apparitions to Bernadette Soubirous in 1858). Something was different this time. I've prayed the Rosary many times with different Priest/s while watching E.W.T.N. at this particular site. Today I noticed flickering of lights and lighting in different places. It must have rained recently because parts of the hill/rocks were shiny, like it was still wet after a drenching rain. They always have a massive stand with large white candles, starting at the top with one candle and increasing in the number of candles at the base. The reflection of these lit candles were shining on the walls of the grotto and above where there stands a beautiful statue of the Virgin Mary. The name Mary gave of Herself to Bernadette in 1858 was 'I am the Immaculate Conception'; meaning She was born without original sin. We are all born with original sin; given to us when Adam and Eve sinned against God by eating of the fruit from the tree of good and evil (the one thing that was forbidden) then casted out of the Garden of Eden.

In order for Mary to be the new 'Ark of the Covenant' meaning the womb in which our Savior was to be conceived, carried and birthed had to be free from all sin…God cannot be harbored in a vessel stained by sin. Therefore Mary was born without original sin. The Virgin Mary, the Mother of Christ our Savior is 'The Immaculate Conception'.

Back to the lighting at today's Rosary recitation. The large golden crown by the Shrine in honor of our Lady from Heaven also was flickering with lights that I've never noticed before… brisk bursts of lights lasting only 1–2 seconds…on/off…on/off…continual. This sequence of lights from the crown to the grotto and statue got my attention but I didn't know what to make of it. Directly after the Rosary recitation, I walked away from my television towards the kitchen and noticed the sunlight from outside flickering from my dining room. Maybe several small clouds were passing overhead causing this brief flickering of natural sunlight to shine through my windows. Devine or coincidence?! The Rosary we recited was the Joyful mysteries. The first 3 decades of the Joyful mysteries cover the 1). The Annunciation: Conception of Jesus 2). The Visitation: Jesus in Mary's womb/carrying our Lord Jesus 3). The Nativity: the birth of our Savior

Jesus Christ. These first 3 decades of the Joyful mysteries show us Mary honoring God's Will for her and all of humanity; becoming 'The Immaculate Conception' and the Mother of God (because God is 3 persons in one God (The Father/the Son/the Holy Spirit). Mary is the Mother of our Savior Jesus (the second person in The Holy Trinity); She is known as the Mother of God.

Somehow I feel like the Holy Spirit was sending a message of light. Have you ever been in a class of students and everyone is talking. In order to get control of a room full of people that is in complete chaos, someone will flicker the light switch on and off to get everyone's undivided attention. Instantly, the room becomes quiet and then someone will make an announcement.

Consider the lights flickered and I am now going to point out why our Heavenly Mother, the Virgin Mary, the Queen of Peace has been appearing for over 35 years to the 6 visionaries in Medjugorje, Bosnia. These 6 children have grown up and continue to spread the messages from our Heavenly Mother to lead Her children (all of us) back to Her Son Jesus and to live as God commands us to do. You can go on-line to see the messages or order books, newsletters etc…at Caritas of Birmingham (100 Queen of Peace Drive, Sterrett, Alabama 35147 U.S.A.)

These visionaries say that most of the time Mary appears in a gray dress because she has been sent to clean up a mess. These are the last apparitions in which visionaries can talk, see, touch Her; when these apparitions are over Mary says Her services will no longer be needed. I wonder if that means Her children will obey God's Commandments or if we will have to go through a purification because of disobedience to our Father in Heaven.

St. Faustina's diary states that God is reluctant to punish aching mankind.

If we of free will, continue to live our lives doing our will (mortal sin separates us from God) and go against any of the 10 Commandments and never repent…at some point God may choose to intervene in ways He has never done before; Divine Intervention! When we decide to use our own solutions and devices instead of following the Word of God, we are telling God that we do not need Him or His ways. We act like we have the things under control (birth control, no fault divorce, divorce, abortion, euthanasia, fornication, not honoring God on the Lord's Day, not praying to God because we are too busy, paying into a healthcare insurance plan that forces us to cover other peoples mortal sin/s (birth control, abortion and euthanasia). Healthcare is not the only way government is forcing us to go against God…no fault divorce, condoning same sex marriage, this insane bathroom issue, now trying to force physicians to perform surgery on children to change their sex (if the child might be gender confused; an issue that usually works itself out naturally). God is being pushed aside as people try to convince others that the secular view is the right way.

I look at the homosexual political agenda; even though they are such a small part of the population…the push (massive steam roller machine) to get everyone to accept abominable lifestyles is over whelming. Everywhere you look (television shows, movies, music, video games etc…); children's programming (television shows, movies, video games and in the schools and scouting). Sex is for procreation within the context of married couples according to God's Will. God loves all of His children, including all those with homosexual tendencies. Turn to God and live chaste lifestyles according to your station in life. The Catholic Church has a ministry for those with homosexual tendencies call Courage. The Catholic Church will meet you where you are at; teaching Truth to lead all towards our eternal home in Heaven. From what I've seen on television (the Catholic channel) the Courage program helps you determine where these homosexual tendencies came from (individually) and offers support/techniques to deal with your lifestyle.

By this I mean living a lifestyle pleasing to God. The Catholic Church does not condone living an active homosexual lifestyle; they will help you with your homosexual tendencies and to reconcile with God. There are different pathways for men and women that have surfaced during research of those suffering from homosexual tendencies that lead to that lifestyle. Science has proved that there is not a gene that predisposes a person to homosexuality; therefore it must be something after birth that leads a person to seek same sex attraction/ desire. If you have same sex attraction issues, and want help; find a Courage program through the Catholic Church close to where you live. I would imagine that these groups are compassionate, kind and welcoming. Remember Jesus Christ came for sinners, not the righteous who are not in need of a spiritual physician. I'm pretty sure that the Priest/s and others leading these programs (helping those with homosexual tendencies) know the people will not return if not treated well and with compassion. The rest is up to the individual seeking help. When I look at the amount of propaganda to convince the whole wide world that homosexual lifestyles are natural and must be accepted; I immediately think that all these individuals must be in a great deal of pain. They have no peace down deep in their soul/s. It must be exhausting to carry this turmoil of their soul around every day, struggling with unrest. Probably most of the people struggling with homosexual tendencies are not the main ones pushing the gay agenda. Trust in Jesus Christ; Jesus is the Way, the Truth and the Life. We must all turn away from the solutions and devices of the secular culture and come back home to the Truth in the Catholic Church; otherwise you will never find true lasting peace.

The 10 COMMANDMENTS are not burdens, they are gifts! Our Father in Heaven knows what we need and we are to obey Him. We must all learn the ways of God (Father/Son/ Holy Spirit) by reading the word of God in the Bible, practicing our faith, and spreading the Truth by words and actions. All confirmed Catholics are Soldiers of Christ and must defend the faith even if called upon to be a white or red martyr. Start praying now for the grace of final perseverance if you are called upon to be a red martyr defending the Catholic faith. Don't go looking for trouble. Remember we are to follow Jesus carrying the cross, not try to lead Him. However we are all to defend the Truth of our faith. Each of us has but one life to live and our eternity depends on how we lived that precious life given to us by God. Life is a gift from God.

I look at the homosexual agenda, even though it affects such a small percentage of the population; the overwhelming push to promote this abominable lifestyle screams 'We need help'. If these beautiful people are having to work this hard to convince everyone to accept their sexual desires; it means their souls are in constant turmoil and not at peace.

Come to the Catholic Church and learn the Truth. The Catholic Church will meet you where you are at and then the rest is up to you. Everyone attending the Catholic Church is a sinner (some more than others). This does not mean the Catholic Church agrees with an active homosexual lifestyle; it means it will help you reconcile with God. Come in, sit and listen; when ready to learn more then ask about R.C.I.A. classes. If you are already Catholic (once Catholic, always Catholic)…Come Home…Jesus and His Bride the Catholic Church love you and we want you back. God loves all of His children. God knows what is best for all His children. Turn to God and live chaste lifestyles for your station in life.

Now let's tackle abortion. God is our creator. God created you and your life started at conception. How has our government decided it has a right to overshadow God and allow the people to kill their unborn children; because 'we the people' voted for it! We the people need to vote to reverse Roe vs. Wade. We also need to support, by action to have a culture of life by bringing back chastity for your state in life. This means no sex until after married in a holy matrimony marriage. Also no birth control because that is a major component of lax standards and unwanted pregnancies. Our own solutions and devices (no fault divorce, birth control pills and other forms of birth control, abortion, euthanasia etc…) have led to a world of dishearted people wandering why we feel so lost. The answer is because we need God. Our Father in Heaven loves each one of us, but we must invite Him into our lives. God does not force Himself on anyone. We of free will must invite God to live in us.

The people trying to get everyone to agree that abortion is a solution; need to view an ultrasound of an unborn child in the womb of its mother. Observe how the baby moves his or her arms, legs and head. Look at the baby's fingers. Unfortunately these people might need more evidence of an innocent human being under attack; there is a video taken of a baby being aborted. I have not seen this video and do not plan to do so because it would hurt me to watch someone go through so much pain. I've heard that the child tries to get away from the intruder, you can see how having the arms and legs ripped off while still alive the child is fighting for their life… then you are unable to watch the rest due to the amount of blood in the mother's womb.

If people wanted their children, then abortion would be practically nonexistent. How do we get a society to want their children. Provide an atmosphere where the child is welcomed. People that think that birth control (other than N.F.P.) is the answer to providing an atmosphere where a child is welcome are dead wrong! Statistics prove that our own solutions (birth control pills, I.U.D.'s etc…) have produced a world that children are not welcomed. Promiscuity brought on by the birth control pill and other means of birth control have led to the breakdown of the family and abortion is a product of lax standards of morality. God has already provided an answer; if only we as a society would live according to God's Laws. Holy Matrimony Marriage of a couple (mother and father) that plan to spend their life together with love and want fruitful additions to their family. This is God's plan for us. Children thrive better when wanted and loved and the basic necessities are provided. People that are pushing their anti life agenda on the world and labeling it as a solution, need to think about why so many people are trying to kill their own children through abortion. A real solution would involve a culture of life. I see that these misguided people are fighting so hard to justify their behaviors or are making money off the killing of unborn (but fully alive) children.

If they keep trying to prove to themselves that they are right to terminate life against the Fifth of God's Commandments; then they are not at peace deep down in their souls. The only way to achieve peace is to admit they are wrong and ask God for forgiveness with true sorrow. Come to the Catholic Church, the Church will meet you where you are, then it is up to you to reconcile with God. Come in, sit down and listen to the word of God, watch as those who are suppose to be in the state of grace receive Jesus Christ into their bodies during Holy Eucharist. When you are ready then ask to sign up for classes R.C.I.A. so you can come into full communion with the Catholic Church which is the Bride of Jesus Christ. If you are already Catholic (once Catholic, always Catholic), then Come Home…Jesus Christ and His Bride the Catholic Church are waiting for you. Go to Confession to free yourself of this burden you've been carrying around, trying to justify…but down deep you know you need God's forgiveness and mercy. Once you repent with true sorrow, the healing will begin. Only then will you have the peace you desire. Reconciling with God is the only way to true peace. This applies to anyone in the state of mortal sin. You may have big changes to make in your life but remember…it was you who veered from God. God has always been the same. You will have to weather the storm while changing your ways. Mary Magdalene did it! Saint Augustine did it! and you can do it! All of Heaven is waiting for your 'Yes' to God's Will. Reconciling with God is the only way to true peace. God's Will and your will must match. So, roll up your sleeves and get to work; go towards the light. After you go to confession and have a firm purpose of amendment for your sins…but fall again…don't despair. The confessional is not a jail cell (where the door is slammed shut), it is a tomb where you leave your sins, and as you leave are resurrected to new life.

Now back to the visionaries in Medjugorje, Bosnia. Prayer, fasting, Bible reading, confession and receiving Holy Eucharist (in the state of grace only) are the main messages from the Virgin Mary (Queen of Peace) to clean up this mess.

Our Heavenly Mother has all of the virtues. When I think of our Heavenly Mother, I'm instantly lifted up! I think of her virtues (like gentleness, kindness, love, joy) and know how much She loves all of us. The love of Jesus (My Lord and my Savior, my big brother and best friend) and Mother Mary make me happy to be a part of God's family. Someday hopefully we will all be at the banquet table in Heaven. Remember we all have free-will and it is up each one of us to choose to do God's Will over our will. We must ask for forgiveness with true sorrow in order to get forgiveness. The sin/s against the Holy Spirit shall not to be forgiven (if you are not asking God for forgiveness with true sorrow then you will not be forgiven).

There have been many apparitions of the Virgin Mary all over the world. Currently in Ireland there is a visionary named Christina Gallagher, and her spiritual advisor is Reverend McGinnity. Since this book is a story of a little Irish Catholic girl; I decided to include a story about the visionary from Ireland.

Both Jesus and Mother Mary have appeared to Christina Gallagher (visionary from Ireland). This information was told to me by a woman I met at the 'Our Lady Queen of Peace House of Prayer' in Lake Placid, Florida. Jesus appeared to Christina Gallagher and asked her to build Houses of Prayer; one in every state in the United States. I'm sure Jesus wanted other Houses of Prayer in other places, but I'm focusing on the United States. Also Jesus gave her a deadline to get these Houses of Prayer. No money was to be borrowed. I don't think Jesus likes it when we are slaves of material things (like borrowing money from bank etc…). These Houses of Prayer must be completely paid for up front. This met the money and/or land must be donated before the deadline. One state had funding that would be coming through a few days after the deadline (the transaction was in progress); but Jesus refused to compromise. A deadline is a deadline. God means what He says! Only a few states had the Houses of Prayer by the deadline. There are 4 Chain Houses of : Our Lady Queen of Peace House of Prayer (Leander, Texas; Lake Placid, Florida; Humboldt, Kansas; Sauk Centre, Minnesota). These places can be added to later, but had to be started by the deadline. There will never be any more of these Houses of Prayer. Maybe someday all of these places will have big beautiful shrines built to honor our Heavenly Mother (Queen of Peace). Maybe these Houses of Prayer might someday include large hospitals to serve the faithful who refuse to pay into healthcare insurance that forces us to go against God (on birth control, abortion and euthanasia). That's the nurse in me coming through. Wouldn't that be wonderful to go to a place of spiritual and physical healing at the same time. However, these are called Houses of Prayer and that would be the main purpose for these places. I wonder why Jesus wanted these Prayer Houses. The logical answer is that we need to pray. We need to pray and do the Will of God.

I encourage the faithful Catholics to explore NOW the messages from 'Our Lady Queen of Peace' through the visionary Christina Gallagher of Ireland. Look into 'Our Lady Queen of Peace 3D Image with White Roses'.

Message from Our Lady Queen of Peace:

July 16th 2010 "Those who venerate Me by means of this picture in their homes and pray the Rosary will obtain protection from the purification. It will be like the times of the Angel of the Passover. The purification will pass over the houses where I am venerated by means of this picture and the Rosary prayed daily."

Also seek information about blessed rose petals if they are still available; once gone there will be no more. Rose Petals cannot be processed through shop order; please call the Texas House of Prayer. Maybe you are one that is being called to have one of these rose petals before events proceeding the purification.

The visionaries from Medjugorje, Bosnia will release secrets 10 days before they happen to the Priest/s assigned to them; and 3 days before the secrets happen to anyone who is interested. The best thing to do is BE READY; meaning to be in the state of grace.

Remember we must be in line with God's Will. God's Will and our will must match. Mortal (serious, grave) sin is the only thing that separates us from God; therefore it would only take one mortal sin to be separated from God. God puts no one in Hell…we do it to ourselves by doing our will over God's on serious (mortal, grave) sin and then never repenting with true sorrow. It feels good to reconcile with God, the weight of the world seems to be lifted from your shoulders, mind and soul.

All are welcome in the Catholic Church (the Bride of Jesus) even if you have never stepped foot in any church for any reason. The Catholic Church will meet you where you are at…but then you must start your conversion to God's Will by obeying the 10 COMMANDMENTS and the teachings of Jesus Christ and the teachings of the Magisterium of the Catholic Church.

No more birth control (other than Natural Family Planning in a Holy Matrimony Marriage and for a good reason according to God); no more watching anything on television/ movies/books/social media/music that is immoral or leads to the culture of death; no more putting other things/events in front of God, meaning GO TO HOLY MASS on Sundays and Holy Days of Obligation and don't do anything that causes others to work on these days (like going out to eat at restaurant or fast food, movies, sporting events, grocery shopping, gas stations etc…) unless essential jobs (like police, fire fighters, hospital workers etc…).

I have one more issue to bring up since we are sort of on the subject of essential jobs. OB-GYN physicians, what alternatives to birth control methods that are damnable to Hell, do you offer to your patients who are practicing Catholics? Catholic OB-GYN physicians, what alternatives to birth control methods that are damnable to Hell, do you offer to your patients who are practicing Catholics? Does your office and the hospital/s that you practice teach N.F.P.

(Natural Family Planning)? A Catholic physician (Once Catholic, always Catholic) cannot prescribe birth control in any form other than N.F.P., yet very few seem to be honoring the teaching of the Catholic Church (and this is a mortal sin). I've heard people joke about the profession of lawyers; that there aren't any lawyers in Heaven. If mortal sin is the only thing that separates us from God, and birth control (other than N.F.P.) is mortal sin, then how many OB-GYN physicians will be in Heaven if they don't stop what they are doing and come up with a new better plan for their patients. In-vitro fertilization, artificial insemination, surrogate motherhood and other procedures are mortal sins also. There are alternatives available that are in line with Catholic teaching. Please explore and promote these ways to treat your patients. It's your eternity, how do you plan to spend it? You have free will, the choice is yours.

> If the purification is coming soon,
> the Great Warning followed by the Great Miracle,
> then will come the purification.

Remember the closing prayer to the Divine Mercy Novena and Chaplet.
This prayer will offer consolation and give hope.

Your sister in Christ,   Virginia

THE END

Made in the USA
Las Vegas, NV
15 March 2022

45694861R00157